Literary Las Vegas

Literary LAS VEGAS

THE BEST WRITING ABOUT AMERICA'S MOST FABULOUS CITY

Edited by Mike Tronnes
Introduction by Nick Tosches

Henry Holt and Company   New York

Henry Holt and Company, Inc.
Publishers since 1866
115 West 18th Street
New York, New York 10011

Henry Holt® is a registered
trademark of Henry Holt and Company, Inc.

Library of Congress Cataloging-in-Publication Data
Literary Las Vegas: the best writing about America's most fabulous city /
edited by Mike Tronnes; introduction by Nick Tosches.—1st ed.
p.   cm.
1. Las Vegas (Nev.)—Social life and customs—Literary
collections.   2. City and town life—Nevada—Las Vegas—Literary
collections. 3. American literature—Nevada—Las Vegas.
I. Tronnes, Mike.
PS574.L37L58   1995   94-43199
830.8'032793135—dc20   CIP

ISBN 0-8050-3669-5
ISBN 0-8050-3670-9 (An Owl Book: pbk.)

Henry Holt books are available for special promotions
and premiums. For details contact: Director, Special Markets.

First Edition—1995

Designed by Betty Lew

Printed in the United States of America
All first editions are printed on acid-free paper. ∞

1   3   5   7   9   10   8   6   4   2
        5   7   9   10   8   6
                    (pbk.)

Dedicated to my parents, Lula and Erling Tronnes

Special thanks to Jessica Johnson and Tom McKusick and thanks also to the following fabulous individuals and organizations for their help: Everyone in my family, especially Beverly and David Tronnes, Jane Aurthur, Beverly Brannan, Jerry Brennan, Chris Calhoun, Deke Castleman, Maxi Cohen, Andrew Danish, Don English, Laurie Gray, Josh Glenn, Anthony (Big Tony) Goshko, John Habich, Dave Hickey, Jeanne Hoene, Shelley Holl, Mark Juergens, Neal Karlen, Dougie Kiner, John Kinsock, Geof Kern, Donn Knepp, Peter Kohlsaat, Michael Konik, Lynette Lamb, Elizabeth Larsen, Buddy Lester, Libby Lumpkin, Tom Montgomery, Charles Morgan, Mark Murphy, Kristie Nelson-Neuhaus, Bryan Oettel and everyone at Henry Holt, Sylvia Plachy, Vicki Reisenbach, Ellen Ryder, Jack Ross, Susan Sanford, John Schultz, Howard Schwarz at the Gambler's Book Club, Fred Sigman, William Bronson Simonet Jr., Greg Smith, Phil Stern, David Stratton, Marlene Strom, Mary Swanson, Robert Stupak, Jim Tronnes, Mr. Tunafish, Chris Waddington, Karen Silveroli and Myram Borders at the Las Vegas News Bureau, Kathy War and Sue Jarvis at the UNLV Special Collection, everyone at the Minneapolis downtown and Walker libraries, all of the eco-gamblers at the Felt Jungle, including Vic Gaia (appearing nightly in the rainforest room), and all of the writers and photographers in the collection, especially Nick Tosches and Michael Ventura. Also, thanks to everyone at the publishing houses, magazines, and photo agencies for their help in securing the rights to the articles and photographs.

CONTENTS

x   Contents

PREFACE
by Mike Tronnes

Las Vegas has always been a magnet for great writers, drawn to the city for the inspiration provided by its symbols and characters, and for what it says about us and our society. It doesn't matter if a writer views the town as a cesspool for the crass or a pleasure palace for the masses, this neon outpost and its denizens provide plenty to spark the imagination. It is not so surprising to learn then that there has been a wealth of brilliant writing produced about Las Vegas over the last half century. What is perhaps more interesting, however, is that these individualistic, often idiosyncratic pieces, when viewed as a mosaic, provide a remarkably entertaining and insightful portrait of this one-of-a-kind place. I've tried to capture this more fascinating, nuanced picture in *Literary Las Vegas*.

There is, of course, the town itself, with the famous casinos, the all-night wedding chapels, and the Strip. But behind the neon and the glitter, there is also an incredible array of colorful characters who enhance the town's mystique. Like everything else here, they're larger than life. Their tales are taller, their winnings and losses—in life as well as at the tables—are bigger, and their extremes of experience are greater.

Literary Las Vegas introduces us to these characters—both real and imagined, famous and obscure, from Bugsy Siegel, the founding father of Las Vegas, to Jackie Kasey, the unknown lounge comic who opened for all the big names—Frank, Dino, and Elvis—but whose own name no one remembered. Then there are the public relations hucksters who turned atomic testing into a tourist attraction, the world's best and worst gamblers, the ladies' room attendants, mobsters and their families, tourists and conventioneers, showgirls, casino cheats, Howard Hughes, Dr. Gonzo, FDR, JFK, high rollers, low rollers, Mormons, and wine goddesses, all of whom give this place a special aura.

Most of Las Vegas's residents have come from somewhere else. In the early days, many came because what they were doing illegally at home was legal in Nevada. By simply crossing state lines, they were transformed into upstanding citizens. While the modern transplants might be a more diverse lot, Las Vegas remains a place unconstrained by the bounds that define most communities. As a result, Las Vegas has been free to reinvent itself as the market dictates. In its rapidly evolving history, Las Vegas has gone from "mobster and starlet hideaway, to haven of sin and vice, to its present incarnation as low-roller heaven." This hyperhistory is presented here, from the modern-day pioneers who opened the Flamingo in the '40s, to today's fanny-packers who come by the tens of millions each year to visit "Disney in the desert."

From Nick Tosches's brilliant introduction to Tom Wolfe's classic "Las Vegas (What?) Las Vegas (Can't hear you! Too noisy) Las Vegas!!!!" to Marc Cooper's hilarious '90s update of *Fear and Loathing*, "Searching for Sin City and Finding Disney in the Desert," this collection captures a place through a multiplicity of views and voices. So whether you are looking for the classic kitschy Vegas of yesteryear, or the contemporary reality of America's fastest-growing metropolitan area, or the hidden world beyond the popular image, you will find it in *Literary Las Vegas*.

INTRODUCTION

Nick Tosches

....

The Holy City

Dante did not write in the age of malls, but he would have recognized Las Vegas, in any age, for what it is: a religion, a disease, a nightmare, a paradise for the misbegotten.

It is a place where fat old ladies in wheelchairs, like wretched, disfigured supplicants at Lourdes, roll and heave in ghastly faith toward the cold, gleaming maws of slot machines. A place where Jerry Lewis maketh the heart merry with the guffaw of the abyss, where Barbra Streisand lendeth wings to the soul with the unctuous simulacrum of pay-as-you-go sincerity. A place where the Wagnerian evocation of Zarathustra brings forth Elvis in a girdled bodice and rhinestone cape. A place where Ken and Barbie can go to be bad, to samba be-

neath the artificial tree of unknowing. A place where every man can
be Dino if he uses the right styling mousse and buys enough lobster
fra diavolo for the seeing-eye bimbo in whose tow he swaggers. A
place where a theology of profoundest mediocrity makes of every
Saul a Paul. A place where miracles do happen, along the line of
Frank Sinatra's hair.

America alone among nations conceived of her destiny as a
dream. The first temple of that American Dream, the heart of what,
with a straight face, she calls her culture, was invented by Jewish immigrants and the sons of Jewish immigrants—Fox, Goldwyn, Loew,
Zukor, and others—who founded the cheap dreamland of Hollywood
firmly upon the principles and aesthetics they had learned from their
shared background in the garment industry of New York.

And the *via sacra* of that dream led through the desert to Las Vegas. Like Hollywood, Vegas had been nothing. It was a forgotten
Pueblo wasteland that the noble white man had not even passed
through until 1829. In 1911, when it was incorporated as a city, its
population was barely fifteen hundred. Gambling, outlawed in
Nevada in 1915, was legalized again in 1931, when state legislation
also eased divorce laws to increase state revenues. This made
Nevada the only lawful game in America. But Vegas remained little
more than a forsaken railroad-depot town. The gambling rooms,
most of them located downtown in a two-block area around
Freemont and Second streets, drew much of their profits from the
paychecks of the workmen who were building the Boulder Dam
southeast of town. It was another Jew from New York, Bugsy Siegel,
who made Las Vegas a temple town of the American Dream.

In the summer of 1941, Siegel sent his henchman Little Moe Sedway to reconnoiter the Nevada territory. By then, the first of the fancy
joints, the El Rancho Vegas, had opened in the desert outside town.
Late in 1942, it would be joined by another. Built on the stretch of
Highway 91 that came to be known as "the Strip," the Last Frontier,
in addition to its casino, offered a showroom, a swimming pool, tennis courts, riding stables, and a hundred and seventy air-conditioned rooms with private baths.

The Last Frontier was nothing compared to the vision of Siegel's dream. In September 1945, a Vegas widow quitclaimed her failed dilapidated motel and thirty acres outside of town to Little Moe Sedway. The property was transferred indirectly to an entity named the Nevada Projects Corporation. In December 1945, ground was broken for Siegel's dream, the Zion he envisioned as the greatest gambling casino in the world. It was to be called the Flamingo.

The other major shareholder with Siegel, the true power behind him, was Meyer Lansky. Like Louis B. Mayer of Hollywood, Lansky had come from White Russia to the land of dreams, and now both were in the business of dreams, each in his own way. And there were other partners as well, such as Frank Costello. For the dream of America was not that of the Mogen David alone. Christ also had a wad to be reckoned with. Frank Capra, the Hollywood director whose work most reflected and influenced the mythos of the American dream, was from Palermo. He and Lucky Luciano, a habitual moviegoer, were born in Sicily in the same year, 1897. Luciano returned there as a deportee in 1946, the year of Capra's *It's a Wonderful Life*, the year of the Flamingo's grand opening.

The Flamingo, which opened the night after Christmas, 1946, was a bust. Siegel had drained the Nevada Project's shareholders of roughly six million dollars, and the casino in its first weeks took a beating for close to three quarters of a million. By late January, there was no choice but to shut it down. Siegel raised money to reopen in March, and by May the casino was showing a profit and Siegel felt sanguine. But his days had been numbered since the previous December, before he had ever opened the joint. There had been a meeting then of disgruntled shareholders, held behind Siegel's back, at the Hotel Nacional in Havana, where Frank Sinatra was performing as the Christmas attraction. They had all been there: Lansky, Costello, even the exiled Luciano, in from Italy. At that meeting, it had been decided that Bugsy had fucked them, and that Bugsy was wood.

In June, within twenty minutes of the carbine blasts that rendered Siegel so in Beverly Hills, Moe Sedway and two other men, Morris Rosen and Gus Greenbaum, representing Costello and Lansky, strode into the Flamingo, gathered the staff, and announced that the joint was under new management. In the year that followed, the casino showed a profit of over four million dollars. Gus Greenbaum, in 1950, was officially proclaimed the first mayor of Paradise, the name of the valley through which the Strip runs.

And the Flamingo begat the many. The Thunderbird came in 1948, the Desert Inn in 1950. The Sands and the Sahara in 1952; the Riviera, the Dunes, and the Royal Nevada in 1955.

If Las Vegas can be said to have had a golden era, it began with the Flamingo and reached its zenith in 1960, when John F. Kennedy and the Rat Pack, symbols and spirit of a blithe, benighted day, together lighted the showroom of the Sands. By the end of that decade, the paradigm shifted. In 1969 Elvis, who had failed miserably in Vegas in 1956, effectively ascended to his kingship in that holy city of old-guard cool where Dino and Sinatra had reigned supreme for a decade and more. He had, in other words, become truly, majestically mediocre.

For that—malignant banality, the pestilent have-a-nice-day smile of devouring venality—is the spirit of Vegas, the spirit of the dream itself. Just as the schlock manufactured by the dream merchants of Hollywood came to be exalted, in this land of hoi polloi, as art, so the slick and sleek mediocrity of the Vegas showroom came to be embraced and emulated as cool.

In fact, the more popular a mecca it became, the less cool Vegas got. The theogony illustrates this. In the beginning were Dean and Jerry, who opened at the Flamingo in September 1949. Eden was new then, and the Flamingo still its jewel, the pleasure dome of the new prefab promised land: a land of chrome, not gold; of Armstrong linoleum, not Carrara marble; of heptalk, not epos or prophecy. There, married by God and state, anointed in the blood of Bugsy, Un-terwelt and American dream lay down together in greed. Martin and Lewis were beloved of that dream, embracing and embraced by the spirit of a post-heroic, post-literate, cathode-culture America. And Dean, burdened even by the unnatural growth of Jerry, was as cool as it got: the idol not only of the suckers who bought the dream, but of the men who had built it as well. But as Vegas grew, the pilgrims of its suckerdom became less elite. After Dean and Jerry came Louis Prima and Keely Smith. This was the Mosaic age of hep. Indeed, in 1955, when a full-page ad in *Variety* for the Sahara quoted Howard Hughes on Louis and Keely, his words seemed less uttered than carved in stone: "The more I see them, the more I enjoy them." Then came the Rat Pack, caricatures of hip selling themselves to the pseudo-hip. (Who were the hipper charlatans of that day: Frank, Dean, and Sammy, or Burroughs, Kerouac, and Ginsberg? It's a close call, but high-roll collars and mohair britches certainly have held up better than berets and bongos.) Then, returned from out-and-out unhip ignominy, came Elvis. And just as surely as Dean and Frank were usurped by him, so Elvis himself ceded to Wayne Newton.

With popularity came crass legitimacy too. In 1963, when Ed Reid and Ovid Demaris published *The Green Felt Jungle*, Vegas was still ruled by the great Judeo-Christian shadowland consortium that had raised it from the desert in the late forties. Today it is a corporate-run nightmare draped in the cotton candy of family values, a theme park where dead souls drift amid medication Muzak, believing, *knowing*, in their hearts that people who need people are the luckiest people in the world and that one should never, ever, double down on a ten when the dealer shows a face card.

But its sleazy soul remains the same. It represents the darker emanation of that other, older dreamland. Both sell the same delusion, the same narcotic. In fact, we can look at America as the sum, the garish metastatic necrosis, of that narcotic's effects. This at least serves to explain the collective sense of beauty we embrace as we follow Mandy Patinkin's siren song, or the brain-dead blare of rap, across the bridges of Madison County—or is it the information superhighway?—to the Astroturf shores of Lethe beyond. In the end, *It's a Wonderful Life*, or this season's computer-enhanced, bare-tit equivalent, and the flashing glow of the programmed slots are one in the same to he who peddles them. And it is the same sucker who falls for both rackets.

It may not be a wonderful life, but it's a wonderful nightmare. The best pieces in this book—scabrous, absurd, perceptive—illuminate that nightmare and offer a guide, a Baedeker to the bizarre, a Virgil in shades, not only to the holy city but to the off-the-rack soul that we, one nation under Frankie's toup, so strangely and so fatally share.

Literary Las Vegas

Tom Wolfe

....

Las Vegas (What?) Las Vegas (Can't hear you! Too noisy) Las Vegas!!!!

Hernia, hernia, hernia, hernia, hernia, hernia, hernia, hernia, hernia, hernia, hernia, hernia, hernia, hernia, HERNia; hernia, HERNia, hernia, hernia, hernia, hernia, HERNia, HERNia, HERNia; hernia, hernia, hernia, hernia, hernia, hernia, hernia, eight is the point, the point is eight; hernia, hernia, HERNia; hernia, hernia, hernia, hernia, all right, hernia, hernia, hernia, hernia, hard eight, hernia, hernia, hernia, HERNia, hernia, hernia, hernia, HERNia, hernia, hernia, hernia, HERNia, hernia, hernia, hernia, hernia

☞ From Esquire, *February* 1964, *and* The Kandy-Kolored Tangerine-Flake Streamline Baby (*Farrar, Straus and Giroux*, 1965).

"What is all this *hernia hernia* stuff?"

This was Raymond talking to the wavy-haired fellow with the stick, the dealer, at the craps table about 3:45 Sunday morning. The stickman had no idea what this big wiseacre was talking about, but he resented the tone. He gave Raymond that patient arch of the eyebrows known as a Red Hook brushoff, which is supposed to convey some such thought as, I am a very tough but cool guy, as you can tell by the way I carry my eyeballs low in the pouches, and if this wasn't such a high-class joint we would take wiseacres like you out back and beat you into jellied madrilene.

At this point, however, Raymond was immune to subtle looks.

The stickman tried to get the game going again, but every time he would start up his singsong, by easing the words out through the nose, which seems to be the style among craps dealers in Las Vegas—"All right, a new shooter . . . eight is the point, the point is eight" and so on—Raymond would start droning along with him in exactly the same tone of voice, "Hernia, hernia, hernia; hernia, HERNia, HERNia, hernia; hernia, hernia, hernia."

Everybody at the craps table was staring in consternation to think that anybody would try to needle a tough, hip, elite *soldat* like a Las Vegas craps dealer. The gold-lamé odalisques of Los Angeles were staring. The Western sports, fifty-eight-year-old men who wear Texas string ties, were staring. The old babes at the slot machines, holding Dixie Cups full of nickles, were staring at the craps tables, but cranking away the whole time.

Raymond, who is thirty-four years old and works as an engineer in Phoenix, is big but not terrifying. He has the sort of thatchwork hair that grows so low all along the forehead there is no logical place to part it, but he tries anyway. He has a huge, prognathous jaw, but it is as smooth, soft and round as a melon, so that Raymond's total effect is that of an Episcopal divinity student.

The guards were wonderful. They were dressed in cowboy uniforms like Bruce Cabot in *Sundown* and they wore sheriff's stars.

"Mister, is there something we can do for you?"

"The expression is 'Sir,' " said Raymond. "You said 'Mister.' The expression is 'Sir.' How's your old Cosa Nostra?"

Amazingly, the casino guards were easing Raymond out peaceably, without putting a hand on him. I had never seen the fellow before, but possibly because I had been following his progress for the last five minutes, he turned to me and said, "Hey, do you have a car? This wild stuff is starting again."

The gist of it was that he had left his car somewhere and he wanted to ride up the Strip to the Stardust, one of the big hotel-casinos. I am describing this big goof Raymond not because he is a typical Las Vegas tourist, although he has some typical symptoms, but because he is a good example of the marvelous impact Las Vegas has on the senses. Raymond's senses were at a high pitch of excitation, the only trouble being that he was going off his nut. He had been up since Thursday afternoon, and it was now about 3:45 A.M. Sunday. He had an envelope full of pep pills—amphetamine—in his left coat pocket and an envelope full of Equanils—meprobamate—in his right pocket, or were the Equanils in the left and the pep pills in the right? He could tell by looking, but he wasn't going to look anymore. He didn't care to see how many were left.

He had been rolling up and down the incredible electric-sign gauntlet of Las Vegas' Strip, U.S. Route 91, where the neon and the par lamps—bubbling, spiraling, rocketing, and exploding in sunbursts ten stories high out in the middle of the desert—celebrate one-story casinos. He had been gambling and drinking and eating now and again at the buffet tables the casinos keep heaped with food day and night, but mostly hopping himself up with good old amphetamine, cooling himself down with meprobamate, then hooking down more alcohol, until now, after sixty hours, he was slipping into the symptoms of toxic schizophrenia.

He was also enjoying what the prophets of hallucinogen call "consciousness expansion." The man was psychedelic. He was beginning to isolate the components of Las Vegas' unique bombardment of the senses. He was quite right about this *hernia hernia* stuff.

Every casino in Las Vegas is, among the other things, a room full of craps tables with dealers who keep up a running singsong that sounds as though they are saying "hernia, hernia, hernia, hernia, hernia" and so on. There they are day and night, easing a running commentary through their nostrils. What they have to say contains next to no useful instruction. Its underlying message is, We are the initiates, riding the crest of chance. That the accumulated sound comes out "hernia" is merely an unfortunate phonetic coincidence. Actually, it is part of something rare and rather grand: a combination of baroque stimuli that brings to mind the bronze gongs, no larger than a blue plate, that Louis XIV, his ruff collars larded with the lint of the foul Old City of Byzantium, personally hunted out in the bazaars of Asia Minor to provide exotic acoustics for his new palace outside Paris.

The sounds of the craps dealer will be in, let's say, the middle register. In the lower register will be the sound of the old babes at the slot machines. Men play the slots too, of course, but one of the indelible images of Las Vegas is that of the old babes at the row upon row of slot machines. There they are at six o'clock Sunday morning no less than at three o'clock Tuesday afternoon. Some of them pack their old hummocky shanks into Capri pants, but many of them just put on the old print dress, the same one day after day, and the old hob-heeled shoes, looking like they might be going out to buy eggs in Tupelo, Mississippi. They have a Dixie Cup full of nickels or dimes in the left hand and an Iron Boy work glove on the right hand to keep the callouses from getting sore. Every time they pull the handle, the machine makes a sound much like the sound a cash register makes before the bell rings, then the slot pictures start clattering up from left to right, the oranges, lemons, plums, cherries, bells, bars, buckaroos—the figure of a cowboy riding a bucking bronco. The whole sound keeps churning up over and over again in eccentric series all over the place, like one of those random-sound radio symphonies by John Cage. You can hear it at any hour of the day or night all over Las Vegas. You can walk down Fremont Street at dawn and hear it without even walking in a door, that and the spins of the wheels of fortune, a boring and not very popular sort of simplified roulette, as the tabs flap to a stop. As an overtone, or at times simply as a loud sound, comes the babble of the casino crowds, with an occasional shriek from the craps tables, or, anywhere from 4 P.M. to 6 A.M., the sound of brass instruments or electrified string instruments from the cocktail-lounge shows.

The crowd and band sounds are not very extraordinary, of course. But Las Vegas' Muzak is. Muzak pervades Las Vegas from the time you walk into the airport upon landing to the last time you leave the casinos. It is piped out to the swimming pool. It is in the drugstores. It is as if there were a communal fear that someone, somewhere in Las Vegas, was going to be left with a totally vacant minute on his hands.

Las Vegas has succeeded in wiring an entire city with this electronic stimulation, day and night, out in the middle of the desert. In the automobile I rented, the radio could not be turned off, no matter which dial you went after. I drove for days in a happy burble of Action Checkpoint News, "Monkey No. 9," "Donna, Donna, the Prima Donna," and picking-and-singing jingles for the Frontier Bank and the Fremont Hotel.

One can see the magnitude of the achievement. Las Vegas takes what in other American towns is but a quixotic inflammation of the senses for some poor salary mule in the brief interval between the flagstone rambler and the automatic elevator downtown and magnifies it, foliates it, embellishes it into an institution.

For example, Las Vegas is the only town in the world whose skyline is made up neither of buildings, like New York, nor of trees, like Wilbraham, Massachusetts, but signs. One can look at Las Vegas from a mile away on Route 91 and see no buildings, no trees, only signs. But such signs! They tower. They revolve, they oscillate, they soar in shapes before which the existing vocabulary of art history is helpless. I can only attempt to supply names—Boomerang Modern, Palette Curvilinear, Flash Gordon Ming-Alert Spiral, McDonald's

6   Tom Wolfe

Hamburger Parabola, Mint Casino Elliptical, Miami Beach Kidney. Las Vegas' sign makers work so far out beyond the frontiers of conventional studio art that they have no names themselves for the forms they create. Vaughan Cannon, one of those tall, blond Westerners, the builders of places like Las Vegas and Los Angeles, whose eyes seem to have been bleached by the sun, is in the back shop of the Young Electric Sign Company out on East Charleston Boulevard with Herman Boernge, one of his designers, looking at the model they have prepared for the Lucky Strike Casino sign, and Cannon points to where the sign's two great curving faces meet to form a narrow vertical face and says:

"Well, here we are again—what do we call that?"

"I don't know," says Boernge. "It's sort of a nose effect. Call it a nose."

Okay, a nose, but it rises sixteen stories high above a two-story building. In Las Vegas no farseeing entrepreneur buys a sign to fit a building he owns. He rebuilds the building to support the biggest sign he can get up the money for and, if necessary, changes the name. The Lucky Strike Casino today is the Lucky Casino, which fits better when recorded in sixteen stories of flaming peach and incandescent yellow in the middle of the Mojave Desert. In the Young Electric Sign Co. era signs have become the architecture of Las Vegas, and the most whimsical, Yale-seminar-frenzied devices of the two late geniuses of Baroque Modern, Frank Lloyd Wright and Eero Saarinen, seem rather stuffy business, like a jest at a faculty meeting, compared to it. Men like Boernge, Kermit Wayne, Ben Mitchem and Jack Larsen, formerly an artist for Walt Disney, are the designer-sculptor geniuses of Las Vegas, but their motifs have been carried faithfully throughout the town by lesser men, for gasoline stations, motels, funeral parlors, churches, public buildings, flophouses and sauna baths.

Then there is a stimulus that is both visual and sexual—the Las Vegas buttocks décolletage. This is a form of sexually provocative dress seen more and more in the United States, but avoided like Broadway message-embroidered ("Kiss Me, I'm Cold") underwear in the fashion pages, so that the euphemisms have not been established and I have no choice but clinical terms. To achieve buttocks décolletage a woman wears bikini-style shorts that cut across the round fatty masses of the buttocks rather than cupping them from below, so that the outer-lower edges of these fatty masses, or "cheeks," are exposed. I am in the cocktail lounge of the Hacienda Hotel, talking to managing director Dick Taylor about the great success his place has had in attracting family and tour groups, and all around me the waitresses are bobbing on their high heels, bare legs and décolletage-bare backsides, set off by pelvis-length lingerie of an uncertain denomination. I stare, but I am new here. At the White Cross Rexall drugstore on the Strip a pregnant brunette walks in off the street wearing black shorts with buttocks décolletage aft and illusion-of-cloth nylon lingerie hanging fore, and not even the old mom's-pie pensioners up near the door are staring. They just crank away at the slot machines. On the streets of Las Vegas, not only the show girls, of which the town has about two hundred fifty, bona fide, in residence, but girls of every sort, including, especially, Las Vegas' little high-school buds, who adorn what locals seeking roots in the sand call "our city of churches and schools," have taken up the chic of wearing buttocks décolletage step-ins under flesh-tight slacks, with the outline of the undergarment showing through fashionably. Others go them one better. They achieve the effect of having been dipped once, briefly, in Helenca stretch nylon. More and more they look like those wonderful old girls out of Flash Gordon who were wrapped just once over in Baghdad pantaloons of clear poly-ethylene with only Flash Gordon between them and the insane red-eyed assaults of the minions of Ming. It is as if all the hip young suburban gals of America named Lana, Deborah and Sandra, who gather wherever the arc lights shine and the studs steady their coiffures in the plate-glass reflection, have convened in Las Vegas with their bouffant hair above and anatomically stretch-pant-swathed little bottoms below, here on the new American frontier. But exactly!

❦   ❦   ❦

None of it would have been possible, however, without one of those historic combinations of nature and art that creates an epoch. In this case, the Mojave Desert plus the father of Las Vegas, the late Benjamin "Bugsy" Siegel.

Bugsy was an inspired man. Back in 1944 the city fathers of Las Vegas, their Protestant rectitude alloyed only by the giddy prospect of gambling revenues, were considering the sort of ordinance that would have preserved the town with a kind of Colonial Williamsburg dinkiness in the motif of the Wild West. All new buildings would have to have at least the façade of the sort of place where piano players used to wear garters on their sleeves in Virginia City around 1880. In Las Vegas in 1944, it should be noted, there was nothing more stimulating in the entire town than a Fremont Street bar where the composer of "Deep in the Heart of Texas" held forth and the regulars downed fifteen-cent beer.

Bugsy pulled into Las Vegas in 1945 with several million dollars that, after his assassination, was traced back in the general direction of gangster-financiers. Siegel put up a hotel-casino such as Las Vegas had never seen and called it the Flamingo—all Miami Modern, and the hell with piano players with garters and whatever that was all about. Everybody drove out Route 91 just to gape. Such shapes! Boomerang Modern supports, Palette Curvilinear bars, Hot Shoppe Cantilever roofs and a scalloped swimming pool. Such colors! All the new electrochemical pastels of the Florida littoral: tangerine, broiling magenta, livid pink, incarnadine, fuchsia demure, Congo ruby, methyl green, viridine, aquamarine, phenosafranine, incandescent orange, scarlet-fever purple, cyanic blue, tessellated bronze, hospital-fruit-basket orange. And such signs! Two cylinders rose at either end of the Flamingo—eight stories high and covered from top to bottom with neon rings in the shape of bubbles that fizzed all eight stories up into the desert sky all night long like an illuminated whisky-soda tumbler filled to the brim with pink champagne.

The business history of the Flamingo, on the other hand, was not such a smashing success. For one thing, the gambling operation was losing money at a rate that rather gloriously refuted all the recorded odds of the gaming science. Siegel's backers apparently suspected that he was playing both ends against the middle in collusion with professional gamblers who hung out at the Flamingo as though they had liens on it. What with one thing and another, someone decided by the night of June 20, 1947, that Benny Siegel, lord of the Flamingo, had had it. He was shot to death in Los Angeles.

Yet Siegel's aesthetic, psychological and cultural insights, like Cézanne's, Freud's and Max Weber's, could not die. The Siegel vision and the Siegel aesthetic were already sweeping Las Vegas like gold fever. And there were builders of the West equal to the opportunity. All over Las Vegas the incredible electric pastels were repeated. Overnight the Baroque Modern forms made Las Vegas one of the few architecturally unified cities of the world—the style was Late American Rich—and without the bother and bad humor of a City Council ordinance. No enterprise was too small, too pedestrian or too solemn for The Look. The Supersonic Carwash, the Mercury-Jetaway, Gas Vegas Village and Terrible Herbst gasoline stations, the Par-a-Dice Motel, the Palm Mortuary, the Orbit Inn, the Desert Moon, the Blue Onion Drive-In—on it went, like Wildwood, New Jersey, entering Heaven.

The atmosphere of the six-mile-long Strip of hotel-casinos grips even those segments of the population who rarely go near it. Barely twenty-five-hundred feet off the Strip, over by the Convention Center, stands Landmark Towers, a shaft thirty stories high, full of apartments, supporting a huge circular structure shaped like a space observation platform, which was to have contained the restaurant and casino. Somewhere along the way Landmark Towers went bankrupt, probably at that point in the last of the many crises when the construction workers still insisted on spending half the day flat on their bellies with their heads, tongues and eyeballs hanging over the edge of the tower, looking down into the swimming pool of the Playboy Apartments below, which has a "nudes only" section for show girls whose work calls for a tan all over.

Elsewhere, Las Vegas' beautiful little high-school buds in their buttocks-décolletage stretch pants are back on the foam rubber upholstery of luxury broughams peeling off the entire chick ensemble long enough to establish the highest venereal disease rate among high-school students anywhere north of the yaws-rotting shanty jungles of the Eighth Parallel. The Negroes who have done much of the construction work in Las Vegas' sixteen-year boom are off in their ghetto on the west side of town, and some of them are smoking marijuana, eating peyote buttons and taking horse (heroin), which they get from Tijuana, I mean it's simple, baby, right through the mails, and old Raymond, the Phoenix engineer, does not have the high life to himself.

I am on the third floor of the Clark County Courthouse talking to Sheriff Captain Ray Gubser, another of these strong, pale-eyed Western-builder types, who is obligingly explaining to me law enforcement on the Strip, where the problem is not so much the drunks, crooks or roughhousers, but these nuts on pills who don't want to ever go to bed, and they have hallucinations and try to bring down the casinos like Samson. The county has two padded cells for them. They cool down after three or four days and they turn out to be somebody's earnest breadwinner back in Denver or Minneapolis, loaded with the right credentials and pouring soul and apologiae all over the county cops before finally pulling out of never-never land for good by plane. Captain Gubser is telling me about life and eccentric times in Las Vegas, but I am distracted. The captain's office has windows out on the corridor. Coming down the corridor is a covey of girls, skipping and screaming, giggling along, their heads exploding in platinum-and-neon-yellow bouffants or beehives or raspberry-silk scarves, their eyes appliqued in black like mail-order decals, their breasts aimed up under their jerseys at the angle of anti-aircraft automatic weapons, and, as they swing around the corner toward the elevator, their glutei maximi are bobbing up and down with their pumps in the inevitable buttocks décolletage pressed out against black, beige and incarnadine stretch pants. This is part of the latest shipment of show girls to Las Vegas, seventy in all, for the "Lido de Paris" revue at the Stardust, to be entitled *Bravo!*, replacing the old show, entitled *Voilà*. The girls are in the county courthouse getting their working papers, and fifteen days from now these little glutei maximi and ack-ack breasts with stars pasted on the tips will be swinging out over the slack jaws and cocked-up noses of patrons sitting at stageside at the Stardust. I am still listening to Gubser, but somehow it is a courthouse where mere words are beaten back like old atonal Arturo Toscanini trying to sing along with the NBC Symphony. There he would be, flapping his little toy arms like Tony Galento shadowboxing with fate, bawling away in the face of union musicians who drowned him without a bubble. I sat in on three trials in the courthouse, and it was wonderful, because the courtrooms are all blond-wood modern and look like sets for TV panel discussions on marriage and the teenager. What the judge has to say is no less formal and no more fatuous than what judges say everywhere, but inside of forty seconds it is all meaningless because the atmosphere is precisely like a news broadcast over Las Vegas' finest radio station, KORK. The newscast, as it is called, begins with a series of electronic wheeps out on that far edge of sound where only quadrupeds can hear. A voice then announces that this is Action Checkpoint News. "The news—all the news—flows first through Action Checkpoint!—then reaches You! at the speed of Sound!" More electronic wheeps, beeps and lulus, and then an item: "Cuban Premier Fidel Castro nearly drowned yesterday." Urp! Wheep! Lulu! No news a KORK announcer has ever brought to Las Vegas at the speed of sound, or could possibly bring, short of word of the annihilation of Los Angeles, could conceivably compete within the brain with the giddiness of this electronic jollification.

The wheeps, beeps, freeps, electronic lulus, Boomerang Modern and Flash Gordon sunbursts soar on through the night over the billowing hernia-hernia sounds and the old babes at the slots—until it is 7:30 A.M. and I am watching five men at a green-topped card table playing poker. They are sliding their Bee-brand cards into their hands and squinting at the pips with a set to the lips like Conrad Veidt in a tunic collar studying a code message from S.S. headquarters. Big Sid Wyman, the old Big-Time gambler from St. Louis, is there, with his eyes looking like two poached eggs engraved with a road map of West Virginia after all night at the poker table. Sixty-year-old Chicago Tommy Hargan is there with his topknot of white hair pulled back over his little pink skull and a mountain of chips in front of his old caved-in sternum. Sixty-two-year-old Dallas Maxie Welch is there, fat and phlegmatic as an Indian Ocean potentate. Two Los Angeles biggies are there exhaling smoke from candela-green cigars into the gloom. It looks like the perfect vignette of every Big Time back room, "athletic club," snooker house and floating poker game in the history of the guys-and-dolls lumpen-bourgeoisie. But what is all this? Off to the side, at a rostrum, sits a flawless little creature with bouffant hair and Stridex-pure skin who looks like she is polished each morning with a rotary buffer. Before her on the rostrum is a globe of coffee on a hot coil. Her sole job is to keep the poker players warmed up with coffee. Meantime, numberless uniformed lackeys are cocked and aimed about the edges to bring the five Big Timers whatever else they might desire, cigarettes, drinks, napkins, eyeglass-cleaning tissues, plug-in telephones. All around the poker table, at a respectful distance of ten feet, is a fence with the most delicate golden pickets. Upon it, even at this narcoleptic hour, lean men and women in their best clothes watching the combat of the titans. The scene is the charmed circle of the casino of the Dunes Hotel. As everyone there knows, or believes, these fabulous men are playing for table stakes of fifteen or twenty thousand dollars. One hundred dollars rides on a chip. Mandibles gape at the progress of the battle. And now Sid Wyman, who is also a vice-president of the Dunes, is at a small escritoire just inside the golden fence signing a stack of vouchers for such sums as $4500, all printed in the heavy Mondrianesque digits of a Burroughs business check-making machine. It is as if America's guys-and-dolls gamblers have somehow been tapped upon the shoulders, knighted, initiated into a new aristocracy.

Las Vegas has become, just as Bugsy Siegel dreamed, the American Monte Carlo—without any of the inevitable upper-class baggage of the Riviera casinos. At Monte Carlo there is still the plush mustiness of the 19th-century noble lions—of Baron Bleichroden, a big winner at roulette who always said, "My dear friends, it is so easy on Black." Of Lord Jersey, who won seventeen maximum bets in a row—on black, as a matter of fact—nodded to the croupier, and said, "Much obliged, old sport, old sport," took his winnings to England, retired to the country and never gambled again in his life. Or of the old Duc de Dinc who said he could win only in the high-toned Club Privé, and who won very heavily one night, saw two Englishmen gaping at his good fortune, threw them every mille-franc note he had in his hands and said, "Here. Englishmen without money are altogether odious." Thousands of Europeans from the lower orders now have the money to go to the Riviera, but they remain under the century-old status pall of the aristocracy. At Monte Carlo there are still Wrong Forks, Deficient Accents, Poor Tailoring, Gauche Displays, Nouveau Richness, Cultural Aridity—concepts unknown in Las Vegas. For the grand debut of Monte Carlo as a resort in 1879 the architect Charles Garnier designed an opera house for the Place du Casino; and Sarah Bernhardt read a symbolic poem. For the debut of Las Vegas as a resort in 1946 Bugsy Siegel hired Abbott and Costello, and there, in a way, you have it all.

I am in the office of Major A. Riddle—Major is his name—the president of the Dunes Hotel. He combs his hair straight back and wears a heavy gold band on his little finger with a diamond sunk into it. As everywhere else in Las Vegas, someone has turned on the air conditioning to the point where it will be remembered, all right, as Las Vegas-style air conditioning. Riddle has an appointment to see a doctor at 4:30 about a crimp in his neck. His secretary, Maude McBride, has her head down and is rubbing the back of her neck. Lee Fisher, the P.R. man, and I are turning ours from time to time to keep the pivots from freezing up. Riddle is telling me about "the French war" and moving his neck gingerly. The Stardust bought and imported a version of the Lido de Paris spectacular, and the sight of all those sequined giblets pooning around on flamingo legs inflamed the tourists. The Tropicana fought back with the Folies Bergère, the New Frontier installed "Paree Ooh La La," the Hacienda reached for the puppets "Les Poupées de Paris," and the Silver Slipper called in Lili St. Cyr, the stripper, which was going French after a fashion. So the Dunes has bought up the third and last of the great Paris girlie shows, the Casino de Paris. Lee Fisher says, "And we're going to do things they *can't* top. In this town you've got to move ahead in quantum jumps."

Quantum? But exactly! The beauty of the Dunes' Casino de Paris show is that it will be beyond art, beyond dance, beyond spectacle, even beyond the titillations of the winking crotch. The Casino de Paris will be a behemoth piece of American calculus, like Project Mercury.

"This show alone will cost us two and a half million a year to operate and one and a half million to produce," Major A. Riddle is saying. "The costumes alone will be fantastic. There'll be more than five hundred costumes and—well, they'll be fantastic.

"And this machine—by the time we get through expanding the stage, this machine will cost us $250,000."

"Machine?"

"Yes. Sean Kenny is doing the staging. The whole set moves electronically right in front of your eyes. He used to work with this fellow Lloyd Wright."

"Frank Lloyd Wright?"

"Yes. Kenny did the staging for Blitz. Did you see it? Fantastic. Well, it's all done electronically. They built this machine for us in Glasgow, Scotland, and it's being shipped here right now. It moves all over the place and creates smoke and special effects. We'll have everything. You can stage a bombardment with it. You'll think the whole theatre is blowing up.

"You'll have to program it. They had to use the same mechanism that's in the Skybolt Missile to build it. It's called a 'Celson' or something like that. That's how complicated this thing is. They have to have the same thing as the Skybolt Missile."

As Riddle speaks, one gets a wonderful picture of sex riding the crest of the future. Whole tableaux of bare-bottomed Cosmonaughties will be hurtling around the Casino de Paris Room of the Dunes Hotel at fantastic speed in elliptical orbits, a flash of the sequined giblets here, a blur of the black-rimmed decal eyes there, a wink of the crotch here and there, until, with one vast Project Climax for our times, Sean Kenny, who used to work with this fellow Frank Lloyd Wright, presses the red button and the whole yahooing harem, shrieking ooh-la-la amid the din, exits in a mushroom cloud.

The allure is most irresistible not to the young but the old. No one in Las Vegas will admit it—it is not the modern, glamorous notion—but Las Vegas is a resort for old people. In those last years, before the tissue deteriorates and the wires of the cerebral cortex hang in the skull like a clump of dried seaweed, they are seeking liberation.

At eight o'clock Sunday morning it is another almost boringly sunny day in the desert, and Clara and Abby, both about sixty, and their husbands, Earl, sixty-three, and Ernest, sixty-four, come squinting out of the Mint Casino onto Fremont Street.

"I don't know what's wrong with me," Abby says. "Those last three drinks, I couldn't even feel them. It was just like drinking fizz. You know what I mean?"

"Hey," says Ernest, "how about that place back 'ere? We ain't been back 'ere. Come on."

The others are standing there on the corner, squinting and looking doubtful. Abby and Clara have both entered old babehood. They have that fleshy, humped-over shape across the back of the shoulders. Their torsos are hunched up into fat little loaves supported by bony, atrophied leg stems sticking up into their hummocky hips. Their hair has been fried and dyed into improbable designs.

"You know what I mean? After a while it just gives me gas," says Abby. "I don't even feel it."

"Did you see me over there?" says Earl. "I was just going along, nice and easy, not too much, just riding along real nice. You know? And then, boy, I don't know what happened to me. First thing I know I'm laying down fifty dollars. . . ."

Abby lets out a great belch. Clara giggles.

"Gives me gas," Abby says mechanically.

"Hey, how about that place back 'ere?" says Ernest.

". . . Just nice and easy as you please. . . ."

". . . get me all fizzed up. . . ."

"Aw, come on. . . ."

And there at eight o'clock Sunday morning stand four old parties from Albuquerque, New Mexico, up all night, squinting at the sun, belching from a surfeit of tall drinks at eight o'clock Sunday morning, and—marvelous!—there is no one around to snigger at what an old babe with decaying haunches looks like in Capri pants with her heels jacked up on decorated wedgies.

"Where do we *come* from?" Clara said to me, speaking for the first time since I approached them on Fremont Street. "He wants to know where we come from. I think it's past your bedtime, sweets."

"Climb the stairs and go to bed," said Abby.

Laughter all around.

"Climb the stairs" was Abby's finest line. At present there are almost no stairs to climb in Las Vegas. Avalon homes are soon to go up, advertising "Two-Story Homes!" as though this were an incredibly lavish and exotic concept. As I talked to Clara, Abby, Earl and Ernest, it came out that "climb the stairs" was a phrase they brought along to Albuquerque with them from Marshalltown, Iowa, those many years ago, along with a lot of other baggage, such as the entire cupboard of Protestant taboos against drinking, lusting, gambling, staying out late, getting up late, loafing, idling, lollygagging around the streets and wearing Capri pants—all designed to deny a person short-term pleasures so he will center his energies on bigger, long-term goals.

"We was in 'ere"—the Mint—"a couple of hours ago, and that old boy was playing the guitar, you know, 'Walk right in, set right down,' and I kept hearing an old song I haven't heard for twenty years. It has this little boy and his folks keep telling him it's late and he has to go to bed. He keeps saying, 'Don't make me go to bed and I'll be good.' Am I *good*, Earl? Am I *good*?"

The liberated cortex in all its glory is none other than the old babes at the slot machines. Some of them are tourists whose husbands said, *Here is fifty bucks, go play the slot machines*, while they themselves went off to more complex pleasures. But most of these old babes are part of the permanent landscape of Las Vegas. In they go to the Golden Nugget or the Mint, with their Social Security check or their pension check from the Ohio telephone company, cash it at the casino cashiers, pull out the Dixie Cup and the Iron Boy work glove, disappear down a row of slots and get on with it. I remember particularly talking to another Abby—a widow, sixty-two years old, built short and up from the bottom like a fire hydrant. After living alone for twelve years in Canton, Ohio, she had moved out to Las Vegas to live with her daughter and her husband, who worked for the Army.

"They were wonderful about it," she said. "Perfect hypocrites. She kept saying, you know, 'Mother, we'd be delighted to have you, only we don't think you'll *like it. It's practically a* frontier town,' she says. 'It's so *garish*,' she says. So I said, I told her, 'Well, if you'd rather I didn't come. . . .' 'Oh, no' she says. I wish I could have heard what her husband was saying. He calls me 'Mother.' '*Mother*,' he says. Well, once I was here, they figured, well, I *might* make a good baby-sitter and dishwasher and duster and mopper. The children are nasty little things. So one day I was in town for something or other and I just played a slot machine. It's fun—I can't describe it to you. I suppose I lose. I lose a little. And *they* have fits about it. 'For God's sake, Grandmother,' and so forth. They always say '*Grand*mother' when I am supposed to 'act my age' or crawl through a crack in the floor. Well, I'll tell you, the slot machines are a *whole lot* better than sitting in that little house all day. They kind of get you; I can't explain it."

The childlike megalomania of gambling is, of course, from the same cloth as the megalomania of the town. And, as the children of the liberated cortex, the old guys and babes are running up and down the Strip around the clock like everybody else. It is not by chance that much of the entertainment in Las Vegas, especially the second-stringers who perform in the cocktail lounges, will recall for an aging man what was glamorous twenty-five years ago when he had neither the money nor the freedom of spirit to indulge himself in it. In the big theatre-dining room at the Desert Inn, The Painted Desert Room, Eddie Fisher's act is on and he is saying cozily to a florid guy at a table right next to the stage, "Manny, you know you shouldn'a sat this close—you know you're in for it now, Manny, baby," while Manny beams with fright. But in the cocktail lounge, where the idea is chiefly just to keep the razzle-dazzle going, there is Hugh Farr, one of the stars of another era in the West, composer of two of the five Western songs the Library of Congress has taped for posterity, "Cool Water" and "Tumbling Tumbleweed," when he played the violin for the Sons of the Pioneers. And now around the eyes he looks like an aging Chinese savant, but he is wearing a white tuxedo and powder-blue leather boots and playing his sad old Western violin with an electric cord plugged in it for a group called The Country Gentlemen. And there is Ben Blue, looking like a waxwork exhibit of vaudeville, doffing his straw skimmer to reveal the sculptural qualities of his skull. And down at the Flamingo cocktail lounge—Ella Fitzgerald is in the main room—there is Harry James, looking old and pudgy in one of those toy Italian-style show-biz suits. And the Ink Spots are at the New Frontier and Louis Prima is at the Sahara, and the old parties are seeing it all, roaring through the dawn into the next day, until the sun seems like a par lamp fading in and out. The casinos, the bars, the liquor stores are open every minute of every day, like a sempiternal wading pool for the childhood ego. ". . . Don't make me go to bed. . . ."

Finally the casualties start piling up. I am in the manager's office of a hotel on the Strip. A man and his wife, each about sixty, are in there, raging. Someone got into their room and stole seventy dollars from her purse, and they want the hotel to make it up to them. The man pops up and down from a chair and ricochets back and forth across the room, flailing his great pig's-knuckle elbows about.

"What kind of security you call that? Walk right in the god-dern room and just help themselves. And where do you think I found your security man? Back around the corner reading a god-dern detective magazine!"

He had scored a point there, but he was wearing a striped polo shirt with a hip Hollywood solid-color collar, and she had on Capri pants, and hooked across their wrinkly old faces they both had rimless, wraparound French sunglasses of the sort young-punk heroes in *nouvelle vague* movies wear, and it was impossible to give any earnest contemplation to a word they said. They seemed to have the great shiny popeyes of a praying mantis.

"Listen, Mister," she is saying, "I don't care about the seventy bucks. I'd lose seventy bucks at your craps table and I wouldn't think nothing of it. I'd play seventy bucks just like that, and it wouldn't mean nothing. I wouldn't regret it. But when they can just walk in— and you don't give a damn—for Christ's sake!"

They are both zeroing in on the manager with their great insect corneas. The manager is a cool number in a white-on-white shirt and silver tie.

"This happened three days ago. Why didn't you tell us about it then?"

"Well, I was gonna be a nice guy about it. Seventy dollars," he said, as if it would be difficult for the brain to grasp a sum much smaller. "But then I found your man back there reading a god-dern detective magazine. *True Detectives* it was. Had a picture on the front of some floozie with one leg up on a chair and her garter showing. Looked like a god-derned athlete's foot ad. Boy, I went into a slow burn. But when I am burned up, I am *burned up*! You get me, Mister? There he was, reading the god-derned *True Detectives*."

"Any decent hotel would have insurance," she says.

The manager says, "I don't know a hotel in the world that offers insurance against theft."

"Hold on, Mister," he says, "are you calling my wife a liar? You just get smart, and I'm gonna pop you one! I'll pop you one right now if you call my wife a liar."

At this point the manager lowers his head to one side and looks up at the old guy from under his eyebrows with a version of the Red Hook brush-off, and the old guy begins to cool off.

But others are beyond cooling off. Hornette Reilly, a buttery-hipped whore from New York City, is lying in bed with a bald-headed guy from some place who has skin like oatmeal. He is asleep or passed out or something. Hornette is relating all this to the doctor over the Princess telephone by the bed.

"Look," she says, "I'm breaking up. I can't tell you how much I've drunk. About a bottle of brandy since four o'clock, I'm not kidding. I'm in bed with a guy. Right this minute. I'm talking on the telephone to you and this slob is lying here like an animal. He's all fat and his skin looks like oatmeal—what's happening to me? I'm going to take some more pills. I'm not kidding, I'm breaking up. I'm going to kill myself. You've got to put me in Rose de Lima. I'm breaking up, and I don't even know what's happening to me."

"So naturally you want to go to Rose de Lima."

"Well, yeah."

"You can come by the office, but I'm not sending you to Rose de Lima."

"Doctor, I'm not kidding."

"I don't doubt that you're sick, old girl, but I'm not sending you to Rose de Lima to sober up."

The girls do not want to go to the County Hospital. They want to go to Rose de Lima, where the psychiatric cases receive milieu therapy. The patients dress in street clothes, socialize and play games with the staff, eat well and relax in the sun, all paid for by the State. One of the folk heroines of the Las Vegas floozies, apparently, is the call girl who last year was spending Monday through Friday at Rose de Lima and "turning out," as they call it, Saturdays and Sundays on the Strip, to the tune of $200 to $300 a weekend. She looks upon herself not as a whore, or even a call girl, but as a lady of assignation. When some guy comes to the Strip and unveils the little art-nouveau curves in his psyche and calls for two girls to perform arts upon one another, this one consents to be the passive member of the team only. A Rose de Lima girl, she draws the line.

At the County Hospital the psychiatric ward is latched, bolted, wired up and jammed with patients who are edging along the walls in the inner hall, the only place they have to take a walk other than the courtyard.

A big brunette with the remnants of a beehive hairdo and decal eyes and an obvious pregnancy is the liveliest of the lot. She is making eyes at everyone who walks in. She also nods gaily toward vacant place places along the wall.

"Mrs. ———— is refusing medication," a nurse tells one of the psychiatrists. "She won't even open her mouth."

Presently the woman, in a white hospital tunic, is led up the hall. She looks about fifty, but she has extraordinary lines on her face.

"Welcome home," says Dr. ————.

"This is not my home," she says.

"Well, as I told you before, it has to be for the time being."

"Listen, you didn't analyze me."

"Oh, yes. Two psychiatrists examined you—all over again."

"You mean that time in jail."

"Exactly."

"You can't tell anything from that. I was excited. I had been out on the Strip, and then all that stupid—"

Three-fourths of the 640 patients who clustered into the ward last year were casualties of the Strip or the Strip milieu of Las Vegas, the psychiatrist tells me. He is a bright and energetic man in a shawl-collared black silk suit with brass buttons.

"I'm not even her doctor," he says. "I don't know her case. There's nothing I can do for her."

Here, securely out of sight in this little warren, are all those who have taken the loop-the-loop and could not stand the centripety. Some, like Raymond, who has been rocketing for days on pills and liquor, who has gone without sleep to the point of anoxia, might pull out of the toxic reaction in two or three days, or eight or ten. Others have conflicts to add to the chemical wackiness. A man who has thrown all his cash to the flabby homunculus who sits at every craps table stuffing the take down an almost hidden chute so it won't pile up in front of the customers' eyes; a man who has sold the family car for next to nothing at a car lot advertising "Cash for your car—*right now*" *and* then thrown that to the homunculus, too, but also still has the family waiting guiltlessly, guilelessly back home; well, he has troubles.

". . . After I came here and began doing personal studies," the doctor is saying, "I recognized extreme aggressiveness continually. It's not merely what Las Vegas can do to a person, it's the type of person it attracts. Gambling is a very aggressive pastime, and Las Vegas attracts aggressive people. They have an amazing capacity to louse up a normal situation."

The girl, probably a looker in more favorable moments, is pressed face into the wall, cutting glances at the doctor. The nurse tells her something and she puts her face in her hands, convulsing but not making a sound. She retreats to her room, and then the sounds come shrieking out. The doctor rushes back. Other patients are sticking their heads out of their rooms along the hall.

"The young girl?" a quiet guy says to a nurse. "The young girl," he says to somebody in the room.

But the big brunette just keeps rolling her decal eyes.

Out in the courtyard—all bare sand—the light is a kind of light-bulb twilight. An old babe is rocking herself back and forth on a straight chair and putting one hand out in front from time to time and pulling it in toward her bosom.

It seems clear enough to me. "A slot machine?" I say to the nurse, but she says there is no telling.

". . . and yet the same aggressive types are necessary to build a frontier town, and Las Vegas is a frontier town, certainly by any psychological standard," Dr. ——— is saying. "They'll undertake anything and they'll accomplish it. The building here has been incredible. They don't seem to care what they're up against, so they do it."

I go out to the parking lot in back of the County Hospital and it doesn't take a second; as soon as I turn on the motor I'm swinging again with Action Checkpoint News, "Monkey No. 9," "Donna, Donna, the Prima Donna," and friendly picking-and-swinging for the Fremont Hotel and Frontier Federal. Me and my big white car are sailing down the Strip and the Boomerang Modern, Palette Curvilinear, Flash Gordon Ming-Alert Spiral, McDonald's Hamburger Parabola, Mint Casino Elliptical and Miami Beach Kidney sunbursts are exploding in the Young Electric Sign Company's Grand Gallery for all the sun kings. At the airport there was that bad interval between the rental-car stall and the terminal entrance, but once through the automatic door the Muzak came bubbling up with "Song of India." On the upper level around the ramps the slots were cranking away. They are placed like "traps," a word Las Vegas picked up from golf. And an old guy is walking up the ramp, just off the plane from Denver, with a huge plastic bag of clothes slung over the left shoulder and a two-suiter suitcase in his right hand. He has to put the suitcase down on the floor and jostle the plastic bag all up around his neck to keep it from falling, but he manages to dig into his pocket for a couple of coins and get going on the slot machines. All seems right, but walking out to my plane I sense that something is missing. Then I recall sitting in the cocktail lounge of the Dunes at 3 P.M. with Jack Heskett, district manager of the Federal Sign and Signal Corporation, and Marty Steinman, the sales manager, and Ted Blaney, a designer. They are telling me about the sign they are building for the Dunes to put up at the airport. It will be five thousand square feet of free-standing sign, done in flaming-lake red on burning-desert gold. The d—the D—alone in the word Dunes, written in Cyrillic modern, will be practically two stories high. An inset plexiglas display, the largest revolving, trivision plexiglas sign in the world, will turn and show first the Dunes, with its twenty-two-story addition, then the seahorse swimming pool, then the new golf course. The scimitar curves of the sign will soar to a huge roaring diamond at the very top. "You'll be able to see it from an airplane fifteen miles away," says Jack Heskett. "Fifty miles," says Lee Fisher. And it will be sixty-five feet up in the air—

because the thing was, somebody was out at the airport and they noticed there was only one display to be topped. That was that shaft about sixty feet high with the lit-up globe and the beacon lights, which is to say, the control tower. Hell, you can only see that forty miles away. But exactly!

Daniel Lang

Blackjack and Flashes

Of the many atomic-energy installations now in operation throughout the country, probably the only one that tallies to any great extent
with the layman's conception of such projects is the continental
proving ground for nuclear weapons, which was started sixty-five
miles northwest of here, in the desert of southern Nevada, a little
over a year and a half ago. The other manifestations of the thriving
new industry—factories producing radioactive fuels, piles cooking
fissionable materials, laboratories housing novel research equip-
ment, and so on—have thus far turned out to be eerily silent and

☞ From The New Yorker, *September* 20, 1952.

generally as well-behaved as a hosiery mill. Here, on the other hand, there is a bit of action. Neither the tight security watch that is maintained over the government-owned proving ground nor the distance between it and Las Vegas has prevented taxpayers in these parts from getting at least a sketchy idea of the nature of the product they are helping to finance. On numerous occasions, a piercing flash of light, many times the intensity of the sun's, has burst over the proving ground in the very early morning, momentarily transforming a gloomy Nevada dawn to a dazzling noon. The same light, pale and diminished, has been seen simultaneously as far away as San Diego, on the Pacific Coast, and Kalispell, Montana—three hundred and fifty and a thousand miles, respectively, from the proving ground. The atomic clouds, with their unearthly hues, that accompany nuclear detonations have been plainly visible from Las Vegas, and sound, in the form of shock waves, has hurtled into this mecca of gamblers, divorcées, and elopers, cracking hotel walls and demolishing restaurant china. Merchants have seen the panes of their display windows shattered and strewn on the sidewalk. Last fall, the owners of Allen & Hanson, a local haberdashery, placed a barrel filled with plate-glass fragments outside their shop and posted a sign over it: "ATOM BOMB SOUVENIRS—FREE!" Within an hour, the barrel was empty. At last report, four hundred and twenty-six people in this region have collected damages from the government, amounting to nearly fifty thousand dollars, and additional claims are pending. The detonation of one bomb broke a vase in Modesto, California, five hundred miles from the testing area.

Thanks to their new neighbor, Las Vegans have picked up a little physics. When they see an atomic flash in the sky, they immediately consult their watches, for they have learned that it takes the ensuing shock wave about seven minutes to reach their town from the proving ground. They know, too, that the low-pressure wave that follows a shock wave does not push windows in but sucks them out, and that the best thing to do to escape damage from both waves is to open a window or door. Despite all the rainless lightning and thunder the Las Vegans have been subjected to, it is possible to find among their other reactions a certain pride in their proximity to the proving ground. "It annoys me to read about some statesman saying that the *world* is living with the atomic bomb," a divorce lawyer here told me the other day. "Damn it, it's not the world. It's Las Vegas."

Late in 1950, when word got around that the government was planning to detonate atomic bombs in the desert near Las Vegas, the news was greeted here with as much enthusiasm as would have greeted the news that gambling, the principal local industry, has been legalized in California, the state from which this town draws its most prodigal players. The general feeling was that the nearby bombing range would scare visitors away, disastrously upsetting the local economy. In its own peculiar way, Las Vegas, at the time, was going quite well. It had become so popular as a divorce center that some of its more optimistic inhabitants were looking forward to the day when it would pull even with Reno in that respect. An increasing number of couples from southern California, too impatient to bother with the blood tests required by their own state, were eloping to Las Vegas, to be married in such chapels as the Hitching Post, Gretna Green, and the Wee Kirk o' the Heather. (A typical sign outside one of these chapels reads, "ORGAN MUSIC—FLOWERS—PHOTOGRAPHS—IMMEDIATELY!") But while it would be bad enough to lose the marriage-and-divorce trade, Las Vegans were concerned above all lest the proving ground impair their town's standing as the gambling capital of the only state in the Union where gambling is legal. The gambling business in Las Vegas was flourishing. Western Air Lines was providing non-stop service for players from Los Angeles, three hundred miles away, and gambling members of the affluent movie crowd were showing up with gratifying regularity. So was Nick the Greek. Along the Strip—a short stretch of Highway 91, about two miles south of the center of town, that is flanked by the more elaborate hotel-casinos—the revenue from gambling was substantial enough to enable hosts to favor their patrons with lagniappe. Leading entertainers, such as Josephine Baker, Jimmy Durante, and Joe E. Lewis, could be seen going through their routines in hotel night clubs where there was never a cover or minimum charge, and the same hotels strove to outdo one another in the magnificence of the fare they provided on their so-called chuckwagons—buffets at which, from midnight to eight in the morning, the customers could help themselves to all they wanted for a mere dollar and a half. "If a man loses enough money, we'll even pay his fare back home," a stick man at the Thunderbird told me. "It's a wonderful town, all right! Where else can a fellow gamble all day, get drunk, go to sleep, get up at four in the morning, and find plenty of company when he walks into the lobby?"

On January 11, 1951, the government officially confirmed the reports of its plans to build the proving ground, and shortly thereafter the Las Vegas Chamber of Commerce printed up some publicity releases intended to allay the qualms of future visitors. One showed a girl sporting an Atomic Hairdo, the product of a Las Vegas beauty parlor. Another heralded the Atomic Cocktail, invented by a bartender in one of the hotels here, and consisting of equal parts of vodka, brandy, and champagne, with a dash of sherry. In a third, a girl wearing a Bikini suit was brandishing a Geiger counter as she checked the beard of a grizzled desert prospector for radioactivity. "The angle was to get people to think the explosions wouldn't be anything more than a gag," a Chamber of Commerce official explained to me.

During the early days of the proving ground, I have been told, the heads of two or three of the casinos tentatively discussed some rather special civil-defense plans. "We were afraid the bombs might shake the tables so hard that the dice would be tipped over and the roulette balls would bounce out of one number into another," one of them recalled. "We thought we might have to post signs warning players that in such an event the house man's ruling, as always, would be final." Such precautions were subsequently found to be unnecessary, and they would have been unavailing anyway on the one occasion when the physicists out at the proving ground did disturb Las Vegas gamblers. That was last November, when a plate glass window near a crap game in the El Cortez Hotel was broken by a shock wave. The players turned briefly to see what had happened and, when they got back to their game, found that the pot was shy twenty dollars.

As word of what was in store for Las Vegas spread, motoring tourists began making it a point to stop here long enough to shop for merchandise, which, they calmly explained, they wanted not for utility but as mementos of a town that archeologists would in all probability soon be exploring. "It got to be pretty grim," a salesman at the local Sears, Roebuck store said to me. "One morning during those last days of waiting, an elderly lady from Los Angeles came in and told me to hurry up and sell her two shirts, that her husband was waiting outside in the car with the motor running. She said she wanted to hand them down to her grandsons, as heirlooms that had come from Las Vegas just before it was wiped off the face of the earth."

To add to the general apprehension, it began to appear that the Commission had decided not to make known in advance the hour, or even the day, when its bombs were to be exploded (a policy it later discarded). Provoked by this, some Las Vegans, upon learning that the local office of the Civil Aeronautics Authority would be responsible for clearing air lanes near the proving ground several hours prior to a detonation, took to calling that office daily, pretending to be pilots of private or commercial planes and asking for the latest reports. Others called the Bonanza Air Lines, in Las Vegas, to inquire whether its Reno-bound flights, which would be halted by the C.A.A. when a shot was impending, were leaving on schedule. The movements of known scientists staying at Las Vegas hotels were carefully observed by bellhops and guests. "It got so that, besides worrying about gambling takes, we were worrying about our own skins," an assistant manager of one of the hotels told me.

The members of the Atomic Energy Commission, being quite unconcerned about either the marriage-and-divorce business or the comings and goings of Nick the Greek, proceeded unhesitatingly with their project, convinced that they had chosen a site that was ideal for their purpose. To be sure, the Commission already had a proving ground at Eniwetok, out in the Pacific, but that was five thousand miles from its weapons headquarters, at Los Alamos, New Mexico. While the isolation Eniwetok affords was—and still is—considered advisable for the testing of certain bombs, the A.E.C. people felt that the majority of shots, to use the trade term, could be safely run off closer to home. Ralph Carlyle Smith, the Assistant Director of the Los Alamos Scientific Laboratory, enumerated for me some of the considerations that prompted them to establish the Nevada proving ground. "It's a terrible waste of valuable time to have our scientists spend all those days travelling to and from Eniwetok," he said. "Since the island is hardly within commuting distance of New Mexico, whenever they go there, they stay there—for six months or so, without their families or any of the amenities of life. And it's a nuisance to have to keep the island free of pests by continually spraying it from the air. Screens are useless there. The corrosion caused by that tropical climate is something fierce. I've seen buildings practically disintegrate before my eyes. Apart from all this, it's important for us to be near our laboratories, with their instruments. Some of the radioactive samples that have to be analyzed are extremely short-lived."

The Nevada site, which, as at least one of the blasts has proved, is within hearing distance of Los Alamos, had several things besides its handiness to recommend it, Smith went on. Consisting of six hundred and forty square miles of unpopulated land, it was looked upon as large enough to accommodate experiments with most kinds of atomic weapons. By the time radiation resulting from the explosions reached the nearest inhabited places, the A.E.C. figured, it would be sufficiently dissipated to cause no ill effects. (The A.E.C. also figured that if radiation in lethal strength *should* drift toward populated areas, there would be ample time to alert and evacuate the threatened citizens.) Furthermore, it was felt that delays caused by the weather would be fewer in the equable desert climate than in most other parts of the United States. Because rain tends to concentrate radiation, the desert's scant rainfall was regarded as an asset. So was the circumstance that strong winds, capable of carrying radioactive matter quickly to populated areas, are rare in this part of Nevada. And the almost daily clear blue skies over the desert would simplify the task of Air Force crews charged with precision bombing and with the tracking and sampling of atomic clouds. Moreover, the tract was already owned by the government (it had been bought during the war for an Air Force bombing range), so it would cost the Commission nothing. Finally, Las Vegas was considered both near enough to and far enough away from the proving ground—near enough for supplies to be delivered to the freight yards of the Union Pacific Railroad, on the town's outskirts, and for its population of twenty-five thousand, to furnish the labor needed for constructing and maintaining the proving ground, and far enough away to insure the isolation required for reasons not only of safety but of security. "Out on the desert, anything that moves, animal or human, is an event," Smith said. "It can be seen for miles."

On January 26, 1951, the Commission let it be known that two nights earlier there had been a "dry run" to test the proving ground's communications and other facilities. At this point, the atmosphere of suspense in Las Vegas became almost unbearable, but it was dispelled at dawn the next day by an incredibly brilliant flash and, seven minutes later, a whacking blast that left a trail of broken glass from downtown Las Vegas clear out to the Strip. Operation Ranger—the name the A.E.C. gave its first series of tests—was under way. Most of the residents were awakened by tumbling window shades and shaking walls; some of them were tossed out of bed. Nobody was hurt, but one of the town's two daily newspapers, the *Review-Journal*, indulged its readers' dire expectations with the front-page headline "VEGANS ATOMIZED." All that day, there was worried speculation as to whether this might be only a tame curtain-raiser, but on the following morning a second shot came off and turned out to be no worse, and the atomized Vegans began to take their obstreperous neighbor in stride. Some of them expressed their relief by filing damage claims, of varying validity. Several homeowners declared that the shock waves had cracked the walls of their houses, but in more than one instance investigators found an accumulation of dust and cobwebs in the fissures. Others wanted reparations for broken water pipes, a few of which had obviously been corroding for years. The government was asked to provide new roofs to replace roofs that had been patched and repatched. A rancher in an area where no shock wave had struck charged that his chimney had been shaken loose and his house set on fire. A hermit living miles from town complained that his farm implements had been stolen "in the general excitement."

Operation Ranger consisted of five shots, which occurred on an average of one every forty-eight hours. Out along the Strip, the gamblers and divorcees took to throwing what became known as dawn parties—drinking and singing sessions that began after midnight and ended, if there was a shot that morning, with the sight of the flash or, if there was no shot, by just petering out around breakfast time. The Desert Inn's Sky Room, a glass-enclosed cocktail lounge with a sweeping panoramic view, was an especially popular spot for dawn parties. "It was a wonderful place for what the customers wanted," a waitress there told me. "They could sit around and listen to our piano player and look out the big windows and see the pretty hotel fountain and the guests swimming in the pool and the traffic speeding by on Highway 91, and then, just when they were starting to get tired, the A-bomb." The patrons at bars without views had to keep on their toes. As a bartender in one of these places recalled the other day, "Some fellow who'd been sitting around with his girl all night would suddenly look at his watch and say, 'Guess it's time for the bomb.' They'd grab their drinks and dash out, and then the rest of the crowd would follow them. After the damn thing went off, they'd all disappear, but by that time we'd have done more business than if we had television out here."

One night early in February, at the proving ground, Carroll L.

Tyler, the Test Manager, and Dr. Alvin C. Graves, the Test Director, received a weather report from their meteorologist that led them to postpone a shot originally scheduled for the coming dawn. The two officials drove back to Las Vegas, arriving at their hotel—it was the Last Frontier, and they were well known there—at about three in the morning. Before turning in, they decided to breakfast in the hotel's Gay Nineties Bar, which was jammed with the usual dawn-party set. They had hardly sat down when they had the place to themselves and a hotel official was at their table pleading with them never to stop by there at that time again. "He said that we should have gone right upstairs and that he'd have been delighted to present us with breakfast in our rooms," Tyler recalls.

The townspeople didn't go in for dawn parties. They had less turbulent ways of greeting the unnatural daylight that was breaking spasmodically over their community. "Around five-thirty in the morning, the lights would start going on in my neighborhood," I was told by Doris Leighton, who is an administrative assistant at the Nevada Construction Company, a contracting firm. "Some of us would come out on our porches with cups of coffee and wait there. We'd be wearing heavy wrappers, because those winter mornings were quite nippy, you know. Sometimes husbands would back their cars out of the garage and into the street to get a better view. They'd let the motor run until the car was warm, and then their families would come out and join them. I used to see parents pinching small children and playing games with them to keep them awake. I guess they wanted to be sure their kids would see history in the making. People all looked expectant, but in different ways. Some, you could see, were afraid. Others smiled and acted nonchalant."

"There was one dawn test I saw from a rooftop, and I'll never forget it," Mrs. Donald Lukens, the wife of a Las Vegas journalist, told me. "When I could see again after the blinding, terrifying flash, I was looking at the sun. It was just coming up over the mountains. The sun, you know, isn't always kind to us here in the desert, but at that moment it seemed like an old friend. It made me feel safe."

Operation Ranger came to an end with a shot at dawn on February 6th. Last October, the second series—Operation Buster-Jangle, seven shots—started up. During Operation Buster-Jangle, Las Vegans displayed little of their earlier skittishness. Less worried now about their own skins, they showed a tendency to regard the proving ground as a good thing. Many heads of families were holding down steady, well-paying jobs with the Commission, and, far from scaring visitors away, the experiments, and the resulting publicity, were actually attracting more. To the joy of the shopkeepers, many of the new visitors turned out to be of a different breed from the accustomed ones who passed up the town in favor of the Strip and spent their time and money out there. Now Las Vegas was besieged by people who cared little about room service and gambling; they bought their own groceries, and cooked them in trailers or motels. They were not interested in getting married or divorced; they simply wanted to be on hand for an explosion. When a detonation was in prospect (by this time the Commission was disclosing its plans), they got into their autos and, along with numbers of Las Vegans, headed for Mount Charleston, a forty-two-hundred-foot vantage point about fifty miles southeast of the test area. "Bumper to bumper, just like a ball game," an attendant at a gas station along the way said in describing the cavalcade.

Meanwhile, business at the big hotels was excellent, too. "I don't know exactly how much the bomb had to do with it, but around shot time the play in our casino seemed to go up and the drinking got heavier," I was told by Wilbur Clark, the head of the Desert Inn. "The curious thing was that guests would drive here from Los Angeles to see a shot and then not bother to look at it. I'd instruct my pitmen to let the players at their tables know when it was about time for the flash, but the players would go right on with their games."

A shot that took place on the morning of November 1st sent Las Vegas its most jolting shock. Over two hundred damage claims were filed as a result—a record number to date. "That was another time we had an especially good take on gambling," Clark recalled. "Same for liquor. Hell, I took an extra drink myself."

Most of the shots of the second series went off between 7 and 8 A.M., instead of at dawn, but that was no bar to dawn parties. One of the parties turned out to have nothing to celebrate, but everybody there had a fine time just the same. "That was quite a night," Ted Mossman, the pianist at the Sky Room, told me one evening. "Standing room only. They were drinking like fish. Some of them had cameras for photographing the flash—a thing they couldn't have done even if they'd been sober. It's too bright. Everyone wanted to sing. They requested all the old numbers—'Margie,' 'The Sidewalks of New York,' 'Bye, Bye, Blackbird,' 'Put Your Arms Around Me, Honey.' They sang as if they were on the Queen Mary and it was going down—loud, desperate voices. After a while, I couldn't take it any more, so I improvised some boogie-woogie that I called 'The Atom Bomb Bounce.' I kept playing it and playing it, until I thought my fingers would fall off. Seven o'clock in the morning, we get word there's been a circuit failure out at the proving ground and the bomb's called off. The crowd took the news fine. They all started betting when the next bomb would be exploded—the week, the day of the week, the hour of the day."

By no means everyone in Las Vegas and its environs has become resigned to the Commission's activities. Certainly no one can blame a rancher by the name of Carroll, whose water hole was found to be dangerously close to the test area, if he is inclined to bridle at the mere mention of the A.E.C. Carroll had already had to move his herds once, back in 1945, when the Manhattan District requisitioned his grazing land in New Mexico for the first atom-bomb test. When the authorities informed him he would have to move a second time, and why, it was almost too much for him. "Oh, Lord, no, not again!" he cried out as he grasped the significance of the deputation that had come to wait upon him. Some of the A.E.C.'s security guards turned cowhand for a day to help drive Carroll's cattle to a new range, but that did little to assuage the rancher's exasperation.

Among the other people who wish the government had located its proving ground elsewhere, some are convinced that a variety of melancholy events are attributable to the explosions. There is a tendency among people who have recently been afflicted with any disease to blame it on the bomb. Governor Charles Russell, of Nevada, told me that one Las Vegan had written to warn him that if the explosions weren't discontinued soon, the minds of southern Nevadans would be addled by the tremendous light and sound waves. The Governor also said that he knows of an old prospector who is living in perpetual dread lest his small outcropping be hit by a bomb. A woman in California has telephoned the Governor several times to express her conviction, in the face of his repeated denials, that federal prisoners are deliberately being exposed to the weapon's radiation, "like the mice and goats on Bikini." The experiments were widely regarded as responsible for last winter's abnormal severity in northern Nevada. During one particularly cold spell, nine manganese miners, whose work was being hampered by snow and ice, petitioned Governor Russell to put a stop to the detonations, and he, in turn, asked some meteorologists at the University of Nevada to look into the matter. They assured him that, far from being localized, the bad weather conditions prevailed throughout Montana and the Dakotas, and, as far as they knew, had nothing to do with the bombs.

Still, the Governor said, every now and then, while reading his mail, he finds himself wondering who is right—the nuclear physicists or his correspondents. "The whole field of atomic energy is so new," he went on. "Perhaps the scientists will eventually come around to agreeing with the beliefs of some of the people who write to me. But no matter who's right, it's exciting to think that the submarginal land of the proving ground is furthering science and helping national defense," the Governor added. "We had long ago written off that terrain as wasteland, and today it's blooming with atoms."

By now, a third series of shots has come and gone, and the predominant attitude in Las Vegas toward the proving ground is one of casualness. In fact, this series, which ended in June, is generally dismissed as having been something of a dud. There were eight shots, and none of them gave the town more than a mild tremor. Only twenty-odd damage claims were filed. The townspeople didn't bother to climb up on their rooftops to sight billowing atomic clouds, and dawn parties went out of style. "Bigger bombs, that's what we're waiting for," said one night-club proprietor. "Americans have to have their kicks." The local A.E.C. offices, according to Marjorie Allen, a secretary there, have received several complaints that the third series was a let-down. "After one of our shots, we got a phone call from a sweet old man who had heard about this grousing and was afraid we were taking it to heart," Miss Allen went on. "He just wanted to let us know that he'd been fishing out at Lake Mead at the time of the shot and that the shock wave had come in nice and strong there."

Many Las Vegans have become nostalgic connoisseurs, pining for the days of the unannounced, robust dawn shots of Operation Ranger. "Good bangs, and so pretty coming at sunrise like they did" is the way one veteran recalls the early tests. Others, less aesthetically inclined, fondly remember the concussive quality of the November 1st shot. One day during the most recent series, Joe McClain, a columnist for the *Review-Journal*, which once had Las Vegans atomized, used his space to accuse the A.E.C. of "gypping its public."

Time was when a nuclear detonation took place, people knew about it [McClain wrote]. . . . People seemed to enjoy the show. But the good old days of Operation Ranger have passed. The scientists, to speak loosely, seem to have a little more control on the old fireball. . . . Yesterday afternoon we had several calls wondering when "the A-bomb was going off." The people were real sore when they learned it already had been detonated. We think it might be good for the town's spirit if the scientists would send a few effects down Vegas way. Just to keep people happy.

These days, Las Vegas is a shrill, restless resort town. While this is as true when tests are not in progress as when they are, Governor Russell, Chamber of Commerce officials, and hotel people attribute the community's present condition in large part to the publicity that the proving ground has given it. "We're in the throes of acute prosperity," one hotel man informed me. "Before the proving ground, people just heard that this was a wide-open town. Now that we're next door to the atom bomb, they really believe it." The pangs of prosperity are especially perceptible to visitors trying to book rooms in Strip hotels. Even when one of them is successful in making a reservation, his triumph may not last if the degree of his gambling isn't sufficiently impressive. The other afternoon, an acquaintance of mine who was staying at one of the larger hotels was hailed by a desk clerk as he passed through the lobby, and brusquely asked to give up his room. The guest took the matter up with a managerial assistant, who simply said, "We've got a ten-thousand-dollar player waiting for that room. What do you think keeps the doors open?" The guest packed up and left. At another hotel, an Eastern scientist, just arrived in Las Vegas for the first time, felt that he was on the verge of landing a room when, spotting some crapshooters in the lobby, he was reminded of a mathematical technique known in scientific circles as the Monte Carlo method and used by physicists to estimate the odds on such eventualities as a neutron's escaping from a pile or causing fission. He started discoursing on this to the desk clerk, whose face at once took on a bored expression. "I informed him that I preferred gambling with the Monte Carlo method, a rather ingenious form of nuclear craps," the scientist told me later. "The next thing I knew, he was informing *me* that he had a lot of mail to sort—and no rooms."

Some of the scientists hereabouts, however, are on occasion quite willing to indulge in the more conventional forms of gambling. The evening following a shot, when the strain under which they have been working eases up for a while, they are likely to be far less interested in computing nuclear odds by the Monte Carlo method than in letting off steam by the accepted Las Vegas method. At such times, a number of them are to be seen playing blackjack in the casino of the Last Frontier. There they while away the evening at the green baize tables, sipping highballs and chain-smoking. They weigh the purchase of a card with as much concentration as if they were pondering a problem in nucleonics, and become too absorbed to take notice of the crowd around them—townspeople who, having watched the hotel's night-club show for the price of a cup of coffee, are killing a few dollars at the slot machines; divorcées in long evening dresses, cheerfully rolling dice; shrewd-faced Hollywood figures at the roulette wheels; impecunious soldiers ordered to Nevada for atomic maneuvers, who play blackjack vicariously by staring at the cards in the gamblers' hands. Finally, soothed by the unpredictability of the cards, the scientists go off to their rooms. On such evenings, when the scientists are at the Last Frontier and it may be taken for granted that no atomic bomb will explode in the desolate wilderness to the northwest, Las Vegas, for all the heavy play at its tables, seems less of a gambling town than usual.

Jane O'Reilly

In Las Vegas:
Working Hard for the Money

Eight o'clock in the evening is a slow, sullen hour in Sin City, a.k.a. Lost Wages. "I'm tired," whines a member of the United States Twirling Association. "C'mon, we're supposed to be having fun," snaps her companion, a clone. In razor-crease jeans and stiletto heels they stamp into the ladies' room, flounce around the corner past the polished wash-basins and disappear into the two long rows of toilet stalls. They are the kind of girls who obey their mothers' warnings never to sit on strange toilet seats. Attendants have to nip in after that type, making sure the next woman will have no un-

☞ From Time, *August 27, 1984.*

pleasant surprises. That is the sort of job specification that made Donna Summer's song about a ladies' room attendant, *She Works Hard for the Money*, a big hit, especially in the neon city.

A circle of flattering pink mirrors catches multiple reflections of the plaster statue of Diana. On the dusty-rose settee, two elderly ladies in Orlon lace sweaters tell each other racist jokes and giggle. The attendant, who is black, has just unwrapped twelve rolls of toilet paper and is now dragging two huge bags of trash out the door. She passes an aghast English-speaking European tourist, who apparently expected Las Vegas to be more in the style of James Bond at Monte Carlo.

Two women on the far side of 45 stand next to each other before the wash-basins, excavating makeup from the inside corners of their eyes. Vision restored, they notice they are wearing the same velour jogging suit. The turquoise version is from Pasadena, Calif., the deep pink from Evanston, Ill. Imagine that! Instant sisterhood. Evanston, who is in real estate and relaxes by playing the slots, says, "Have you got one of those rooms with the round bed and the mirror on the ceiling? Just out of curiosity, I asked the bellboy what it would cost me to get some company. He said, 'It's hard to get any kind of a sharp looker in here for less than $100. But you shouldn't have any trouble on your own.' So I checked out the craps tables. This adorable guy, my type, with the Southern drawl, the boots and the $500 chips, told me to step right up and be his good luck. Well, after ten minutes I realized I'd have to stand there all night to shift his attention away from the table."

"Yeah," says Pasadena, "I'm married to one of those kind of guys." Pause. "Did you say $100? That seems sort of high." Both women scrub hands blackened from pushing hundreds of coins into slot machines, and then each takes one thin quarter from the paper cup holding her slot-machine supplies and deposits it on the tip plate. An attendant, sweeping together the wreckage of paper products they have left behind, says, "Women don't tip like men. Sometimes I don't take home more than $6 in tips."

❧   ❧   ❧

At 11 o'clock everyone is friendly, wide awake and ready for action. A response of "Nice dress" to "You like that mascara?" leads, within minutes, to "So I told him, if he wants to see those children, he has to stop tearing them up emotionally." A circle of strangers, all intricately wielding lip pencils, choruses sympathetically, "Baby, I know just what you mean." A dealer from another casino drops in to visit a friend, who looks at the dealer's name tag and says, "Bernadette? Since when?" The real name is Pamela, but, she says, "I'm sick of it. I tried Edith one time and all I got was 'Oh ho, Edith, have your cake and Edith too, eh?' Mona is best. It sounds sort of untouchable." The false Bernadette says she had dinner with "someone influential, very prominent in town." This is code for someone with reputed underworld ties. "It was boring, I'm not going out again until I find someone as smart as my ten-year-old son."

A classic bimbo comes in, a sincere (as opposed to commercial) bimbo, a woman who has chosen her life-style and works hard at it. She is accompanied by a bimbo-in-training, a young woman who has not yet imagined all the places blusher can be applied. Both wear draped and beaded jersey jumpsuits. It is hard to go to the bathroom in such garments, and the subsequent readjustment involves lots of friendly bantering with the attendant. "We came with some degenerates who went straight to the tables. They haven't even been up to our rooms." ("Degenerate" is an acknowledged category of gambler in Las Vegas, one step ahead of "compulsive" on the road to ruin.) In perfect synchronization, the two women lean over with brushes in both hands, and each beats her hair into a froth. Upright again, both declare, "Ugh! Straw!" The little bimbo says, "I'd never put color on my hair. People would think I was phony." Her mentor, wiser and blonder, lets the remark pass. She takes out a small bottle and sprays her face. "Baby oil. Gives you that fresh, dewy look." But doesn't it smudge? "Oh, you never let them play kissy face—it ruins your makeup." They depart from the premises, the big bimbo's cleavage prompting admiring stares from a mother and daughter in wind-breakers. Says Mom to newlywed daughter: "How'd you like to have a pair like that?"

At 2 o'clock in the morning the tourists are as blurred and fading as children allowed up past bedtime. The women who work the graveyard shift sneak in for a cigarette. Says a cocktail waitress: "We're supposed to go to designated areas for our breaks, and otherwise the bosses want us out on the floor all the time." "The bosses" is the Las Vegas equivalent of "the Man," covering every rank of power from a floor supervisor to a casino manager to the Mob to God. The bosses are, almost without exception, men. "Dorks, all of them," says a cashier. "A boss asked me out last week. We'd go to the mountains, he said. You guessed it. No mountains. Halfway through dinner he says, 'Are we going to get between the sheets or not?' Cute, huh? Lucky thing I brought my own car." She takes out a tube of Super Glue and, in a surrealistic gesture worthy of Buñuel, reattaches a thumbnail that is one and a half inches long.

Fingernail maintenance seems to fill the hours women once devoted to straightening stocking seams and rolling pin curls. The ladies' room crowd admires a tourist, the owner of a nail shop in California, who reveals a gold nail set with diamonds on her left ring finger. But the home champ is Leta Powers, whose nails are polished, striped with silver and pierced with little gold circles and charms. Leta works as a Goddess, which means she is a cocktail waitress at Caesars Palace, a hotel and casino organized around a spurious Greco-Roman theme. Locally, the Goddesses are dubbed coneheads, after the shape of the false hairpiece that is part of the costume. Unchanged since the hotel opened in 1966, the uniform, with its uncomfortable corset top and cutie-pie short pleated skirt, is as archaic as the clothes in a Currier & Ives print. The Goddesses, carrying a tray of drinks in one hand, give a thin gloss of glamour to that job that is a grueling eight-hour hike in high heels. But, says Goddess Bonnie Arrage, "I'm one of nine sisters, born in Kentucky. I was working as a secretary in Michigan, and I got laid off. I decided I wanted to go where there was money left in the world. For someone like me, with only a high school education, this is opportunity city."

All night the conversation threads along: aching feet, daughters' weddings, chemotherapy, whether or not it will rain that weekend— and men. A coffee-shop hostess says, "You know Howard? My old boyfriend? He's seeing a new girl. She's 30, with two kids. They've already got an apartment together. Well, last night he comes into my place. I gave him one of my superduper dirty looks. He says I've got to talk to him because the two of them need money. He wants to borrow some. Can you imagine?"

Jean Brown is the attendant from 2 A.M. to 10 A.M., and she knows what to say: "You keep a positive outlook. Don't give up. Keep faith in yourself. You never know when Mr. Right will show up."

The hostess sighs. "I never thought I'd be carrying menus at 35." And then, "What do you think I ought to wear when he comes back to get the money?"

John Gregory Dunne

··

Vegas:
A Memoir of a Dark Season

Jackie Kasey was taking some steam. It was three P.M. on a Monday afternoon, he had a cold and he had done two shows the night before. Sunday night was a bad night for a lounge comic. The weekend mob had cleared out and the convention crowd was still settling in, getting their plastic name tags and drinking gin and orange juice or Seagram's Seven and Seven in the hospitality suite. The insurance wives compared corsages and hair spray, their husbands the latest full-coverage floaters.

"Just tied up Ben Maddox."

☞ *Excerpted from* Vegas: A Memoir of a Dark Season (*Random House*, 1974).

"He still got that Chrysler-Plymouth agency over in Stockton?"

"No, sirree. He's into mobile homes. Ten thousand a whack."

"Discount pricing."

"And seven locations. New and used product. Newports, Vikings, Ramadas, all sizes and models."

"Synthetic shrubbery?"

"That's an extra. You know what his slogan is?"

"What's that?"

" 'The Mobile Home That Looks Like a Home.' "

"Good slogan."

"I think so."

All of which made the lounge comic's life more difficult. The convention crowd was not a high-rolling crowd in any case, and the first night in town they were too busy setting up prospects to look in on the lounges or to give the tables much play. The lounges were full only on weekends and so deserted the rest of the week that many of the hotels on the Strip were turning them into keno rooms. A keno room was open twenty-four hours a day and was therefore a profit center, much more so than an empty lounge where a $10,000-a-week comic spent Sunday to Thursday nights playing to audiences consisting mainly of hookers cruising for johns.

The empty house at the second show Sunday night had not made Jackie Kasey's cold any better. There was a black hooker with a gold left front tooth and a small American flag decaled to her bag working the bar and maybe forty other people scattered around a room that sat six hundred. The jokes just sat there.

"Why don't you all get at one table so I can talk to someone," Jackie said.

Nothing.

"One thing I found traveling around the country is that a night when no one is here you're in trouble."

Nothing.

❧   ❧   ❧

The second show broke at two-thirty and Jackie wandered around the casino until five A.M. He was too revved up to go to bed and the cold was working its way down into his chest. This was his first shot as the headliner in the lounge at the hotel and he had worked up a whole new act and the act was not going. He was forty years old and had spent twenty years working one-night stands at bowling alleys and smokers and automobile dealers' district sales meetings. He had learned his trade the hard way in places like the Chart House in Milwaukee and Leo's Supper Club in Peoria, Illinois, and the Cool Club in Cairo and the Brentwood Country Club in Lexington, Kentucky. They were Mob joints mainly, with a line of girls out front and a private game in the back, and he worked on his Harold, the Homo Halfback routine and his Girl with the Itchy Twitchy routine and his Dangerous Dan, the Used Car Man routine. They went over big at the Pink Panther Room in Akron and the Club Capri in Cincinnati and the Aware Inn in Sioux City and Great Lakes Social Club in Buffalo, N.Y., but he flopped at the Copacabana in New York and was canceled out of the Town & Country in Brooklyn after one night. He was doing a flamenco routine at the Town & Country and when he twirled his cape it knocked the wig off a woman sitting down front and the woman was the best friend of the boss's wife. He went back to club dates and worked out of Detroit and Miami and played four different spots a night in the Borscht Belt. He started in Vegas downtown on Fremont Street and then was the comedian in an ice show on the Strip, and then was signed to warm up for Frank and then for Dean, and then Colonel Tom Parker caught his act and hired him to warm up for Elvis. He went on tour with Elvis and bought a house in Beverly Hills, south of Wilshire, east of Doheny, but still Beverly Hills, and the year before he had grossed $108,000 and no one knew his name. Now he was headlining in the lounge at the hotel, he was making $10,000 a week, he had a cold, his act was not working and there was still no one who knew his name.

Jackie got up early Monday afternoon, had some breakfast and decided to take some steam for the cold. He did not play golf, it was too hot to play tennis and there was nothing else to do. The walls of the health club were lined with autographed eight-by-ten glossies, "To Lew Foxx, Best regards, Sandra Dee" and "To Lew, One great guy, Roman Gabriel" and "To Lew, Many thanks, Gene Tunney." Lew Foxx ran the health spa. He was a very healthy pink-skinned man in his mid-fifties, barrel-chested, with generous clumps of hair growing out of his nostrils and creeping out of the back of his shirt over the collar. He was not by trade a masseur. He had once run some parking lot in Cleveland and was very well connected.

"What do you mean 'well connected'?"

"He knows some people."

"What people?"

"Guessssss," was the irritated reply, the all-purpose Vegas reply when someone wished to imply a connection with the People.

His connections had won Lew Foxx the health-club franchise. He showed up at every opening night on the Strip, sitting at a table down front with his wife, an ex-Vegas show girl who was six inches taller than he was. Or perhaps she was two inches shorter and had eight inches more hair. Lew Foxx said that he was a two-time loser before he met his present wife. Her name was Valerie and he always referred to her as his "present wife."

"The first time I was just a kid," Lew Foxx said about his first marriage. "I didn't know any better." His second wife was someone his first wife caught him fooling around with when he was running the parking lots in Cleveland. "I figured she was the cause for the divorce, I might as well marry her." The heel of his hand slapped against his forehead. "Oi veh."

"I see what you mean, Lew."

"You know what my second wife used to do?" Lew Foxx said. "She used to stick a pair of rosary beads up my ass before I came. A broad does that you can come for a week. She was a Catholic girl."

Jackie stripped and wrapped a towel around his middle. The

steam room at three P.M. Monday afternoon was full of middle-aged men with bad muscle tone and good-sized tits, the kind that would cause a woman to be described as small-breasted. The routine was unvarying. Steam, sauna, whirlpool, Scotch douche, massage. In the Scotch douche, masseurs in white ducks, white T-shirts and white shower clogs play high-velocity hoses over the body, up one leg, down the other, over the back muscles, down the arms and then a playful stream at the privates. "Don't move," the masseur would say, and the water would ease down the stomach, stopping a safe couple of inches away from the joint, then a quick squirt. "You moved."

"Jesus, you see him jump?"

"Lower and slower, Arnold."

"It may be small, but it's a willing little devil."

The conversation in the health club was slow and desultory, as if each word were enveloped in the steam before it was released. The talk was of life and the community and it was the dialogue of the used-car tycoon and the parking-lot mogul.

"Joe E. Jason's going to warm up for Tom Jones."

"No kidding."

"Never made it in the lounge, Joe E."

"He's a hard man to employ, Joe. Not big enough to be a head-liner, too big for a warm-up."

"He can only go with a headliner like Al Martino. Then he gets equal billing."

The muscles are kneaded, pounded, pushed into shape. Blow jobs are compared and private games in Chicago and Pittsburgh and Seattle.

"I went on a junket in London."

"Meet George Raft?"

"Sure I met George Raft."

"I heard about that junket. I heard one of the guys lost twenty-nine grand in a private game at the Mayfair. And he knew it was crooked."

"He just liked the action."

"I can understand that."

Silence, and then: "I knew a guy once in Gary, Indiana, and this guy, he called his root Jane. It's a funny name for a guy to call his joint, I mean, he wasn't a fairy or nothing, so I says to him, 'How come you call your root Jane?' And he says to me, 'I heard of a book once, it's called *Jane's Fighting Ships*, so I started to call my joint Jane.' "

"That makes sense."

Again the muscles are bruised into shape, the masseur's fingers pushing the pouches of fat up toward the shoulders, then smoothing them back down again.

"I did twenty-six shows over the weekend."

"No shit. What's the show?"

" 'Bowling With the Stars.' "

"You know something, I bet I've seen it."

"It's on all over. Syndicated."

"Peter Lawford, guys like that."

"Superstars."

"You know something, I never thought Peter Lawford bowled."

"Why's that?"

"He's English, right."

"You figured him for tennis?"

"Right."

"That makes a lot of sense."

"I thought it did."

"So anyway, I put these twenty-six shows together over a weekend and I didn't have to take any time off for my publicity clients."

"You in publicity?"

"That's right."

"You know Mickey Rooney?"

"I know a lot of people who know him."

"I bet he's a nice guy."

"That's what I hear."

"You hear that, huh?"

"Yeah."

"That's nice to hear."

2

The first time I ever saw Jackie Kasey he was warming up for Elvis Presley. In the history of the Strip, there had never been a bigger draw than Elvis. Right by the front door in the lobby, there was a booth set up to sell souvenirs of Elvis—records, pins, eight-by-ten glossies, even bumper stickers that read, VISIT ELVIS' BIRTHPLACE—TU-PELO, MISSISSIPPI. The main room was packed tighter than a subway in a rush-hour summer thunderstorm, and the minimum was fifteen dollars a person, and for that fifteen dollars you got four drinks, which average out to $3.75 per Scotch whiskey, or a bottle of bilious California champagne, pink champagne which in the bizarre lighting in the International Ball Room turned an even more bilious lavender. And that was all you got because the room was too crowded for the waitresses, old girls with pencils stuck in their blue-tinted hair buns, to serve you any more, and so you were stuck with four drinks with all the ice melted even before the houselights went down.

It sometimes seemed to me that nothing so exactly expressed the feeling that Vegas was in a time warp as the appearance of Elvis on the Strip. The audience that first night I saw Jackie consisted mainly of the groupies of 1956, now thirty-some-year-old matrons with Alberto VO-5 bouffant hairdos and Empire dresses and strapless bras and gardenia corsages. It was hard to imagine that these matrons with the propped-up falsie tits were the same teenagers who a decade and a half earlier had torn off Elvis' clothes and traded in that photograph of him in *Life* magazine, the one with the succulent carbuncle decorating the middle of his back. Now they had husbands in the dental-supply game and kids who were not turned on to the thirty-five-year-old Elvis, kids who wanted to boff the lead guitarist in the Three Dog Night and who could not comprehend that their mothers were once pimple freaks.

It was a tough audience for a warm-up comic, and the job was already tough enough. The warm-up comic has forty-five minutes and functions basically as a high colonic, getting the audience through dinner, one trip to the john, a little juice on board, loosening them up for the headliner. He stands up there, a guy with six tuxedos in his closet, every one with the sky-blue lining, and he opens the tuxedo and gives the audience a hint of the lining and it looks like he's hustling After Six. He snaps the microphone cord as if it were a bullwhip, shoots out the pinky finger and launches a fusillade of one liners.

"Speaking of Italians . . ." He had not been speaking of Italians, but there is not a stand-up comic in Vegas who does not change his line of thought with the phrase, "Speaking of . . ."

"Speaking of Italians, they had birth control long before the pill." A beat. "They called it garlic." Another beat. "Even the Pope uses it."

The audience laughs, mechanically at first, then more appreciatively. The minutes are passing, the headliner is getting ready backstage, the creamed chicken has not started to react chemically with the crème de menthe parfait to block the lower intestinal tract.

"And speaking of Jews, I got so many caps on my teeth my mother's chicken soup bends my mouth."

Back and forth across the stage, the sweat soaking through the blue lining of the After Six. "And listen, you ever see a Jew schlepping with the football? The Jew is the team treasurer."

He is the liege of the star, funny but not too funny, the headliner must never be upstaged. "And look at the teams. Everyone is represented. Our Indian brothers—the Redskins. Our feathered friends—the Falcons. The fish in the sea—the Dolphins. Even the Commies—the Cincinnati Reds, right? What about the Jews? So why don't they call a team the Miami Beach Accountants or the Newark Optometrists?"

The dishes are being cleared away, it is time to go. "And speaking of fags, excuse me, laze and gemmen"—the voice becomes sibilant—"gay liberation it's called today. I'm a honkie, my brother-in-law's a pig, but I can't call a fag a fag. But speaking honestly, laze and gemmen, you know what the gay cathedral is called?" A beat. "St. Bruce's."

Time is up, the star awaits. "God love you, laze and gemmen, you've been a great audience." The two-handed kiss. "Peace and love, peace and love."

Upstairs to the second-floor dressing room, coated with sweat, temper out of sorts. "The headliner comes out, the people have finished their dinner. I come out, all I can hear is the waiters saying, 'You want the parfait or the mousse, the mousse is the soft stuff.' "

A quick shower, then three hours to the next show. Stomach in knots, can't eat, can't drink, can't nap, no time to fuck even except with a hooker and it is very tough to go back onstage after forty-eight minutes with a hundred-dollar hooker who washes your joint the first thing she does, no matter how many times she has been with you, and after something like that it is difficult to make with the jokes about the Miami Beach Accountants.

3

"Who wants to ball a spade hooker?" Jackie Kasey said. He was standing in the lobby of the hotel, a short man with dark crinkly hair, smelling of expensive toilet water and wearing a beige jump-suit ensemble. It was after the second show Sunday night and I was telling him about the black prostitute in the bar, the one with the gold front tooth and the American flag decal on her bag. She had been propositioning a trick when I walked into the lounge where Jackie was playing, and without turning away from the prospective john she had motioned me to the other stool beside her. As I ordered a drink, she lit a cigarette, and from behind her cupped hand she said to me, sotto voce, "I'm just keeping you in the bull pen in case this one doesn't work out." Dramatically blowing a smoke ring, she then turned back to the other man and began negotiating price and specialties, the little gimmicks that would make the time with her well spent. I heard her say that the gold tooth ought to be worth something, she bet that he had never been given head by a girl with a gold front tooth. The man thought for a moment and then said no, he guessed he hadn't.

All the while, Jackie had been up onstage, sweating profusely, a very nervous man making $10,000 a week in his first headline appearance in the lounge, but only playing harmony, it seemed from the bar, to a hooker with a gold tooth. The few people in the room for the second show were spread out instead of all grouped down front, in order that each waitress could get a crack at a tip. It did not at all improve Jackie's disposition that the waitresses' tips were considered more important than an audience for him to play against. He had worked up a new routine for his shot in the lounge. No more the stand-up comic in an After Six with a sky-blue lining. No more Harold, the Homo Halfback, no more Dangerous Dan, the Used Car Man. Jackie was a theme comic now: check that—a theme *comedian*. Corbett Monica and Pat Henry, they were comics, but a comedian dealt not in jokes but in *character*, a character who was *characterized*, a character with *characterization*, and the characterization gave the comedian what he never had before, and that was an *identity*, and what the identity did was make you *identifiable*, and if you were identifiable, you could be *marketed*, turned into a product.

The product that Jackie Kasey hoped to become was Brother JayJay. Brother JayJay was an evangelist. Seedy, conniving, opportunistic, the epitome of likable low cunning, the major-domo of a moth-eaten Elmer Gantry tent show. Jackie had planned his wardrobe with extreme care. A tambourine, cheap rings covering every knuckle, a lavender silk frock coat and matching pants. Singing and clapping from a white-robed sisterhood of black gospel singers. The only trouble was the room was empty, there was no playback from the audience. That, and also the act was not very good, it needed work.

First there was the overture from the gospel singers:

> "Way down south
> In the land of cotton
> Brother Jay am not forgotten

Here he come, here he come, here he come
Brother Jay."

Clapping and hooraying from the gospel singers as Brother JayJay
bounced on stage, a mendacious look in his eye:

"Thank you, sisters. Thank you, brothers. Thank you,
saints. And hallelujah, you sinners. I'm partial to sinners—being no saint myself. "But the good Lord loves
the sheep who strays from the flock. And I stray so
much I get an awful lot of loving."

"Amen, brother," said the gospel singers.

"You know, just last week I went to a sin-o-teria.
In the interests of research, of course. I tried a little
of everything—and a second helping of lust. YOU
HEAR ME, LORD? YOU, THE CAT UP THERE WITH
THE FUZZ ON YOUR FACE AND THE GROOVY WHITE
CAFTAN."

"Amen, brother."

"Then I seen the error of my ways and decided to
cleanse myself. They wanted to bathe me in the river,
but ohhhh, that water was so cold. I went through a car
wash instead. With the windows up. Got the soul and
the white walls done in one operation."

"Amen, brother."

It was like a revival played to an empty tent. I watched fascinated
from the bar. Watching a comic flailing against an indifferent audience seemed a refraction of my own depression. Vegas has a way of
co-opting burned-out cases; there is a sense that failed expectations
are the mean, the norm. Here was a jester to the affluent proletariat;
here was comedy essentially prejudiced, not in the racial sense, but
in reinforcing resistance to change. It seemed no accident that kings
employed jesters; they deflated individual pretensions, deviations
from established values.

I felt the hooker's hand slide over mine. The prospective trick had left, ostensibly for the men's room, but he had not returned. He had left a full drink and a freshly opened package of Larks.

"I guess he never went with no colored girl," she said. She tapped her glass against her gold tooth. "You want to date?"

I assured her I wished to remain in the bull pen.

She picked up his Larks. "I'll trade you these for your Salems. I like menthol."

The exchange was made. She beckoned the bartender. "He pay for my drink?"

The bartender shook his head.

"The cocksucker," she said pleasantly. She patted my hand. "Settle it for me, honey," she said. "And dream about what you're missing." And then she was gone.

In the lobby after the show, Jackie Kasey was unimpressed by my account of the black hooker. "What was she, some kind of Watusi with the gold tooth?" The vowels were all flattened out, the diction slightly nasal. He wore glasses offstage. "Twenty dollars and a catheter up your cock. Stick with the white stuff."

His eyes roamed the casino restlessly. There were brochures of Brother JayJay scattered about the lobby and he checked every location to make sure that the supply was not running out. His conversation was manic, like a nonstop LP. He had a tendency to exaggerate in the most meaningless manner. He would try a story out on me, then repeat it slightly changed a few seconds later, as if I had rematerialized before him tabula rasa, and then with a slight change of emphasis a third time. "You know, there's these nuns staying at the hotel and they thought I was an evangelist."

"They come in the lounge and see your act?"

"No, you see there's these nuns in the hotel and they asked this bellhop if there was an evangelist staying here."

He dropped a Brother JayJay brochure into every empty chair in the lobby. "You see, there's these nuns here and they asked the bell-hop why an evangelist was holding a revival in the hotel."

The story seemed to satisfy him now. "They wanted to know who this Brother JayJay was, you know, what church he belonged to. I guess they wanted to come to the meeting, you know, in their nun's suit."

It was nearly four A.M. and he bounded across the casino, stopping at each table, saying, "You wanna be saved, sister? I is Brother JayJay. The Lord may be your shepherd, but Brother JayJay says you stay with a soft seventeen."

He settled into a chair in the Persian Bar, clapping his hands for a drink. "Honey, I'll have a Scotch and soda pop-a-lop-a-dop and a couple of cube-a-loob-boobs, heavy on the bevy, the light kind." The double talk was something he used with strangers and menials, almost as a way of making connections. Out of my own inertia I found myself carried along on the pointless tide of his compulsion to connect.

He rattled on, his conversation a compendium of triumphs, story after story about best friends who had to step aside and watch him rise, because that was the nature of the business, friends who did not have it on nights when he did. I watched and said nothing, with a rising sense of exhilaration that I was onto a good thing, the $10,000-a-week never-was and never-will be, and I tried not to think how ultimately I would use him.

"Like with Frank at the Riviera. That's when it all started, that's where I busted through. Frank was my best friend and I was opening up for him. I mean, he said he wouldn't go to the Riv unless I was on the bill with him. And I left him for dead. A standing ovation on opening night. I mean, how could he follow a standing ovation."

Trying to interrupt was like trying to hold back a tidal wave with a sieve. He would stare open-mouthed as if I had been speaking Urdu, eyes dead, jaw slack, then he would snap his finger at a waitress. "Dis is Brudda JayJay, you wanna be saved?"

The waitress was balloon-bosomed. "Amen, Brother JayJay."

Benediction with a leer. "I do my saving in Room 2529."

"Oh, Jackie."

Again the double-talk order for another drink. "You see what I mean?" Jackie Kasey said. "You got to get the little people behind you. The waitresses and the bartenders. They talk about you, the lit- tle people. They tell the customers to come to the show. You can't make it in Vegas without the little people."

It was as if he were talking about a serving class of three-foot-two midgets.

"The thing about Brother JayJay, he can be marketed. You know, like a product. T-shirt, records, Brother JayJay games. Dolls, balloons, not just the saloons, into the stores. A product. Lunch boxes, di- aries, comic books. You ever heard of Monopoly? It's a game. We can do something like that with Brother JayJay's land company or Brother JayJay's insurance company. Fun things."

It was nearly five in the morning and it did not seem the time to talk about the apathy of the audience at the second show. "I got to take a leak," he said.

He burst through the door of the men's room, dismayed at first because there was no attendant, no one at whom to fire a joke, no one to ask if he wanted to be saved. He stood in front of the urinal, unzipping his beige jump suit; he practically had to undress to take a leak. "It's not easy being a semi-name," he said, flexing his knees in front of the urinal. "You got to wear shit like this."

He peed generously, flexed his knees again and re-zipped. "I hate dribblers," he said. "I like guys who really take a piss. Show me a guy who dribbles down the side of his pants and I'll show you a loser, I'll show you a guy who three-putts his way through life. You got to give it a good shake."

He washed his hands like a surgeon scrubbing for an operation, the soap easing over the manicure into the cuticles, the suds thick and enticing. Then the rinse, hands under the hot water until the steam rose. He wiped his hands, looked into the mirror and blew himself a kiss off his wrinkled fingers.

"There is nothing," Jackie Kasey said, "like a good piss."

.   .   .   .

A. Alvarez

....

The Biggest Game
in Town

Nine o'clock on a Tuesday morning at the end of April, 1981, and
according to the giant illuminated figures at the top of the Mint Hotel the temperature was already ninety-two degrees. At the entrance
of Binion's Horseshoe Casino stood the famous horseshoe itself,
seven feet high, painted gold, and enclosing within its arch a million
dollars in ten-thousand-dollar bills. The hundred bills are neatly
ranked and held, for whatever foreseeable eternity, in some kind of
plastic, bulletproof, fireproof, bombproof—the perennial dream of

☞ Excerpted from The New Yorker, March 7, 1983, and The Biggest Game in Town
(Houghton Mifflin, 1983).

the Las Vegas punter visible to all, although not quite touchable. If you come too close, one of Binion's giant security guards, leather straps polished and creaking over his beige uniform, gun in his holster, moves quietly forward.

The million-dollar horseshoe reflected the glare of the morning sun on Fremont Street. Behind it were gloom and movement: a long, low, rather shabby room, full of noise and smoke, and, unlike the other casinos at this early hour, full of people. Women in halters and men in cowboy boots and Stetsons jostled each other around the roulette and craps tables, rattled the armies of slot machines, and perched in semicircles before the blackjack dealers; even the seats in the little keno lounge were mostly taken. At the back, there was already a crowd along the rail that separates the casual punters from the area that, for about four weeks every year, is set aside for poker. Fixed to one wall of this makeshift poker room was a large yellow banner, announcing in red, "BINION'S HORSESHOE PRESENTS THE WORLD SERIES OF POKER 1981." Opposite was an equally large blackboard, listing across the top the side games being played that day while the official tournament was in progress: "HOLD 'EM, NO LIMIT —5, 10, 25;" "HOLD 'EM, NO LIMIT—25, 25, 50;" "7 STUD—50, 100;" "7 STUD—200, 400." Under each set of figures was a column of names and initials. The larger the number, the shorter the column beneath.

The game just inside the rail seemed to have been going on all night. The players were gray-faced and unshaven. They shifted about uncomfortably in their seats, yawned, scratched vaguely at their grubby shirts, lit one cigarette from the stub of another. They looked, most of them, like the uneasy sleepers on the benches in railway stations, sitting there because they could not raise the price of a hotel room. Only the dealer seemed dressed for the occasion: he wore a gleaming white shirt and a narrow black bow tie with two long tails, Western style, inscribed with the word "Horseshoe." He checked the bets in front of the three players who remained in the pot, and raked those chips into the pile of chips at the center of the table; then he discarded the top card of the deck he held, and turned over a communal card, to join four already exposed in front of him. A cowboy to his left tapped twice on the table with his forefinger. To the cowboy's left, an elderly man in a bulging T-shirt stared meditatively at the exposed cards, took two black chips from the stack in front of him, and tossed them toward the center. He seemed utterly uninterested, as if the matter were somehow beneath his attention. "Two dollars," said the dealer, in a bored voice. The next player, a nervous young man with a Zapata mustache, cupped his hands around two cards face down in front of him, squeezed up their corners, and flicked them toward the dealer, elegantly, like a fop making a conversational point. Only the cowboy was left. He tilted his Stetson back an inch and stared at the elderly man, unblinking, for a full minute. While he stared, he juggled a pile of black chips up and down on the baize in front of him—up and down, in and out, like a yo-yo on a string. His fingers were agile and surprisingly long. Then his hand stopped abruptly, he lifted seven chips off the pile without seeming to count them, and pushed them into the center. "Raise it up a nickel," he said. The fat elderly man crossed his arms on his chest, sank his chin toward them, and considered the cowboy. There was a long pause. In the same bored voice, the dealer said, "Five dollars to you."

A nickel? Five dollars? This was my first morning in Las Vegas, so I leaned forward to see the markings on the black chips. In the middle of each was a white disc decorated with the casino's symbol, around which was printed "HORSESHOE CLUB, LAS VEGAS, NEV." Inside the horseshoe was a portrait of the owner, Benny Binion, in a cowboy hat, smiling encouragingly over his signature. Below that was the figure "$100." So now I knew. Later, I was told that serious gamblers always leave off the zeros when they announce bets. Perhaps it is a way of showing their indifference. The bigger the bet, the more zeros omitted. In gambling parlance, a nickel is five hundred dollars, a dime is a thousand, a big dime is ten thousand. "It makes it simpler," I was told. It also makes it more unreal.

Unreal. Over in the back corner of the enclosure, as far from the spectators as they could decently manage, another group of men was settling down to a new game. Their clothes were pressed, their hair was brushed, and they moved in an aura of aftershave and talcum powder. I recognized some of the faces from newspaper photographs and from pictures in Doyle Brunson's book "Super/System," a large treatise on advanced poker techniques, strictly for postgraduates. I had studied the book like a Biblical scholar before I left my home in London, but now I found, to my irritation, that I could remember the faces more vividly than I could remember the advice and the card analysis. Brunson himself was at the table, and Bobby Baldwin and Puggy Pearson, all of them winners, in their turn, of the World Series Poker Championship, and there were four others, whose faces I vaguely recognized but whose names I could not place. The big league was settling down to a morning's entertainment. The men chatted while they nonchalantly unloaded their racks of chips and arranged them at their places at the table: massed towers of black, a couple of towers of gray five-hundred-dollar chips, and then, as an afterthought, a lower bastion of green twenty-five-dollar chips. Each player seemed to have his own architectural plan in mind, but the final effect was of so many grim desert fortresses. Then they fumbled around in their trouser pockets and pulled out packets of money, which they set between the chips and the raised leather edge of the table, like the garrison that the fortifications were protecting. The packets were of hundred-dollar bills, as freshly laundered as the players, and each belted with a paper band on which was printed "5,000 DOLLARS." It was a quarter past nine on a weekday morning, and the boys were settling down for a quiet game of cards.

Welcome to Dreamland.

.   .   .   .

Las Vegas has the highest, hardest poker games in the world, twenty-four hours a day, seven days a week, fifty-two weeks a year. It also has Binion's Horseshoe—the one casino where none of the usual limit rules apply. The gambler at the Horseshoe is allowed to set his own limit with his first bet. In 1980, for example, someone drove in off the desert carrying two suitcases, one empty, the other containing seven hundred and seventy-seven thousand dollars in hundred-dollar bills. He took the suitcases to the cage at the back of the casino and changed the neat packets of money into chips, and then, escorted by security guards, he carried his racked chips to a craps table, bet the lot on a single throw of the dice, won, returned to the cage with his double load of chips, filled both his suitcases with money, and drove away. His only comment was "I reckoned inflation was going to eat that money up anyway, so I might as well double it or lose it all." He has not been back.

It could have happened nowhere in Las Vegas except at Binion's. The big casinos on the Strip, despite their apparent opulence and glamour, would not even have considered a bet of that size, because most of the men who run them are merely employees of business organizations with their offices elsewhere. The Horseshoe, however, is a family concern, which was founded by Benny Binion and is run by him and his two sons, Jack and Teddy. One or another of them is always there when a decision has to be made. . . .

. . . The Binions themselves are gamblers and the high rollers who come to the Horseshoe are mostly their friends. The Binions have played cards with them, or golf or tennis; they have even staked some of them when they were broke. "In the gambling world, your social life and your business life become so interrelated that they are one and the same," Jack Binion said to me one day. The gamblers themselves put it more strongly. "For the serious player, the Binions *are* gambling in Vegas," I was told. The professional poker players I spoke to were unanimous only in their attitude toward the Binion family: not just admiration but—an even rarer feeling in that edgy and exclusive world—affection. That attitude permeates the casino itself—shabby, ill-lit, and crowded at all hours "We're small," said Jack Binion. "Therefore, everyone is jammed together. But people are having a good time, and that gives the place an atmosphere of its own. We've been here a long time, and I like to think of us as a gamblers' gambling house. Not that the other places are just catering to tourists, but the guy who comes here is the sophisticated player. We're like a discount house: no frills, a kind of self-service, but you get the best deals."

That down-home, family atmosphere would not be possible among the grisly Hollywood-style palaces of the Strip, nor would it be appropriate. The Horseshoe belongs to downtown Las Vegas, a geographically separate entity, otherwise known as Glitter Gulch— eight dollars by taxi from Caesars or twenty minutes by bus—to which the punters are ferried in from Los Angeles by the coachload, like migrant workers to the California fruit farms, and where the hotels have no tennis courts or golf courses or gymnasiums, and when I was there only a couple of them had swimming pools (smaller than average back-yard pools in suburban Phoenix) tucked away on their roofs. Downtown Las Vegas is strictly for gambling: there is nothing else to do, nowhere else to go. Fremont Street is lined with shops peddling cheap clothes and hideous souvenirs and zircon rings and pornography. In an area of about four blocks, there are more pawnshops than in the whole of Greater London. But I discovered only one drugstore, one five-and-ten, and nowhere at all to buy groceries or fruit. Ordinary shops are banished, like ordinary life, to the shopping centers and the suburbs.

Glitter Gulch is for transients, most of them elderly and dressed to kill: old women in lime-green or banana-yellow or Florida-orange pants suits, clutching Dixie Cups of small change in one hand, the lever of one of Vegas's fifty thousand slot machines in the other; old men with plastic teeth and sky-blue plastic suits shooting craps for a dollar, playing fifty-cent blackjack and three-dollar-limit stud poker; wrecks in wheelchairs or with walking frames, the humped, the bent, the skeleton-thin, and the obese, cashing in their Social Security checks, disability allowances, and pensions, waiting out their time in the hope of a miracle jackpot to transform their last pinched days. All of them are animated by a terrible Walpurgisnacht jollity—gamblers' optimism compounded by nostalgia. "THE GOOD OLD DAYS" say the neon signs, and "50¢ BAR DRINKS," "WIN A CAR 25¢," "FREE

ASPIRIN & TENDER SYMPATHY." For the Snopeses of this world, Glitter Gulch is the absurd last stop on the slow train to the grave.

The young are fewer and not much more presentable. The trim, straight-backed young people who roam with such extraordinary grace and confidence around the rest of the United States and seem to be America's most triumphant export to Europe have mostly by-passed downtown Vegas. Instead, the rule for both sexes is big bottoms, beer bellies, and skin muddied by greasy burgers and French fries. The boys have tattoos on their arms, and the girls' heads are permed and dyed so relentlessly that a natural head of hair seems like a visitation; you stare after it, thinking, Now, who is *that*?

These people are essentially no different from the tourists on the Strip; they are simply less obviously affluent and considerably more single-minded. For Glitter Gulch is where the real action is, the thing in itself, with no pretensions to glamour or luxury, or even holiday-making. The people are there purely to gamble, and most of them, sooner or later, try their luck at the Horseshoe. It is the natural setting for the World Series of Poker.

Benny Binion is now seventy-eight years old, a genial, round-faced, round-bellied man, like a beardless Santa Claus in a Stetson, benign and smiling. Yet when he left Texas, thirty-six years ago, his police record included bootlegging, gambling, carrying concealed weapons, and two murder charges. (One was dismissed as "self-defense," and for the other he was given a suspended two-year sentence.) Like his contemporary and longtime friend Johnny Moss, three times World Poker Champion, Benny came from a dirt-poor family—his father was a stockman—and made his fortune the hard way, by his wits, starting as a "hip-pocket bootlegger." Moss explained to me, "He kept his stuff in a stash car round downtown Dallas. He'd go get a pint, put it in his hip pocket, sell it, and go get another pint." After the repeal of Prohibition, he moved into gambling, which was then, as it is now, illegal in the state of Texas. By the time the Second World War ended, he had become "kind of the boss of gambling down there in Dallas," his son Jack said. He left town precipitately in 1946. "I had to get out," he is reported to have said. "My sheriff got beat in the election that year." So he moved to Las Vegas, where gambling was legal, and eventually bought the Horseshoe, a shabby little casino that had begun life in 1937 as the El Dorado Club. As for the illegalities in his past, he says, "Tough times make tough people."

In 1953, the tough times caught up with him again: he was sentenced to five years in the federal penitentiary at Leavenworth for income-tax evasion. The casino was sold to a man from New Orleans, and the Binion clan did not regain complete control of it until 1964. Even then, the law was not quite finished with Benny, although he had become, I was told, the third-most-powerful man in Nevada. In the mid-seventies, he appeared before a grand jury to testify about money he had given to the local sheriff. "That wasn't no bribe," Benny said. "If that there sheriff hadn't paid it back, I'd have made him wash dishes for me in the kitchen." (The sheriff, incidentally, was said to be the second-most powerful man in Nevada.) Later, when he was asked why he gave money to political candidates, including Gerald Ford, he replied, "For favors, what else?" The sheriff was indicted on a tax charge but the case was dismissed.

Tough times may make tough people, but age, reputation, and great wealth turn tough people into lovable old characters. Although the running of the casino is now in the hands of Jack Binion, when I was there Benny, wearing a cowboy shirt with solid-gold buttons, still held court every day in the Sombrero Room, the Horseshoe's restaurant, at a table overlooking the casino that was permanently reserved for him and his cronies. He eyes the people coming through the door, greets some, and spends a great deal of time on a private telephone that hangs on the wall behind his chair. In April of 1981, he was back in the news following the publication of a book by a Mafia informant who alleged that Benny had once taken out a two-hundred-thousand-dollar contract with a hit man. "Two hundred

grand, never," an indignant friend said. "Two, maybe. In casino credits." Benny himself seemed unperturbed by the allegation.

That, too, was in character. "He doesn't care," said Jack Straus,
one of the most formidable of all the poker professionals, and certainly the wittiest. "I get tired of hearing gamblers tell hero stories
about themselves—how four big guys jumped them and they
whipped the four dudes and seduced all the beautiful women. When
Benny tells a story, he's the fool, he's the coward. I finally got to re-
alizing that here is a man who knows exactly where he's at: He isn't
the least bit interested in impressing you, because he knows who he
really is. And he pays you the compliment of assuming that you
know, too."

During the month of the World Series of Poker, Benny also has no
time to try to impress anyone. Journalists and photographers flood
into the Horseshoe from all over the world, television teams trail
their cables around the poker room, stick the snouts of their cameras
over the players' shoulders, and fuss with the lights, while the players arrive from every corner of America and also from London, Paris,
Athens, Sydney, Oslo, and Dublin. "In the Old West, they used to
have trappers' rendezvous every year," said Straus. "All the mountain
men and people who lived up in the wilderness would get together
in a certain spot to swap stories, have wrestling matches and canoe
races, and see their friends. This is our trappers' rendezvous."

The World Series was first held in 1970, but the idea of it was born
in 1949, when Nick the Greek Dandolos arrived in Las Vegas looking
for a high-stakes poker game. There were big games in town even
then, but all of them were ring games—that is, they consisted of
seven or eight players—and all were played with limits on the betting. The Greek wanted to play no-limit, head-up poker—with a single opponent. Benny Binion, with a shrewd eye for free publicity for
his recently acquired casino, offered to set up a game, provided it
was played in public. When the Greek agreed, Binion called Johnny
Moss, in Dallas.

Moss, who now has the face of an irritable basilisk, was forty-one
at the time, smooth-cheeked, thin-haired, with wide-set, hooded

eyes and a thin, scrolled mouth. He had been brought up on the streets of Dallas, a newsboy when he was eight, a telegraph messenger at nine. If you ask him when he learned to play cards, he tells you, with relish, that he learned how to cheat before he learned how to play. "Dealin' from the bottom of the pack, dealin' seconds, usin' mirrors, markin' cards, fadin' the dice—everything about cheatin'," he says. "We thought we were smart. Everybody we looked at was a sucker. The suckers had money an' we didn't. I could make a living, but it warn't a good livin'. I could never get hold of a lot of money, like a sucker could, so in time I come to see it was better to be a sucker. For sixty years now, I've been a sucker. But I'm hard to beat." At the age of fifteen, like a reformed criminal turning state's evidence, he quit cheating and went to work in a gambling house called The Otter's Club in Dallas as a lookout man, to protect the players against cheaters. It was there that he began to play cards seriously, and by the age of nineteen he was a road gambler, playing all over the Southwest, wherever the action was good, often staked by Benny Binion. But it was a precarious existence. "Every time I go into a game, the cheaters are there, the thieves are there, the hijackers are there, the police are after you, the rangers are after you," he says. "Then you have to get in an' beat the cards. You have to win an' get out with the money." For years, he played with a revolver in his jacket pocket at the table and a double-barrelled .410 shotgun on the back seat of his car. "I've been arrested five or six times for carryin' that there shotgun," he says. "I tell 'em I'm out bird huntin', an' I pay a two-hunnerd-dollar fine. But I have buckshot in my shells, an' they say, 'You shoot a bird, you blow it all to pieces.' I say, 'This is for a two-legged human bird, not a hummingbird.' On the road, you jus' have to be prepared. If they know you carry a shotgun into your hotel room with you, they better not be there waiting. Some places are easier to stick up than others." Then he adds, mildly, "Not that I'm mean or nothin'."

Moss played through the East Texas oil boom, and he played through the Depression. He also took up golf, which he played as brilliantly as he did poker and for equally exorbitant sums of money—sometimes for as much as a hundred thousand dollars a round, often for a thousand dollars a hole. But he had never been to Las Vegas, and when Benny Binion called him in 1949 he was exhausted from a four-day poker marathon. Nevertheless, he drove non-stop from Dallas straight to the Horseshoe, shook hands with the Greek, and sat down immediately to play.

In the weeks that followed, the Greek got his action and Binion got his publicity, to a degree that neither of them could have imagined. The game lasted for five months, with breaks for sleep every four or five days, although the Greek, who was thirteen years older than Moss, spent most of his non-poker time at the craps tables and needled Moss about his frailty, saying, "What are you going to do, Johnny—sleep your life away?" But even before the first break the table, which Benny had thoughtfully positioned near the entrance to the casino, was surrounded by crowds six-deep, drawn by rumors of the biggest game the town had ever seen.

They began by playing five-card stud—"not my real strong game," Moss says—and during the weeks of this, while occasional players came and went, buying themselves in with a minimum stake of ten thousand dollars, Moss and the Greek played what has since become one of the most famous and expensive hands in the history of poker.

Five-card stud is the most classic of the games. Each of the players antes an agreed sum and on the first deal receives two cards— one face down, or in the hole, the other face up. They bet, and are then dealt three more cards face up, one at a time, checking (that is, not betting), betting, or folding after each card. As Moss and the Greek were playing it, each anted a hundred dollars, and the man with the lowest exposed card "brought it in"—that is, was forced to bet two hundred dollars. Before this particular deal started, each had about a quarter of a million dollars' worth of chips in front of him; by the time it was over, the entire half-million dollars was in the pot.

Moss's first two cards were a nine in the hole and a six exposed; the Greek was showing an eight. Moss tells the story now, as he has told it often before, with a kind of chewed-up satisfaction. His Texas drawl is so thick and slurred that it sounds at times like a foreign language, but the sentences are as economical as telegrams: "Low man brings it in. I bet two hunnerd with a six, he raises fifteen hunnerd or two thousand, I call him. The next card comes, I catch a nine, he catches a six. I got two nines then. I make a good bet—five thousand, maybe—an' he plays back at me, twenny-five thousand. I jus' call him. I'm figurin' to take all that money of his, an' I don't wanna scare him none. The next card comes he catches a four, I catch a deuce. Ain't nuttin' he got can beat my two nines. I check then to trap him, an' he bets, jus' like I wanted. So I raise him *wa-ay* up there, an' he calls. I got him in there, all right. There's maybe a hunnerd thousand dollars in that pot—maybe more; I don't know exactly—an' I'm a-winnin' it. On the end, I catch a trey, he catches a jack. He's high now with the jack an' he bets fifty thousand. I cain't put him on no jack in the hole, you know. He ain't gonna pay all that money jus' for the chance to outdraw me. I don't care what he catches, he's gotta beat those two nines of mine. So I move in with the rest of my money."

Nick Dandolos was then fifty-three years old, tall, trim, and polite. He is reputed to have had a degree from an English university and to have broken all the gamblers on the East Coast, including the legendary Arnold Rothstein, winning sixty million dollars in the process. In the moments of silence after Moss pushed what remained of his quarter of a million dollars' worth of chips into the center, the Greek eyed him, upright and unblinking, and then said softly, "Mr. Moss, I think I have a jack in the hole."

"Greek," Moss replied, "if you gotta jack down there, you're liable to win yourself one hell of a pot."

There was another aching silence, and then the Greek carefully pushed his own chips forward and turned over his hole card. It was the jack of diamonds.

"He outdrawed me," Moss says now. "We had about two hunnerd an' fifty thousand dollars apiece in that pot, and he win it. But that was all right. I finally broke him anyway."

That is the old man talking, secure in his fame and his investments, as remorseless now as he was then, the kind of character that John Wayne was fond of portraying—true grit without forgiveness, to be admired, but from a safe distance. Even now, only the hardest players are willing to sit down with him. In the course of their marathon, Moss and Nick the Greek played several forms of poker. They switched from five-card stud to draw, and both forms of lowball—ace-to-the-five and deuce-to-the-seven—and, gradually, Moss wore his opponent down. After almost exactly five months, the Greek lost his last pot, smiled courteously, and said in his soft voice, "Mr. Moss, I have to let you go." He bowed slightly and went upstairs to bed. Precisely how much he had lost is not certain; the rumor says two million.

In 1970, the Binions decided to restage a battle of the giants by inviting the top professionals to play in public. There was no official prize money, and the champion was elected democratically by the assembled players. The man they chose was Johnny Moss. . . .

Since that first meeting at Binion's, in 1970, when the top professionals elected Moss champion, the tournament has expanded and the rules have changed. The contestants now buy themselves into each game—the stakes vary from four hundred dollars for the women's seven-card high to ten thousand dollars for the main event—and play freeze-out; that is, they play until they have no more chips in front of them, and one man has won them all. In 1971, Moss won the main title outright from six fellow-professionals; he was beaten in the final by Puggy Pearson in 1973; and he won it again the following year, at the age of sixty-seven. By 1981, there were thirteen separate competitions, and the number of contestants for the world title had risen to seventy-five, the three-quarters of a million prize money being divided on a sliding scale among the nine players who reached the final table, the winner taking half, the runner-up twenty per cent, and so on down to two percent each for the seventh, eighth, and ninth places.

Nearly all forms of poker are played during the tournament except five-card stud, which now seems too slow-paced and inflexible to interest the top players. But the game that decides who will win the title of World Champion is hold 'em, which originated in Texas toward the end of the last century and is still regarded with suspicion outside the Southwest. (I myself have tried, and failed, to introduce it into two regular New York poker games. In London, oddly, poker players are less rigid.) Hold 'em is a variation of seven-card stud with communal exposed cards. Each player antes and is dealt two cards face down; the man to the left of the dealer is forced to bet blind—without looking at the cards he has been dealt. (In casinos, where there is a professional, non-playing dealer, an object like a small hockey puck, called the button, is placed in front of each player in turn to indicate that he is "dealer" for that hand.) The other players either see the bet, raise it, or fold. Then three communal cards, called the flop, are dealt face up in the center of the table, and there is another round of betting, but this time the players may check. Then two more cards—known as Fourth Street and Fifth Street—are dealt face up, one at a time, with a round of betting after each. The five cards in the center are common to all the players, who use them in combination with their hole cards to make the strongest possible hands.

The variations and subtleties are infinite. A pair of aces in the hole is the strongest start, but after the flop anything is possible: a small pair in the hole suddenly becomes three of a kind (in Vegas, called a set); two connecting or suited cards turn into a straight or a flush. The complexities are so great that Doyle Brunson devotes two hundred pages of "Super/System" to hold 'em—three or four times the space allowed for any other form of poker. "Hold 'em is to stud and draw what chess is to checkers," Johnny Moss has said. It is a game of wits and psychology and position, of bluffing, thrust, and counterthrust, and depends more on skill and character than on receiving good cards. Like Kenny Rogers' gambler, "You've got to know when to hold 'em, Know when to fold 'em, Know when to walk away, And know when to run."

❦   ❦   ❦

. . . There are estimated to be over fifty million poker players in the United States alone, and only two or three hundred of them ever graduate to the games at Binion's; of those players, perhaps twenty would stand a chance in the really big games. Even so, the casualness and imperturbability with which that elite handles huge sums of money is beyond ordinary understanding. It is a question not just of a different level of skill but of a different ordering of reality. . . .

"The sums involved are beyond reason. They blow your mind." That was said to me not by an outsider but by A. J. Myers, a regular and successful player, who in 1981 won the biggest of the seven-card-high competitions, walking away with sixty-seven thousand five hundred dollars in prize money. Myers, a retired real-estate investor, who looks like a fleshy West Coast version of Saul Bellow—professorial half-glasses perched on the end of his nose, red floral band around his straw hat—plays regularly in the big seven-stud games with the top professionals, and commutes from his home in Beverly Hills, sometimes as often as a dozen times a year. Yet he still finds it hard to adjust to the professional gamblers' indifference to money. "They look at me, and there is absolutely no understanding between us," he told me. "They will bet on a ball game—football, basketball, baseball—sums that stagger the imagination. I know many wealthy people, some of them worth well over a hundred million, who would never bet more than a couple of hundred dollars on a game, because they would feel terrible if they lost. Yet some of the gamblers here, who are worth nothing compared with those people, will bet a hundred thousand without blinking. Most of them are average golfers—they shoot in the middle eighties—but at the end of a match they regularly settle up for fifty or a hundred thousand dollars. Even the golf pros don't play for that kind of money, and if they did they probably wouldn't be able to hold a putter. If a golf pro who shot seventy played a gambler who shot eighty-two and gave him the right handicap, he would lose every time. The pressure would be too much for him; for the gambler, it is a stimulus."

"Right," said Straus. "I even drive farther when the stakes are high."

In poker, as in golf, at least gamblers are betting on their own skills. The cards go round, but in the end the best players win. When the poker players bet on sports, however, they are putting down gigantic sums on events wholly beyond their control. Even the late Arnold Rothstein managed to fix baseball's World Series only once. "Players who make tremendous amounts of money through their talents at the poker table go out and destroy it betting on things they have no control over," Myers said.

We were sitting in the Sombrero Room with Myers' wife and his daughter, a California Matisse odalisque, who had recently returned from a grand tour of Europe. They nodded understandingly, knowing that Myers had earned his right to disapprove by surviving a gambling fever as virulent as any junkie's addiction. He first came to Las Vegas to shoot craps some years before. He had a princely credit line at all the major hotels and was comped—provided with a free luxury suite, free food and drink, and whatever other indulgence he fancied ("all the fringe benefits of being a big sucker," he called it)—wherever he went. He had run through a fortune "in taxed money" before he realized that his dream life in Vegas was endangering his real life at home.

"So I stopped."

"Just like that?"

"I believe in will power. And in responsibility to my family. If I'd been alone, perhaps I wouldn't have quit. But with a wife and child I had to take stock of myself. I knew there was nothing in the world that could support the habit I had."

"Then what?"

"I learned to play blackjack, which afforded me the luxury of sitting down while I gambled rather than standing at a craps table and wearing myself out. In very short order, I was an expert, and the casinos wouldn't allow me to play."

So he turned to poker, which he had played for years in relatively small stakes games in California. "At first, I was very much in awe of the professionals, and consequently found it hard to compete," he told me. "I'm not really talking about the level of their skill, I'm talking about money. The games were of a size I wasn't used to, and until you get used to the high stakes you pull in your horns and play too conservatively. The money freezes you up, and you become tight-weak. You try not to play until you have an unbeatable hand, and when someone makes a big bet at you you automatically assume the worst. The tight-weak player is the kind the pros most love to play with; they run rings around him. But in time I got used to the size of the game. It is a question of respect, not fear. I'm a wealthy guy, and I don't believe I was ever really afraid of the big money. But it took me a while to realize that if I had too much respect for the money I couldn't play properly. Chips are like a bag of beans; they have a relative value and are worthless until the game is over. That is the only attitude you can have in high-stakes poker. Even so, I still prefer a medium-sized game, like the two-hundred-dollar-and-four-hundred-dollar limit, where if you're going bad you can lose twenty or thirty thousand dollars. The highest I've played is five-hundred-and-a-thousand, where you can easily lose a hundred thousand dollars. They've begged me to play in the thousand-and-two-thousand-dollar game, but I have always refused. It was just too high; I didn't want it to affect my game. And the truth is, I don't even like the five-hundred-and-a-thousand-dollar limit. There is too much money involved. It offends my sensibilities. Yet time and again I've been in medium-sized games with players who don't look as if they could afford to play fifteen-and-thirty-dollar limit, and they have pleaded with me to raise the stakes. God knows where the money comes from, yet if they lose they always pay."

It offends his sensibilities. His wife nodded, the odalisque daughter smiled, and Myers' eerie resemblance to Saul Bellow increased. His judgment seemed, in the circumstances, the right and proper one. Yet in the noisy gloom of Binion's, with the midday heat blasting the street outside and the signs blazing and jumping like a fever, the words he used were as foreign as Urdu—like the exhibition of pictures painted by local schoolchildren which lined the corridors of McCarran International Airport when I arrived. "KIDS LIVE IN VEGAS, TOO," the signs repeated, but the only kids I saw were the stunned waifs half asleep on the carpeted sidewalk outside the Golden Nugget, waiting for their parents to blow the week's housekeeping, and the lost souls, faces sticky with ice cream, wandering around the mezzanine of Circus Circus. Las Vegas is no more a place for childhood than it is a place for sensibility. It is a town without grace and without nuance, where the only useful virtues are experience, survival, and money.

"In Vegas, they weigh you up in gold," said Straus. "They call it the golden rule: the man who has the gold makes the rules." They also say that it is the only town where visitors are made to think that a hundred-dollar bill will not buy a loaf of bread. Ulvis Alberts, for example, is a free-lance photographer who has covered the poker tournament for the last five years, and whose marvellously atmospheric portraits of the players were published in 1981 in a collection called "Poker Face." During his first visit to Binion's, a number of the contestants asked to buy blowups of the pictures he had taken of them. "That will be seventy-five dollars," he said, and suddenly there was a problem: when the gamblers pulled out their giant wads of cash, none of them had change. "So I charged a hundred dollars," he told me, "and everyone was happy."

Another example: Chip Reese has been in Las Vegas since 1974. His hair is blond and unruly, his plumpness is turning to fat, and his round face appears jolly until you see his eyes. He dresses in extravagantly colored velvet track suits, but this Vegas dishabille is misleading: his background is solid upper-middle-class Ohio, and he graduated from Dartmouth. At Dartmouth, however, the pattern was already set; after he left, the Big Daddy Lipinski Poker Room at the Beta Theta Pi house was renamed the David E. Reese Memorial Card Room, and a plaque was put up in his honor, listing the names of the fraternity brothers he had fleeced during his four years' residence. To raise money for law school, he took a job as a manufacturer's representative, but he hated it, despite the pay, and quit after nine months. On his way out to see a friend in California, he stopped off in Vegas for a weekend. He had four hundred dollars in his pocket when he sat down in a twenty-dollar limit seven-card-stud game; at the end of the first day he had won eight hundred dollars; the next day he won a thousand dollars; within a fortnight he was twenty-five thousand dollars ahead. He has been in Vegas ever since, and went on to run the poker room at the Dunes. Reese is rumored to have won a couple of million dollars in his first three years in town. This may or may not be true. What is certain is that the continual move-ment of huge sums of money across the poker table has fractured his sense of reality. "I'd like to be able to say I'm in tune with world af-fairs and worried about my budget," he told me. His years in Nevada have not affected his accent; his voice is crisp and Ivy League, with-out a trace of drawl. "But when I play poker for hundreds of thou-sands of dollars a day what do I care if a Popsicle costs ten cents here and twelve cents there? Big-limit poker is a separate world, and makes it hard to relate to other aspects of what's going on. Hundred-dollar-bills in Vegas are like one-dollar bills anywhere else. I don't even carry dollar bills except to tip the cocktail waitresses, and I can't remember the last time I had coins in my pockets. In other towns, these habits can cause a problem: I've stopped at a drive-in for a hamburger, and when the bill came for five dollars I've pulled out a hundred-dollar bill. They look at me as if I were some kind of thief, and say, 'We can't change this.' You don't think about these things until they happen to you."

The degree to which Reese fails to think about these things is fa-mous around town. He is rumored to have lost in his own house every piece of jewelry he has ever owned, and for a period to have paid without question a monthly water bill of two thousand dollars. After some time, the water company discovered that the pipe sup-plying his house had broken and was flooding the area for acres around. Reese himself had not noticed.

"Money means nothing," he told me. "If you really cared about it, you wouldn't be able to sit down at a poker table and bluff off fifty thousand dollars. If I thought what that could buy me, I could not be a good player. Money is just the yardstick by which you measure your success. In Monopoly, you try to win all the cash by the end of the game. It's the same in poker: you treat chips like play money and don't think about it until it's all over."

It is this money element that makes poker different from all other card games. According to Terence Reese, who has captained the English bridge team, there is little to choose between bridge and poker in terms of skill. Yet poker looks like a gambling game—and was classified as such by the British Gaming Act of 1968—because, unlike bridge, it must be played for money. Chips are not just a way of keeping score; they combine with the cards to form the very language of the game. What you do with your chips—how and when you bet or check or raise—is a way of communicating with your opponents. "You ask subtle questions with your chips," said the subtle Crandall Addington. The questions you ask and the answers you receive may be misleading—a gigantic bet may be a sign of weakness, an attempt to drive the other players out of the pot because you do not have the hand you purport to have—but the combination of cards and money and position at the table creates a complex pattern of information (or illusion) that controls the flow of the game. In poker, betting and what is called money management are as much an art as reading the cards and judging the probabilities.

"In order to play high-stakes poker, you need to have a total disregard for money," Doyle Brunson said to me. "It is just an instrument, and the only time you notice it is when you run out." Among the top players, however, running out of money is a relative concept. Although they all announce, with pride, that every real pro has gone broke more times than he can count, being out of money does not seem to affect their spendthrift habits. Johnny Moss told me that when he was younger he had had no difficulty in borrowing ten thousand dollars to play poker but had known no one he could ask for five hundred dollars simply to get out of town. He also said that gamblers drove the best cars, wore the best clothes, stayed at the best hotels, got the best-looking women, and lived like millionaires even when they were broke; the amount of money they had at any particular moment did not alter their habits one jot. . . .

"I'd go to the moon if they were anteing high enough," said Bobby Baldwin, another young World Championship winner. Meanwhile, he commutes the eleven hundred and eighty miles to Las Vegas from his home, in Tulsa, and reckons to spend twenty thousand dollars a year on air fares. "One night, I chartered a Learjet and then found the game had broken up while I was airborne," he told me. He shrugged laconically. "Dry run." As for his living expenses, he said, "I have to make fifteen to twenty thousand dollars a month to break even. To tell you the truth, my wife and I never go near a supermarket. Our groceries are delivered to our home and put in the kitchen cabinets by the delivery boy." Baldwin is not given to boasting; he has a student's small, bespectacled face under a halo of curls, and his manner—away from the poker table—is preternaturally modest. He was merely indicating the degree to which high-stakes poker inoculates the players against economic reality. Money is no longer money to the professionals; it is like a wrench to a plumber—a tool of the trade. It is also, most often, not a green treasury bill validated by a President's face but a colored plastic disc stamped with a number and the name of a casino. A New York gambler who goes by the name of Big Julie once remarked sagely, "The guy who invented gambling was bright, but the guy who invented the chip was a genius." The chip is like a conjurer's sleight of hand that turns an egg into a billiard ball, a necessity of life into a plaything, reality into illusion. Players who freeze up at the sight of a fifty-dollar bill, thinking it could buy them a week's food at the supermarket, will toss two green chips into the pot without even hesitating if the odds are right. "Chips don't have a home," said Jack Straus. "People will play much higher with chips than they will with cash. For some reason, it is hard for inferior players to turn loose of money, but give them chips and they get caught up, mesmerized by the game."

Chips, in fact, are the currency of Las Vegas. When a gambler arranges a line of credit with a casino, he takes the money in chips. You tip with them, pay for meals and drink and sex with them, and in more relaxed times you could buy goods with them in the stores. The better adjusted to them you become, the further reality recedes.

To hand over a couple of pieces of unimposing black plastic and receive for them a two-hundred-dollar jacket is no longer a business transaction, it is magic. "This town hypnotizes people," Doyle Brunson said. "Guys who won't bet twenty dollars at home come out here and bet five hundred or a thousand without even thinking—particularly during the poker tournament. Playing constantly for a month or more is like being in a pressure cooker. If you are not careful, you reach boiling point and explode. Then you just throw your money away. They keep hammering and hammering at you, until you lose touch with reality about everything. That's when people go off and lose huge sums." . . .

A couple days later, Eric Drache wandered into the Sombrero Room, looking as cheerful as always but vaguely preoccupied. Drache, who is one of the world's best seven-card-stud players, is from New York and New Jersey. He went to Rutgers on a chemistry scholarship but dropped out after two years (he was at the race track on the day of a vital examination), learned to play poker seriously while serving as an M.P. in Vietnam, ran his own game in and around New York, came out to Vegas for a weekend with six hundred dollars, and has never returned East. He won seventy thousand dollars in his first three months in town, lost seven hundred and fifty thousand in the next two years, won it back, lost, won, and has been on the roundabout ever since. He now organizes the World Series for the Binions. He is a witty, highly articulate man with a beautiful English wife—the daughter of a retired colonel from Crediton, Devon, who is studying at Columbia and also plays a mean game of seven-card stud—and apparently limitless reserves of charm and affability.

"How goes it?" I asked.

He shook his head. "Terrible."

"How terrible?"

"One-sixty. I hit a bad streak and threw off ten thousand an hour." He shrugged, laughed, and moved off through the crowded restaurant, chatting and joking with the other players. Twenty minutes later, he returned and paused by my table near the entrance, deep in discussion with another professional. I heard him say, "He owes me ten and a half, plus one-eight from Reno . . ." Then he noticed me still sitting there. "Excuse me," he said. "I didn't see you. Money tends to close your mind to common civility, and I'm negotiating a loan. The worst thing is to play poker with your own money." He and the other man both laughed, then drifted off to the poker tables outside.

That insouciance is the test of the true professionals, but they do not necessarily acquire it from a psychopathic deformation of character, or even from the strong inoculation against the value of money that every visitor receives, willy-nilly, from Las Vegas. It comes, instead, from painful experience. "We used to bet all we had, day after day," said Doyle Brunson. "And every other day we went broke." Out of that emerges a kind of bedrock endurance that manifests itself as an attitude toward money. . . .

As usual, it was Straus who put this matter in a human perspective. "If money is your god, you can forget no-limit poker, because it's going to hurt you too much to turn loose of it," he said to me. "The way I feel about pieces of green paper is, you can't take them with you and they may not have much value in five years' time, but right now I can take them and trade them in for pleasure, or to bring pleasure to other people. If they had wanted you to hold on to money, they'd have made it with handles on."

People like Straus gravitate to Las Vegas because it is the one place where that total disregard for money essential to the high roller precisely matches the fever that the town induces in everyone. At one end are Straus, Brunson, Baldwin, Drache, Ungar; at the other, the little old ladies with their Dixie Cups of change in one hand and work glove on the other, priming the slots hour after hour, waiting for the shower of jackpot gold that will transform their shabby lives: deus ex machina.

To the poker professionals, the god appeared a couple of years ago in an odd disguise. Jimmy Chagra was a cocaine dealer who is now serving thirty years in the federal penitentiary at Leavenworth for his "continuing criminal enterprise." He came to town for a final fling while he waited for his case to come up before a judge known in Texas as Maximum John. (Shortly before the trial, Maximum John was shot dead, and Chagra was duly indicted for plotting that, too, but was acquitted.) Chagra was to Vegas what the Arab princes are to the London casinos: a platonic ideal incarnate, a high roller with no tomorrow, backed by the virtually unlimited and untaxed resource of the narcotics business. In the town's early days, before the operators realized that they could make more profits by scrupulous honesty than they could decently cope with, the casinos were rumored to have been used by the mob for laundering dirty money. Chagra's money was as black as pitch, but he was not interested in cleaning it up—only in enjoying it while he had time. Naturally, the only casino willing to allow him to gamble for the deranged sums he insisted on was Binion's Horseshoe. He played there every night—craps, blackjack, roulette—and during the day he took a little fresh air out on the Dunes golf course with the boys, sometimes for half a million a round. Since he was a good gin-rummy player and Binion's poker room was open for the World Series, he decided to learn hold 'em and deuce-to-the-seven, or Kansas City lowball.

The professionals were delighted to teach him, but even they were awed by the size of the games he wanted to play. The minimum table stake was fifty thousand dollars, but few of them risked sitting down with so little, because time after time Chagra would throw in twenty-thousand-dollar bets blind, which he said were "just to liven the game up a little." Once the action was properly under way, there would be an average of two million dollars on the table every night—"so many checks," said Jack Binion, "that you couldn't see the green baize." Jack Binion does not impress easily, but even now he speaks of Chagra's gambling in puzzled, hushed tones, as he might speak of some inexplicable natural phenomenon. With reason: in the weeks Chagra was there, it is said, he beat the Horseshoe for between two and three million dollars at craps and blackjack. Early one morning, he got up from a bad session at poker, strolled across to the blackjack table, bet a hundred thousand dollars on a single hand, won, and went to bed. Chagra's legend goes right down through the casino hierarchy: during one particularly stormy poker game, he tipped a cocktail waitress ten thousand dollars—two packets of fifty hundred-dollar bills—when she brought him a complimentary bottle of Mountain Valley water.

"In poker, money is power," said Alvin Thomas, alias Titanic Thompson, alias Damon Runyon's Sky Masterson, an old-time road gambler, now deceased, who would bet untold amounts on anything if he thought he had a sufficient edge. But money is power only in the hands of an expert. An innocent journalist once asked Amarillo Slim why a Texas oil millionaire who could not be scared out of a pot would not eventually see off the professionals. "Son," replied Slim, who has a reputation for vivid, folksy imagery, "that millionaire would have as much chance in a game with us as you would of getting a French kiss out of the Statue of Liberty." Likewise Jimmy Chagra: the two or three million he won at craps and blackjack he lost back remorselessly and with interest at the poker table. And the crazed action he inspired brought in another high roller, a local named Major Riddle (Major was his first name, not his rank), who owned the Silverbird and a hefty share of several other Las Vegas casinos. Riddle was in his early seventies when Chagra appeared, but chose to ignore this fact. At one point, he played against Chagra for three days and three nights without a break, until he was called out to a board meeting at the Dunes, of which he was president. He left only on the condition that the game not break up while he was away. "Naturally, you want to beat the guy," said Eric Drache. "But you don't want to kill him." As it happened, Riddle died a few months later, having happily dropped three million while Chagra was in town.

When I asked who won all the money, I was given a neutral, poker player's answer: "The cash got distributed pretty good." Only Straus was more forthcoming. He told me, "It was like that TV program 'Fantasy Island.' I kept waiting for Tattoo to come on and say it was all a dream: Look, boss! The plane! The plane!' " . . .

. . . According to Mickey Appleman, it is the element of imagination that separates the true high rollers from those who merely grind out a living from cards. Appleman is the odd man out at the tournament—a New York intellectual among the cowboys, clever eyes peering out from under a Harpo Marx mop of blond curls, clothes like a hippie's unmade bed. He grew up on Long Island and emerged from graduate school at Case Western Reserve and Cleveland State with qualifications that he is reluctant to mention in the hearing of the other poker players: an M.B.A. in statistics, and an almost completed master's in education. "I was supposed to go into the business world, but I didn't want to get a short haircut and wing-tipped shoes," he told me. So he took up community work: in Washington, D.C., after the riots of 1968; at a treatment center for alcoholics in Harlem. He also spent years in assorted styles of psychoanalysis, but when I asked him if analysis had helped his addiction to gambling he answered sharply, "Gambling was never an addiction. On the contrary, it helped me more than analysis. I suffered from depression—I was so entwined with my inner world I never had a chance to enjoy myself. For me, activity was the answer. I took up gambling professionally *after* I finished with psychoanalysis, and the depressions never returned."

But the habit of introspection dies hard, and Appleman has thought about gambling as intently as he has thought about more orthodox subjects. Indeed, introspection and the openness to experience that goes with it are, he thinks, the qualities that distinguish the great players from the pedestrians. "There are no soft spots out here," he said. "They are all good players, with sophisticated techniques that you have to analyze and incorporate into your own play. It's like any other field: you have to develop yourself *and* your game. Poker is a skill, it's an art, it's a science. You have to improve continually and know your own weaknesses. To be successful, you must be realistic. Up to a certain point, you have to believe you're a really good player, but you also have to realize what you're up against. There can be no self-deception. But confidence is a double-edged sword. It's the down side of a gambler that ruins him, not his up side. When you're playing well, you can be as good as anybody, but how you handle yourself under pressure when you're playing badly is the character test that separates the men from the boys. Yet the strange thing is, to be a high roller necessarily means having a down side. Certain individuals come here just to make money: they grind, grind, grind in the small-stakes games, they make a living, and they have no down side. But they have no gamble in them, either, so they will never know the enjoyment of the high roller, the romance of gambling. Poker playing is strictly a business to these small-stakes players, but to the high rollers it's business and it's also pleasure; it's fun, it's a game, it's gamesmanship. After all, what are we all here for at the Horseshoe? When you are playing for hundreds of thousands of dollars, it's not the money. I mean, how much do you need? It's the gamesmanship, the competition, the thrill of letting it all hang out. Poker for big money is a high-risk sport, like driving a racing car. I've always appreciated the high rollers, because pettiness has no part in their lives. The technicians who do well in the small games will never derive the same thrill from it as somebody who is willing to roll it out there. Of course, different types of people look for different levels of satisfaction. I'm a romantic, and for me gambling is a romance. That's what I enjoy; the rest is by the way. I play and I play and I play; then I pick up the pieces and see how I did. It's only at that moment that I realize I was playing for real money. How could I play at all if I started thinking about the sums involved? Can you measure the goods and services a ten-thousand-dollar bet is going to buy? No. But you can measure the intrinsic feeling you get from gambling. Everybody has these subtle energies floating around inside. Some people get through their whole lives sublimating them, repressing them. But there are gamblers here who don't sublimate them; they let them out. That's what high rolling is about."

The Sombrero Room is as far from community centers in the slums as the poker games that Appleman now plays are from the quarter-and-fifty-cent-limit games in which he started, "where fifty dollars was a fortune." It is also a long way from the analyst's consulting room, although "sublimation" is a word much favored by Freudians when they discuss gambling. Appleman, however, is using it without any narrow, disapproving psychoanalytic connotations; the sublimation he is talking about is a passport to freedom from the choking constrictions of self. W. H. Auden once wrote of a young poet, "One has the impression that, on returning from a walk, [the inhabitants of his poems] could tell one more of what they had worried about than of what they had seen." Poker was Appleman's way out of worry into alertness and objectivity. When he said, "Gambling is a romance," he was not referring to the smoke-filled rooms, the sullen tribal faces, or the stilted backchat that passes for conversation; he meant the art of the game at its highest level and the romance of personal liberty.

It is a romance that mesmerizes all the high rollers. They pride themselves on the fact that they survive spectacularly well outside the system: no bosses or government bureaucrats on their backs telling them what they should do and how they should do it, no routine that is not of their own choosing, no success that is not the result of their own unaided talents. Also no failure. They are mesmerized by the romance of big losses as much as by that of big wins, and are not interested in compromise. Jack Binion told me of one old-timer who, like all serious gamblers, had been broke more times than he could count. But at the age of seventy-three he had one final lucky streak and found himself seven hundred thousand dollars ahead. Everyone—even the other gamblers—told him to buy himself an annuity policy. A hundred thousand dollars would assure him of a good living for the rest of his life and leave him six hundred thousand to gamble with. "But he didn't even consider it," Binion said. "He would rather take his chances of going broke. Which he did, and it didn't bother him at all. And, when you think about it, he was right. If you go broke here in America, you don't really starve to death. From the financial point of view, there is a far greater difference between you and some poor native in Africa than there is between you and the richest man in the world. We all eat much the same food and sleep on the same brand of mattress as the Hunt brothers down there in Dallas. This shirt of mine is one hundred percent cotton, and that's all Bunker Hunt is going to be able to wear. So maybe he can take a private jet while I have to stay home. But that's no big deal. Once you reach the lower middle class in the

United States, there is no great difference between the top and the bottom. Here at the Horseshoe, if these guys go broke they are going to have to play cheaper. That's the only difference."

"Cheaper?" I said. "There are fortunes changing hands every day."

Binion shook his head. He seemed disappointed in me. We had appeared to be understanding each other, but now, as though for the first time, he registered my English accent and realized that, after all, I was just another uncomprehending foreigner. "In the free-enterprise system, you have to assume that each guy is the best judge of what he does with his own money," he explained patiently. "I've often thought, If I got really hungry for a good milkshake, how much would I pay for one? People will pay a hundred dollars for a bottle of wine; to me that's not worth it. But I'm not going to say it is foolish or wrong to spend that kind of money if that is what you want. So if a guy wants to bet twenty or thirty thousand dollars in a poker game that is his privilege. Society might consider it bad judgment, but if that is what he wants to do you can't fault him for it. That's America." And that, too, is Las Vegas—the only place on earth where they justify gambling as a form of patriotism.

.   .   .   .

"Las Vegas is like a parasite that feeds on money," said a man from Texas. "It sits here in the middle of the desert and produces absolutely nothing, yet it supports half a million people. It depends on the rest of the United States to feed it money, which it channels through the casinos to those five hundred thousand people. I guess it's a kind of modern miracle something like the loaves and the fishes. I see the Casinos packed with tourists telling themselves they are having a good time losing their money and it's beyond my comprehension. Yet they're always full."

"And you continue to come."

"Poker is how I make my living. And I approve of the location. The desert cuts Vegas off from the real world. You have to make an effort to come here, you have to have money to lose. If the casinos were in a metropolitan area, the people who couldn't afford to lose—construction workers, taxicab drivers, housewives, mail clerks—would gamble because the opportunity was there. In Vegas, suckers are suckers by choice. Without them, there wouldn't be a gambling economy." He glanced at his watch and rose to his feet. "Time to play." He paused, glanced at me quickly, and looked away, as though embarrassed. "Still, I'd hate anyone to think I was bad-mouthing the old place."

In the first years of the World Series of Poker, everything about the occasion was amateur except the players. Word went around, although no one was actually invited, and the events were not even scheduled. "If seven seven-card-stud players arrived at the Horseshoe at the same time, they'd play the seven-stud contest—provided one of them wasn't asleep," Eric Drache told me. Despite the haphazardness, the event grew steadily, and after five years Jack Binion asked Drache to organize it for him. "I don't take a fee," Drache said. "Jack has done me so many favors I could do this for the rest of my life and still be in his debt. Anyway, I like organizing things."

Now a schedule is sent out a couple of months in advance to a mailing list of players all over the world; there are thirteen separate events; a public-relations firm from Los Angeles issues daily press releases, and they are regularly picked up by the wire services; television cameras film the highlights of the main events; even the *London Times* and *Observer* carry the results.

Meanwhile, the players keep on coming. By 1981, the number of experts willing to put up a ten-thousand-dollar stake to compete for the title of World Poker Champion had grown from the original six to seventy-five. There were hundreds of aspirants for the other titles, and still more who came to the Horseshoe simply for the side games that are played day and night while the tournament is in progress.

By late afternoon on May 5th, the end of the second week of the World Series, only two players remained of twenty-seven who had anted five thousand dollars each—plus a fifty-dollar buy-in for table time and dealers—to enter the seven-card-high (limit) World Championship. Johnny Moss, Doyle Brunson, Puggy Pearson, and Stu Ungar had all been eliminated on the first day. Other big names, including Chip Reese, had followed them during the second morning, and only Eric Drache and A. J. Myers were left for a final showdown under the inhumanly bright lights set up by the television crew.

The contestants' appearance suggested that they had reached a secret agreement to stage the game as a confrontation between the East and West Coasts. Myers' gaudily-patterned shirt was open halfway to his navel, showing gray chest hair and a heavy gold chain around his neck. His straw hat with the wide scarlet band printed with white flowers was tilted at a rakish angle, his half-glasses were perched on the end of his nose, and he was chewing a gigantic cigar. A second cigar, wrapped in cellophane, lay on the table beside his stacked chips. Drache, in contrast, was a model of Eastern discretion: subdued sports jacket of herringbone Harris tweed, Viyella shirt, sober woollen tie. He looked more like an Oxford don than like a gambler. He also looked bored.

"I feel I'm anteing myself to death," he had said to me a couple of days before. "If they made a film of my life, half the footage would be of my hand throwing in ante after ante after ante. As if it had a life of its own, like Dr. Strangelove's. And every ante is one step closer to the grave. O.K., I'm winning at the moment, so it's easy to enjoy it, because I can kid myself that I will use the money for something more interesting than poker, like travel. But I won't, of course, and I wonder where this is going to end. I'm never going to have a job now. I mean, who is going to pay me three hundred thousand dollars a year? I'm at the top of my profession, and there aren't many opportunities at the top. I'd probably be good in public relations, but I'm not prepared to start at the bottom and work my way up—even if I had the qualifications. So poker is my only security. Some security—though Johnny Moss is a great inspiration: in his mid-seventies, still playing every day, and still winning. Even so, I'm thirty-eight now, and I wouldn't want to think my next thirty or forty years are going to be spent in a poker game. I've already been playing professionally for twenty years. In the same game, really. I mean, how long is a poker game? If you play for a living, there is no end to it. Just because it breaks up doesn't mean it ends. The players may go away, but they are still thinking about it, replaying hands, working out their strategy. And they'll be there again the next day. Them or someone else.

"It's utterly unproductive. You can't even carry on a conversation. The losers say, 'Shut up and deal,' and anyway how much input can there be with guys who play twelve hours, then go home and sleep? What's happened to them? What are they going to talk about? Their dreams? A few years back, there was one old guy, a regular, who didn't even know there was a war on in Vietnam. That's why we all enjoy it when someone comes in from out of town. But we don't get many of them, because the game is too high.

"So we have our family of Vegas professionals. Part of the tension of the game is not created by the size of the stakes; it's a family tension, a terrible intimacy. It's like being stir crazy, doing time with the same seven guys in a cell day after day. If someone told me I had to go to the Horseshoe and play for forty-eight hours straight, I'd wonder what I'd done wrong that merited two days in jail. You're just stuck there. There's nothing to see, and, for me, there's not even that much interest in the game anymore. I've seen it all before. Everything that could happen has happened: I've fallen asleep in the middle of a deal; I've played an entire hand without being dealt any hole cards. I've not yet had a guy die on me at the table, though others have. Apart from that, you name it, I've seen it.

"I would willingly pay a hundred dollars a day to have a news ticker go by, so I'd have something to occupy my mind. As it is, I try to manufacture interest. Sometimes I pick up my cards and look at all three at once. Sometimes I squeeze them very slowly to keep myself in suspense. Sometimes, if I'm drawing to a flush, I arch them up so that the upper card reflects on the back of the lower; then I can tell whether it's black or red and narrows my chances down to even money. Anything to alleviate the boredom. I look at every pretty girl who passes, and every well-dressed guy. That's not good for my

poker; you're supposed to concentrate. But I'm so bored I do it anyway."

. . . But now he had made it to the final showdown, and he
seemed bored again, despite the occasion, despite the money involved, despite the overwhelming competitive urge to win. When all
was said and done, it was just another poker game.

Drache and Myers lounged nonchalantly in their chairs and made
jokes to each other sotto voce. The television producer fussed
around them irritably, trying to create the impression of seriousness
and strain he considered appropriate to the worth of the chips—a
hundred and thirty-five thousand dollars—divided between them on
the table. . . .

Drache leaned back and said to me, "In the last year, I've spent
more time with A.J. than I have with my wife."

Myers nodded cheerfully, while his wife and his odalisque daughter, sitting behind him, smiled their approval.

Drache was probably not exaggerating. He and Myers seemed to
know each other's game so intimately that they might as well have
been playing with all the cards exposed. Drache bet on an open pair
of aces—a very strong hand—but when Myers raised him back,
showing nothing higher than an eight, he folded immediately.

"Pity," said Myers, and turned over his hole cards: two more
eights.

"Surprise, surprise," said Drache.

The cards were not running for Drache, and Myers was "on a
rush," hitting hand after hand, as if by magic. There was nothing
Drache could do except endure it stoically, retrench, risk nothing,
and hope that his chances would come before the antes ate him up.

"It's a war of attrition," he said. "And it's costing me seven hundred and fifty dollars a hand." But he did not seem perturbed. . . .

Finally, Drache won a hand. "Watch it," he announced. "I'm on a
rush." He won the next hand, too, but then began folding again.

"End of rush," said Myers.

For two hours, the game dragged on uneventfully, and then it
flared briefly to life for one hand. On the sixth card, Drache was

showing a nine, a deuce, and a pair of fours, and he had two more nines in the hole, giving him a full house. Myers was showing a jack, a seven, and a pair of fives; he had a second jack in the hole, giving him two pairs. But when Myers bet after the seventh card Drache did not raise him. Correctly. Myers' last card was another jack, giving him a higher full house.

After that, it was only a matter of time before Drache was frozen out—"like Broomcorn's uncle," as they say in Texas, chewed up by the antes. Twenty minutes later, he "went down the river" (took all seven cards) on an open-ended straight, nine to the queen, and did not make it. Myers took the hand and the championship with aces up. His prize money was sixty-seven thousand five hundred dollars, Drache's twenty-seven thousand dollars.

Within a couple of hours, they were facing each other again across the poker table, but for much higher stakes than were allowed in the official championship.

.   .   .   .

. . . The high-stakes poker games always have their groupies loitering at the edges, attracted by the aphrodisiacs of big money and risk. But the atmosphere at Binion's during the poker tournament, despite all the din and razzle-dazzle and tough talking, is strangely sexless. For a month each year, the place becomes a world of men without women. Or, rather, the women are there but—except for the few who sit down to play the men on equal terms—only as color in the background, like the voice of the hotel operator over the intercom or the rattle of chips. There is no trace at all of the sensual charge that usually bristles in the air of a holiday resort. The women who do connect seem to spend most of their time listening morosely to passionate but obscure accounts of how some freak tried to run a bluff with pair of sixes: "I mean, what's two lousy sixes?" The women smile and nod and glance furtively around for relief.

One evening, I was in the elevator the Golden Nugget with a tall, middle-aged cowboy with the aquiline profile and fierce beard of a

Spanish conquistador—a man who that afternoon, in true conquistador fashion, had been destroying the nonprofessional hold-'em event. I had seen him seated unmoving behind two gigantic towers, one of black hundred-dollar chips, the other of gray five hundreds capped with three blacks. Each tower was over a foot high and perfectly symmetrical, rising from a base of three chips set side by side. They looked like giant space-age architectural fantasies built in Lego by a patient child—appropriately, patience being what the game is about. But the tournament was over for the day, and now the cowboy was ascending majestically to his room with an Anita Loos blonde in a low-cut pink dress and very high heels, who held a drink in one hand, a cigarette in the other. She hummed "Nowhere Man" to herself and smiled vaguely while the elevator rose and he analyzed for me a key hand I had watched him play. He seemed utterly unaware of her. "When he raises in an early position," he was saying, "I have to read him for nothing better than ace-jack." The elevator stopped, the doors slid apart. The blonde started forward, then hesitated. He raised his hand like a traffic cop, pressed the button to hold the doors open, and continued, "Two aces, two kings, ace-king, he'd have sent it around in the hope of getting in a reraise." Then he moved courteously aside, bowing slightly to the girl as she stepped out in front of him. As the doors closed again, he took her silently by the arm to guide her down the hall. A couple of hours later, when I came down after a nap, the girl was drinking alone at the bar of the Golden Nugget and he was playing poker again across the road at the Horseshoe.

The little old-fashioned courtesies (he was, after all, a man in his fifties), the silence, the firm, businesslike hand gripping the girl's elbow and guiding her to his room were all part of a formal exchange: sex without sensuality, without even much interest; sex bought as one might buy a drink—as a way of winding down after the tension and concentration of gambling, as a hunger to be assuaged, like other hungers, for a fixed price.

Brothels are legal in Nevada, and sexual hypocrisy is the one vice that Las Vegas has never aspired to. At the bus stops along the Strip, there are give-away newspapers offering every variety of playmates, of both sexes. The bordellos and the call-girl agencies ("No need to leave your hotel room") take full-page spreads with blurred, stylized photographs, credit-card logos, and dreadful double-entendres: "The perfect way to climax your stay in Las Vegas." There are also columns of coy personal ads for free with names like Sherri, Terri, Lori, and Desarya. A topless bar just off the Strip not only has dancing girls to cater to most tastes—one fat, one thin, one tough, one yielding—but also offers to customers who can no longer manage the four steps up from the parking lot to the bar a ramp for wheelchairs. There seems no end to the depression induced in the name of pleasure by the entrepreneurs of Clark County, Nevada, and it spreads outward, to professionals and nonprofessionals alike. "I feel that the women here have been hardened," Mickey Appleman said. "They're not vulnerable, like the women back East. It's like they've had their insides stripped out. I guess it's tragic in its own way, but this town is hard on everybody. It strips away your spirituality. In order to be successful on a continual basis out here, you have to remain nonemotional. But when a gambler is nonemotional, then he becomes detached from the person he really is. That's the basic problem of living in Las Vegas: you become despiritualized."

Despiritualized, depersonalized, one-dimensional: that is how life in any Disneyland must always be. But during the World Series of Poker the atmosphere at Binion's Horseshoe is as unwavering and concentrated as that of an Olympic training camp. I have never seen so many apparently healthy men gathered together in one place for so long with such single-mindedness: no sex, no drink, just the turn of the cards hour after hour and the little thrill of excitement and expectation at each new deal.

Robert Alan Aurthur

Hanging Out

Las Vegas may be defined as a unique community devoted to excess on every conceivable level, and with the addition of six hundred and twenty-eight guest rooms The Hilton Las Vegas will be the largest resort hotel in the world. Even now, with distant jackhammers chattering toward that transcendent day, the hotel is an imposing self-contained city, a Sodom to its newest neighbor and competitor, the MGM Grand's Gomorrah. Where better than the Hilton to establish a brief lookout to observe certain aspects of Vegas, especially since the (transient) director of entertainment for the Hilton Hotels in America is an old friend, Harvey Orkin.

☞ From Esquire, February 1974.

Until four or five years ago, perhaps when Howard Hughes began buying in, Las Vegas hotels, mostly mob-controlled, offered the best buy in the world for vacationers who could stay away from the gaming tables. No longer. As more legitimate management has taken command, prices have risen to where Las Vegas is not a bargain. Yes, the high rollers still come, brought in on free junkets, wined and dined on the cuff, but the overwhelming bulk of today's visitors is increasingly Middle America on a spree, paying prices for rooms and meals no less than at any other resort. And they do come: package tours and conventions; charter flights from all over the Mid- and Southwest. Packed buses leave Los Angeles on a Saturday morning at six A.M., with resident guitar and accordion players, arrive in Vegas at eleven, depart at two A.M. on Sunday. No need for a hotel room. Little possibility of getting one, anyway; on most weekends Vegas hotels and motels are about one hundred five percent overbooked.

With only slight fear of contradiction, it can be said that show business in America has been reduced to television, pop records and Las Vegas. The film industry is shattered, theatre dead, nightclubs, except for Las Vegas, practically nonexistent. For live entertainment, seven days a week, twenty-four hours a day, Vegas is *the* Apple, the only game in town. So the building continues, MGM's one hundred and six million dollar Grand Hotel being the latest addition. As the competition for customers mounts the question of attractions becomes more and more critical.

Harvey Orkin called late last fall and, in a hoarse whisper, said, "I'm sitting here looking at Johnny Cash's contract. This is a new kind of show business. Tell me how much he makes here." A calculated guess: fifty thousand dollars a week. The whisper gets hoarser. "Wrong. *One hundred and twenty-five thousand dollars* a week. And five suites of rooms. And two chauffeur-driven Mark IVs."

Johnny Cash?! "And that's not even the top," Harvey continued. "Elvis gets a hundred and fifty, plus God knows how much for Colonel Parker [Presley's longtime manager] to promote the engagement. Streisand also gets the top, *and* they built her a private tennis court." A new kind of show business, indeed—numbers that are out of sight. A closer look is obviously needed here. Not only will there be material for a couple of columns, but with just a little luck, the right turn of a few cards, steely eyes facing down hardened pit bosses, word will go out: Stand by! The last of the great low rollers is back in town.

When, after just forty hours in Las Vegas, you've dropped your entire bankroll, *hundreds* of dollars, there is little to do in the daytime but lounge at the Hilton pool and stare at the other losers. The fall sun is still a burner. The pool is huge, in the exact shape of the hotel's guest tower, a sort of triangle with collapsing sides. Cocktail waitresses, some from Detroit, most with husbands who are dealers at other hotels, shuttle between the lounges and the various food-and-drink facilities that rim the pool. Several lounges down from where the Loser lies next to his friend The Entertainment Director is what appears to be a small child wearing a striped caftan and a big, floppy hat. A child with platinum hair and orange lipstick who, when she gets up, is clearly not a child but one of the littlest lady midgets in the whole world. Completely unselfconscious, ignoring impolite stares, she moves to the edge of the pool, lifts the caftan to reveal perfectly formed if tiny legs, sits to dangle her feet in the water, and at the same time lights a cigarette. As a voice over the P.A. pages Harvey Orkin to a nearby phone, the Loser's eyes are diverted from the little person, and he is suddenly aware of the constant background of various sounds. In addition to the phone paging, which never stops, there is the overlapping Muzak, the thud of tennis balls on adjoining courts, the cries of children playing in the pool. "All that noise," Harvey Orkin says, returning from his call. "Including the music in the halls and elevators . . . *that* becomes your silence in Las Vegas." He sits. "That one was from Arthur Park." Park is a prominent agent who represents such clients as Dean Martin, Shirley MacLaine, Julie Andrews. "Dean is signed to the Grand, Shirley doesn't have an act, so I asked him about Julie," Harvey says. "He said they've been negotiating nearly two years with Caesars Palace, which may even build her a house here. He offered me a Russian variety show, and I asked if they did it with subtitles." Once again he is paged to the phone, and the Loser reflects that the insistent paging and not hearing one's own name can make a person a little paranoid. And even knowing, while visiting the Flamingo the night before, that one of the lounge acts is Paul Revere and The Raiders, it is still disconcerting to hear a disembodied voice calling, "Paging Mr. Paul Revere. Mr. Paul Revere, please."

Back from the latest call. "That was a lady named Leona," Harvey says. "She and her husband have an act, songs and comedy, and they're auditioning at eleven on Wednesday at the Musicians Union. She says they've been in Asia four years and no one knows them here. I'll go if I can. Who knows?" Does he get such calls day and night? "The other morning I was awakened at two-thirty by Evel Knievel. He said, 'Mr. Orkin, I have an act.' Another night I got a two A.M. call from Wilson Pickett. He was playing the lounge and wouldn't go on for the late show because he said *They* were taking money from his check. I had to get dressed and go down and prove *They* weren't. Tapped-out comics want their markers okayed at four in the morning." He sighs, looks gloomily past the lady midget who has gotten up to put out her cigarette. Most of the poolsiders are middle-aged women whose husbands are at either convention meetings or the tables. "When Elvis was here," Harvey says, "this place was filled with two thousand hysterical thirty-year-old groupies." He points toward the roof of the guest tower where almost the entire top floor is the Imperial Suite. "There he was, Elvis, with a parade of women, in and out, sixteen hours a day. It was unreal. All I could do was picture him sitting up there in his spangles, mumbling, 'Send me broads.' And they never stopped."

From another lounge comes a loud moan of protest. The moaner is a forty-seven-year-old junketeer named Sal, a building contractor from New Jersey. He is dressed in tennis whites and cradles his racket, but, tending a hangover and mourning a sixteen-thousand-dollar loss in four days, he has not the strength to get on the courts. "Don't remind me of when Elvis was here," Sal says. "I dropped twenty-one thousand on that junket." The lady midget has left her lounge and now prances by on her way to the ice cream bar. She glances briefly at Sal, who gives her a long look, then turns away. "Oh, God, what I was just thinking," he says when she's passed. "Back home I would never have such thoughts about little midget ladies, but here in Vegas. . . ." A man in pain, he closes his eyes.

"Superstars," Harvey says. "They all want the Imperial Suite. They can make a hundred thousand dollars a week, but if they don't get the Imperial Suite they think they've been put down. It's the carrot on the stick. Like the only way to book our rooms in places other than Vegas, say the Waldorf for fifteen or twenty thousand a week, is to tie it in with a hundred thousand here *and* the Imperial Suite. You find yourself treating them like insatiable children, giving more and more because they demand more and more. Like Ann-Margret. Ninety thousand a week, and the day following her opening I get a note complaining that the last time she played here there were free peanuts in her dressing room. Where were they now? When I ignored the note, the next day I got a call from her lawyer in Beverly Hills, her lawyer for crissake, asking where are the free nuts? How did it end? Well, the lawyer admitted, yes, at ninety grand a week she should be able to afford to buy them, and I sent the nuts over."

The lady midget returns to her lounge, an ice cream cone looming large in her tiny hands, and, while Harvey takes another call, Sal plans how he will recover from both his hangover and his losses. First a long nap and then one more shot at baccarat, just one more, before his junket jets out in the morning. Harvey is back from the phone. "That was Donna Fargo's husband, who's also, by some coincidence, her manager." Donna Fargo is a country singer coupled on an incoming bill with Glen Campbell. "He's found the only billboard in Las Vegas that doesn't have her name on it. Wait 'til he sees where her name *is* listed, and she has only seventy-five percent of Campbell's billing." Harvey explains that the previous booker had negotiated individual contracts with Campbell and Fargo promising each sole hundred-percent billing, an obvious impossibility. How will it be worked out? "She'll be offered more money for less billing," Harvey says. "Otherwise Glen won't play."

Any other superstar idiosyncrasies? "Well, there's Tony Bennett,"

Harvey says. "I love him, and he's the best. No trouble except, even at seventy-five thousand a week, he refuses to open or close on a Monday night, which creates all kinds of scheduling problems. Also, he won't work on Jewish holidays, says he doesn't want to insult his Jewish friends. I guess the best of them is Cosby. He, too, gets seventy-five, but he comes out all by himself, sits on a chair, and talks about when he was a kid."

Enter Henri J. Lewin, senior vice-president of Hilton Hotels. A tall, imposing-looking man in his fifties, Lewin dresses impeccably and expensively, has an extensive collection of gold jewelry. For poolside he wears a tailored jump suit, and around his neck is a chain given him by Elvis Presley that bears the letters TCB (Take Care of Business). Headquartered in San Francisco, Lewin has been overseeing construction and planning of the new wing, and this weekend has entertained a party of Japanese who will open an expanded Benihana of Tokyo, to move from their present location in the hotel. A former refugee from Germany, Lewin came to the United States through the Far East, and still speaks with a precise accent. A devoted hotelman, he appears to be slightly uncomfortable with casino operations, and is often heard to point out that as much revenue is made in the Vegas Hiltons on food, drinks and rooms as is made in gaming.

Now he sits on the foot of Harvey's lounge. "You're going to do a lot of business tonight," Lewin says. "Over at the Sahara Sonny decked Cher, and their shows are canceled for a couple of days."

"Some of these people do behave strangely," Harvey says.

Lewin nods. "There was what's her name. . . . She went into our jewelry shop, picked out three pieces, sent me word she'd accept one. I sent back word I was in the Suez. Pay these people a hundred and twenty-five thousand dollars a week, and they expect you to say 'Thank you.' Superstars!"—the word comes out like a curse. "On the other hand there are the guys you could pay any amount, and they'd wind up with no money. They leave it at the tables, the schmucks."

As if paged, Sal opens his eyes. "Listen, Henri," he says. "Last night in the Imperial Room we waited twenty-five minutes for our main course." Lewin looks at him implacably. "So?" "So that's a long time," Sal says. Now Lewin's expression is one of undisguised contempt. "Sal, I can't figure people like you at all. You come out here on junkets, everything's comped, and every morning I see on the computer what each one of you has eaten and drunk, how much paper you've signed for the tables. Now, you've lost some on this trip, right?" Sal nods truculently. "Okay," Lewin goes on, "so you eat five meals a day, drink only champagne, and you think that's the way to get even. If you ate and drank like that for a couple of weeks at home you'd die. Right?" Without waiting for an answer, he ticks off his fingers. "So far you've eaten meals in Benihana, the Bavarian Inn, the Steak House and Leonardo's. Overall, have you ever eaten better food?"

"No, but . . ." Sal starts to say. "But nothing," Lewin interrupts. "Last night the Imperial Room, gourmet food, one of the great restaurants in America. Everything cooked to order. *Of course you waited twenty-five minutes!* In one of the great restaurants do you expect the blue-plate special?"

Sal, who leaves a lot of money in this hotel, is cornered but not intimidated. "It wasn't just the wait, Henri," he says. "It was *how* we were made to wait." He seems to have conveyed a message, because Lewin abruptly rises. "Ill see about *that*," he says, and you know he will.

The lady midget is slowly collecting her belongings, preparing to leave. "Here's the main problem booking this place," Harvey says. "You're always roughly a year ahead. Half the talent now playing Vegas is rock or country-western recording stars I've never heard of, so when an agent tells me about a hit record, well, I have to figure a year from now will the guy still be hot?" Reflectively. "The hardest art form is knowing good from bad. You see someone great and, if the artist hasn't had a hit record or exposure on TV, the public isn't prepared to accept him. then you see someone very hot, and you say, well, he's no good, just no damn good, and you're told he's *got* to be good, because he sold two million records last week or played arenas, doing a hundred seven thousand in two nights here, a hundred twenty-three thousand in two nights there, or he's a smash on the Carson show. So what do you say?

"Another thing, we have the largest room in Vegas, twenty-one hundred seats, and there's the specter hanging over the star that he'll look out and see four hundred empty seats. In another hotel where the room seats fifteen hundred he'll be turning them away."

There's the feeling that Harvey Orkin will not be an ace booker for very long. "I don't know," he says. "I live in luxury in a great hotel, eat and drink the best. I look out my window and see a huge swimming pool, tennis courts, hills to ride a horse, and not a drop of rain since I arrived. I say to myself, 'What's so bad?' Then I burst into tears."

It's now obvious that the lady midget is headed directly for Sal. She pauses at the foot of his lounge, barely able to see over the edge, and they stare at each other. "Pardon me," she says in a little, squeaky voice, "but isn't your name Sal?"

Sal's eyes squint a bit. "Yeah, it is," he admits, and the little lady smiles. "I thought it was you," she says. "The last time you were out, when Elvis was here, didn't you take out my cousin Velvet?"

A long moment, and then Sal says, "Yeah, Velvet, right, how is she?"

"She's fine," the lady midget says, and there's another long pause, both at a loss. Sal is the first to speak. "Funny thing," he says, "I saw you walking around before . . . but I didn't recognize you."

Susan Berman

Memoirs of a
Gangster's Daughter

It was 1957, and I was twelve. They said it was the largest funeral Las Vegas had ever seen—there were thousands of mourners. The pallbearers were men I had known: Gus Greenbaum, whose throat would later be slashed in Phoenix; Willie "Ice Pick" Alderman, who would die on Terminal Island while serving time in a mob extortion rap; Joe Rosenberg, one of my father's partners, who was known as his mouthpiece; Nick the Greek, the famed odds-maker. Squat Jewish men surrounded Uncle Chickie and me at the funeral, saying, "We don't expect trouble." My father, Davie Berman, 54, lay in an open

☞ Excerpted from New York, July 27, 1981, and Easy Street (Dial Press, 1981).

casket while a rabbi intoned, "It is a sad day for all of Las Vegas. Davie Berman, one of our original pioneers who made this city bloom, is dead. There will never be anyone like him. Davie Berman had a vision. He saw a boomtown where others had just seen desert. He was Mr. Las Vegas. Davie Berman, beloved by all of Las Vegas, beloved husband and beloved father, is gone."

Hundreds of mourners held me and kissed me. One man I didn't know grabbed me and said, "Susie, your dad was the greatest gangster that ever lived. You can hold your head up high." Then there was just the Kaddish, uttered by all, most of them crying. It sounded louder than any floor-show orchestra I had ever heard. My voice blended with the others as the rabbi recited, "*Yisgadal Vyiskadash, Sh'me Rabbo.*"

Another man said to me, "Susie, your dad was a stand-up guy." I had never heard the word "gangster" before in connection with my father; I didn't know what "stand-up guy" meant—someone with a strong commitment to the underworld who wouldn't crack under pressure.

To me he was just my father, but to the world he was Davie Berman, one of the founders of the syndicate, a trusted partner and confidant of Meyer Lansky, Frank Costello, and Bugsy Siegel. He was the man a crime book said "was so tough he could kill a man with one hand tied behind his back."

The son of a Russian-immigrant rabbinical student, he built his own gambling empire when he was just sixteen, and went on to become a bootlegger and bank robber whose face appeared on dozens of "wanted" posters. He was the brazen kid who engineered one of the first kidnaps for ransom, escaped death in a Central Park shoot-out, and was described by a detective on the front page of the *New York Times* as "the toughest Jew I ever met." He was the mob visionary who helped convince his eastern associates that there was money to be made in that honky-tonk town called Las Vegas, and he went on to turn a desert full of sagebrush into a gambling bonanza.

After my father's funeral, my Uncle Chickie, his younger brother, gave me a cup of coffee. He was sitting on a bed in the Riviera Hotel's largest suite. Always a sport, with his dark olive skin, his jet-black hair, and his perfect monogrammed silk shirts and suits, Chickie looked uncharacteristically rumpled that day. His shiny hair wasn't slicked back with its usual Brylcreem sheen. He held his ever-present English Oval in the very tips of his manicured nails, but he had forgotten to light it; he had no energy to take a drag. It was the first time I had seen him without a smoky halo around his face.

Tears ran down his red silk Sulka pajamas and robe, but he didn't seem to care. The phone rang off the hook, there were constant knocks on the door, and the headlines on the newspapers scattered around the room screamed DAVIE BERMAN DEAD. Uncle Chickie was in a daze. By nature jaunty, he moved very slowly that day. His hazel eyes finally comprehended that I was waiting for him to tell me what to do, and he rose slowly from the bed.

"Baby, put on a clean dress and I'll brush your hair," he said shakily. He took a silver brush out of a brown alligator suitcase and turned it over. It had his initials, CMB, on it. He started to brush my hair, and I knew Brylcreem was getting on my bangs, but I didn't care.

As a first-generation Las Vegan, I had known only the life my father had chosen to give me. The sounds of my childhood were the crunching of slot machines, the click of dice, the songs of Sophie Tucker and the Andrews Sisters, and the voices of pages at the Flamingo Hotel insisting, "Davie Berman, calling Davie Berman." The cactus-strewn desert invigorated me, and hotel coffee shops and floor shows gave me an exhilarating sense of security.

I would watch my father from the sidelines of the hotel, the casino patrician, strolling so elegantly in the pit, glancing at the gaming tables and issuing commands in a soft, staccato voice that knew no hesitation. His daily rounds included not only his partners but such people as Jack Benny and Jimmy Durante, producer Harry Cohn, businessmen, foreign nabobs, and Las Vegas's highest rollers. He was called the ambassador of gambling.

A legendary gangster in his youth, my father was a forceful and feared head of the syndicate by the time I knew him. He lived in a world that was dangerous, violent, and severe. But he crafted my illusory childhood to seem all-American and completely normal.

I thought we had no house key because "somebody is always home." Mob members never carry keys, because if they are kidnapped, a rival could get to their families. I thought we had no checking account because "everybody knows us here; we just use cash." Mob members prefer to keep cashboxes and few visible assets.

My father was austere—he didn't gamble, drink, or smoke. He told me he didn't like to stay in small rooms for a long time because he felt confined. I later learned that he had served seven years in Sing Sing, four in solitary confinement, on a twelve-year sentence.

He told me our late-night jaunts to Los Angeles were a vacation. He'd wake me and tell me to get dressed; we'd drive to McCarran Field and fly to L.A. I'd be kept at the Beverly Wilshire Hotel for a few days with a couple of his men friends. The suite was filled with Mission Pak fruit and flowers. They took me to Uncle Bernie's toy store, in Beverly Hills, to drink lemonade from the lemonade tree, and we ordered coffee ice cream in our room from MFK's drugstore, in the hotel. Then my father would reappear magically after two days and take me to the Brown Derby for dinner. We'd sit under Ingrid Bergman's picture, and he'd order "lamb chops with pink skirts for Susie" and put me on a red leather child's seat so I could join in the conversation. In fact, those "vacations" were flights to freedom when there was mob unrest and I was endangered.

My father always told me to "follow the rules," yet he had broken so many he had lost count. I thought the black spot on my father's ankle was where a horse had kicked him, as he'd told me; it was a bullet wound. I thought the men who lived with us when I was very young were just friends; they were bodyguards.

Most days after school, the driver would take me to the Flamingo Hotel to be with my father. I'd run into the casino and head for the pit, ducking under the burgundy velvet cord and announcing, "Daddy, Daddy, I'm here." Gamblers would look annoyed when they heard a child's shrill voice in this most grown-up of places, but once they saw whose child it was, they seemed delighted. My father was always dressed in a stylish suit. He had a ruby mezuzah that hung on a gold chain from his pocket, and he always smelled of French cologne.

My father's eyes would twinkle and he would reach down and throw me in the air, catching me in a hug on the way down. Then he'd head off to the counting room in back of the pit, where we'd get down to the serious business of homework. The counting room always smelled awful to me—the odor of old cigarette butts and paper money clung to the walls.

He had decided to concentrate on improving my math. He'd clear off a space and we'd begin. My father hit on an inventive approach—he started a coin collection for me. He bought me the coin books and had hotel sheriff Dave Schuman bring in handfuls of change from the slots for me to sort, catalogue, and total up. It was a lesson in casino economics.

As math got more complicated, he bought me a slot machine, one of the old ones, without the neon lights, recently retired for a newer model.

"Now, Susie, here is $5 worth of nickels and a key to the back. Memorize how many nickels you can get for a jackpot, practice your multiplication tables on the nickels, figure how many times you need three cherries to get all the nickels out of the back. And I don't want you making money off of anyone else—everyone is to play with these nickels."

At five o'clock, I'd run to the front desk and ask for a key to an empty room. The hotel would get busy at that hour, and I had to fend for myself. Then I'd skip up the six floors to the room, turn on the radio (there was no TV yet), and order room service. I adored waiters and their tables on wheels. I'd always get chocolate ice cream and tomato soup with crackers. I'd sign "Susie Berman" on the check.

❧   ❧   ❧

In 1944, the year before I was born, my father made the biggest move of his career: He went to Las Vegas to help run it for Meyer Lansky and the mob. After a long and dangerous career spanning every mob venture from the 1920s through the 1940s, he was rewarded with a big piece of the action in what he envisioned as a mob jackpot town.

He went to Las Vegas to front for his East Coast associates—Lansky, Frank Costello, Lucky Luciano, and Joe Adonis. None of them wanted to live in this desert boomtown, but they needed a few men they could trust to run the business for them. My father was one of those men.

He had first visited Las Vegas in 1940 with his friend Bugsy Siegel. Siegel was an original member of the Bugs and Meyer gang, partners with Lansky in a group that started Murder, Inc., and founded the Jewish component of organized crime. Siegel was from the Lower East Side in New York. He had begun his career by bootlegging, organizing the transport of liquor from the New York City docks to the underworld warehouses during Prohibition. He had been sent to California in 1930 by Lucky Luciano to open up the West Coast for the mob. He was to set up a centralized horse-betting system, direct narcotics to the United States from Mexico, and look for new ways to invest syndicate money on the West Coast.

After World War II, my father came back to stake his claim. He brought a suitcase with $1 million—money he had raised from his associates in Minneapolis and St. Paul and in northern Minnesota. With the blessings of his East Coast backers and his promise that they would get 25 percent of everything, he bought his first club downtown, the El Cortez. There was no strip yet. He brought his best friend, Willie Alderman, with him from Minneapolis, joined old friend Moe Sedway, who had come from New York, and met a new partner put in by Siegel, Gus Greenbaum from Phoenix.

Meyer Lansky and Frank Costello had already staked their claims, and they were taking in partners. Before my father left Minneapolis, he had to square my Uncle Chickie's debts. But even with Chickie's debts paid, Chickie wasn't safe in Minneapolis. He had angered too many people this time, so Davie took his brother to Las Vegas with him.

Once he got to Las Vegas, he negotiated with the owner of the El Cortez and got approval to buy. Then he flew to Omaha to meet with Lansky to get official syndicate permission to close the deal and head the new group at the El Cortez. Lansky was in Omaha trying to get dog racing legalized. He was going to Las Vegas every month, complaining of the heat; he didn't want to live there and was delighted to have trusted lieutenants like my father run the city for him. At that time, Lansky and Frank Costello had the whole country. Lucky Luciano was facing deportation to Italy, and there were shifting territories and new opportunities. Lansky asked my father for $160,000 up front and gave his permission.

Back in Las Vegas, Chickie and Davie shared a room at the El Cortez during the negotiating. Finally, all that remained were the signatures and payments. Davie went upstairs to get the money he had asked Chickie to guard. When he got upstairs, Chickie and the suitcase were gone. He feared the worst.

He called everyone he knew to find Chickie. Moe Sedway sent all his boys, and they scoured the town. They finally found Chickie in a small downtown joint. He had lost the $1 million in a high roller's crap game. My father probably would have destroyed anyone else for such a transgression, but Chickie was his brother, and he loved him. Chickie threatened to kill himself if Davie never spoke to him again. My father just looked at him, punched his fist into the wall, peeled off a few bills, and said, "Go to Miami till all this dies down."

Then my father flew back to the Midwest, where he raised another $1 million and promised to make good on the first million. He hurried back to Las Vegas to the El Cortez. Early in 1945, Davie closed the deal; he was in big action in Las Vegas, and he was exultant. The owners included Ben Siegel, Moe Sedway, Gus Greenbaum, Dave Berman, Charles Berman, Meyer Lansky, and Willie Alderman.

◆   ◆   ◆

I knew my father's partners only from a child's perspective—the same way I knew my father. There was Willie Alderman, called "Ice Pick Willie" in his youth because he allegedly killed people with an ice pick. Willie was my favorite, a big, lumpy, silent man who greeted me every day with "How ya doing, Susie?" He was always at my father's side.

There was Gus Greenbaum, a junkie and alleged killer. Gus was an older dark-skinned man who smoked cigars and growled. He never paid any attention to me and never smiled. Once, I kicked him as hard as I could in the ankle just to prove I existed. He said, "Davie, the kid takes after you." I asked my father if he had kicked "big mean men" too, but my father said no, and not to kick Gus again.

Gus lost his temper at everyone and started yelling in a slow, raspy voice. Different parts of his face would get red, and then the whole face would be completely discolored. My father would calm him down but would always tell me to go out by the pool and leave the counting room immediately. Sometimes, Gus would be sleeping on the couch in the back, but not sleeping like my father or Willie. You just couldn't wake Gus.

The FBI files, in colorful language, described my father's partner Moe this way:

> Moe Sedway, born Morris Sidwirtz and called the Little Giant, is a dwarf Jewish boy with all the worst traits of his nationality overemphasized. While not an independent operator in the underworld, [he] is a distinctive individual maintaining a position on the fringes of the smart money. Catered to big names on Broadway, was quick to capitalize on the opportunity to put other persons under obligation to him. Prone to be a snappy dresser, vain to the point of being boresome and in his own mind a terrific woman killer. Being deprived of physical power, Sedway relied on his natural tendency

to bargain and frequently followed the bribery theory. During periods of stress he wrings his hands, becomes wild eyed and resembles a small dog about to be subjected to the distasteful procedure of being bathed. Sedway's obsessions are monogrammed silk shirts and silk underwear as well as manicured nails. Sedway has been a front man for Bugsy Siegel for fifteen years. He was head of illicit liquor and gambling in New York.

My father, Gus, Willie, and Moe would always file into the counting room together, looking grim. At the end of a late night (if I was there because of a floor show), I would notice my father's three partners looked rumpled and haggard and somewhat dazed, but he was immaculate and affable as usual. "What's wrong with them, Daddy?" I'd ask. "Just *tsuris* [trouble], Susie," he'd say. I always thought *tsuris* was a stomachache, because they all looked like they had one.

I didn't know what really went on in the counting room when I wasn't doing my homework there. Three times a day—3 P.M., midnight, and 3 A.M.—my father brought in the money and counted it in that room. Then he made sure the eastern group got its share. At the Flamingo, as in his downtown hotels, he was the pit boss, the man in charge of all gambling in the casino.

What I remember most about my father with his partners is that none of them liked to lose at card games or golf. They despised losing, since they considered themselves winners in life. If the four of them were playing gin rummy, one team had to lose; even I knew that. But they didn't seem to expect it. If my father and Willie lost, my father would throw his cards at the ceiling and stalk off. If Gus lost, he would slam his cards into the wall. When they were on the golf course, it was worse. My father and Willie usually played with a hotel owner and a revolving fourth. About midway through the game, there would be a dispute on the score. The caddie would be asked to referee. He always looked as if he would have given anything to be in another country at this time. If my father lost, he would break his clubs over his knee and walk off. The others would toss golf

balls into the trees, throw their golf bags on the ground. By the fif-
teenth hole, the foursome was not speaking. I'd look blasé as I
watched the caddie turn pale. I knew that by the next Sunday it
would all be forgotten as my father and three others would be cheerfully heading for another disaster.

My father's mother, Clara, or Bubby to me, would show up unannounced at our home in Las Vegas once a month for her "pay-as-
you-eat Shabbes dinner." Around 2 P.M. on a Friday, Bubby would
pound on the front door, yelling, "Davie, Lou, Susie, let me in, hurry
up." Or course, my father was never home from the hotel in the afternoon, but she'd act as if he should have been. She'd run all over
the house looking for him, then go right into the kitchen and sneer,
"So where's Davie? Working again?"

Without waiting for an answer, she'd throw down her shawl and
start unpacking two huge needlepoint bags full of groceries. She was
in a frenzy, her white hair standing up in wisps as it came out of her
bun. She was short and stout and smelled like old rouge. As soon as
she washed the carrots for the matzo-ball soup, she yelled at our
bodyguard Lou to "come and chop these carrots into little pieces."
Lou dutifully went into the kitchen. She took an eggbeater from her
purse and started making matzo balls and washing the chicken. After about an hour of intense preparation, during which she yelled at
me "to stay out of my goddamn way" and said "ach" several times and
"oy vay" if Lou wasn't fast enough on the chopping, Bubby hit the
telephone and had all my father's friends paged in the casino.

"Hello, Gus? Clara Berman. I'm making a Shabbes meal at Davie's
tonight. Be here at sundown. You eat good," she'd say as she rang up
Willie, Joe, Mickey Cohen, and others, usually about eight men.

It took her all afternoon to cook the Shabbes meal. Finally she
laid out the matzo-ball soup, the chicken, stuffed cabbage, challah,
vegetables, and strudel for dessert.

Around 6 P.M., the sleek, dark Cadillacs would roll up. Gus, Joe,
Mickey, Willie, and others arrived, and the hungry Jewish men took

their places around our table. My father entered with an expression that said, "Oh, no, not again!" but he kissed Bubby hello and sat down too. They ate with the gusto of men starved for a matzo ball. It was always a silent dinner except for slurping noises from the soup bowls. Bubby lit the menorah on the mantel.

She kept shoving food onto my father's plate, saying, "Davie, you're too thin," and Gus came in for chiding if he didn't finish every drop: "Whatsa matter? You got an ulcer from the hotel business? You can't finish the *tsimmes*?" When the strudel was gone, Bubby would remove her apron and announce, "Fine, first you eat, then you pay. I need gelt for my City of Hope project," and she'd go to each man and hold out a fat hand.

My father looked embarrassed to death and said, "Mama, I'll give you the money. You promised you'd never do this again. Please!" But she knew her victims. Hundred-dollar bills flowed out of their pockets while I watched in fascination. She put a rubber band around the take and threw it into her needlepoint bag.

Soon after my father started a synagogue, he had an idea for Passover services. Since none of our mothers was Jewish, and no one lived in a house big enough to hold a Seder, he decided that it should be held at the Last Frontier Hotel. My father even brought Bubby in for it; she taught our mothers to mix haroseth and make other traditional foods.

He'd have special Passover matzos sent to us from New York, and he'd always take me with him to pick up the shipment at the airport. My father would see to it that any employees who were Jewish would be invited; on the way to the hotel, he read their names to the rabbi so that he would be familiar with their children.

He would walk me through the casino, where as usual I'd be straining to see who was winning a jackpot, but my father would say, "Not tonight, Susie. Tonight is special. It's Passover."

The dining room would be transformed, all the small tables lined up in long rows. In their *shiksa* zest, our naïve mothers decorated the ceiling with streamers from all the Jewish holidays; silver decorations picturing dreidels and Chanukah nights mixed with those of Passover and Rosh Hashanah. The rabbi would introduce himself to any new children, and those of us who knew him trailed along to meet the new celebrants.

The rabbi walked onto the stage and yelled the four questions in the microphone. "Why is this night different from all other nights?" My father led us in the answers. A few other fathers had imported their small, fat mothers too. Yiddish accents, the recitation of the four questions, and our two or three attempts at Jewish songs led by the cantor drifted from the room. Occasionally, confused guests would wander in and ask why there was no floor show that night, and we kids would laugh hysterically at their mistake.

I found the whole experience exhausting and usually wound up falling asleep on my father's lap. I'd be awakened when he whispered in my ear, "Susie, the *afikomen.*" This was the highlight of the evening: Whoever discovered the hidden matzo in the napkin got a picture book on Israel. As soon as the rabbi told us to get started, the 30 or so of us dived into the dining room. Trouble was, the rabbi didn't have much of an imagination; he always hid it in one of three places: under the microphone stand, in the orchestra pit, or backstage. I never got there first, a fact that I blamed on my father. He held on to my dress sash until the rabbi said "Go," and there were always two other girls who got a head start. Then it was over. We would all pitch in to take down the decorations from the sparkly ceiling, because the late floor show would go on as usual afterward. In fact, the guests were already lining up as we left. I always gave the waiting guests a superior grin. They were mere tourists; *we* were Las Vegas.

I was surrounded by middle-aged men who helped my father raise me, because my mother was ill. I never knew she was sick, only that she was away most of the time and that when she was home she was usually very sad and very quiet. I thought of her as a beautiful painting that was becoming dimmer and dimmer as she became more and more diminished. There were framed pictures of her all over, pictures of a tall, vibrant young tap dancer dressed in glamorous costumes, with shiny blue-black hair and smiling red lips. In those pictures, she had a gossamer quality, and she seemed to glide rather than walk. I knew that had been my mother, but I could hardly believe she had ever been like that.

When she was well, she would be joyful and loving. But much of the time she lay in her bed, tears running down her cheeks, that black hair the only vivid thing about her. I didn't know why this delicate creature looked like a frightened doe and lay in her white satin bathrobe day after day. Would she ever be that other person, the one in the photographs, again?

When she was at home in that room, it seemed like a museum. Her closet was stuffed with dozens of gowns; all her colorful high-heeled pumps stood at attention, waiting for her to leap into them, but she never did. When she wasn't at home I could never bring myself to go into that room. I was afraid of it, afraid some of that terrible sadness would get on me and drag me down. I used to have nightmares that the sadness would move down the hall into my room and grab me. I imagined struggling against it and losing. My death would come like a gradual paralysis, and I would lie still, crying as she did.

I didn't know that my mother was having a series of nervous breakdowns caused by her realization of just what her life was about. I didn't know that she lived in terror day and night that something would happen to me or my father. I didn't know that she was traumatized and finally immobilized by her life with the mob. All I knew was that she was so very unhappy, and I thought somehow I had caused it. Maybe I was too rambunctious—my father told me not to climb on her. Maybe I bruised her—how could I make it up?

I knew my father loved her very much, because he kissed her all the time and stroked her hair. He used to sit on the edge of the bed—when she felt a little better, I was allowed in to sit there too—and talk to her about all the things they had done together in the past, and he would tell her how wonderful things were going to be.

He'd urge her to get up just for two hours, to go to a floor show with him, or to go to the piano, where they would play a duet. He would pick at the piano, singing, "Come to me, my melancholy baby,/Cuddle up and don't be blue." Then he'd kiss her cheek as he sang the line "Every cloud must have a silver lining." My father was a man of popular tastes. He could play show tunes on her piano by ear, and he loved music. She liked to sing "Frankie and Johnny were lovers" to him. Sometimes she would look happier. I would watch breathlessly, thinking, "He's going to make that bad thing go away, he's going to do it," but then he never did, and I thought it was his fault too. She didn't like me to see her crying, and she'd say, "Susie, don't look at me—I don't want you to see me like this. Go and play." But I was so fascinated by her that I wanted to be around her whenever I could. When I wouldn't leave, she'd tell me she had a headache and ask me to fetch the blue goggles from the refrigerator. I'd dutifully get the plastic goggles filled with blue liquid and think, "That's it, she has headaches."

When she felt good, she would drag her big scrapbooks out of the cupboard and show me hundreds of pictures of her as a dancer.

My mother was 26 when she gave birth to me, on May 18, 1945, in Minneapolis. The man who feared nothing was shaking as he drove her to the hospital. "Keep calm, baby," he kept saying. "Keep calm."

She would answer, "I am calm, Davie," but he didn't hear her; he was terrified. The minute she was wheeled into the delivery room, he called all his friends to the hospital to help calm him down.

Chickie, Willie, Chief, Flippy, Rabbit, and Lou paced back and forth with him, making the waiting room at Abbott Hospital look almost as menacing as the scene of the Saint Valentine's Day massacre in Chicago. In fact, they looked so ferocious that the nurse was afraid to come out and announce my birth—the doctor had to. My father shook his head in disbelief when he first saw me, and tears streamed down his face. My mother was holding me, and she said, "Dave, this is Susan Berman."

When I was two months old, my mother brought me out to Las Vegas on the train. It was the middle of a sweltering July, and she was dressed in a white linen suit and big-brimmed hat, and she had me clothed in a white silk dress. She got off the train and handed me to my father with a look of shock on her face. She uttered the words every midwestern wife would say: "Where is the town?" There was nothing to see but sagebrush, cactus, and the carcasses of prairie dogs. She had expected something more like Los Angeles. . . .

My mother had barely been out of St. Paul, except for a few trips with my father. Las Vegas had a population of about 16,000 and consisted of just two areas—the raggedy downtown, called "Glitter Gulch," where my father had his clubs, and a small residential area. Many people lived in trailers and cinder-block houses, there was a large Indian reservation on the outskirts of town, and most of the town's blacks lived on the west side under a cement structure called "the cement curtain."

It was a cowboy town. Men with deep sunburns and sweaty underarms walked the streets in silver spurs. Grizzled prospectors and tapped-out gamblers looked up with wonder as my father and his partners brought their fancy city manners and suits to town. Alligator shoes started to take the place of cowboy boots.

The strip was just a two-lane highway then; lizards and snakes decorated the landscape. Most of the action was at the downtown gambling clubs, but the Western Union office always held some drama. There, cast-off spouses hoped for a second chance; divorce and marriage were second only to gambling as a town attraction. Entrances to the town in each direction were lined with wedding chapels.

The gaudy patchwork of gambling clubs—the Old Rex, the Sal Sagev, the Las Vegas Club, the Boulder Club, the El Dorado, and the

Pioneer Club—sprang up in the early 1940s. The famed D4C ranch was on the outskirts of town. Everything was authentic cowboy— even the crap dealers at the Last Frontier wore chaps and leather jackets, and steer horns decorated the walls.

.   .   .   .

The "town" was firmly established only in my father's mind. With ardent resolve, he told her how it was going to be the jewel of the desert—with luxury hotels everywhere, sophisticated entertainers, patrons from around the world. He stood on the railroad platform in his tailored suit, pointed at the cowboys hanging around the depot, and vowed, "Gladys, honey, this is only the backdrop."

Katharine Best
and Katharine Hillyer

....

Fanciful Press Agentry

220,000 gallons of Martinis in the swimming pool wouldn't have been fair to the public. . . .

—Stan Irwin

Las Vegas has learned in the space of a few short years how to get its picture on the nation's front pages every day without benefit of gambling or atomic explosions, though both help. The Dunes, for instance, installed an enormous electric sign on top of the Capitol Theater at Fiftieth Street and Broadway in New York City, a sign that

☞ From Las Vegas: Playtown U.S.A. (*David McKay Company, 1955*).

costs the hotel $56,000 annually for location, lease, and maintenance. There is the usual gaudy replica of a sheik whisking over the sands. There are the words "Dunes" and "Las Vegas" in great glittering neon. And then there is a roulette wheel, bigger than life itself, that spins and spins and spins and then stops, sometimes on red, sometimes on black. Newspapers regularly report unusual traffic jams in the vicinity, and even on occasion have noticed certain wagering activities.

Atomic explosions not only provide Las Vegas with lovely visitors' statistics, but have served from time to time as stunning photographic tie-ins.

Wilbur Clark, whose primary enterprise is the sprawling, gambling superden, Desert Inn, timed the opening of his other Strip venture, the chaste (no gambling) and unique (unneonized) Colonial Inn for the atomic blast of March 1953. Papers everywhere had trouble deciding which was the more earth-shattering event, and ended by carrying both.

Lili St. Cyr, the Strip's delectable resident stripper, postponed her wedding to Ted Jordan three times so that it would coincide with the blast that rocked the town in the early morning hours of February 21, 1955. By the time the flash had faded and champagne glasses stopped jingling, the couple had exchanged vows and were cutting an atomic-blast-mushroom-shaped wedding cake. Newspapers found this romanticized angle on nuclear fission irresistible and captioned their photographs with the additional information that "the couple are honeymooning near the atomic proving grounds." Since the nearest unrestricted living area to the atomic proving grounds is Las Vegas itself, it may be presumed that the happy couple didn't even bother to leave the elegant premises of El Rancho Vegas.

Each gambling establishment on the Strip has a press agent, and in some of the posher places, the press agents have press agents. Competition is intense and unending, and the bigger the star across the road, the brasher must be the stunt on this side. Harvey Deiderich, promoting the Gabor sisters a year or so ago at the Frontier, found himself competing with Stan Irwin across the highway at the Sahara, whose current promotion sinecure was releasing news stories and pictures on Marlene Dietrich's famous "peek-a-boo" costume and her then all-time-high salary of $30,000 a week. Zsa Zsa Gabor was sporting nightly a black eye patch, a facial ornament she claimed was necessary because of a luscious 2-$\frac{1}{2}$-by-1-$\frac{1}{4}$ inch shiner reportedly given her by international playboy Porfirio Rubirosa. Mr. Deiderich merely provided black sequin eye patches for sisters Eva and Magda and all the chorus girls and so startling was the sister act from then on that national coverage took care of itself.

Stan Irwin, a dapper and superenergized ex-actor, and presently state assemblyman, is possibly the suavest publicist of all the Strip's big-name droppers. When he doesn't have a practically naked Dietrich to promote, he still manages to get the name of the Sahara before the public. Once, just for the hell of it, he talked one of the hotel's current headliners, an acrobat named Karl Carsony, into doing a one-arm handstand on a cane on top of the Sahara's fifty-foot tower sign outside the hotel. He insured the fellow with Lloyd's of London for $100,000, enticed all photographers within telephone range to bring their cameras along, and watched smugly as Mr. Carsony balanced himself against a wild desert wind on a cane atop the tower for ten seconds. The stunt cost the Sahara $400 and was worth some $10,000 in free newspaper space.

Nor is Stan Irwin one to overestimate a headliner's power with the press. Once, when Red Skelton and Anna Maria Alberghetti were playing in his Congo Room, he ordered a miniature replica of the Sahara's Garden of Allah swimming pool constructed into a gargantuan billboard at the intersections of Sunset Boulevard and Doheny Drive near Los Angeles. It wasn't enough to fill this roadside swimming pool with water that glistened and high-lighted the names of Skelton and Alberghetti. No indeed. He hired eight beautiful girl swimmers whose jobs were to leap and cavort around the pool for eight hours a day in shifts of four hours each. The stunt cost $30,000, resulted in $1,000,000 worth of publicity, and brought only the Bureau of Internal Revenue knows how many paying customers from the City of the Angels, but that isn't all that makes Mr. Irwin happy. The billboard won commendations for "originality" from advertising men all over the country.

It's sometimes debatable in Las Vegas whether pools are constructed for swimming or for publicity purposes. Helicopters from someplace like Forth Worth, Texas, are likely to whirl down beside any pool on the Strip any day with a honeymooning couple aboard who invariably appear surprised that hordes of cameramen are on hand. Stan Irwin one time seriously considered filling the 220,000-gallon pool at the Sahara with Martinis and little bright-colored straws sticking out, and only abandoned the idea when he learned that more vodka than gin is drunk in Las Vegas. "It wouldn't have been fair to the public" was his cryptic remark on this occasion.

At one time the New Frontier, in the interests of nation-wide demand for Las Vegas whoop-de-do, built a glass-enclosed observation chamber at the bottom of its swimming pool so that nonswimming customers could sit therein sipping Gibsons while watching health fiends frolic in the water outside. "Where else in all the world but Las Vegas," cried the captions to the inevitable pictures that appeared in home-town papers everywhere, "could Mr. and Mrs. Joe Doakes, of Wichita, Kansas, enjoy cocktails under water?" The Flamingo, slightly envious of all the newspaper space given to atomic tests at Yucca Flat, edged advantageously into the act by commemorating the destruction of Doom Town by filling its pool with 2,000 mushrooms. And the Sands, in an effort to lend credence to Las Vegas's Chamber of Commerce's loudly touted "Have Fun in the Sun" ballyhoo, floated a roulette table in its pool, complete with swim-suited players.

Perhaps the most imaginative of all Las Vegas swimming pool pranks was one that never saw the light of a darkroom. At the Flamingo a professorial-type subpublicist, who was able to flex his promotionwise muscles only when his boss was away, meticulously worked out a scheme to fill the Flamingo pool with Jello and have lovely maidens named Miss Raspberry and Miss Orange and Miss Lemon and so on leap in from time to time. Photographers were practically poised at the pool's edge when the hotel's maintenance engineer in desperation wired absent boss publicist Abe Schiller to put a stop to the stunt; it would ruin the hotel's drainage system. Mr. Schiller wired these memorable words back to his engineer: "Tell Al if he fills that pool with Jello, he'll have to empty it with a spoon." Mr. Schiller's assistant left the Flamingo shortly thereafter, a frustrated and disheartened man. When last heard from, he was teaching Techniques of Public Relations at a West Coast university.

Promotion stunts on the Strip run in cycles, sometimes in vicious cycles. When one hotel institutes the idea of having an ex-champion boxer as official greeter, all the hotels hurry and get ex-champion boxers for official greeters. When the Riviera made its famous Liberace show into the first live nonatomic telecast from Las Vegas, all the other hotels instantly inaugurated live nonatomic telecasts with *their* stars. When one hotel hires a social director, all the hotels hire social directors.

These innovations are perhaps expensive at first but exceedingly profitable in the long run. The ex-champions lure big-gambling sports fans to Las Vegas. Live telecasts make names like Riviera, Sands, Thunderbird, Flamingo household words from Wytopitlock, Maine, to Rough and Ready, California. And social directors keep the little women and the kiddies happy while daddy loses his sport shirt at the crap table.

The position of social director is new to Las Vegas, a post created rather flamboyantly a while back by a young woman named Bunny Ehrenberg, who came out to El Rancho Vegas from New York City to get a divorce. Mrs. Ehrenberg was so gay and charming around El Rancho's swimming pool that when her six weeks were up, owner Beldon Katleman urged her to stay on as social director at a reputed $10,000 a year. Nothing could have pleased Bunny Ehrenberg—now Bunny Schloss—more. She loved the West. She loved Las Vegas. She loved being gay and charming around the swimming pool. And she could use the $10,000.

The scene now shifts to New York City, where El Rancho's New York press representative is trying to sell the idea of a Strip hotel social director to a national magazine as a picture feature. "It's a lulu for glamour," he proclaimed to the editors. When they did not seem especially overcome with the idea, he began to gild the lulu.

"She's known as the Golden Girl," he extemporized. "Works at a gold desk, uses a gold telephone. Rides in a golden Cadillac. Hands out gold swizzle sticks to drinkers. . . ."

"Yeah," said the editors, perking up.

"Yeah," said the press agent. "She . . ." and on and on he went.

By the time he concluded, nobody could blame the editors for falling for the story. It sounded glamorous and exclusive and thoroughly Las Vegan, and they bought it. Then the press agent called El Rancho with the glad tidings. In the excitement he didn't go into details, only that Miss Schloss should appear as soon as possible in New York with a gold evening dress so that preliminary pictures of her might be taken on her home stamping grounds being social with Broadway personalities on TV and what not. Nobody can blame the delight that swept over El Rancho at the thought of getting a spread in a national magazine, delight enlivened with laughter and tempered with mystification over the fact that their Golden Girl was darkest brunette, and aside from her recently discarded wedding ring was not unusually endowed with gold habiliments. So they packed Bunny off to New York, equipped with a gold lamé evening dress, and laughed some more. This was money for jam.

Miss Schloss arrived back in Las Vegas one jump ahead of an editor and photographer. She was breathless. Also, she now had a gold streak in her hair and gold-tipped eyelashes.

"I don't know exactly what golden tricks our press agent has sold the magazine," she reported tensely, "new things kept coming up. But I do know this much. He said I rode around in a golden Cadillac and worked at a golden desk and used a golden telephone. What are we going to do? The magazine people arrive tomorrow."

She added that her eyelashes hurt. The editor in charge of the story had insisted she get a gilt hair- and lash-do.

El Rancho management swung into action. A Cadillac was borrowed from the town's dealer, James Cashman, and sprayed with a rich, sticky gold. A knotty pine desk became a Cinderella sunburst overnight. Ditto a telephone. By morning everybody was too tired to be nervous. Miss Schloss drove out to the airport in the golden Cadillac to greet the editor and photographer and all went well due to careful herding of the visitors into the still-wet painted car. Back at the hotel Miss Schloss posed for pictures at her golden desk and except for the fact that she couldn't get the paint-stuck drawers open and didn't dare pick up the glistening telephone, this particular photographic chore went off successfully. And then:

"Where are your gold jeans?" the editor inquired. "We'd better get some outdoor Western shots of you in them."

Bunny Schloss was, fortunately, on her recently painted golden toes. "They're—they're at the cleaners," she stammered.

That night El Rancho's wardrobe mistress sat up until dawn stitching little bright yellow sequins all over a pair of blue jeans.

That morning Miss Schloss's patience began to slip. She discovered that the magazine thought the name Shaw would be more glamorous than Schloss, and she didn't like that one bit. Her eyelashes stung. And the sequined jeans were too small. Furiously she declined to don them until the wardrobe mistress threatened to quit. "After I've spent the whole night sewing itsy-bitsy gold so-and-so's on them things," she roared, "you're going to wear 'em!"

Wardrobe mistresses are hard to come by. Miss Schloss was crammed into the sparkling pants and spent as much of the day as possible standing up. Probably her finest hour came when she swung one seemingly cement-encased leg over a horse and sat with stomach pulled back to spine long enough for gay pictures of her cantering across the desert to be taken.

The net result was that the photographs were stunning and made a splendiferous feature for the magazine and a handsome addition to El Rancho's publicity album, but folks around the hotel can't to this day look at them without shuddering. Nor can they bear the sight of James Cashman cruising about town in his returned Cadillac. Mr. Cashman liked his gilded job so much he just kept it that way. As for Golden Girl, she quit her job the week the magazine hit the stands.

A. J. Liebling

Dressed in Dynamite

The long stoppage of the New York newspapers—four-sevenths strike against the *Times*, *News*, *World-Telegram*, and *Journal-American*, and three-sevenths sulks by the *Herald Tribune*, *Post*, and *Mirror*, which declined to publish while the printers struck their colleagues—has enabled me to catch up on news in Las Vegas, Nevada, which is livelier than it is around here, even when all seven papers are publishing. . . .

. . . by good fortune I have for the past eight years been on the subscription list of the Las Vegas *Sun*, Southern Nevada's Only

☞ From The New Yorker, January 12, 1963.

Home-Owned Daily Newspaper (circulation 22,000). My justification is that I want to know what odds the professionals out there are laying on future political events and prizefights. My true reason, though, is that the *Sun* offers a grand escape when I weary of the graying world around me. Opening its pages is like buying a small stack of chips at the Sands or Tropicana; the pleasure does not last long, but you get a change. Between these vicarious fugues there are weeks when the *Sun* just piles up on top of my "in" basket, successfully hiding all bills, and all the telephone messages that I do not wish to answer. Several days of the stoppage elapsed before I remembered that the newer deposits on this mountain of newsprint might, like the slag heaps by the old workings in Virginia City, also Nevada, contain retrievable ore.

The first number I looked at with these new eyes, the December 15th one, after one newspaperless week in the metropolis, carried a press-association story about cold weather on the Atlantic Coast, which I already knew about, being here, and one headed "GUNMEN KILL TWO OFFICERS IN BANK HEIST"—in Montreal. (Unfavorable Eastern weather and gunmen anywhere are always sure of a good play in Las Vegas.) There were also bits about the Chinese in India and the fall of a Brazilian airliner that made me feel I had lost little by not reading the papers that weren't published. Airliners fall so casually now that I don't notice them unless I have to duck. But it was when I reached Walter Winchell, on page 4, that I realized why my days without the *Mirror*, which carries him here, had seemed so flat. (Winchell's version is that he carries the *Mirror*, but it has not for many years been carried in the style to which it once was accustomed.) Winchell had had to send the essential news of New York clean out to Las Vegas via his syndicate to get it back to me via the *Sun*! Without his "Memos of a Midnighter" I would never have known who was "Frank Sinatra's new No. 1 Favorite Flame"—I have since forgotten, but maybe Sinatra has, too. Nor would I have learned that "When the newspaper strike ends one of the eve'g blatts expects a shakeup of execs"—a tip that bowled me over, because shakeups on evening newspapers are as rare as hiccups in Glasgow. And without "The Broadway Lights," another Winchell department, I wouldn't have known that James Stewart, the cinemillionaire, had been at the Tower Suite, or Ginger Rogers, full of vintage "shelectricity," at the Forum of the XII Caesars.

After that I kept *au courant* with life around me by reading my rediscovered pal. An eight-column headline announced:

VEGAS
'MARRYING SAM' RACKET
DRAWS BLAST

in two-inch red type over the front page of the *Sun* in which I found Winchell. Hank Greenspun, the *Sun's* publisher, threw away all headline type less than very big when he bought the paper, for a thousand dollars, in 1950. (He found twenty-five hundred dollars in the till.) It was like stripping a poker deck of the low cards.

A Marrying Sam, it appears from the story, is a person who performs only marriages, like a barber who does only haircuts. Las Vegas is great territory for impulsive marriages; the wedding chapels, like the casinos, are open twenty-four hours a day, because single people who stay up all night gambling feel lonely when they have to go to bed. A minister out there gets a license, valid indefinitely, to perform marriages, whenever he can convince a district judge that he *is* a minister. The test question is whether he has a congregation and a place to sit it down. Having got the license, he can shuck the congregation and put in full time marrying, which pays a high rate per minute and provides high ancillary profits, since the wedding chapels advertise—in neon lights—packaged weddings that include a choir, bridesmaids, and (if required) refreshments. The marrier usually owns at least a piece of all these concessions.

The Clark County (which includes Las Vegas) Ministerial Association, the *Sun* said, was accordingly petitioning the state legislature to put marriers on a yearly-license basis, so that a *soi-disant* pastor would have to prove annually that he still had a flock. A Dr. Roger Sawyer, appearing as a witness before the Clark County legislature, which meets at Carson City, said, as quoted by the *Sun*, that many a Marrying Sam had left his flock in the bulrushes. This, he implied, worked prejudice to those who had to expend time in preparing sermons, preaching, burying and visiting with parishioners, as well as just splicing. He felt this was a horse on the regulars. "He cited an amusing incident," the *Sun* said, "in which a would-be minister, not yet a resident, attempted to obtain a certificate to perform marriages to finance his own divorce six weeks later." (Six weeks' residence is mandatory for a divorce there, but you have to stay six months for a license to shoot sage hen.) "Also on the amusing side," the *Sun* went on, "was the instance of a 'seminary on wheels' in Las Vegas, selling 'ministerial degrees' from his station wagon. Another practice related to the legislators was that in which the 'minister' certified to his own ordination in order to be able to get in on the lucrative Las Vegas marriage business. Dr. Sawyer continued to cite examples of the racket among itinerant men of the cloth, by telling of the person whose only congregation was his own family, and another who assembled the required 'congregation' by serving free meals." Asked if the association could rally support behind legislation from ministerial groups elsewhere in Nevada, Dr. Sawyer said that "it is favored throughout the state, and that some are in favor of even stronger regulations."

This, I felt sure, was cheerier than most of the church news I would not have read anyway in the *Times* and the six others, and the Las Vegas crime story of the day:

BOWDEN'S FATE
DELIBERATED BY
LAS VEGAS JURY

introduced me to a procedure in trial reporting that I had never encountered in less enterprising papers anywhere. "As the jury of nine men and three women commenced its deliberation at 3:40 yesterday afternoon on whether to send Edward J. Bowden to the gas chamber for the murder of his wife," the *Sun* began, in boldface (the usual body type for the top half of the paper), "alternate jurors, dismissed after hearing the trial since Monday morning, agreed the defendant was guilty." Interviewing the two alternates, who are excused before the others even begin to argue, provides a sneak preview, or cross-section poll, of what the effective jury will decide. It expedites the process of communication and serves the public, whose anxiety over the official verdict is thus shortened. As at the race track, the apparent winner's number goes up, but it does not become official until it is confirmed by the judges. In the meantime, bettors are warned not to tear up their tickets.

The account continued:

> One [alternate juror] felt inclined toward the extreme penalty, the determining factor being the non-introduction into evidence of proof of accidents the defendant claimed he was in that produced headaches and blackouts.

Apparently the other fellow didn't favor the gas room.

> Highlight of yesterday's session was the dramatic power-packed plea noted for its brevity and quiet, serious appeal to reason delivered by defense counsel Albert Stewart, which commenced with "A man's life will be placed in your hands." Stewart ended his summation in a whisper as he asked the jury: "Do not return to this courtroom with a doubt that will haunt you forever—'Did I send an innocent man to his death?'" District Attorney John Mendoza . . . retorted . . . by shouting: "Was he (pointing to Bowden) guided by God when he killed her? Who is this man to judge his wife's life?" The de-

fense had relied on sworn testimony of witnesses that Bowden was drunk the afternoon and night of Sept. 9, when he pumped five shots at his estranged wife, Louella Mae Kendall Bowden, as she tended bar at Honest John's in midtown Las Vegas.

This sounded as if he had pumped the first, at least, in the afternoon and the last at night, but I took it that he had been less deliberate. (The regular jurors, kinder than the cited alternate, decided not to be haunted forever by a doubt. They found Bowden guilty in the first degree, but recommended life.)

In this corner of the effete East, the judge, when dismissing the alternates, tells them not to talk to anybody about the case, and interviewing them for quotation might, even the *News* has always assumed, lead to a charge of contempt of court. I telephoned Las Vegas and got the city editor of the *Sun*, a Mr. Dave Bradley. He said he had always thought it was the same out there until the reporter covering the Bowden trial had tried it out—just a case of individual enterprise. "This is a very informal part of the country," Bradley added. He said there had been no reactions from the Bench. It is an innovation that, if it became standard procedure, would add a lot to the fun of a murder trial. In the event that the regular jurors reversed the alternates, the losing lawyer would at least have credit for a split decision, which might help him get a return match for his man.

The next day's *Sun* topped my first sample—and, in fact, topped just about any crime thriller I have recently read—with a local story headed:

DYNAMITE-CLAD
ROBBERY SUSPECT
NABBED IN VEGAS
(By *Gene Tuttle, Sun Staff Writer*)

That is the kind of headline that makes you look twice to be sure. But it was no fake; "dynamite-clad" the man had been. The lead said (starting in boldface, of course):

A woman's intuition led local FBI agents to the capture of a human bomb late Friday night at Alamo Airways. He arrived in a chartered plane carrying loot from a bank robbery committed earlier in the day.

Allen Ray Lisenbury, 27, was arrested as he stepped into the main office of Alamo Airways after arriving in Las Vegas. He was highly wired with dynamite electric blasting caps and six sticks of dynamite fastened within his attache case which also contained $20,000 in $10 and $20 bills plus a cashier's check for $9,890 taken from the Security First National Bank, 102 Pine Avenue, Long Beach [the California one].

A touch of his fingers to the attache case could have caused a tremendous explosion and possibly killed a great number of persons. . . . Lisenbury didn't seem to care about himself, though he had taken many safety precautions.

Special agent in charge, Dean W. Elson of the Las Vegas office of the FBI, led his agents to Alamo Airways and captured the wanted criminal after a telephone call from Fullerton, Calif., FBI office warning them that Lisenbury was flying to Las Vegas.

Lisenbury had robbed the bank at 4:15 P.M. Friday. He spent about 75 minutes in the bank with the bank manager, brandishing a snub-nosed revolver and threatening to blow up the bank with his bomb device that he had concealed in his attache case. He demanded $29,890 from the bank manager in small bills. [Why that precise amount, I wonder.] The manager gave the cash and check to Lisenbury and he left.

Several hours later, Mrs. Bette Pastor, who with her

husband operates the Sunset Beach Charter Service, received a call from a man who claimed he was a writer
and wanted to fly to Las Vegas to obtain background for
a story.

This last touch is the kind of detail that I do not think would have
survived in any wire story that reached New York. The wire services,
keen to save money by sending as few words as possible, would almost surely have eliminated it. Yet it constitutes social commentary;
criminals and pilots' wives alike, basing their notions about the literary life on films they have seen, think of writers as persons of af-
fluence. A *writer's* wife, had she received a call from a man posing as
a writer who was prepared to spend more than fifty cents, would
have immediately recognized him as an imposter and called the
cops. Lisenbury's choice of a story and Mrs. Pastor's response to it
place them both in the world that gets its *Anschauung* from the media of romance—whodunits, television, and the flicks.

Mrs. Pastor [without summoning the cops] told him her
husband was on a flight, but would return shortly.
    Lisenbury arrived at the airport, and Mrs. Pastor fur-
nished coffee and they talked. She noticed a large bulge
under his coat and was a little suspicious. [She probably decided, though, that he was carrying a built-in
muse, or—like many of the current corp of interview-
ers—a recording device.] After Lisenbury and Pastor
took off for Las Vegas, Mrs. Pastor picked up a late edition of the newspaper [had it been lying, just arrived
and neatly folded, on her table as she talked to Lisenbury?] and read of the robbery and the $10 and $20
bills. She checked the cash Lisenbury had paid and it
was new $10 and $20, so she called the FBI immediately, fearful of her husband's life.
    FBI agents reported at Alamo Airways to Pat Stanley,
night manager, who then contacted the McCarran Field

tower for the plane to land at Alamo where the FBI
agents would wait.

But did they yet know how Lisenbury was rigged? They had part
of the truth if Fullerton had relayed the bank manager's story of the
robber's threats. But how much? The flight of the two men would
make a wry sequence in the movie that someday must be made from
Tuttle's text, with Lisenbury wondering whether he had been identified after the takeoff, Pastor at first pleased to get the unexpected
charter and then, perhaps, puzzled by his odd passenger. Or had Pastor received a message over the earphones, and had it included the
dynamite bit? There is no evidence in the story that he had. The
stranger must have held on to his case all the way, huddled against
Pastor in the front seat.

Lighting troubles caused by fuses kept the lights going
on and off at Alamo during the long wait. Morton Cutler, flight line service attendant at Alamo, waited and
met the incoming plane with Lisenbury and Pastor and
guided them to the pumps by the building.
As Lisenbury alighted, the lights went on and he
started to leave, but Cutler offered to get him a taxi, and
as they started toward the office, the lights went off.
Lisenbury became suspicious, but Cutler said:
"Bosses here can't pay their light bills—so we have
to work in the dark."

This for me was one of the high moments; would the small joke
reassure the human bomb, or would he touch his fingers to the at-
taché case and blow up the air terminal? And I wondered whether, as
Lisenbury got out of the plane, Cutler had offered to carry the case
or whether he had feared that this would give the game away. And
how did he plan to get Lisenbury within reach of the F.B.I. men un-
detonated? It surprised me that an F.B.I. man had not substituted for
the airport worker. But the joke worked: "This took Lisenbury off

guard as he chuckled." Reading, I was as relieved as the airport man must have been. And now: "He paused as they started through the doorway into the office, but Cutler gave him a shove with his flashlight and he fell forward into the waiting grasp of the F.B.I. agents who quickly pinned him to the floor."

I especially liked this part of the story, because Mr. Tuttle had not given away Cutler's plan until he acted. I was as much surprised as Lisenbury must have been, walking gingerly because of his explosive condition, and perhaps, because of that, paying insufficient attention to the joker's movements; to refuse to go first into the office as Cutler opened the door would have seemed unnatural, in any case, and Lisenbury had wanted above all things to avoid attention.

> Lisenbury had his left arm wrapped with surgical tape with wires running down from his shoulder to his wrist. He had electrical blasting caps on his fingertips which were metal covered and he wore a specially constructed rubber insulated glove. He also wore heavy rubber insulated shoes. The moment he made contact with the case which held the six sticks of dynamite, it could have blown up an area of 50 feet or more.
>
> Chief of Detectives William J. O'Reilly, Clark County Sheriff's office, was with the FBI agents and quickly deactivated Lisenbury. O'Reilly is an expert in handling explosives. [I wondered, though, how he felt as he worked; had he been a booby-trap man in the war?] The agents quickly stripped Lisenbury. They found many dynamite caps upon his person and in his hip pocket was a good supply of bullets for his revolver, which was fully loaded.

There the prize was, landed, and now there was a touch of banality that the robber, not the narrator, introduced:

> "Well, it took five of yuh to get me," he snarled at the officers. "If I'd been arrested a little earlier, I'd a blown yuh all to hell."

These do not sound like the words of an arch-criminal impersonating a literary man, but perhaps Lisenbury had abandoned his role. It is possible also that he was misquoted by the arresting officers, for cops often make criminals sound the way cops think they should. I take it that Tuttle was not there.

> Being careful not to cause an explosion [the story continued, adding an extra touch of science and modernity], the FBI agents took Lisenbury to Nellis Air Force Base for complete deactivating; then he was booked in the Clark County jail on $50,000 bail. During the trip to Nellis, all law-enforcement agencies were requested not to transmit over the air for fear of static in the air which could cause an explosion.

This is a point that I don't understand, being a complete electronic square, but that entranced me as much as the rest. "Why couldn't *any* emanations—the "Late Late Show," for example—set the guy off as readily as law-enforcement transmissions? Did the officers call for nationwide radio silence?

There was a coda:

> Officers yesterday were trying to determine why Lisenbury selected Las Vegas as his destination.

Several possible answers occur. Perhaps he wanted to change those new tens and twenties into chips, and the chips into assorted money, which would be harder to identify. This can be done fast in a gambling town, without attracting any attention, if each transaction is held down to several hundred dollars. And I think a cashier's check could be negotiated there with less formality than almost anywhere else—after banking hours, especially, since the big gambling houses keep masses of cash around and are eager to oblige prospective customers. A cashier's check cannot bounce, unless it is a phony, and so inspires confidence.

Or he may have felt he had an infallible system for beating roulette, for which he had to have a minimum starting stake—the amount he brought to Las Vegas with him. The odd sum suggests that. Perhaps he had planned, after winning all the money in Las Vegas, to repay the bank and then go on to Monte Carlo. He may even have planned the most spectacular grab in history—to seize the million dollars in cash that used to be displayed in the window of a gambling place there after threatening to blow the joint up if the guards interfered. I can see him backing, a lone Untouchable, his arms loaded with ten-thousand-dollar bills, through the crowd of players toward the alley entrance, where an explosive confederate awaits him at the wheel of an explosive Ferrari, all wired like Lisenbury. But most probably, I think, he just saw one of those Las Vegas Chamber of Commerce ads like the one I read in the *Wall Street Journal* the other day, about Las Vegas, the great "Convention-Vacation Location . . . *Wonderfull* Las Vegas . . . Year-round boating, fishing, golfing, swimming, hunting, sunning, star-studded entertainment, excitement . . . the *wonder* of the resort world." The poor guy needed a holiday.

Reading about ordinary crime again will seem pretty tame when the New York papers come back, if ever. There are parts of the country where people have more fun.

Michael Herr

The Big Room

$\mathbf{P}$robably no place else in the history of modern city building was developed on a single idea the way Las Vegas was. The closest thing to it is Hollywood, which grew by exporting its idea, but the Vegas idea can't leave town. It has nothing for export but its promise. Its growth was not only conspicuous, conspicuousness was the only medium of its growth. You can't touch conspicuousness, it's like efflorescence. You can feel it and walk around in it and, when you're in Vegas, hold the more than reasonable hope that it will materialize for you; the Passion According to St. Nick the Greek. When the town

☞ Excerpted from The Big Room (Summit Books, 1986).

finally raised itself up above the desert floor and began radiating and broadcasting itself, the rebounding waves drew millions in, and not just the loose pins and shavings of a restless moneymad tourist population, but Personalities, men and women of tremendous stature, and weight, and density. They pronounced it fabulous, and inimitable, and never stopped to ask why it was, and has always been, that almost everybody who comes here for the first time has the feeling that they've been here before. And not just before, but all along.

Arriving off the long trail of a thousand cities and towns, one so much like the others as to be indistinguishable, into the packaged premeditated trumped up (true) West, Howdy do drop in, come as you are, do what you want, what you'd never dare to do back home, at least not openly, piss away the hours with the nickles and dimes or get in deep, too deep, even drown, if that's your pleasure. Roaring in from L.A. and New York, Dallas, Detroit, Miami, New Orleans (London, Paris, Tokyo, Caracas, Bahrain, New Delhi) engorged and dying to pop, driven over the earth by undifferentiated wants into the receptacle and outlet, material gulag and dream terminal, to breathe the air of license and "personal" freedom: a few laughs, a few drinks, company, and all of it legal, or most of it, a lot of it, sort of. Your money is as good as anybody else's money, and it doesn't come fairer than that, or more democratic. Protracted Helldorado, where the only inhibitor of your appetites is your means, and the only thing that isn't promiscuous is the percentage.

When they talk about luck in Las Vegas, it's just the way they have there of talking about time. Luck is the local obsession, while time itself is a sore subject in the big rooms and casinos. It's a corny old gag about Las Vegas, the temporal city if there ever was one, trying to camouflage the hours and retard the dawn, when everybody knows that if you're feeling lucky you're really feeling time in its rawest form, and if you're not feeling lucky, they've got a clock at the bus station. For a speedy town like Vegas, having no time on the walls can only accelerate the process by which jellyfish turn into barracuda, grinders and dumpers become a single player, the big winners and big losers exchange wardrobes, while everyone gets ready for the next roll. The whole city's a clock. The hotels change credit lines as fast and often as they change the sheets, and for a lot of the same reasons. The winners and the losers all have identical marks on them, bruised and chewed over by Las Vegas mitosis, with consolation prizes for anybody left who's not already inconsolable. Don't laugh, people. It could happen to you.

F.D.R. / BUGSY SIEGEL

There has never been another place like it for connecting the unconnectable, and if you doubt it look at this pair, dealt spontaneously from the great American deck. One off the top, a king with the value of four aces, and one from the bottom, the wildest card in the pack. The patrician, destiny's giant and history's client, in the books and on the dime, not just another president, and president of more than the United States president by a landslide of the Twentieth Century itself. And this menace, this lowlife gutter-snake mobster, but not just another mobster; the outlaw *par excellence*, from his baby blue eyes down to his alligator shoes, his Broadway/Hollywood pals, and his tender-hardboiled love story, co-starring Virginia Hill.

F.D.R. and Bugsy Siegel were far from bedfellows, but they weren't complete opposites either. Each had developed his patented blend of seductiveness and iron, each acquired a legendary stature (like Honest Abe and Billy the Kid, although the Bug probably killed a lot more people than the Kid), and each, in his time and in his way, was a traitor to his class. Roosevelt was the most uncontrollably democratic man that American privilege had ever produced, and Ben Siegel longed endlessly (well, extensively) for greater exclusivity. Each man had his own idea of where the equalizer lay, and what steps he could take to arm and activate it. Maybe Las Vegas never had a mother, but it was rich in fathers, and these two, in dreams and in fact, were first among them.

Franklin Roosevelt was the ceremonial father, presiding as he did at the opening of Hoover, née Boulder, Dam in September, 1935. When he threw the switch and the juice came down like paternal grace it ran straight to Las Vegas, twenty-five miles away, just as the dam builders themselves had been doing nights and weekends for the five years it took to complete the work, establishing the town's usage for all time.

Benjamin Siegel was the practical father, although his associates in the east didn't think he was being very practical at all, pouring their money like that into his outrageous plan. How those dark eyebrows went up when he told them it would take two million to build, and how they came down again when the cost eventually reached six million. In fact, from the day in 1945 when he first pulled off of Highway 91 and pointed towards the emptiness and said, decreed, fatally *insisted*, that right there in the middle of what looked just like nowhere to everyone else, he would build his fabulous Flamingo Hotel, they really wondered about him. And when he told them that once his movie-star and society friends from L.A. started the ball rolling, the rich, powerful and famous would come there from all over the world, and by a transfer of much more than their money would make the Flamingo rich powerful and famous (and the man behind it would rise up so classy and legitimate that his gruesome past would dissolve, except for the least controlled whisper, for glamour), they thought that he was madder than the maddest drifter in the desert, and, being Bugsy, a thousand times more dangerous.

The dam had not been Roosevelt's idea, but he was quick and inspired to see what it was good for. First of the seven wonders of the modern world, it was the massive poured concrete substitute for the miracle Depression America needed, and fully expected; so tremendously potent and good-looking that many people accepted it for the miracle itself. It's strange to think how devotional they became about something as thick, hard and present as Boulder Dam. For F.D.R. it was the pumping, working symbol of a whole new deal: Power not only to the southwest, but to all the people; a great field of federal warmth; shelter and nourishment to the poor, the weak, the disenfranchised; the return of the grail to American Capital.

The Flamingo, on the other hand, was entirely Ben Siegel's idea. In his desert rapture he dreamed up everything we mean when we say Las Vegas, and though he never saw it realized, he came closer to getting what he wanted than Roosevelt did. In spite of a disastrous opening on the night after Christmas, 1946, when practically no one from L.A. showed up (George Raft was one of the few exceptions, driving the three hundred miles through freak storms that had closed the L.A. airports, and against the orders of the studio bosses, who in turn were responding to pressure from William Randolph Hearst to boycott the Flamingo); in spite of heavy losses for the house during the first six months, nothing could reduce his faith in the hotel. He believed in it against common sense, against counsel from his stockholders and increasingly unambiguous warnings, until the warnings stopped, and he, of all people, could see what was coming. He just believed in it even more then, faithful right up to the minute that they came down from headquarters and shot him, making sure to put a couple into those blue eyes, so that everyone who saw the papers next day would understand that this one was personal. Twenty minutes later, the stockholders walked in and took over the Flamingo.

Ninety-nine men lost their lives in the construction of Boulder Dam, and for years there was the strange but popular belief, that the bodies of those men were buried inside the dam, as though the United States Government would have stood still for such a thing. There's no way of knowing how many lives were lost during the building of the Flamingo and its aftermath, or where those bodies might be buried, since all of those costs were well under the table and occurred, like Siegel's death in Beverly Hills, out of town and across state lines, and were strictly intramural. ("We only kill each other," Siegel used to say.) Whether considered as works of art or as generators of the new life, Boulder and Flamingo were very expensive projects. All these years later, there's hardly anyone around who would suggest that they were too expensive.

It's appropriate, even romantic, that the two men should have passed each other here in the corridors outside the big room, where F.D.R.'s search for less and less class intersected Ben Siegel's search for more and more. Except in historical hallucination, of course, there's no possibility that the two men ever actually met, or even appeared for a moment together in the same place. But it's certain that on several occasions, F.D.R. shook a hand that shook the hand of Bugsy Siegel. A dubious relationship, but, skin being skin and non-retractable, a definite connection.

J.F.K.

The greatest of the historic Summit Meetings was being held at the Sands Hotel in late 1959. Frank's name was on the marquee outside, but the stage was so crowded those nights you could hardly tell whose engagement it was, or where the stage ended and the audience began. The whole Clan was there. They worked on their movie during the day and then did two shows every night. There were names everywhere you looked. They came down from the stage to sit at the tables, while others ran up to replace them, taking their drinks with them. Frank was in the middle of a ballad when Dean came weaving across the stage pretending to be loaded. Sammy jumped up doing his Jerry Lewis voice, "Dean, Dean, I made a boo boo," and they all broke up. Joey Bishop stood off to one side and heckled, while Berle and Rickles schpritzed them from ringside. Lawford was completely deadpan, looking on in mock disbelief at this madness.

Nothing would make him crack until Sammy came flying on, tap-dancing and snapping an imaginary rag. He made like he was shining Frank's shoes, and Lawford broke up too. The audience screamed, even when the gags were so inside that they didn't get them. They say you could hear gusts of laughter outside blowing across Highway 91 as you drove by, and nobody laughed harder or seemed to be having a better time than Frank's friend and personal guest, the Senator.

The apple didn't fall far from the tree. Made in the shade, he was the most successful of his father's many successful enterprises, and by far the most attractive. Ever since he was a boy he'd liked his fun, and known where, when and how to have it, if not always who to have it with. Which didn't matter much. There's nothing more becoming in a serious man than a developed sense of play.

He loved his brief visits to Las Vegas, and not only because it was so far from his constituency. He was the most starstruck of stars, (that never changed, even when he became the most famous man in the world), and his Vegas friends arranged everything there for him, especially seeing to it that his privacy would be respected, and he was always happy there. (It's an interesting question, more than a footnote but less than a thesis: Did they make him feel at home there, or did he just feel that way?) True, half the people he met there thought that "Senator" was just his nickname, but that's one of the things he liked about it. The smart money saw right away that it would not only be possible to run a Catholic for President, but totally all right, so long as it was as obvious to everyone else as it was to them that he was not a dogmatic Catholic.

Everybody was immediately charmed by the graceful yet forceful yet diffident way he spoke, and by his smile, which could have meant anything, but certainly meant something. In the informality of the place he could unwind, relax, and mix business with pleasure in the easy earnest way of a sharp young head completely on the make, making friends and probably promises that he wouldn't be able to keep for very long, at least not openly. Because even then his kid brother was around like a mongoose on Benzedrine, watching, keeping tabs and running the connections down to their root-ends, to see exactly who was friends with who, and who to play up, or down, or chop completely. The older brother's playground was the younger brother's nightmare. Still, the action was invigorating. It's possible that more of the New Frontier was inspired here at the Sands than back on the Massachusetts bedrock or looking dreaming out of the office window at the Jefferson Memorial.

"Hey what the hey!" Frank said. Dean was carrying Sammy onstage in his arms.

"Hallo dere," Dean smirked. "Congratulations. The NAACP wants that you should have this beeyoodiful award . . . " He dropped Sammy at Frank's feet.

Frank picked him up and hugged him. "This is a very great honor," he said. "I'm gonna take him home with me . . . Say, what do you people *eat*?" The audience screamed.

It was almost impossible to book a room anywhere in Vegas, and to get into the Sands you need more money than juice, and plenty of both. The town had never seen anything like it before, and never would again. There would be steady commercial increases over the next fifteen years, but what's money? There would never be the hyperglamour of those weeks again. It was the Sun at Noonday by which all decline is measured.

Those of us who only read about it in the columns and the magazines were sorry we weren't there, more than sorry, envious. But it wasn't as bad for us as it was for the losers who actually came so close, who saw the show and then got the Rat Pack brush, Let's Lose Charley, and were left downstairs when the party moved from the stage to Frank's suite, where it went on all night.

The atmosphere was so charged that nobody could take it all in. The events of those evenings turned into vacant nostalgia almost as they were happening, people woke up the next day and remembered the night before as though it had been ten years ago. And the room was so full of stars and star impulses that they cancelled each other out, turning themselves into mere people and even the shadows of mere people, and out of those shadows stepped a minor, purely parochial celebrity, so young and dishy that instead of everybody looking at Cary Grant, everybody was looking at Jack Kennedy.

Hunter S. Thompson

···

Fear and Loathing
in Las Vegas

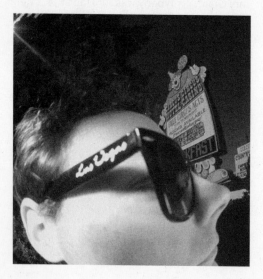

A Night on the Town . . .
Confrontation at the Desert Inn . . .
Drug Frenzy at the Circus-Circus

Saturday midnight . . . Memories of this night are extremely hazy.
All I have, for guide-pegs, is a pocketful of keno cards and cocktail
‸ins, all covered with scribbled notes. Here is one: "Get the Ford
‸nd a Bronco for race-observation purposes . . . photos?

g Stone, *November 11, 1971, and* Fear and Loathing in Las
se, 1971).

. . . Lacerda/call . . . why not a helicopter? . . . Get on the phone, *lean* on the fuckers . . . heavy yelling."

Another says: "Sign on Paradise Boulevard—'Stopless and Topless' . . . bush-league sex compared to L.A.; *pasties* here—total naked public humping in L.A. . . . Las Vegas is a society of armed masturbators/gambling is the kicker here/sex is extra/weird trip for high rollers . . . house-whores for winners, hand jobs for the bad luck crowd."

A long time ago when I lived in Big Sur down the road from Lionel Olay I had a friend who liked to go to Reno for the crap-shooting. He owned a sporting-goods store in Carmel. And one month he drove his Mercedes highway-cruiser to Reno on three consecutive weekends—winning heavily each time. After three trips he was something like $15,000 ahead, so he decided to skip the fourth weekend and take some friends to dinner at Nepenthe. "Always quit winners," he explained. "And besides, it's a long drive."

On Monday morning he got a phone call from Reno—from the general manager of the casino he'd been working out on. "We missed you this weekend," said the GM. "The pit-men were bored."

"Shucks," said my friend.

So the next weekend he flew up to Reno in a private plane, with a friend and two girls—all "special guests" of the GM. Nothing too good for high rollers. . . .

And on Monday morning the same plane—the casino's plane—flew him back to the Monterey airport. The pilot lent him a dime to call a friend for a ride to Carmel. He was $30,000 in debt, and two months later he was looking down the barrel of one of the world's heaviest collection agencies.

So he sold his store, but that didn't make the nut. They could wait for the rest, he said—but then he got stomped, which convinced him that maybe he'd be better off borrowing enough money to pay the whole wad.

Mainline gambling is a very heavy business—and Las

makes Reno seem like your friendly neighborhood grocery store. For a loser, Vegas is the meanest town on earth. Until about a year ago, there was a giant billboard on the outskirts of Las Vegas, saying:

> ## DON'T GAMBLE WITH MARIJUANA!
> ## IN NEVADA: POSSESSION—20 YEARS
> ## SALE—LIFE!

So I was not entirely at ease drifting around the casinos on this Saturday night with a car full of marijuana and head full of acid. We had several narrow escapes: at one point I tried to drive the Great Red Shark into the laundry room of the Landmark Hotel—but the door was too narrow, and the people inside seemed dangerously excited.

We drove over to the Desert Inn, to catch the Debbie Reynolds/Harry James show. "I don't know about you," I told my attorney, "but in my line of business it's important to be Hep."

"Mine too," he said. "But as your attorney I advise you to drive over to the Tropicana and pick up on Guy Lombardo. He's in the Blue Room with his Royal Canadians."

"Why?" I asked.

"Why *what*?"

"Why should I pay out my hard-earned dollars to watch a fucking corpse?"

"Look," he said. "Why are we out here? To entertain ourselves, or
~~h?"~~

~~urse,"~~ I replied. We were driving around in circles,
~~rking~~ lot of a place I thought was the Dunes,
~~e~~ the Thunderbird . . . or maybe it was the Ha-

scanning *The Vegas Visitor*, looking for hints of action. "How about " 'Nickel Nick's Slot Arcade'?" he said. " 'Hot Slots,' that sounds heavy . . . Twenty-nine cent hotdogs . . ."

Suddenly people were screaming at us. We were in trouble. Two thugs wearing red-gold military overcoats were looming over the hood: "What the hell are you doing?" one screamed. "You can't park *here*!"

"Why not?" I said. It seemed like a reasonable place to park, plenty of space. I'd been looking for a parking spot for what seemed like a very long time. Too long. I was about ready to abandon the car and call a taxi . . . but then, yes, we found this *space*.

Which turned out to be the sidewalk in front of the main entrance to the Desert Inn. I had run over so many curbs by this time, that I hadn't even noticed this last one. But now we found ourselves in a position that was hard to explain . . . blocking the entrance, thugs yelling at us, bad confusion. . . .

My attorney was out of the car in a flash, waving a five-dollar bill. "We want this car parked! I'm an old friend of Debbie's. I used to *romp* with her."

For a moment I thought he had blown it . . . then one of the doormen reached out for the bill, saying: "OK, OK. I'll take care of it, sir." And he tore off a parking stub.

"Holy shit!" I said, as we hurried through the lobby. "They almost had us there. That was quick thinking."

"What do you expect?" he said. "I'm your *attorney* . . . and you owe me five bucks. I want it now."

I shrugged and gave him a bill. This garish, deep-orlon carpeted lobby of the Desert Inn seemed an inappropriate place to be haggling about nickel/dime bribes for the parking lot attendant. This was Bob Hope's turf. Frank Sinatra's. Spiro Agnew's. The lobby fairly reeked of high-grade formica and plastic palm trees—it was clearly a high-class refuge for Big Spenders.

We approached the grand ballroom full of confidence, but they refused to let us in. We were too late, said a man in a wine-colored tuxedo; the house was already full—no seats left, at *any* price.

"Fuck seats," said my attorney. "We're old friends of Debbie's. We drove all the way from L.A. for this show, and we're goddamn well going in."

The tux-man began jabbering about "fire regulations," but my attorney refused to listen. Finally, after a lot of bad noise, he let us in for nothing—provided we would stand quietly in back and not smoke.

We promised, but the moment we got inside we lost control. The tension had been too great. Debbie Reynolds was yukking across the stage in a silver Afro wig . . . to the tune of "Sergeant Pepper," from the golden trumpet of Harry James.

"Jesus creeping shit!" said my attorney. "We've wandered into a time capsule!"

Heavy hands grabbed our shoulders. I jammed the hash pipe back into my pocket just in time. We were dragged across the lobby and held against the front door by goons until our car was fetched up. "OK, get lost," said the wine-tux-man. "We're giving you a break. If Debbie has friends like you guys, she's in worse trouble than I thought."

"We'll see about this!" my attorney shouted as we drove away. "You paranoid scum!"

I drove around to the Circus-Circus Casino and parked near the back door. "This is the place," I said. "They'll never fuck with us here."

"Where's the ether?" said my attorney. "This mescaline isn't working."

I gave him the key to the trunk while I lit up the hash pipe. He came back with the ether-bottle, un-capped it, then poured some into a kleenex and mashed it under his nose, breathing heavily. I soaked another kleenex and fouled my own nose. The smell was overwhelming, even with the top down. Soon we were staggering up the stairs towards the entrance, laughing stupidly and dragging each other along, like drunks.

This is the main advantage of ether: it makes you behave like the village drunkard in some early Irish novel . . . total loss of all basic motor skills: blurred vision, no balance, numb tongue—severance of all connection between the body and the brain. Which is interesting, because the brain continues to function more or less normally . . . you can actually *watch* yourself behaving in this terrible way, but you can't control it.

You approach the turnstiles leading into the Circus-Circus and you know that when you get there, you have to give the man two dollars or he won't let you inside . . . but when you get there, everything goes wrong: you misjudge the distance to the turnstile and slam against it, bounce off and grab hold of an old woman to keep from falling, some angry Rotarian shoves you and you think: What's happening here? What's going on? Then you hear yourself mumbling: "Dogs fucked the Pope, no fault of mine. Watch out! . . . Why money? My name is Brinks; I was born . . . born? Get sheep over side . . . women and children to armored car . . . orders from Captain Zeep."

Ah, devil ether—a total body drug. The mind recoils in horror, unable to communicate with the spinal column. The hands flap crazily, unable to get money out of the pocket . . . garbled laughter and hissing from the mouth . . . always smiling.

Ether is the perfect drug for Las Vegas. In this town they love a drunk. Fresh meat. So they put us through the turnstiles and turned us loose inside.

The Circus-Circus is what the whole hep world would be doing on Saturday night if the Nazis had won the war. This is the Sixth Reich. The ground floor is full of gambling tables, like all the other casinos . . . but the place is about four stories high, in the style of a circus tent, and all manner of strange County-Fair/Polish Carnival madness is going on up in this space. Right above the gambling tables the Forty Flying Carazito Brothers are doing a high-wire trapeze act, along with four muzzled Wolverines and the Six Nymphet Sisters from San Diego . . . so you're down on the main floor playing blackjack, and the stakes are getting high when suddenly you chance to look up, and there, right smack above your head is a half-naked fourteen-year-old girl being chased through the air by a snarling wolverine, which is suddenly locked in a death battle with two silver-painted Polacks who come swinging down from opposite balconies and meet in mid-air on the wolverine's neck . . . both Polacks seize the animal as they fall straight down towards the crap tables—but they bounce off the net; they separate and spring back up towards the roof in three different directions, and just as they're about to fall again they are grabbed out of the air by three Korean Kittens and trapezed off to one of the balconies.

This madness goes on and on, but nobody seems to notice. The gambling action runs twenty-four hours a day on the main floor, and the circus never ends. Meanwhile, on all the upstairs balconies, the customers are being hustled by every conceivable kind of bizarre shuck. All kinds of funhouse-type booths. Shoot the pasties off the nipples of a ten-foot bull-dyke and win a cotton-candy goat. Stand in front of this fantastic machine, my friend, and for just 99¢ your likeness will appear, two hundred feet tall, on a screen above downtown Las Vegas. Ninety-nine cents more for a voice message. "Say whatever you want, fella. They'll hear you, don't worry about that. Remember you'll be two hundred feet tall."

Jesus Christ. I could see myself lying in bed in the Mint Hotel, half-asleep and staring idly out the window, when suddenly a vicious nazi drunkard appears two hundred feet tall in the midnight sky, screaming gibberish at the world: "Woodstock Über Alles!"

We will close the drapes tonight. A thing like that could send a drug person careening around the room like a ping-pong ball. Hallucinations are bad enough. But after a while you learn to cope with things like seeing your dead grandmother crawling up your leg with a knife in her teeth. Most acid fanciers can handle this sort of thing.

But *nobody* can handle that other trip—the possibility that any freak with $1.98 can walk into the Circus-Circus and suddenly appear in the sky over downtown Las Vegas twelve times the size of God, howling anything that comes into his head. No, this is not a good town for psychedelic drugs. Reality itself is too twisted.

❧   ❧   ❧

Good mescaline comes on slow. The first hour is all waiting, then about halfway through the second hour you start cursing the creep who burned you, because nothing is happening . . . and then ZANG! Fiendish intensity, strange glow and vibrations . . . a very heavy gig in a place like the Circus-Circus.

"I hate to say this," said my attorney as we sat down at the Merry-Go-Round Bar on the second balcony, "but this place is getting *to* me. I think I'm getting the Fear."

"Nonsense," I said. "We came out here to find the American Dream, and now that we're right in the vortex you want to quit." I grabbed his bicep and squeezed. "You must *realize*," I said, "that we've found the main nerve."

"I know," he said. "That's what gives me the Fear."

The ether was wearing off, the acid was long gone, but the mescaline was running strong. We were sitting at a small round gold formica table, moving in orbit around the bartender.

"Look over there," I said. "Two women fucking a polar bear."

"Please," he said. "Don't *tell* me those things. Not now." He signaled the waitress for two more Wild Turkeys. "This is my last drink," he said. "How much money can you lend me?"

"Not much," I said. "Why?"

"I have to go," he said.

"Go?"

"Yes. Leave the country. Tonight."

"Calm down," I said. "You'll be straight in a few hours."

"No," he said. "This is serious."

"George Metesky was serious," I said. "And you see what they did to him."

"Don't fuck around!" he shouted. "One more hour in this town and I'll kill somebody!"

I could see he was on the edge. That fearful intensity that comes at the peak of a mescaline seizure. "OK," I said. "I'll lend you some money. Let's go outside and see how much we have left."

"Can we make it?" he said.

"Well . . . that depends on how many people we fuck with between here and the door. You want to leave quietly?"

"I want to leave *fast*," he said.

"OK. Let's pay this bill and get up very slowly. We're both out of our heads. This is going to be a long walk." I shouted at the waitress for a bill. She came over, looking bored, and my attorney stood up.

"Do they *pay* you to screw that bear?" he asked her.

"What?"

"He's just kidding," I said, stepping between them. "Come on, Doc—let's go downstairs and gamble." I got him as far as the edge of the bar, the rim of the merry-go-round, but he refused to get off until it stopped turning.

"It won't stop," I said. "It's not *ever* going to stop." I stepped off and turned around to wait for him, but he wouldn't move . . . and before I could reach out and pull him off, he was carried away. "Don't move," I shouted. "You'll come around!" His eyes were staring blindly ahead, squinting with fear and confusion. But he didn't move a muscle until he'd made the whole circle.

I waited until he was almost in front of me, then I reached out to grab him—but he jumped back and went around the circle again. This made me very nervous. I felt on the verge of a freakout. The bartender seemed to be watching us.

Carson City, I thought. Twenty years.

I stepped on the merry-go-round and hurried around the bar, approaching my attorney on his blind side—and when we came to the right spot I pushed him off. He staggered into the aisle and uttered a hellish scream as he lost his balance and went down, thrashing into the crowd . . . rolling like a log, then up again in a flash, fists clenched, looking for somebody to hit.

I approached him with my hands in the air, trying to smile. "You fell," I said. "Let's go."

By this time people *were* watching us. But the fool wouldn't move, and I knew what would happen if I grabbed him. "OK," I said. "You stay here and go to jail. I'm leaving." I started walking fast towards the stairs, ignoring him.

This moved him.

"Did you see that?" he said as he caught up with me. "Some son-ofabitch kicked me in the back!"

"Probably the bartender," I said. "He wanted to stomp you for what you said to the waitress."

"Good *god*! Let's get out of here. Where's the elevator?"

"Don't go *near* that elevator," I said. "That's just what they *want* us to do . . . trap us in a steel box and take us down to the basement." I looked over my shoulder, but nobody was following.

"Don't run," I said. "They'd like an excuse to shoot us." He nodded, seeming to understand. We walked fast along the big indoor midway—shooting galleries, tattoo parlors, money-changers and cotton-candy booths—then out through a bank of glass doors and across the grass downhill to a parking lot where the Red Shark waited.

"You drive," he said. "I think there's something wrong with me."

J. Randall Prior

Casino Queen

Patty Lane has had it with gambling, had it with Vegas. For a hustler of her stature, that may sound unlikely. She is, after all, one of the legends, famous up and down the Strip for her encyclopedic knowledge of scams and her sangfroid in putting them into practice. From when she first started gaming, at the age of 16, until she quit in 1984, Patty says, she helped stage 6,000 slot-machine jackpots and hustled 3,500 blackjack games. That's a track record that puts her in the Vegas pantheon with the likes of Bugsy Siegel.

☞ Excerpted from Spy, October 1993. Some of the names and identifying details in this story have been changed.

When a legendary casino hustler leaves town, even her enemies get sentimental. "She worked in a group of the best slot cheats in the world," reminisces Ron McAllister, former chief investigator of the Nevada Gaming Control Board. "She was very clever and very cool. And you can have respect for a crook you're trying to catch." "She's a Damon Runyon character, without a doubt," muses another law-enforcement type nostalgically. "I mean, how many women do you know who smoke Pall Mall reds, butt hanging from their mouth just right?"

She still smokes heavily, but you might have a hard time pegging Patty as a 24K "crossroader" from her appearance alone. Five foot three, a little over 100 pounds, a mother of four: not your typical profile of a high roller, even a reformed one. Padding around her suburban Vegas apartment in sweats, she looks like a regular midwestern matron, a homebody, albeit a little more youthful and a little shapelier than her 53 years. But then, it's been a while since Patty worked the baize or the reels. In her heyday, she thought nothing of raking in tens of thousands of dollars over a weekend; on one occasion she knocked off 20 jackpots in a single day.

Even if she hadn't been caught, it still would have been time to leave that life behind. Las Vegas isn't what it used to be, in Patty's opinion. The casinos have been bringing in efficiency experts to advise them on cutting costs: Only the high rollers get free drinks these days, and some places have stopped printing the customized matchbooks people used to take home as souvenirs. "The places that used to be very elite casinos are becoming hokey and downtown," Patty says. "They just keep adding on to them until they look like a hodgepodge. When I came to Las Vegas, there were about eight casinos on the Strip. Since that time they've built all the rest of them. And they were berry patches when I first got here." . . .

Patty moved to Las Vegas from Newport, Kentucky, in 1961, after exposés billing Newport as Sin Town USA forced the police to shut down Newport's seedy but profitable illegal gambling industry. Patty had been making $20 a night since she was 16 working as a shill in blackjack games, feeding information to the dealers about how much money was in gamblers' wallets and what cards they held. The dealers taught her how to deal deuces—dealing the next-from-the-top card in the pack to keep players from winning.

When she was 17 and working at clubs in Newport, Patty married a 31-year-old safecracker named Hank. "This was a town full of pimps, whores, thieves and gamblers," Patty says. "A safecracker was an elite citizen compared with some of the other scum." Hank cracked safes and blew the loot gambling. "One time Hank gave me $26,000 on a Friday night and it was gone by Sunday," Patty says. "That was a lot of money in 1957."

Patty had a baby boy—Joey—and learned how to cook; Hank kept busy getting arrested throughout the Midwest, including for possession of burglary tools, but apparently found time to impregnate Patty again. She named the baby, a girl, Jerry, after a girlfriend of hers. That was before she found out Jerry was sleeping with Hank. Goodbye Hank.

After the police shut Newport down, Patty got a job as a cocktail waitress in a legitimate bar across the river in Cincinnati. She started dating a man named Jack—a con man who posed as an aluminium-siding salesman. After a while Jack skipped town for Bisbee, Arizona, and Patty, then 20, sold her trailer, left her kids with her mother in Chicago and went to join him. Jack and Patty moved to Las Vegas in 1961, and not much longer after that Patty came home to find all Jack's things gone; he'd got back together with his wife.

Then she met Larry. Like Patty, Larry had hung around the gambling scene in Newport before moving to Vegas, and he started asking her to go gambling with him after she got off work. Playing blackjack one night at the Horseshoe, Patty saw that Larry was "handmucking"—he had stolen a card from the dealer's deck and was sneaking it in and out of his hand. If he was dealt a 14, say, and the card facedown was a 4, he would switch the 4 with the queen he had stolen a hand earlier, which would give him a 20, and hide the 4 between his legs.

Larry was raking in the chips when Patty noticed that thin showers of tiny paint flakes were falling, every few seconds, from the ceiling onto the table. Patty looked up and figured out what was going on. In those days there were no cameras in the casinos; when the house thought it was being cheated, it sent a man into the crawl space in the ceiling to look down through a peephole at the game. A security guard grabbed Larry, but just beforehand Patty had grabbed the card out of Larry's lap and sneaked it back into the deck unnoticed, so when the casino boss searched him, there was no evidence that Larry had cheated.

After that Patty started hustling with Larry on a daily basis. They would alternate weekends in Vegas, California and Reno. Sometimes they worked with Roger Grayson, leader of the then-notorious Grayson Gang. "There were times we would go downtown and beat six or seven casinos on a Friday night," Patty says, "go home, get some sleep, go beat another seven or eight casinos starting at 11:00 in the morning, get home around 4:00, rest up until 7:00 Saturday evening, and then hit seven or eight more. We once knocked off 20 jackpots in a day."

When they went handmucking, Patty would steal the card and pass it to Larry or Roger. "When the joint came unglued," says Patty, "it was my job to get the card back. I was the one holding the card when the shit hit the fan. If they count their deck, and they only have 51 cards, you're in trouble, so I wouldn't care how the card went in— bent in half, laid up on the table, kicked in the rack—I did whatever I had to do to put it back. That's why everybody that sat down with me felt at ease."

A much riskier but more profitable way to beat blackjack than handmucking was known as switching in a cooler. Instead of stealing one card, you stole the dealer's *entire deck* and replaced it with a new deck—called a cooler (or a cold deck, or iceberg)—arranged to deal winning hands to a person sitting in a particular seat at the table. Coolers, like handmucking, required a group of cheaters working together: the "mechanic," who switched the deck; "first base," who sat at the far lefthand seat and distracted the pit boss; "third base," who sat at the far righthand seat and distracted the dealer; and the "take-off man," in whose favor the cards were stacked, whose job it was to bet heavily throughout the shoe and collect the winnings. Usually the dealer was in on a cooler, so the trick was to switch decks without being seen by the cameras and pit bosses focused on the table. Working with a cooler could, on rare occasions, yield as much as $100,000 for 45 minutes' work.

"One time—I think it was 1971—I was working with Roger and a crew that was coming through Carson City," Patty recalls. "It was a small casino. . . . At some point I see that the guys have finished with one cooler and they're setting up a *second* cooler, which was pretty ballsy. Well, the pit boss was already suspicious; when he saw the same people sit back down again for another game, he just knew something was going to happen. I look up and see the pit boss running from the pit to the kitchen, which isn't far, because it's a small joint. And there's the fry cook coming down from behind the counter with a *hatchet* in his hand, and the pit boss is on the telephone—we all vacated the joint pretty quickly. Luckily we had cashed in most of our checks."

Other times the run-ins were between Patty and her gambling cronies, such as the time she scrapped with the ex-wife of a hustler named Billy. "We were out at a restaurant and she asks me what kind of food I like," Patty recalls. "And I say white beans and corn and collard greens. And she said, 'Well, I wouldn't know about foods like that, I'm only used to being around people with money.' Well, when she said that, I just saw red."

Patty threw her glass of wine in the woman's face, then seized her by the hair and punched her. Billy and the restaurant's maître d' scrambled to break up the fight, Billy taking hold of his ex-wife and the maître d' grabbing Patty around the waist. But Patty kept her hand locked until she had ripped a hank of hair right out of the woman's head.

Later, out in the parking lot, "I banged her head against the wall a couple of times, and it ended with me sitting on top of her and pounding her and half the people from the bar outside looking at us and laughing. And all the time Larry was yelling at me, 'Don't hurt your hand, punch her in the tit!' But I didn't listen, so afterward I had to go to the hospital and get my hand put in a brace. I ruined my suit too, and my Andrew Geller shoes. I'd say she ended up with some bruises and contusions, but in the long run it probably cost me a lot more money than it did her. But that's the Irish in me.' "

For a while in the 1960s and '70s, card-cheating circles experimented with various ways of "juicing" the deck. One of the more reliable kinds of juice was invisible ink, which the cheaters would apply to the cards while playing at the table, and which would show up black through the infrared contact lenses they'd bought from a doctor in Beverly Hills. "I never liked juice plays," Patty says, "because there was always the danger of losing, and I don't gamble."

For a brief period in 1965, on the advice of a socially challenged scientific type she knew from Berkeley, Patty tried daubing cobalt paste on certain cards, whose positions she would then attempt to determine by means of a small Geiger counter. "It did work," she says, "but we could never get a Geiger counter small enough to schlepp in a joint that could get past the first card." More reliable were the old techniques of sanding and bending: scratching the cards with a tiny piece of sandpaper on the tip of your finger, or bending the cards very slightly in different ways to denote a card's high, low or medium value.

To beat the traditional slot machine, Patty will tell you, you want to have at least five people working. The first person is the mechanic, who opens up the machine door and lines up its reels to the jackpot position. (In a Big Bertha— the six-foot-high, four-foot-wide giant slot machines you find in some of the larger casinos—the reels are so heavy that you need two mechanics to climb *inside* the machine and force them around.) The second person is the lookout, who diverts the attention of any casino personnel looking in the direction of the machine being opened and sounds the alarm if anything goes wrong. The third and fourth people are blockers, who stand in front of the machine, preferably in large fur coats, to prevent cameras and stray pit bosses from seeing what's going on. The fifth person—usually not a member of the crew but a friend with a clean record—is the collector, the figurehead player of the game, who when the jackpot hits and the bells start ringing goes into a frenzy of excitement and collects the money from the casino, to be divided later on in the safety of somebody's house. If a cheater is known to a casino, it's easier to work on the slots than up close with the blackjack dealers, since the cheater is more likely to get away with a disguise. Patty would sometimes dress up as an old woman with a cane: She would spread clear facial mask on her face and hands, wait half an hour until it dried and tightened, and then scrunch her face around until she developed artificial wrinkles.

In the early days of slot machines, the reels were made of a type of metal that could be controlled by a magnet. You brought the magnet into the casino in a purse or inside your coat, leaned up against the machine and, without opening the door, aligned the reels in a jackpot position. In the early 1970s the casinos got wise to this and started buying new slot machines with parts made of brass or plastic—a loss both to cheaters and to cheating's potential for farce, as in the time Roger Grayson and a female associate were escaping from a bad situation and Roger noticed that the woman had stopped running a block behind him and was waving frantically. She had a particularly strong magnet in her purse and had gotten stuck to a lamppost.

"Another time, sometime in the early seventies, a guy I was working with got his tie locked in the machine door, and when he started to run he almost hung himself," Patty says. "A guy we were with had a knife and cut him loose, but now we had a jackpot sitting there with three sevens and a guy's tie hanging out of the machine. The guy whose tie it was just wanted to run. I don't blame him—I probably would've run, too. But we didn't want to lose the jackpot, so we were all over his ass to get the door opened again. He was having a hell of a time opening it, because he was nervous, and he took a good three or four minutes, but he got it done."

❦   ❦   ❦

Beating roulette can be easier or more complicated than beating slot machines, depending on how carefully the casino watches its wheels. If the wheels were left unguarded when they weren't being used, Patty and company would measure a wheel's numbered stripes, cut identical stripes from a sheet of lead, paint them to match the originals and slip them into about a quarter of the slots on the wheel at which they would later be playing. Casinos use ivory balls in roulette games, and when ivory hits lead, the lead kills the bounce. Most of the time, then, the ball would stop on one of the false-bottomed slots, and the cheaters would win.

Another method they used involved stealing the casino's roulette ball and replacing it with a ball with a tiny magnet inside. The cheater would then attempt to control the ball's movement by means of a larger magnet he or she was holding near the wheel, inside a purse or a pocket. In London one time, Patty was working with a man who'd embedded the magnet inside a fake plaster cast on his arm. Alas, the magnet was stronger than anticipated, and the ball leapt off the wheel altogether and stuck to his cast. Amazingly, everyone escaped.

Fred was Patty's third husband. Patty had married Larry in the winter of 1965, and it lasted about a year. She started working with Fred, a crooked dealer, soon afterward, and married him in 1969. "He had a little pimp in him," Patty says now. "I'm sure I was being pimped, although I wasn't selling my body. You don't have to sell pussy to be a whore. He didn't give me my end of the money."

Fred wound up in prison in the early 1970s, and Patty started dating a burglar with no casino experience by the name of Jimmy. By the time Fred's sentence was over, Patty was living with Jimmy and wanted a divorce.

Patty and Jimmy got married in 1975 and bought a house in Alamo, Nevada. "I'm getting very insecure," Patty says of that period. "We're starting to argue all the time, Jimmy beats me half to death." After two years she walked out on him and moved back to Vegas.

"I've got $14,000 cash, four kids [she had a daughter by Fred and a son by Jimmy], no place to live, I don't have towels, I don't have pots, I don't have pans, I don't have a vacuum," Patty says. Jimmy [who is now deceased] burned down the house in Alamo and collected the insurance. Patty went back to work handmucking and cheating slots. Within six months she had enough money to make a sizable down payment on a house.

Patty got busted in 1980 putting in a cooler at the MGM Grand in Reno. The group she was with had tried to recruit a young dealer who turned out to be a policewoman's daughter and turned them in to the FBI. Patty got off lightly—with a year's probation—due to a legal technicality. Probation notwithstanding, Patty continued to work the casinos, and the three years that followed were her most profitable ever.

In the early 1980s the limits on slot-machine jackpots went up by tens of thousands of dollars. In the 1960s it was rare to find a jackpot worth $10,000, but by 1984 jackpots worth $50,000 and $80,000 were relatively common, and you could even find pots worth hundreds of thousands of dollars. Casinos put in machines with larger denominations of coin acceptance: The old-fashioned nickel slots gave way to ones with quarter minimums, and the dollar machines to ones requiring $3 or $5. Many casinos also modernized their slot machines with mechanical anticheating devices and cut down on human floor security, so once Patty learned how to beat the new machines, she could do her work with relative ease. The casinos were installing too few cameras in the early 1980s to catch all the cheating that was going on. "They didn't want to spend the money," Patty says. "They stepped over dollars to pick up pennies."

"One time we got caught on a machine," Patty says. "There was a Big Bertha at Caesar's with a $125,000 jackpot on it. I was out rounding [distracting] this one boss standing maybe 20 or 30 feet away from the machine. I didn't think the two guys were inside yet, because I hadn't given them the signal, but when I look over at one of the blockers, he shrugs his shoulders at me, and I see they have the door of the machine already open. Meanwhile this boss is moving toward them, and he's only about two aisles over.

"I point at the other lookout and signal that he has to stop the boss, but it doesn't work. At this point the boss isn't going to pay attention to some guy. By this time he's coming down the aisle and he's walking directly to the machine that they're inside of—the door is *open* and there are *two guys* inside the machine. So the boss is coming down the aisle and I grab him and begin abusing him—I say the machine he just fixed for me was still taking my money and not paying me and would he please come back and fix it because I'm tired of contributing money to Caesar's Palace, blah, blah, blah, and he's saying, 'Lady, I'll be right there. Lady, I'm sorry, I'll make sure you get your money back. Lady!' Finally he just reaches over and grabs me by the shoulders and shouts in my face, 'Lady, please! I've got to see what these people are doing!' and he pushes me out of the way.

"He runs over to the machine and tries to see what's going on, but he can't see over all the people standing in front of it, so he starts jumping in the air like a jumping jack trying to see what's going on, and finally he pushes one woman out of the way and he hangs over the door of the machine and yells at the two guys, 'What the hell are you doing?' I run over there and I scream to them, 'Get the fuck out of there! It's Tom!' ["It's George": Everything's cool. "It's Tom": Cheese it.] One of the guys throws the boss to the ground and somehow we all got away, everyone by a different door."

As the 1980s economy inflated, people started betting higher. "It used to be a rarity to see green-check [$25] players," says Patty. "People were very conservative. And all of a sudden you started seeing green-check players and black-check [$100] players all over the table." This also made things easier for cheaters. "Naturally they watch the player with the most money," Patty explains. "So if you have a guy who's betting $2,000 or $3,000 a hand, we could bet $1,500 a hand, and they usually wouldn't pay that much attention to us, because the other guy was betting more."

Many of the people Patty worked with in the 1960s and '70s have gotten out of the business. Some the hard way—Roger Grayson served three years in jail in the late '70s. (He has since reformed and is now a shift manager at a Vegas casino.) Others are working for the casinos in security. Nonetheless, cheating is very much on the rise. The casino industry now loses between $40 million and $100 million to cheaters every year. Cheating is also getting more high-tech: Miniature cameras hidden in sleeves or the arms of wheelchairs are used to read cards as they are dealt in blackjack (the camera's signal is transmitted back to a van, where an associate watches the tape and radios back to the player what he sees), and cheating crews have learned how to manipulate the microchips of electronic slot machines.

In 1984, Patty got busted again, for her part in a slot-cheating operation in Nevada. She was indicted on racketeering charges but escaped with no jail time and a fine of $2,500. She felt incredibly lucky. "A lot of people are scared of going to jail because they've never experienced it," she says. "Well, I got locked up in jail in Florida once, so I knew what a jail cell was. That didn't bother me. But somehow, when I stepped in that courtroom and I looked up at that big, awesome insignia behind the judge's bench that said THE UNITED STATES GOVERNMENT, and when I heard them read, 'United States Government versus Patricia Lane,' it scared the bark off of me. Besides, all my life I learned that there were two things you didn't screw around with: You didn't screw around with the FBI, because they had unlimited funds, and you didn't screw around with the outfit [the Mafia], because *they* had unlimited funds. And here I had screwed with Old Whiskers [the FBI] and I didn't know what was going to happen, but I knew that I was going to jail, and then who was going to raise my kids?"

After the indictment in 1984, Patty got out of cheating altogether, mostly in the hope of stopping her youngest son from going into it too. She lived out of state for two years, then moved back to Vegas and found a job at the Dunes, in surveillance. When the Dunes went bankrupt in 1990, Patty started working in a hospital, taking blood.

✺   ✺   ✺

It's now ten years since Patty's last hustle, and the statute of limitations on all her crimes has expired: Patty can recount her history with impunity. Still, she will never be completely free of her past. Her life can be a lonely one. Her old gambling chums no longer associate with her, and her rap sheet makes it hard to find new friends. As one acquaintance puts it, "She doesn't get invited over to too many doctors' houses."

Despite ten years of going straight, Patty still has the know-how and the moxie to turn her hand to cheating. "She could go out. She could still move," says the acquaintance. "And she'd never be recognized. . . . I mean, if you were in a casino, you would never ever suspect this little lady of holding out a blackjack and popping it on you, would you?"

As of August, the jackpot on the Megabucks slots at Caesar's Palace had climbed to more than $6 million.

Just one more score. That's all it would take.

Joan Didion

....

Marrying Absurd

To be married in Las Vegas, Clark County, Nevada, a bride must swear that she is 18 or show parental permission, and a bridegroom that he is 21 or show parental permission. Someone must put up five dollars for the license. (On Sundays and holidays, $15. The Clark County Courthouse issues marriage licenses at any time of the day or night except between noon and 1 P.M., between eight and nine in the evening, and between four and five in the morn-

☞ From Saturday Evening Post, *December 16, 1967, and* Slouching Towards Bethlehem (*Farrar, Straus and Giroux, 1968*).

ing.) Nothing else is required. The state of Nevada, alone among these United States, demands neither a premarital blood test nor a waiting period before or after the issuance of a marriage license. Driving in across the Mojave from Los Angeles, one sees the signs way out on the desert, looming up from that moonscape of rattlesnakes and mesquite, even before the Las Vegas lights appear like a mirage on the horizon: GETTING MARRIED? FREE LICENSE INFORMATION FIRST STRIP EXIT. Perhaps the Las Vegas wedding industry achieved its peak operational efficiency between 9 P.M. and midnight of August 26,1965, an otherwise unremarkable Thursday that happened to be, by presidential order, the last day on which anyone could improve his draft status merely by getting married. One hundred and seventy-one couples were pronounced man and wife in the name of Clark County and the state of Nevada that night, 67 of them by a single justice of the peace, Mr. James A. Brennan. Mr. Brennan did one wedding at the Dunes and the other 66 in his office, and charged each couple eight dollars. One bride lent her veil to six others. "I got it down from five to three minutes," Mr. Brennan said later of his feat. "I could've married them *en masse*, but they're people, not cattle. People expect more when they get married."

What people who get married in Las Vegas actually do expect—what, in the largest sense, "expectations" are—strikes one as a curious and ambiguous business. Las Vegas is the most extreme and allegorical of American settlements, bizarre and beautiful in its venality and in its devotion to immediate gratification, a place the tone of which is set by mobsters and call girls and ladies' room attendants with amyl nitrite poppers in their uniform pockets. Almost everyone notes that there is no "time" in Las Vegas, no night and no day and no past and no future (no Las Vegas casino, however, has taken the obliteration of the ordinary time sense quite so far as Harold's Club in Reno, which for a while issued, at odd intervals in the day and night, mimeographed "bulletins" carrying news from the world outside); neither is there any logical sense of where one is. One is standing on a highway in the middle of a vast hostile desert looking at an 80-foot sign that blinks STARDUST or CAE-SARS PALACE. Yes, but what does that explain? This geographical implausibility reinforces the sense that what happens there has no connection with "real" life. Nevada cities like Reno and Carson are ranch towns, Western towns, places behind which there is some historical imperative. But Las Vegas seems to exist only in the eye of the beholder. All of which makes it a very stimulating and interesting place, but an odd one in which to want to wear a candlelight satin Priscilla of Boston wedding dress with Chantilly lace insets, tailored sleeves and a detachable modified train.

And yet the Las Vegas wedding business seems to appeal to precisely that impulse. "Sincere and Dignified Since 1954," one wedding chapel advertises. There are 19 such wedding chapels in Las Vegas, intensely competitive, each offering better, faster and, by implication, more sincere services than the next: Our Photos Best Anywhere, Your Wedding on a Phonograph Record, Candlelight with Your Ceremony, Honeymoon Accommodations, Free Transportation from Your Motel to Courthouse to Chapel and Return to Motel, Religious or Civil Ceremonies, Dressing Rooms, Flowers, Rings, Announcements, Witnesses Available and Ample Parking. All of these services, like most others in Las Vegas (sauna baths, payroll-check cashing, chinchilla coats for sale or rent) are offered 24 hours a day, seven days a week, presumably on the premise that marriage, like craps, is a game to be played when the table seems hot.

But what strikes one first about the Strip chapels, with their wishing wells and stained-glass paper windows and their artificial Bouvardia, is that so much of their business is by no means a matter of simple convenience, of a late-night union between a showgirl and a baby Crosby. Of course there is some of that. (One night about 11 o'clock in Las Vegas I saw a bride in an orange mini-dress and masses of flame-colored hair stumble from a Strip chapel on the arm of her bridegroom, who looked the part of the expendable nephew in movies like *Miami Syndicate*. "I gotta get the kids," the bride whimpered. "I gotta pick up the sitter, I gotta get to the midnight show." "What you gotta get," the bridegroom said, opening the door of a Cadillac Coupe De Ville and watching her crumple on the seat, "is sober.") But all day and evening long on the Strip, one sees actual wedding parties, waiting under the harsh lights at a crosswalk, standing uneasily in the parking lot of the Frontier while the photographer hired by The Little Church of the West ("Wedding Place of the Stars") certifies the occasion, takes the picture: the bride in a veil and satin pumps, the bridegroom usually in a white dinner jacket, and even an attendant or two, a sister or a best friend in hot pink *peau de soie*, a flirtation veil, a carnation nosegay. *When I Fall in Love, It Will Be Forever*, the organist plays, and then a few bars of *Lohengrin*. The mother cries, the stepfather, awkward in his role, invites the chapel hostess to join them for a drink at the Sands. The hostess smiles professionally and shakes her head; she has already transferred her interest to the group waiting outside. One bride out, another in, and again the sign goes up on the chapel door: ONE MOMENT PLEASE—WEDDING.

I sat next to one such wedding party in a Strip restaurant the last time I was in Las Vegas. The marriage had just taken place; the bride still wore her wedding dress, the mother her corsage. A bored waiter poured out a few swallows of pink champagne ("on the house") for everyone but the bride, who was too young to be served. "You'll need something with more kick than that," the bride's father said with heavy jocularity to his new son-in-law; the ritual jokes about the wedding night had a certain Panglossian character, since the bride was clearly several months pregnant. Shrimp cocktails, the New York Steak Special. Another round of pink champagne, this time not on the house, and the bride began to cry. "It was just as nice," she sobbed, "as I hoped and dreamed it would be."

She meant of course that it had been Sincere. It had been Dignified. She had it on a phonograph record to prove it. All the fears and recriminations and knots in the stomach of the past few months were gone. Smoothed into respectability. She was a girl, and perhaps many of them were, those Las Vegas brides in the detachable modified trains, for whom the sexual revolution was a newspaper phrase, quite without meaning.

Michael Ventura

....

Las Vegas:
The Odds on Anything

Part 1: Up and Atom

*One of the first responses I had coming to Nevada was whether this
was really part of the United States.*

— Joe Yablonsky, Former FBI Chief

Where else but Las Vegas would they make the Atom Bomb a picnic? An honest-to-god picnic. From 1951, when the bright mushroom first bloomed in the desert north of town, to 1962, when some

☞ *From* L.A. Weekly, *February 2, 1990, and* Letters at 3A.M.: Reports on Endarkenment (Spring Publications, *1993*).

killjoy treaty drove the testing underground, the casinos sponsored picnic lunches to view the A-blasts. Maybe the women would wear "The Atomic Hairdo," designed by a hairdresser at the Flamingo: the hair was pulled up over a mushroom-shaped wire form and sprinkled with silver glitter, and maybe they'd drink the popular "Atomic Cocktail": equal parts vodka, brandy and champagne, with a dash of sherry. Thus coiffed and oiled, folks would perch on the hillsides, as near as was allowed (which was pretty near), and make a party of it.

Even if you didn't get *that* close, you could see the explosion pretty good from anywhere in town. One joint called itself the Atomic View Motel, advertising an unobstructed sight line to the bomb blast from the comfort of one's lounge chair.

At that time our president was a bald, competent and (some historians now claim) impotent general named Dwight D. Eisenhower, and he decided that Americans didn't need to know about the dangers of fallout. His successor, John F. Kennedy (not as competent, but notoriously potent), let that decision stand. People downwind as far as Nebraska were contaminated by the blasts. Small farm towns became gardens of leukemia. And our Vegas picnickers, and the unobstructed guests of the Atomic View Motel, thrilled by the bomb's concussion-wind mussing their hair—judging by the effects of the tests on people so much farther away, a lot of those picnickers probably died young.

But who can deny they saw something worth seeing? Wouldn't *you* have gone on a Bomb picnic? Be honest, now. I know I would have.

I can see myself as I was when I first discovered Vegas. In my early 30s, the new money of success hot in my pockets, not caring *too* much that my first film, *Roadie*, was a lousy one, nor that a master of the Hollywood hustle had tricked me out of more money than the government would soon take—in other words, too dumb to know that I was actually broke. (A terrific state of mind for Vegas.) My often-suspect sense of romance drew me, in those days, to three general sorts of women: honkytonk angels, non-separatist lesbians (who were prepared to sleep with me parenthetically, as it were), and the otherwise married. Vegas was an especially delicious place to rendezvous with the otherwise married.

So I can see myself, at the Flamingo maybe, shelling out money that I didn't know I didn't have, tipping big, blowing a couple of hundred a clip at roulette, squandering with a vengeance—the way only a poor kid can—and doing this with an equally vengeful Otherwise-Married Woman. Nobody we knew was likely to run into us in Vegas—we were liberals, *leftists* for heaven's sake, and New Agey to boot. Our crowd never made this scene. So I could make like I was Steve McQueen in *The Cincinnati Kid*, and she could wear something that, if her kids saw her in it, they'd have to spend five years in therapy someday to get over it. And she could pick up this gorgeously cheap outfit in one of those casino sleaze shops because I'd buy it, I'd buy her anything, what did I know? (We'd leave it in the room for the maid when we checked out.) We loved Vegas because we knew the house rules, which are as follows: As long as you don't bother the other customers, you can do *anything*.

That's the promise of Vegas: Anything.

Not that most people have the stuff for Anything—but being in Anything's general vicinity is heady and, in Vegas, not too threatening. (You can always go home, where you think Anything can happen, and where you're wrong.) Being around Anything in a guaranteed controlled situation—guaranteed by the Mafia, no less—is a neat way to do a vacation.

So that's what Vegas is for—to be safe in the presence of Anything. Vegas as we know it was the brainchild of a talented murderer named Bugsy Siegel, who opened the Flamingo, in 1946, on a piece of land that was then five miles away from a small desert pit stop. Siegel financed it with money from a veritable genius of a murderer, Meyer Lansky. The other American institution these two started is now known as Murder, Inc. It took a couple of killers to understand Anything. To dig that everybody's just enough of a killer to harbor a kind of envy for the real killers, and that if everybody's a bit of a killer then everybody's a bit of everything—and that includes Anything.

And that if, in Puritan America, you dedicate a city to the pursuit of Anything, and you put that city far enough away from everywhere—then the Puritans will find a way across one of the most dangerous deserts in the world just to rub shoulders with Anything without ruining their safe lives. The gambling is just an excuse, a way to participate in the Anything.

And you can't get any deeper into Anything than the Theory of Relativity harnessed in the service of inchoate rage. So I can just see me and this Otherwise-Married Woman who's looking pretty good in her see-through chintz of Flamingo neon-pink—and if it had been, say '59, and if the casino had offered an all-you-can-drink picnic on a hill overlooking the *atom bomb*? Oh, yes.

I mean, it isn't everyday that you're invited to a rehearsal for the Apocalypse. And imagine *sharing* that with someone. Doesn't it get you just a little horny: arms around each other's waists, hip to hip, thigh to thigh, a little high, and the ground trembles underfoot, and a hot gust smacks your face as the cloud rises up and up, shimmering with rainbow tints of radiation, and you feel a waft of how it felt to write the Book of Revelation? Yes, the neon of the Strip and the glow of the bomb go well together. They're both about Anything.

Part 2: The Geology of Anything

But Anything is nothing new in the Nevada desert. If you have a big stake in the idea of permanence, then you probably should avoid the Nevada State Museum in Lorenzi Park in Las Vegas, and you should definitely not look at its relief map of Nevada circa 30,000 years ago. Now 30,000 sounds like a lot, but it's a tiny span geologically, and not even a terribly long time in the history of our species. Our molecules have been doing the people-dance for about a million years. Folks like you and me, with the same brain load, were around for what I'm about to tell you.

You can see it on the Nevada relief map: 30,000 years ago Nevada was all lakes! Hundreds of square miles of huge lakes covered about 20 percent of Nevada's surface. A 200-foot-wide river flowed through *in* the Las Vegas Valley. Mammoths and camels roamed here. Nearby Death Valley was an *enormous* lake. The entire place was an environmentalist's wet dream.

Until, only 20,000 years ago (while "civilization" was already under way in several parts of the world), Lake Las Vegas and the other great Nevada lakes "drained suddenly."

That's what it says at the museum. No explanation, just "drained suddenly."

Drained suddenly?! What the fuck are they talking about? Dozens of big lakes, enough moisture to support lots of large mammals and all the plants that they ate, and it just . . . drained? Suddenly?

I don't know about you, but I find that fact incredibly threatening. I'd be happier if there were a bad guy. Like, didn't the developers do it? Wasn't pollution responsible, or the defense budget, or Styrofoam cups? But no. The planet just decided: "To hell with those lakes, those mammoths, that river, those camels, I'm bored with all that. I'm draining all that suddenly."

By 10,000 years ago the place looks like it does today. There isn't a camel for 15,000 miles, and there ain't no mammoths nowhere.

This gets weirder when you realize that this happened about 20,000 years *after* the last Ice Age glacier receded from what we now know as the United States. In other words, while Nevada was drastically changing, most of America (New England, for instance) looked pretty much the way it does now. In other words, the Wild West was wild before we ever set foot in it.

So the people who became the Paiute Indians made the best of things, got used to their new desert, got to love it. Then came *their* Apocalypse. First, just a few Franciscan monks in 1776 (portentous year, that). Then, in 1855, Mormons. In fact, the first building on what is now Las Vegas Boulevard (also known as the Strip) was the Mormon fort. There's still a piece of it left.

Of all the people who've tried to use America as a staging ground for Paradise on Earth, the Mormons have been the most determined and, by any measure, the most successful. And Mormons don't think Paradise is worth a prayer unless you and your whole family can be there pretty much as you are here. You *can* take it with you—a Vegas thought if ever there was one.

As it happened, these particular Mormons bickered among themselves, and Brigham Young called them back to Utah. Lucky for Bugsy Siegel. Or unlucky, maybe. Without disparaging those Mormons at all, it's fair to say that Bugsy, the man credited with starting *our* Vegas, had more than a little in common with them: He was a devout but bickering member of a highly organized, effective and rigid institution (the Mafia); an outfit with superb business acumen, dispensing valuable benefits to its members in return for a strict obedience; an organization dedicated to building its own version of Paradise on Earth. Except that when Brigham Young recalls you, you start fresh somewhere else; when Meyer Lansky and Lucky Luciano recall you, you get shot in the eye.

While recognizing that Mormonism is a profound spiritual movement, while the Mafia is just profoundly evil—still, structurally (and only structurally), there are strong similarities. Odd, isn't it, that such similar social structures were drawn to the same place in the same immense desert, and that each built its first abode on what is, in effect, the same street. Another way to say this is that what Mormon pioneers, the Mafia, *and* the atomic military have in common is a keen, highly developed sense of Anything—a sense of Anything that felt a kinship to the place itself, as though this desert were calling to them.

Connect the dots: atom bombs, "drained suddenly," the Neon Anything. Religious fanatics, Jewish and/or Sicilian gangsters, atomic maniacs. Mammoth Apocalypse, Paiute Apocalypse, rehearsals for *the* Apocalypse. Spiritual Paradise on Earth, carnal Paradise on Earth. Lakes drain suddenly, and some lakes *un*-drain suddenly. Shit sure happens in that part of the Mojave.

It's a scene, see. It didn't start with Vegas. Rather, the concept that culminated in "Vegas" got drawn toward a place where some very strange and not dissimilar stuff has been happening for a very long time. The stuff that is "Vegas" is coming up out of the ground out here. I'm very serious. In other words, Las Vegas as it is presently constituted may *not* be a gross ecological travesty; as an expression of what Lawrence Durrell calls "the spirit of place," Vegas may be what the place *wants.* This is, as they say in Vegas, the "juice," the "action," that this environment itself likes. It's been drawing strangeness to itself for thousands of millennia.

Call it coincidence, or a flight of fancy, or a flash of insight into the human-planet interface, or tabloid nonsense either way, the pattern shimmers.

And stir in this little grace-note of fact: In 1864, President Abraham Lincoln declared Nevada a state—on Halloween. Now, Halloween is not just a children's holiday. Halloween is what survives from the most important celebration of our Pagan European ancestors, the night they celebrated their new year with rituals in which psychic and spiritual forces were unleashed. The Pagan New Year's Eve. And it's Nevada's birthday. (Happens to be mine, too. Hmmmm.) Not that Lincoln was aware of these nuances. It's just that, as I say, the place seems to draw this stuff.

This is how strong I think that draw really is: 400 years before Vegas happened, Spanish Conquistadors kept trying to find it. They were *sure* that somewhere to the north and west, across the great deserts, would be a city of gold and light, incredible riches, eternal youth, exquisite pleasures—an intoxicating city of riches and dreams. Expedition after expedition failed to find it, yet they were sure. They just *felt* it out there. Many of them staked everything on their certainty that a city very like Las Vegas already existed. And they would never know how right they were—right that there was such a city, right that it lay in the great western desert. They were just wrong about when.

The place itself was generating Vegas-vibe, and they felt it and were called by it; but the place would need 400 more years to generate an actual Las Vegas.

Halloween. Unleashed forces. "Drained suddenly." Mormons. Liberace. Boxing. The Bomb. Sinatra. The Strip. Quickie divorce. Legal

whores. Instant marriage. The Mafia. Wayne Newton. Un-drained
Suddenly. Howard Hughes. The Mecca of Anything.

But in the middle of *nowhere*? Because let's not forget we're talking about *nowhere*. The Mojave. 110 in the shade. Where even a
healthy young person can dehydrate so fast that a brisk walk can be
fatal. . . .

This place, this utterly hostile environment, is the fifth fastest
growing city in the United States—and if you count from 1930, when
there were only about 5,000 Vegans, to now, when there are more
than 700,000, it may be the fastest growing city in the Western world.
And more than 17 *million* people visit Vegas each year now—with a
marvelous faith in the ability of electricity and piped-in water to
keep them alive in an environment otherwise capable of killing them
in a matter of hours.

Do I sound a little hysterical? It's just that the level of weirdness
we've come to take for granted (about everything, not just Vegas) as-
tonishes me. Not the weirdness itself—I like that—but how we take
it for granted. That's the weirdest thing about the weirdness.

As for Vegas—it couldn't be much weirder if this town were on
the moon. The place just seems to pulse with whatever it is that
makes the weirdness weird. The place feeds on it. Likes it. And the
weirdest thing is—it always has.

Part 3: One Step Beyond

Mars ain't no place to raise kids.

—Elton John

Not everyone takes the weirdness for granted. Nevada, in general,
and Las Vegas in particular, "ranks highest" (according to *The New
York Times*) in teenage suicides and for every kid who commits suicide, there are a lot more who come close.

They don't seem to care that Vegas is the best city in America
for faces. Etched, walking-photograph faces everywhere, the kind of

faces you see in carnivals and prisons and on ranches. The kids don't sit in off-the-Strip restaurants like Capazzoli's wondering about the lives of the waitresses, bitterly etched tallish women in their 50s and 60s with great bone-structure and coiffed dyed hair who look like they once were chorus-line dancers, beauties from the days of bomb blasts, wisecrackers with hard, tired eyes and smiles that happen by reflex for the customers—but you're dying to ask their stories, you know each one has a story, and that it's something, these days, to be a story, to have a story. More and more people don't. The kids don't.

The kids don't care about the gambling cabbie ("Do you gamble?" "Oh yes, you gotta gamble.") who moved here from Chicago because one day he told his wife, "When I retire I'll move to Vegas," and she said, "Why wait?" They don't care about his inside information: that the best tippers are from the house builders and the heavy-construction conventions, the worst from the doctors' convention. The kids don't think it's funny about doctors being the worst tippers. They don't think anything having to do with Anything is very amusing.

The kids who are dealing with the highest teen suicide rate in America aren't impressed that at the Horseshoe casino downtown there's a million dollars on display, 100 $10,000 bills in a glass case. And whose picture is on the bill? Some guy named Chase. One of the people I was with on my last Vegas run shares my passion for American history; neither one of us had ever heard of the guy. Later I looked it up. It's Salmon Portland Chase (1808–1873), an Ohio senator, secretary of the treasury, and chief justice of the Supreme Court who presided over Andrew Johnson's impeachment hearings and founded the national banking system. So now me and my friend know. And we like knowing. But the kids don't want to know. Because it doesn't help them any. And they're right.

Likewise, the kids aren't impressed that Las Vegas has to be the most racially integrated resort in the world. The casinos are one of the few institutions I can think of in the United States where blacks, whites and Asians mingle without noticeable tension. But you don't see Latinos. This last trip, I don't think I saw any. Not among the guests, I mean. Just among the maids. Like the one who looked at me with such exhausted eyes when I opened the door and told her, "Come back in an hour, we'll be checked out by then," and she came back, but we weren't near ready—we'd ordered something from room service and I said, "I think it'll be another hour," and for a moment the veils lifted and her eyes said, "You rich fuck."

The kids growing up in the ever-present glow of casinos where only money counts—they'd understand that pretty good. And they also wouldn't buy that stuff about "racially integrated resort," because they'd know about where the local blacks actually live, in acres of dismal one-story government housing, featureless, lifeless, and so quiet in the heat.

If I could get them served without hassle I'd like to take them to the Tropicana's bar at about 1:30 in the morning, where the women on the chorus of the Folies Bergere unwind before they go home. Most of the suckers are either alseep by then or drunk at the tables, and almost every seat at the bar is occupied by a leggy woman in jeans, late 20s, early 30s, heavy lines under the eyes, savvy mouth. The Tropicana's where you dance near-naked when you're too old for the chorus at the high-roller casinos but you're still a looker and you can still kick high. (One day you may be a waitress at Capozzolli's, but not yet.) The women banter with the bartenders and talk their back-stage shoptalk. Some of them have great nicknames—"The Alabama Slammer," that's my favorite. She looks like Lainie Kazan; the bartender named her after her favorite drink, and it seems to have stuck, at least for this gig. The scene goes on for about 40 minutes, then within five everybody leaves. You get the impression that it's the best time of their day. I'd like to take the kids there just to show them some down-home, human exchange under all this heartless glitz—but they'd say it's not enough, it doesn't help, and they'd be right again.

But for me, the scene that stands for the worst of Anything (worse than the Bomb, in a way—the Bomb is at least *thrilling*), the scene that goes hand-in-hand with the teenage suicide rate, hangs on just one thing one man said at Whoopi Goldberg's show at the Golden Nugget a few days before New Year's.

The Golden Nugget features an enormous chunk of gold in a heavily guarded case on the casino floor. It's where the *real* high-rollers go, the gamblers who bet thousands. And, with Caesar's and Bally's, it's where the stars play. Lots of tough glitz in that crowd, lots of jewels, furs, thousand-dollar suits. The sick grin of Anything was like static in the air.

Whoopi came on, and she was Something. She started easy, getting a big laugh and applause about Jim Bakker being sentenced to 45 years. Jim Bakker had gotten his, and the crowd was glad. Until they got theirs: "1989 was a bad year for pussy. You couldn't get elected if you fucked *anybody*. That's how George got in. Look at Barbara Bush—you know she don't swallow."

They laughed at that, a laugh of surprise, not fun. You didn't have to look far or hard to see that this was an audience that hadn't experienced much swallowing. Whoopie kept it up, Lenny Bruce-style, making them laugh at what they hated to admit—pussy jokes, the-government's-selling-crack jokes, and edgy jokes about race. Some people stopped laughing. This one guy, his wife was laughing hysterically while he just stared from her to Whoopi and back with a face of stone-cold hate. He would never forget nor forgive either woman for this laughter.

Then Whoopi wisecracked about the reunification of Germany.

"WHY ARE YOU WORRIED? GOT A LITTLE JEW BLOOD IN YOU?"

It was a silver-haired, beautifully groomed man, perhaps 60, in a perfectly cut suit. His voice was strong and cruel.

There certainly must have been Jews in the audience. They said nothing. I said nothing. Whoopi, obviously thrown, danced away from the sentence with some lame patter, but all the life had gone out of her performance—"drained suddenly" would be an accurate description. She was off the stage in five minutes.

Anything had snickered. Anything had caught us off guard. Anything had reminded us that an atom bomb, or a Holocaust, is not a spectacle, not a magazine cover, not a weird thing to read about on the toilet. It's an atom bomb. It's a Holocaust. And it wants the death of everything. Anything had spoken up, lest we forget that a gangster is not a movie star, Al Capone is not Robert DeNiro—a gangster is a reptilian force utterly lacking the quality of mercy. Reptiles, of course, are very much at home in the desert.

"GOT A LITTLE JEW BLOOD?" The voice of the lizard. And, as is said to happen when a reptile stares at you, everyone froze.

As the kids are frozen. And for the same reason. Anything is hissing at them all the time. Especially in Vegas, where they "rank highest" in suicides. And *most* especially in Vegas, where it's more out in the open than most places. And I like that. I have passion for Anything and would love to write a piece saying the more Anything, the better, because it's what I feel in my bones. But the statistics on teen suicide say that my bones may be bad wrong.

They're building Vegas up so fast! It's not just the new gargantuan casinos. (The Mirage alone cost $630 million.) At the rate things are going, the entire Las Vegas Valley will be residential within a few years. It'll still be just a spot in an enormous desert, but it'll be a major spot. Walled-in single-family developments are going up all over, with ludicrous names like "Mountain Springs" and "Rainbow Meadows." Newly paved streets stop suddenly, and beyond them stretches the patient desert, the Mojave that waits to come back, and knows it will. . . .

There's not much graffiti in Las Vegas, hardly any by comparison to most places, but on the wall of one of those streets one of those statistically threatened kids had written: One Step Beyond.

I could see myself as one of those kids, 16, say, out on a hillside, smoking cigarettes and dope, staring at the pulsating neon in the valley down below. It's probably inevitable that I'd have known a few of the local teen suicides. Maybe I'd even thought about doing it myself. Maybe I've got a good friend; maybe we're wrecked together. We keep looking at what, from our hillside, seems a tiny neon city, a perfect plastic model city, with its lights pinprickly clear in the desert air. We stare at it as though we're asking it a question. Its light pulsates

2

back as though it's answering. We've lived in the capital of Anything every day of our lives, we understand the answer, even if we can't articulate it.

But . . . it doesn't apply to us. There's nothing in it about how to grow up or what to do. Anything is about the wildness at the heart of the universe. It's about Kierkegaard saying, "With God all things are possible. God *is* all things are possible. All things are possible *is* God."

Which is a statement utterly beyond good and evil, as terrifying as it is hopeful. But if you're a kid it's hard to hope. You just get the terror or the Anything. And growing up becomes a matter of enduring terror. And some people just don't make it.

Part 4: The Card So High and Wild

Like any dealer he was watching for the card that is so high and wild he'll never need to deal another.

—Leonard Cohen

Next time you're in a gambling town, stand by a roulette game a while and take in the wheel. Make sure it's a good casino—because a cheaply made roulette wheel is a sin against creation. The good ones are beautiful—shining inlaid woods, silver or gold bone numbers. And then the wheel spins, and the colors of the wood grains blend into a smooth, shimmering, rippling circle as the numbers flash their light, and the black and silver or red ball rattles from one groove to the other till a tiny piece of fate, maybe yours, is decided. *Decided.* No argument, no appeal. The wheel is spun, the ball finds a number, and whether you bet one buck or a hundred, something is different afterward—a little different or very different, depending on the bet. And there's no going back. It's a lovely game.

Almost a ritual. Which, in fact, is how wheel, dice, and card games all began (for they are many thousands of years old). Shamans invented dice, cards, and the wheel for divination and to draw powers into and out of their rituals. And the people got such a hit from those rituals that (greedy for the kick but eager to avoid the meaning, like the rest of us) they copied the shaman's tools and secularized, substituting money for spirit.

Those must have been some hellacious rituals, because thousands of years down the road, even our bastardized wheels, dice and cards often radiate of themselves and draw down the powers. I've seen it.

I was walking out of my apartment, bag packed for Vegas, an otherwise married woman already in the air heading from another city in the United States of Anything—and the phone rings. It's a Texas friend subject to psychic flashes. "Three." "That's all you got for me?" "Three."

That night at the roulette table at . . . I think it was the Sands, I went down 180 odd bucks playing the three, playing it slowly, two or three bucks at a time. There are several ways to bet, but the most interesting are the numbers and "the corners." The odds on winning on a single number are 35-to-1. Or you can put your chip on a corner where four numbers meet; if any of these numbers wins, you win, the house paying 8-to-1. I was playing the corner of 2-3-5-6 and, simultaneously, the 3.

Now, whether you're betting numbers or corners, the odds at roulette stink. ("Smart gamblers" never touch the game; they play cards or dice—much better odds.) But I fell in love with roulette the first time I sat down to it, and if I had the money and the drinking capacity I'd probably live at a roulette table and let my life go to hell.

Because of the wheel. The kick of cards is strategy—great card players are strategists, and the raw power of the cards is tempered by their knowledge of the game, their sense of when to push and when to fold, and the struggle of one strategist pitting savvy and luck against another. The kick of dice is the feel of the "bones" in your hand, the static between your body and the dice—and more than that. There are so many ways you can bet craps, and the pros have such a stunning, computerlike grasp of *all* the odds of *all* the ways, that dice-feel becomes secondary to how you scope the table. And it all happens so fast, and it's a group game with shouting and groaning. But roulette—baby, it's just the wheel.

The kick of roulette is the very fact that no strategy or computation is possible. The game simply exposes you to the wheel. That's what it's there for. If you bet the corners your odds are better, but that can hardly be called a strategy. Nothing comes between you and the wheel. In roulette, all you can do is pick your numbers—and await the wheel. It's the thrill of giving yourself up to the wheel that makes a roulette player.

Okay, that's my game and I'm playing the three. Losing $180-odd is losing 30 more dollars than I ever made in a week before the age of 32. It's losing the equivalent of almost five months' rent on our slum tenement in Brooklyn when I was a kid. Fuck it. Let's lose a *year* of that rent. Let's lose a *month* of those salaries. The wheel is making me crazy. Or rather, I'm relishing how my Anything rises in me as the wheel spins. That's why I'm there.

The number three hasn't come up in what seems like 3,000 years, a period with the slow-motion intensity of a car crash. Am I willing to lose my hotel money? My gas money?

Then three hits! Well, it was bound to hit once. But it keeps on hitting. It's like I've finally broken through to the wheel— finally, this once, had what every roulette player sits there for, a hotline to the wheel. The wheel has heard. The wheel, at which over the course of 10 years I will lose a total of several thousand dollars. But because of this one night I won't resent a dime of the money I've lost, because tonight the ancient wheel and I are *together*, together in the cave, together in the temple, together in the energy of Anything. An unforgettable sensation, and worth the cost exacted.

So three kept hitting with fantastic improbability. I go way over a thousand, maybe two—I wasn't counting—then three disappears for a while, I'm down to $500, and then, to show me I haven't been dreaming, the wheel starts giving me the three again. I walk away with nearly $900. But by now, I don't care any more about winning the money than I do about losing it. The money was just my way to the wheel.

In roulette you can put your bets down as long as the wheel is still spinning. Twice, around crowded tables—once at the Marina and once at the Tropicana—I've seen this: a man (not the same man twice) who's walking quickly past the table stops short; looks sharply at the table, the way you turn around when somebody unexpectedly calls out your name; and, without hesitating an instant, reaches out his arm and slams down some chips on a number. And the number wins.

What I saw at those roulette games were two masters of Anything tuned to a pitch of trancelike awareness wherein they could hear the wheel. What a thing that must be for them, to go in and out of. Because the likelihood is that they are not very conscious individuals— it's very hard on your consciousness when the dominant (and not very merciful) culture has no room for your talents and tendencies. In the first place, you tend to accept the culture's definitions—"sick," "crazy," "compulsive," what all—you learned them so young you can't help it. In the second place, what you have a talent for goes on in a shadow world, an underworld where sensitivity and vulnerability are not exactly rewarded.

So you don't know what your powers are for. You think they're for gambling, for money, and they fade in and out, and drive you mad and broke. You don't know that if you had lived a few thousand years ago you might have been a shaman, that the wheel and the dice and the cards would have spoken very differently to your spirit.

Part 5: The Family Slot

LAS VEGAS—THE AMERICAN WAY TO PLAY!
—Santa Monica Freeway Billboard

Until recently the ancient ways of the wheel, the dice, and the cards were how Vegas made its money. Slots weren't considered a draw, and weren't advertised. As one casino owner quaintly put it, the slots were there "for the wives." (To my eye, the male-female ratio for roulette and blackjack is about even, but poker and craps are overwhelmingly male.) But now that the emphasis is on "family casinos," the slots are the big draw.

Wait a minute, hit the pause button—"*family* casinos"? Isn't that a contradiction in terms? Real average American families, with working mothers, overextended credit, where TV's on six to 10 hours a day, where kids score abysmally on tracking tests, where fathers spend less than 10 minutes daily talking to their kids, and where there's a 50-percent chance of the whole shebang ending in divorce? *Those* families? What are they doing here?

Mostly the grown-ups (who plan the vacations, after all) are playing the slots.

An interesting thing about old-timey gambling is that (unless you bet on bridge, which isn't a Vegas game) you bet alone—but the game itself creates a brief community. You play cards *with* people. Craps is pointless with several bettors. As for roulette, there are few things more desolate than being the only one at the table. And couples can play roulette standing beside each other (though I prefer the woman to be across the table where I can see *her* better). Same with craps. And you can have fun, cheer each other on, give each other good or bad luck, get jealous, feel neglected, feel close. You've bet the same number and it wins and you've both won a hundred bucks and are juiced enough to take it for a sign that the wheel approves your love. In short, human contact. Real life. Anything can happen.

But slots and video poker—these are not Anything games. You

don't get excited; you get dazed. Watch these people. Even when they win their expressions don't change. The masturbatory slow-motion pulling of the lever lulls you into a timeless nether-mood. You're not surrendering to even a bastardized technique of divination; you're giving yourself up to a computer into which you have no input but coins. And unlike the wheel or the dice, that computer is not governed by the Goddess' sense of humor. (The ancient games go back to the time of the Goddess religions.) The fix is in, it's been programmed, there are X many times it's going to lose— something decided long before you said, "Honey, let's go to Vegas."

And where *is* honey, by the way? Working a machine on another aisle, usually. Slots are the loneliest way to bet.

No community. No contact. Little to cheer about. Nothing to fight about. Interesting that the family crowd seems to prefer the games you play alone. Most people don't magically transform on a vacation (at least not without a good dose of Anything), so playing-games-alone is probably the way they are at home, too.

And yes, there's lots more for families to do than slots—there's the Gold Coast Casino, for instance, with its 72 bowling lanes, two first-run movie houses, and day care for the kids till midnight. There's Circus Circus, with a different circus act every hour. And lots of places have golf, tennis, swimming, shows, rodeos, an aquatic park for the kids—and all of that not-wildly-profitable stuff is supplied for one very profitable reason: the slots.

The Gold Coast has all those nice family things—and 2,000 video poker and slot machines. Because that's what people mostly do. Dazed. Alone. The way they secretly feel inside their own homes.

And why come to Vegas for it? Maybe it has something to do with Heaven. For to do nothing special in Paradise, to have all your needs tended while you stare and twiddle your thumbs (or pull levers) in the general vicinity of Anything—is pretty much the image most people have of Heaven.

Bugsy's idea of Paradise has mingled with the Mormon family idea of Paradise to attract Christians who've given up all hope of Paradise.

For now that America has gotten so dangerous, now that it can offer no safety, no security, no sense that the future will be worth waiting for—Vegas seems more and more safe. In a U.S. of A. that now stands for the United States of Anything, the way Vegas does Anything is comparatively well-ordered. Not like the Anything at home, unadmitted and repressed and ricocheting off the headlines, from the TV, out of your kids' eyes, and out of the way you hate your job but have to say you love your life or you're not a good American. No, now you can come to Vegas to get away from all that. Here the sex and danger and stealing and phoniness and chintz are completely up front, not repressed at all. You don't have to wonder about them or be afraid they'll ambush you. You can pick and choose among them. Vegas is the shopping mall of Anything. The American Way To Play.

These folks are just hanging out at the mall. And they queue up for the bargain buffets, stand in line for an hour to save the five bucks they'll blow in the next hour on the nickel slots. Anyway, room service would make them too nervous, it's not nickel by nickel; you *know* you're spending money with room service. They want to spend without knowing. (They elect people to run their country that way, too.) Nickels. Quarters at the most. More than a billion bucks' worth per year.

Family casinos. Talk about Anything. Who would ever have imagined family casinos? What fat Rand Corporation futurist would have predicted that someday such a town would draw the average American family to the tune of 17.2 million people a year? And now there are Vegas-style casinos in Atlantic City and Canada. Soon there'll be more in South Dakota, Indiana, Iowa, Kansas and Ohio. While the country *pretends* that it's more and more conservative. Votes for faceless rich people as a way to lie to itself, as a way to convince itself that it *really* still believes in values vaguely associated with the 19th century or the Bible or sitcoms or something. While it sinks deeper and deeper into Anything.

These folks don't play the wheel, but that doesn't matter. The wheel spins. The inlaid woods shine. The numbers flash. There's nothing between you and the wheel. There never was. There never will be. The rest is a lot of rhetoric and bustle. It doesn't matter whether any particular wheel is played or not, the wheel's on fire anyway, the cold fire of Anything, and whether or not you play the wheel, the wheel plays you. Which is, finally, what Vegas has to teach. Not a lesson but a question: Are you playing the game, or is the game playing you?

The desert won't tell and the wheel won't stop.

Albert Goldman

....

Elvis:
Revival at Las Vegas

. . . **W**hen Elvis began to have thoughts about returning to live performance, he gave no consideration to Las Vegas because he saw the
resort as a most unsuitable place for his style of entertainment. How
else, in fact, could he have seen it? Rock music had never attained
any popularity in Las Vegas. All attempts to introduce the style had
failed miserably. Las Vegas was, in fact, the one totally secure bastion of the traditional entertainment idioms, deriving from the
Broadway theater, the New York nightclub and the Parisian follies.
The heroes of Vegas were sophisticated old pros like Frank Sinatra,

☞ *Excerpted from* Elvis (*McGraw-Hill*, 1981).

Dean Martin, Tony Bennett, Sammy Davis, Jr., Don Rickles, Buddy Hackett and Shecky Greene: performers with whom Elvis had no identification. Everything in Vegas was oriented to the "over-thirties," a euphemism for the middle-aged and the elderly. Putting it all together, any sensible person would have said that Las Vegas was the worst place in America for Elvis Presley to attempt a comeback. As if all this were not bad enough, Las Vegas also had the distinction in Elvis's mind of being the only town in America where he had ever bombed.

Back in the spring of 1956, as he was making his spectacular take-off into national celebrity, Colonel [Tom Parker] had booked him into the New Frontier for two weeks. He was the star of a show that featured the silky string arrangements of the Freddie Martin Orchestra and the booze and gambling jokes of Shecky Greene. Elvis cut such an incongruous figure in that company that *Newsweek* likened his appearance to "a jug of corn liquor at a champagne party." The Las Vegas audience was described as sitting through Elvis's act "as if he were a clinical experiment." After two weeks of getting the cold shoulder from the old folks—as well as suffering the humiliation of seeing his name go from the top to the bottom of the marquee— Elvis exploded, telling the press: "I don't want no more nightclubs." For any other entertainer the recollection of this early mishap would have become a joke after the passage of thirteen years, especially if the performer had been as incredibly successful as Elvis and had re-oriented his image and his career to middle-of-the-road comformity with popular taste. This was not, however, the way Elvis Presley's mind worked. He had forgotten nothing and forgiven nothing. At thirty-three he felt about Las Vegas precisely as he had felt at twenty-one; namely, that it was a good place to party but a bad place to play.

What Elvis thought, felt or wanted, was rarely a decisive factor in any decision concerning his career. The important consideration was what the Colonel thought. The joke is that even the Colonel, who spent half his life at Vegas gambling, had never considered booking his boy back into the resort until he received an offer that put the once unthinkable notion of Elvis in a showroom into a new and enticing perspective. To appreciate the significance of this offer, especially from the Colonel's standpoint, one has to recover for a moment a little of the curiosity and excitement that was aroused by the much-publicized announcement by Kirk Kerkorian in 1968 that he was going to lead America's most popular resort into the golden decade of the seventies by providing it with the world's largest and most lavishly equipped hotel.

As the news stories and prospectuses depicted the International Hotel, it sounded like one of those "world of the future" conceptions that used to tease the imaginations of Americans back in the thirties. Every feature of the hotel was colossal: a capacity of 1,500 rooms (two and a half times the size of the reigning favorite, Caesar's Palace), a height of thirty stories ("the tallest building in the State of Nevada"); the pool, a reservoir of 350,000 gallons ("the second largest man-made body of water in Nevada, second only to nearby Lake Mead"); the shopping concourse, with a score of boutiques, offering everything you could buy in a fair-sized town; the dining facilities, half a dozen American and ethnic restaurants—Mexican, German, Italian and Benihana Japanese; the casino, the largest in the world—natch!—with over a thousand slot machines. As for entertainment, the International would have not one but three major facilities—a lounge, a legitimate theater and a showroom—each offering a production that would rival or surpass anything that could be found in the entire resort. Clearly, therefore, the International was the ultimate resort hotel. In fact, it was not so much a resort hotel as it was a resort in a hotel: a totally self-contained, round-the-clock pleasure dome, where one could check in for a weekend or a week and never once feel the need to step out the door.

The Barnumesque grandeur of this conception was certain to have impressed itself on Barnum's foremost living descendant, Colonel Tom. The canny Colonel saw at once the great advantage he could reap by launching the publicity for Elvis's return atop the enormous wave of ballyhoo that would be generated by the hotel's first season. He recognized that the scale of this undertaking corresponded to his favorite billing of Elvis as "The World's Greatest Entertainer." What's more, as a deeply addicted gambler, the Colonel was attracted by the possibility of combining profit with pleasure.

Booking Elvis into the International for two weeks, however, wouldn't solve his career problems. If he were going to match the millions he earned in the movies with income from personal appearances, sooner or later he would have to go where the real money was—out on the road. What this gig would offer was a chance to break in his new act and get back into the rhythm of regular performing. So just when Elvis was starting to kick against the traces of his old routine, the Colonel was readying a new harness and surveying a new track at Las Vegas.

The man with whom the Colonel was dealing was the general manager of the hotel, Alex Shoofey. A tough little Lebanese whose nickname is "The Cleaver," Shoofey had a well-deserved reputation for being one of the shrewdest operators on the Strip. He had come to the Keno Kingdom back in 1948 in the same random manner that characterized the arrival of so many of the greatest figures of this Topsy-grown town. Having become a CPA in New York after the war, he had gone out to California to make his fortune running a gas station. When the business failed, he packed up his gear and started driving home. Going through Vegas, his old car broke down in front of a joint called the Club Bingo. Shoofey strolled inside and—Bingo!—he had a job working for the owner, Milton Prell. When Prell bought the Sahara, he made Shoofey its manager. It was at this time that the astute CPA first met Colonel Parker, the man who was fond of saying, "Fuck capital gains!"

When Kirk Kerkorian decided to build the International, he wooed Shoofey and his whole staff away from the Sahara and established them at the Flamingo, where their job was to recruit and train the staff for the International. Shoofey made such a good thing of the Flamingo that Kerkorian decided he would operate two Las Vegas hotels. Now, Shoofey was looking for big names to lend prestige to the International's first and most critical season.

Colonel and Shoofey couldn't agree on a price. Colonel took the position that his man was vital to the showroom's success; Shoofey argued that Elvis had been out of the game for a long time and was an unknown quantity in Las Vegas. When the Singer Special played, Shoofey was disappointed. "The show was not the big, big success they expected," he recalls. "In fact, it didn't come off. Elvis came on wearing his old leather jacket. It was a throw-back. It was unacceptable for Las Vegas."

When Shoofey did not call the Colonel with the anticipated offer, the Colonel called Shoofey. Once more they negotiated, and this time they made a deal. Shoofey had several acts in mind to open the room. He asked the Colonel if Elvis would like to have the honor. "Absolutely not," snapped the old man. "We will not open under any conditions. It's much too risky. Let somebody else stick his neck out." The Colonel was shrewd in making this stipulation, as events were to prove.

The showroom of the International is comparable in scale to every other feature of the building. Similar in plan to a huge municipal auditorium, one of those dreadful houses that are all spread and no height—the sort of stage that is perfect for only one famous act, the Rockettes—the Showroom Internationale is a solo performer's nightmare. Don Rickles, whom Shoofey had been very eager to engage, took one look at the looming balcony and said there was no possibility that he could do his act in such a vast and impersonal space. Finally, it was decided that the room should be opened by the hottest entertainer of the day, Barbra Streisand.

Elvis was very unhappy about the Vegas booking. Once again, the Colonel had thrown him into the lion's den. Now, it was his job to find a way to lick the beast. The Colonel's decision to keep him off the stage all these years had destroyed Elvis's confidence. No longer a cocksure kid who had but to walk onstage to have the audience at his feet, he was now a young old pro, smart enough to recognize all the pitfalls that lay before him. One big problem was that he had no act. What was he supposed to do—go onstage with a five-piece rock band and start singing "Heartbreak Hotel"? That's what the Colonel wanted him to do. Now, how could Elvis do something as dumb as

that? It would risk typing him as a relic of the past, a campy character out of a rock 'n' roll cartoon. What was even worse was the fact
that he didn't dig the old rock any more; he had gone on to other
things and so had the world. Why should he put himself in a rock
strait jacket when he preferred so many other kinds of music?

What was the alternative? Put on a tux and play Dean Martin?
That was just as ridiculous. Elvis had an image that was bigger than
life. Whatever he thought about rock, people still loved it and he was
its king. He couldn't disappoint the public and risk his neck by suddenly assuming a totally new identity. Then, there were all the problems that related to the Vegas audience. Elvis had spent his great
years driving little girls to tears. Now he would be looking at bouffant hairdos and evening gowns and cleavage. He'd have men out
there who were old enough to be his father and women old enough
to be his mother. He sure as hell couldn't come on to these people
the way he had to the teenyboppers.

He began to haunt the hotels. One night he walked into the
lounge at the Flamingo and found the solution to his problem. The
performer was a young, virtually unknown Welsh singer named Tom
Jones. He was a good-looking, well-built stud dressed in a sharp tux
with a vest and wearing a tight, groovy Afro. His voice was powerful,
though his held notes sometimes wavered unpleasantly. His stance
was commanding. As he would hit the long high notes, he would
bend way back from the waist, giving the women at ringside a good
long look at his crotch. His pants were so tight that they appeared to
have been sprayed on. In the strong stage lights, you could see
clearly the outline of his dick and his balls. In fact, the best word for
his act was "ballsy."

The most astonishing thing about this young man was the effect
he had on the women in his audience. As the show reached its
peaks, stylishly dressed, carefully soignéed young matrons, many of
them seated beside their husbands, would scream and throw their
room keys at the singer. (Afterward the poor husbands would have to
go onstage and retrieve the keys.) Some of them even got so nutsy,

they pulled off their panties and tossed them into the lights. As Elvis looked on in astonishment, he realized that these women were feeling just what the little girls had felt at his shows back in the fifties.

When Elvis checked out Jones, he discovered that he was hot as a murder weapon. His records were going gold, he had a great new TV show in the works, his price was shooting up. The Flamingo was so eager to push him that they had launched a whole promotion keyed to the theme of "Tom Jones Fever." When you sat down at the table, you found a little bottle filled with pink "fever pills." When you turned on your radio, you got the latest report from the "fever clinics." The whole hype. The amazing thing was that it worked! Night after night, Tom Jones packed the room. It was said that the pit bosses and stickmen were complaining, because their wives were pestering them constantly for tickets to the show.

Elvis got very friendly with Tom Jones. He even told the Guys, "Tom is the only man who has ever come anywhere close to the way I sing. He has that ballsy feeling, that 'I'm gonna shove it up your ass attitude.' " The only fault Elvis found in Jones's act was its blatant sex appeal. "I think that's very lewd," Elvis would frown "showing his cock and his balls." "Hell, Elvis," Lamar Fike would carol, "you did the same shit in your time!" "No," Elvis would demur, "I was never vulgar."

All the same, the two men soon became fast friends. Elvis would hang out in Jones's dressing room, even walk out onstage while Jones was working. After the gig, they would go out together and get drunk. Jones drank champagne, Elvis vodka with orange juice to disguise the taste. Then, when they were mellow, Elvis would talk to the young singer, only five years his junior, like a father to a son. At the same time, this father was getting a lot of good ideas from this son.

When Elvis opened in Vegas, the professional show people who worked with both Elvis and with Tom Jones were astonished at how much the famous star had taken from the man he treated as his protégé. Nick Naff, director of publicity at the Flamingo and then at the International, sums up the borrowings neatly:

What Elvis got from Tom was the trick of working the Vegas show stage. Tom showed him that you have to be dynamic and sensual in a way that gets through to the over-thirties. You gotta hit 'em right in the cunt. Tom gave Elvis those head shakes, the vocal accents on the bridges, the freeze poses at the end of the songs, the trick of wiping the sweat with a cloth and then throwing it out in the house—all those things. The big difference was that Tom did all this stuff instinctively. He just didn't know any other way to work. Elvis was much smarter. He wasn't so spontaneous, but he knew a good thing when he saw it. He took Tom's stuff, translated it into his own style, rehearsed his ass off and went over big with it. Elvis was much the brighter of the two.

Tom had given Elvis the key to the house. The rest, for a performer of Elvis's talent and resources, was relatively simple. The whole trick was the image, the attitude. Once Elvis got that straight, he knew just what to do. He wasn't going to stand there in a fancy tux flashing his pecker. He had a better gimmick. For years he had been studying karate. He was a second-degree black belt. Now what was ballsier than karate? Those studs paced around on the mats like big cats. When they attacked, they screamed like jaguars. They had dozens of great moves that were as beautiful as any choreography. They also had that great look in their eyes: that killer look, where the soul, the *ki* comes flashing out of the eye. Finally, there was the karate uniform, the *gi*. If you were going to do karate moves, you couldn't have a better costume.

Calling up Bill Belew, the costume designer whom he had met on the Singer Special, Elvis ordered a number of specially designed *gis* in black mohair. Some were in the traditional two-piece pattern; some were all-in-ones to keep the jacket from flying up and exposing his midriff. For the sash, Belew suggested that he have a macrame belt made by a Hawaiian-Japanese who was into the martial arts and would weave into the belt all the appropriate karate symbols. This idea thrilled Elvis. It was as if he were receiving a magic talisman that would protect him on the stage.

Sartor resartus. When Elvis put on the new *gi*, he assumed instantly his new image. He didn't jiggle and jerk anymore. He took his stand and held it, firm as a statue. He didn't walk in that old butchy style. He padded back and forth like a cat-footed karate killer. When he got into a hard-hitting tune, like "Suspicious Minds," instead of throwing his body into some awkward rendition of the Shimmy or the Camel Walk, he started throwing karate punches: kicks and chops that projected powerfully the force of the music. In no time, he had his new act together.

Now it was time to attend to the music. Elvis started rehearsing a full month before his opening. For the first time in his career, he assembled a band of first-rate Los Angeles studio musicians: no more Nashville cornballs or boyhood pals, like Scotty and D.J. Las Vegas was a big challenge and Elvis was determined to meet the challenge with all the power he could marshal.

Two weeks before opening, Elvis brought all his forces together at the International Hotel for a series of full-scale rehearsals. One of the things that had impressed him about Tom Jones's act, especially when he saw him work in Hawaii in May 1969, was the way the Welsh singer matched his powerful voice with the sonority of a full orchestra, producing those smashing showbiz climaxes that give you goose pimples. Though Elvis had only recently been carping at Steve Binder and Bones Howe about the dangers of "over-producing" his songs with a big studio orchestra, he now became passionately convinced of the importance of working with the largest possible backing. In addition to his five-piece virtuoso rock band, he engaged: the Imperials (a pop gospel quartet); the Sweet Inspirations (a black female soul trio); a harmonizing soprano with an extremely high "angelic" voice; and a thirty-five piece orchestra with a conductor. With Charlie Hodge standing at his side with his acoustic guitar, Elvis mustered onstage *fifty* musicians and singers.

Naturally, the Colonel was furious at this extravagance. In a flash, he saw that Elvis's anxiety would wipe out their joint profits. In fact, he may have suspected that this was Elvis's true intention: an act of revenge inspired by the Colonel's callousness toward Elvis's feelings about Las Vegas. Elvis was heard to say at the time: "I don't care if I don't make any money so long as I give a good show." This was the kind of speech calculated to give the Colonel another heart attack. Colonel, for his part, went about puffing his cigar to a hot glow and demanding of no one in particular: "What the hell does he want all these people for? He doesn't need them! He's just *insecure!*" Ah, a line like that was designed to ricochet back off the Guys to Elvis, where it would hit him square in the balls. Elvis would send back his answer through the same set of human bounce boards "I've got to have my *power!* I've got to have *dynamics!*" he thundered to the Guys. "You saw that stage, you saw what I've got to cover! What the fuck does that old bald-headed bastard think this is all about!"

By the time Elvis arrived in Las Vegas, Barbra Streisand had been working the showroom for two weeks. At this moment, she was at the peak of her career. She had just won an Oscar for *Funny Girl.* Her talents as a singer, an actress, a comedienne and an analyst of public taste promised that her Las Vegas debut would be one of the greatest events in the history of the resort. It was confidently expected that her engagement would establish attendance records, set benchmarks for musical and theatrical excellence and push the whole level of local entertainment onto a higher plateau. Then, the unthinkable happened. Streisand, ignorant of Vegas, puffed up with success, not really at her best before a live audience, came to town with an audaciously simple show. It was essentially a rehash of a program which she had given the previous summer at New York in Central Park. There were no warm-up acts, no jokes, no choreography or sets: just Barbra standing there under the lights with a fantastic hairdo, a splendid gown and the longest fingernails since the Manchu dynasty, singing her heart out into a jeweled hand mike. It was a stunning exhibition of vocal and stylistic virtuosity by the Heifetz of pop song. In New York, it would have killed the audience. In Las Vegas, after the stellar opening night, it produced shrinking houses and even snores.

Elvis slipped into the back of the balcony one night to watch his rival work. He pointed mutely to all the empty seats around him. Then, he settled down to listen to the program. He gave no signs of pleasure. He made sour faces when Barbra got into her Jewish obsessions. When it was all over, he turned to Lamar Fike and said two words: "She sucks!" Then, he went downstairs to the dressing room to tell Barbra how much he had enjoyed the performance. When he was admitted to the dressing room, he was astonished to find the great star alone. Elvis had never been alone for one moment in his entire life. Two or three men always accompanied him even to the bathroom. Streisand made no bones about her disgust with the audience and the hotel. "This place isn't even built yet!" she fumed. "I wouldn't be surprised if some night while I'm out there working some schmuck doesn't walk by with a ladder on his shoulder!" Then, vowing that she would never play Las Vegas again and wishing Elvis well on his engagement (doubtless with the same degree of sincerity as he had evinced with his phony congratulations), the two parted company.

As Elvis was straining every fiber of his being during the final days of rehearsal, even going so far as to strap weights on his legs as he worked to build up the muscles, Colonel Parker was having a field day blitzing the town and the nation with his publicity. Setting up his headquarters in a three-room suite at the end of the hall on the fourth floor, the old boy and his henchmen—Tom Diskin and Jim O'Brien—swiftly seized control of the hotel's public relations apparatus and readjusted it for their style of pitch. The hotel, for example, had wanted the radio spot announcements to be low-keyed and tasteful, with Elvis's voice in the background as the announcer extended an invitation. Colonel Parker would not hear of such a thing.

Soon the airwaves were filled with raucously echoing pitches: "ELVIS!))) ELVIS!)))) ELVIS!))) NOW!))) NOW!))) NOW!))) INTERNATIONAL HOTEL!)))" The roads were lined all the way in from Los Angeles with socko billboard sheets. Every store in town was offered a window placard or a poster. Every unguarded wall was plastered with a quarter sheet. The newspaper ads were not just ads: They were two- and three-page sections devoted entirely to Elvis. You couldn't watch TV for an hour without getting an urgent spiel. All this round-the-clock activity, however, was just the build-up to the circus-hits-town bit the Colonel did the moment Barbra Streisand's engagement ended.

That night, the Colonel was standing in the hotel lobby with a huge crew, equipped with ladders, staple guns, lumber and vast quantities of posters and placards printed up by his old buddy Clyde Rinaldi, in Tampa. Abiding by the rules of professional etiquette, the old man did not permit one banner to be hung announcing Elvis's appearance until the contractual time of the Streisand engagement had run out. Then, at the stroke of midnight, he shouted at his crew: "Hit it!" Instantly, the men went into action. In a matter of hours, they had papered every public room in the hotel with Elvis's name and picture. They had constructed a booth next to the hotel entrance that sold souvenir programs, styrofoam straw hats, teddy bears. They hung banners from the ceiling, they supplied the maids with stand-up announcements to be placed conspicuously in every room on top of the TV set or the dresser. Next morning, when the hotel executives came to work, they were appalled to discover their immaculate new lobby buried under this junk blizzard. What could they do? As the marquee announced, in the largest lettering available and with a silhouette figure of the star, Las Vegas was now under the rule of ELVIS!

Opening night, July 26, 1969, the hotel offered a free dinner show to a specially invited audience. Naturally, the Colonel got control of the guest list and invited all his cronies from Tampa, Nashville and Hollywood, his doctor from Palm Springs, his wife's relatives and other such important figures. Oh, it was a star-studded assembly. The Colonel knew George Hamilton quite well. Minnie Pearl and Earl Scruggs were invited. Fats Domino attracted quite a bit of attention because he was virtually the only man of color among the two thousand guests.

The decor of the Showroom Internationale was just as preposterous as everything else in Las Vegas. Grander than the "Fountain-blue," grosser than Grossinger's, it was adorned with three-dimensional putti stringing yards of swagging chiffon between plastic classic columns. The maitre d' and the captains wore frilly blue shirts under their elaborate tuxedos, and seated each guest according to a vast, astrological-looking chart. The New York rock press had been flown in en masse on Kirk Kerkorian's private DC-9, a stunning two-bedroom aerial yacht. Accustomed to nothing better than a paper plate laden with "soul food" and a plastic cup filled with sour wine, they were overwhelmed by the largesse that characterized the Presley opening. Small wonder that their notices of the event were so rhapsodic.

The two warm-up acts, the Sweet Inspirations and the comic Sammy Gore, can be passed over without comment as they were observed without interest by the audience. Then, the giant gold curtain fell. When it rose again, it revealed the philharmonic-sized forces of Elvis's accompaniment belting out a hot show-time rhythm. Suddenly, without a word of announcement, a figure dressed in black emerged from the wings at stage left. There was a gasp of recognition, then a mounting roar of applause that instantly became a standing ovation. Elvis, meantime, had stridden to center stage, received his guitar from Charlie Hodge and assumed the classic spraddle-legged stance to kick off his first number. The uproar in the house was so great that he was stopped in his tracks. Smiling foolishly but unwilling to break the spell by saying anything, he held the band in check for a few moments. Then, he cried:

"One for the money!" The band shouted back, "Ba-*dum* boom!" "Two for the show!" Ba-*dum* boom! "Three to get ready and go, cat, go!" He was off and running fast on "Blue Suede Shoes."

What followed was a case of old Cokes served up in shiny new cans. Elvis's special arrangements . . . had the effect at fast tempos of seizing the singer, as if in one of those old vibrating belts, and shaking him violently on what sounded like one note until he was breathless. Then, panting, gasping, apologizing—at one point he said, "You all just look at me a couple minutes while I get my breath back!"—he would swig down a cup of Gatorade, like a spent athlete, and return to his musical exercise machine. On the first slow tune, "Love Me Tender," he strolled around the stage apron, kneeling down to kiss one woman after another. He was determined to make contact with the "over-thirties." His first medley—"Jailhouse Rock," "Don't Be Cruel," "Heartbreak Hotel" and "All Shook Up"—betrayed a sarcastic and spoofing attitude, as if he were saying: "I'm not twenty-one anymore and neither are you, so we won't take these old toys too seriously." All the best material appeared in the latter part of the show, where he got into his recent hits, "In the Ghetto" and a six-minute take-out on "Suspicious Minds," which built up to a bacchanalian climax, the trumpets screaming, the drums roaring, the choral voices shouting out their lungs. All in all, it was a show that offered a lot more to the eye than to the ear and a lot more to the viscera than to the mind. Elvis was blowing it out, belting his songs, producing broad, coarse effects that were appropriate to all the broad, coarse sensibilities in his audience. When he walked off that night, the flacks, the fans, the rock critics and the music businessmen hailed the performance as a triumph. As such it was reported the following week from coast to coast.

.   .   .   .

Elvis was destined to return to Las Vegas again and again in the next seven years, falling into one of those treadmill patterns that characterized his entire career. Every August and February, like clockwork, Colonel Parker would throw a switch and the machine would spring into action. At first Elvis got some pleasure from his new success. He tinkered with his image and his repertoire. When he opened for the second time, in February 1970, he had a totally new look.

Not since Marlene Dietrich stunned the ringsiders with the sight of her celebrated legs encased from hip to ankle in a transparent gown had any performer so electrified Las Vegas with his mere physical appearance. Bill Belew, who had been very cautious up to this point about designing any costume that would make Elvis look effeminate, decided finally to kick out the jams. Now Elvis faced the house encased in a smashing white jumpsuit, slashed to the sternum and lovingly fitted around his broad shoulders, flat belly, narrow hips and tightly packed crotch. And then there were his pearls—loads of lustrous pearls, not sewn on the costume but worn unabashedly as body ornaments. Pearls coiled in thick bunches around his neck, pearls girdled his tapered waist in a fabulous karate belt, rope of pearl alternating with rope of gold, the whole sash tied over one hip with the ends dangling down to brush one knee. With his massive diamonds flashing pinks and purples from his fingers and his boyish smile flashing sheepishly through his huge shag of shiny black hair, Elvis looked like a heaping portion of male cheesecake ripe for the eyeteeth of the hundreds of women ogling him through opera glasses or lunging at the stage like gravid salmon hurtling a cataract.

Elvis also relaxed and regained his old confidence. He would kick off the show now James Brown style by collaring the mike and shaking it to the beat of "I'm All Shook Up," the kettle-drumming orchestra shaking its elephantine body behind him. Coming to the guitar break, Elvis would strum the acoustic instrument slung on a white band about his neck with the carelessness of a practiced faker. Then the number would end abruptly with the martial artist snapping into profile and thrusting his guitar bayonet-wise at the chorus.

The rest of the evening would pass smoothly as he glided through medleys of old tunes or lounged in elaborately upholstered versions of his new anthems. Every number would end with a classically struck profile, the white-clad figure with the Grecian features suggesting a spaceage version of the Discus Hurler or the Laocoon. Between numbers he would offer glimpses of his wry humor: "My mouth's so dry, feels like Bob Dylan slept in it all night." Finally, the performance would come to its conclusion with the Vegas equivalent of one of those sunset-in-the-Rockies numbers from the old *Ziegfeld Follies*.

Silhouetted against a cerulian blue cyclorama, the Las Vegas Philharmonic, the front rank of black-clad, guitarslingin' Memphis Mafiosi and the integrated chorus of the Imperials and the Sweet Inspirations would be transfigured by a flood of rich amber light pouring in from the Valley of Loose Gold. As the massed players and singers sustained a mighty cathedral chord, the Sun King would fall on one knee in the classic Jolson-gladiator pose, flinging wide his arms in a grand salute to his assembled court, over which he seemed destined to reign forever in eternal youth and jollity and jamboree. . . .

Noël Coward

The Noël Coward Diaries: "Nescafé Society"

Friday 3 December   *Las Vegas*

This is a fabulous, extraordinary madhouse. All around is desert sand with pink and purple mountains on the horizon. All the big hotels are luxe to the last degree. Even now, in the pre-Christmas slump, there are myriads of people tearing away at the fruit machines and gambling, gambling, gambling for twenty-four hours a day. The lighting at night is fantastic; downtown where "The Golden Nugget" is and the lesser dives, it is ablaze with variegated neon

☞ *Excerpted from* The Noël Coward Diaries, *edited by Graham Payn and Sheridan Morley (Little, Brown and Company, 1982).*

signs. In the hotels, where the casinos are more classy, beams of light shoot down from baroque ceilings on the masses of earnest morons flinging their money down the drain. The sound is fascinating, a steady hum of conversation against a background of rhumba music and the noise of the fruit machines, the clink of silver dollars, quarters and nickels, and the subdued shouts of the croupiers. There are lots of pretty women about but I think, on the whole, sex takes a comparatively back seat. Every instinct and desire is concentrated on money.

I expected that this would exasperate me, but oddly enough it didn't. The whole fantasia is on such a colossal scale that it is almost stimulating. I went from hotel to hotel and looked at the rooms. They are all fairly large and much of a muchness. Expert lighting and sound and cheerful and appreciative audiences who are obviously there to have a good time. I noticed little drunkenness and much better manners than in the New York night-clubs. The gangsters who run the places are all urbane and charming. I had a feeling that if I opened a rival casino I would be battered to death with the utmost efficiency and despatch, but if I remained on my own ground as a most highly paid entertainer that I could trust them all the way. They are curious products of a most curious adolescent country. Their morals are bizarre in the extreme. They are generous, mother-worshippers, sentimental and capable of much kindness. They are also ruthless, cruel, violent and devoid of scruples. Joe Glaser, whom I have taken a great shine to, never drinks, never smokes and adores his mother. He is now fifty-eight and, rather naturally, over the moon with delight at having got me under his wing. My name is big prestige stuff for a brisk little Jewish go-getter who hitherto has mainly booked coloured acts and promoted prize-fights. My heart, and reason, go out to him because he at least took the trouble to fly over to London to see me at the Café and give me a concrete offer. If it all ends in smoke I don't think it will be his fault. I believe him to be honest according to his neon lights. He is shrewd, sentimental, noisy and generous. The situation is that I will appear here for the

first three weeks in May providing all the money part of it is satis-
factorily arranged.

.   .   .   .

Sunday 5 June   *The Desert Inn, Las Vegas*

Coley and I arrived here on Wednesday. The daily temperature is
generally over 100°, which I love. My voice is in fine form and I have
cut down smoking to the minimum. We have been to see dinner and
supper shows at the other hotels. Rosemary Clooney really charming. Jane Powell a very pretty little thing with a fine soprano with a
slight gear-shift. Sammy Davis Jr., a rich talent and a brilliant performer but he goes on too long. All the hotels are on the same pattern. A gambling casino with angular shafts of light falling on to the
gamblers; the perpetual noise of the slot-machines and the cries of
the crap shooters; a bar lounge with a separate four-or five-piece
band playing continually. The din is considerable but you get used
to it. The men's shops here are wonderful, and as everything I buy
can be charged to my hotel bill and is therefore deductible, I am being, most enjoyably, very extravagant indeed. I have hired a car for
$50 a week. It is a yellow and black Ford convertible with automatic
drive and every known gadget. It also shuts and opens itself when
one presses a button.

Sunday 12 June

Well, it is all over bar the shouting which is still going on. I have
made one of the most sensational successes of my career and to
pretend that I am not absolutely delighted would be idiotic. I have
had screaming rave notices and the news has flashed round the
world. I am told continually, verbally and in print, that I am the greatest attraction that Las Vegas has ever had and that I am the greatest
performer in the world, etc., etc. It is all very, very exciting and gen-

erous, and when I look back at the grudging dreariness of the English newspaper gentlemen announcing, when I first opened at the Café de Paris, that I massacred my own songs, I really feel that I don't want to appear at home much more. I have just had a batch of notices from London of Larry and Vivien's *Macbeth* at Stratford, and their ignorance and meanness and cruel, common personal abusiveness have made me sick. I *know* they can't be right, but even if Larry and Viv were not perfect (which I doubt), the tone of the notices is beneath contempt. Much the same as I usually get from the mean, envious little sods.

At any rate—pull the ladder up, Joe, for I'm all right! The place is packed every night at both shows; the audiences, even at the dinner show which is notoriously dull, are quiet as mice and beautifully attentive and they always pull the place down at the end.

Perhaps by the end of my time here I shall be longing for the softer, gentler ways of home, but at the moment I am so fascinated— and helped—by the professional "expertise" in all departments. I am also touched and warmed by the generosity of their reception of me. Here, a rave notice is *not* considered bad news as it is at home. Here also there is a genuine respect for, and understanding of, light music. I am not gibed at for not being a "singer," because they recognize immediately here that not being a "singer" is one of my greatest assets. They know I know how to sing, and they are used to, and largely prefer, performers who perform songs rather than "sing" them. Light music has been despised and rejected in England for years. Modern music, including variations of jazz, is not considered important by the savants. Benjamin Britten, yes, with all his arid, self-conscious dissonances, but then that is "serious" and "significant." Here, light music has its own genuine values, which are recognized not only by the public but by the Press. The orchestral arrangements and variations are incredible—vital and imaginative. Sometimes they go too far for my own personal taste, but I cannot fail to be impressed by the expert knowledge of instrumentation. Pete Matz, at the age of twenty-six, knows more about the range of various instruments and the potentialities of different combinations than anyone of any age

I have *ever* met in England. I suppose music is in the air more here and the mixture of Jewish and Negro rhythms has become part of the national consciousness because it is a goulash of all races. Very exciting and stimulating.

The first night, from the social-theatrical point of view, was fairly sensational. Frank Sinatra chartered a special plane and brought Judy Garland, the Bogarts, the Nivens, etc.; then there were Joan Fontaine, Zsa Zsa Gabor, the Joe Cottens, Peter Glenville, Larry Harvey, etc. The noise was terrific. The next day there was a quarter of an hour's radio talk devoted to me in course of which they all lavished paeans of praise on me with the most uninhibited and heart-warming generosity. The Press have been courteous and the photographers insistent but considerate. On Friday I was driven out into the Nevada desert, where I was photographed for *Life* magazine in my dinner-jacket sipping a cup of tea. The temperature was 118°.

Sunday 19 June

The mood lasted but God in his infinite wisdom struck me down with a violent fever on Monday. I staggered through two performances with a temperature of 103° and on Tuesday the doctor absolutely refused to let me play, so I lay here in bed, sweating and writhing and feeling terrible. Meanwhile the news was flashed round the world and there were cables and telephone calls and great fuss. On Wednesday I tottered back and have not missed a performance since. The weather changed suddenly and a hailstorm happened which flooded the whole place and caused three million dollars' worth of damage. Two days after I got better, Cole went down with the same virus. I am now virtually all right again and he, after thirty-six hours in bed, is up and about.

The triumph continues and is even greater than at first. I receive a screaming ovation at every performance. Last night the Goetzes, Burns and Allen, and the Jack Bennys came. Also darling Kay Thompson. Tonight Joe Cotten again and Jeanette MacDonald. The business is fantastic and hundreds are turned away at every performance. I must say it is very, very gratifying and I am enjoying myself like crazy.

.   .   .   .

Sunday 26 June

One more week to go. The time has certainly passed incredibly swiftly. I don't think I should like any longer playing two shows a night. It is fairly tiring but on the whole I am enjoying myself.

Lots of people come from Hollywood. The Goldwyns came the other night and were wildly enthusiastic. The audiences continue to be wonderful with the occasional exception of a dull dinner show, but even when they are dull they are at least attentive.

Sunday 3 July

On Monday and Tuesday Goddard Lieberson was here with his myrmidons, and four performances were recorded for a long-player of me at Las Vegas. Happily all four audiences were wonderful and applauded and laughed like crazy. The experts are delighted with the recorded results and so at last I shall have a good American LP on the market. I added 'Matelot' and 'A Room with a View' to the repertoire, also 'Alice.'

The Wednesday night supper show was thrilling. Cole Porter came and Tallulah and the Van Johnsons, and it really was sensational. I was so glad because I so wanted Cole to see me at my best and he certainly did. Last night was the let-down of all time, both audiences stuffed cod's heads, but the supper show really vile. I pressed on and got them in the end, but it was gruelling hard work.

I went to a sweet party given by one of our dancing-girls, Jeanne Gregory. Her husband is a handsome young Pole who came to Gerald Road twice during the war when I was giving the GI parties. We sat in the garden under oleander trees and had barbecued hotdogs and potato pancakes with chives and sour cream, and it was delicious and peaceful and I stayed cheerfully until dawn.

Tuesday 5 July

Well, it's all over. The bags are packed, the farewell presents given, and the paper streamers drooping in the hot desert wind. Last night was exciting and strangely moving. The management presented me with a beautiful silver cigarette-box and I made a speech and everyone became very sentimental. Ethel Merman was in the front row and in floods. Then I gave a party in the Sky Room to all the boys and girls plus Merman, Tallulah, etc. At long last, when all goodbyes were said, I lost $15 very quickly at blackjack and went to bed. It has been an extraordinary experience and one of the most reverberant successes I have ever had. I am really proud and pleased that I succeeded in doing what no one suspected I could, and that is please the *ordinary* audiences. Obviously on certain nights crammed with movie stars and chums I had no difficulties and every number went wonderfully, but the dinner shows, filled with people from Kansas, Nebraska, Utah, Illinois, etc., were what really counted and their response was usually splendid. Occasionally they would start dull and remain so, but as a general rule I got them in the end. How much I owe to those hellish troop audiences in the war. After them, anything is gravy. This afternoon we fly to Hollywood. It has all been a triumphant adventure and I feel very happy. . . .

Phyllis Barber

....

How I Got Cultured:
A Nevada Memoir

One morning, about five o'clock, our gray Plymouth drove in the opposite direction from the dawn, toward Las Vegas, out by Railroad Pass where Uncle Tommy played trumpet on Saturday night. Elaine and I kept warm under a friendship quilt and read the embroidered names of Mama's old friends, waiting.

"It's time," Daddy said. "Watch. Don't miss this. We should be able to see everything, even if it is seventy-five miles away."

We waited some more, eating apples and crackers.

☞ *Excerpted from* How I Got Cultured: A Nevada Memoir (*University of Georgia Press*, 1992).

"It's got to be time," he said.

My neck cramped. I looked at the sunrise.

"There it is, there it is," he yelled.

I saw the flash, but mostly my father's face and his brass buttons that seemed to glow red for one instant.

"That's how I came home to you, everybody. Just look at that power."

The cloud flowered, mushroomed, turned itself inside out, and poured into the sky. Red fire burned in the middle of browns and grays, colors that hid the red almost. But it was there—the fire burning at the center, the red fire that charred the North Wind's puffed cheeks and squeezed eyes until it blew itself away, trailing black smoke and its pride. It was there in the middle of the rising columns of earth and clouds boiling over, clouds bursting into clouds, whipping themselves inside out, changing colors over and over. Red, yellow, and black, colors from the fire. Gray, brown, and beige, sand from the desert floor, Daddy said.

And then the picture blurred at its edges, unfocused itself into other shapes—smoke arches, long floating strings, dots and dashes. In no time at all, everything floated away, on the jet stream, Daddy told us.

"I thought it would last longer," I said. "Won't they do it again?"

Daddy laughed, "It's time to go home now and get some hot breakfast. Wasn't that amazing, kids?"

Everyone who had gotten up to watch the blast talked about it in school that day. "Did you see it?" Our desert land had been chosen once again for an important government project.

The front page of that night's newspaper had pictures of the before and after—frame houses before, no frame houses after; dummied soldiers before, no recognizable dummies after. Surprised cattle lay flat out in the dead grass on their sides, their hair singed white on the up side. Yucca Flats. Frenchman Flats. Mercury Test Site. Household words.

"Nobody can get us now," my daddy said.

I don't think about it much, but sometimes when I punch my pillow for more fluff, ready to settle into sleep, the cloud mists into long red airy fingers over everything, reaching across the stark blue.

.   .   .   .

One day when I was at the piano, some show girls from the Strip walked through the front door—no stage makeup or feathered head-dresses. "I long for the Spartan demands of a good studio," they said from behind large sunglasses as they trailed their cardigans and oversized bags across the wooden floor.

Just before class, I walked through the dressing room to go to the bathroom. A show girl stood there, unabashedly naked, her shorts pooled around her ankles. Another was peeling off her toreadors and see-through blouse before I could say excuse me for intruding. I'd been drilled about modesty at the Church of Jesus Christ of Latter-day Saints, but I couldn't take my eyes off their bodies sliding into their tights without any underwear. Then they dashed past me as if no etiquette had been breached, as if their bodies were everyday things, not sacred temples as I'd been taught from childhood.

There was pure defiance beneath their stretched Danskins—a different world from canning peaches with my mother, baking bread, and sniffing golden loaves, Brother this and Sister that when we greeted each other at church meetings. A strange wind blew through the windows of my mind and shook the panes etched with the Sunday School words: "Choose the Right when a choice is placed before you."

I don't remember leaving the dressing room, but during the lesson, I watched the two show girls leap across the wooden floor and land with their arms stretched gloriously over their heads. As they danced, they held their shoulders back until their breasts tilted to prominence. Then they laughed boldly and spun like striped tops. I wondered if God would fetter their wings or demand retribution for their brashness, their boldness with their bodies.

I felt a wild bird screeching from the limb of a tree inside myself. It screeched all through an excerpt from *Coppélia*. It made me want to tear my music into confetti, to lean into the piano keys with my elbows and forearms, to climb up on the piano bench and fly over the heads of the dancers through the large front windows that said Roberts' School of Dancing and spread my legs and arms and become like wind that carried birds. My chest hurt as I played excerpts from ballets.

I turned around to see Mrs. Kranz mending, darning some socks slipped over a rubber ball, buried in her handiwork. What was happening behind her small oval eyeglasses? What did Mrs. Kranz think of show girls? Maybe they made her ask questions. Was this what she wanted for Merry Anne? What did she say to Merry Anne when they drove home in their Dodge?—"Don't forget the difference between classical and popular dancing. One is pure."

She dipped the darning needle over and again into the web of thread on the stocking's heel. She was a mother with a thread, a needle, and a sock. Steadily, in and out. Night and day. Caring. Mending. Guarding with curious determination.

"A dancer's life isn't for you," my mother said when she watched me move furniture in the living room to clear space. "You can dance at the church dances. You've got your piano, and there's school."

"I'm paying for the lessons myself," I said.

"Enough is enough," she said flatly. "You make me tired, and a cheap show girl is the last thing you want to be."

I hadn't mentioned the show girls who'd come to the studio, so she caught me by surprise. I gathered my defense.

"Why are show girls cheap? I've met some, and they're very nice women."

"Give me a break," my mother said. "You know some show girls, do you? Know about the big world out there, do you?"

"I know a few things."

Even as I spoke, I thought of the bare skin beneath the show girls' leotards and their freedom to do with it as they pleased. Lately at night, I'd been thinking maybe my skin could belong to me and no one else. Why did it have to be God's temple when I lived in it? Why did somebody else make decisions about my body? It was mine, after all.

"It's my life," I raised my voice. "I'll do with it what I want."

"Your life is a part of every other life. Don't think you're a solo."

"I want to dance, and I'm going to!"

My mother shrugged her shoulders as if she were dealing with an idiot and shouldn't waste any more energy on the conversation. But she couldn't resist. "Have you ever seen an old show girl? Marriage and family last forever, but legs, waistlines, and breasts don't, your highness."

"So maybe I don't want marriage and family. It's a moving train with no windows or doors."

My mother sighed. "Young people think they're different, that they can break rules. I'm telling you this to help you, my dear. We're all on that train. Nobody gets off. Don't kid yourself, because you'll make things harder if you do."

"But what's wrong with dancing?"

"Nothing," she said. "We dance here at home."

"But I want to *really* dance. Leap up and fly out the window. That kind of dancing."

"You're dancing any time you move to music, dear."

.   .   .   .   .   .

When you wish upon a star, makes no difference who you are. I once believed that line and believed every wish I made would come true. I could ask God. I could ask the stars. Someone or something would answer. But I never took the notion of rhythm into account.

I thought I knew what it was in 1956. My family and I gathered in front of a television set one Sunday night to eat popcorn and watch a performance of a select group of Las Vegas High School girls on Ed Sullivan's variety stage in New York City. The Las Vegas Rhythmettes, the precision marching dance team with their pseudo can-can routine and full line pivots, danced and kicked and snapped their page-boy-hairstyled heads that glistened like shampoo ads.

The camera panned in on each face.

"That's Brother Crane's daughter," my father's voice sounded surprised. "I wonder how he feels about his daughter dancing on the Sabbath."

"I imagine he's ashamed," my mother said, wiping a spill from the coffee table with the corner of her apron. "His daughter parading herself around in that skimpy outfit."

"There's Melba Simmons's best friend," my sister Elaine said. "She's really stuck on herself."

"This is stupid." Mother retrieved the empty popcorn bowl. "Making such a big deal over these girls. I know dancing when I see it. That's not dancing."

But I was mesmerized by the eighteen girls who marched into our home and the full-screen, black-and-white portraits of each of them filling the TV. I would have given anything to be making rhythm with them. I imagined my face on TV, smiling out on the nation, listening to disembodied voices saying, "My, isn't that a beautiful young girl? She could be a star."

At bedtime, the ritual began: "Dear God. I don't ask much, but please, if it's okay with you, let me be worthy." And then, for insurance, I whispered to the sky, "Star light, star bright." I'd take any help I could get.

After I fell into sleep, the black-and-white television images followed me to my dreams and split in halves—legs dancing on the bottom left of the screen, arms synchronized on the upper right side. Marching feet pranced; girls' heads snapped to the right, then to the left on every eighth count; absolute precision, the line of eighteen girls with their hair turned under gently at the tops of their shoulders.

Suddenly, the leg of one of the Rhythmettes snapped off on a high kick and flew through the air. Kicking at the darkness, it landed on a stage swept clean by desert wind. There it danced by itself, until gradually other parts fell into place—an arm, the other leg, a torso—until it was me, Phyllis Nelson, all together, kicking and dancing in the spotlight of the moon on a hill in the middle of the desert, dancing for the snakes, lizards, and cactus blossoms while they stopped and watched. The night sang.

When I entered Las Vegas High School the next year, I watched the Rhythmettes in the girls' locker room slip in and out of the sleeves of their Rhythmette sweaters. I watched them walk gracefully around the school with their long flowing hair and manicured fingernails. I watched them dance at the halftimes of the football and basketball games. And I often paused at the bulletin board in Miss Stuckey's office in the gym. She'd tacked up rows of pictures of *her girls* marching in parades and shaking hands with Frank Sinatra.

"That's all you think about, isn't it?" my mother said after I mentioned tryouts were coming up. We were shelling peas for dinner. "You think you're really going to be something if you're a Rhythmette, don't you? It's ridiculous, everybody clamoring to get into that corny organization, making so much out of nothing. Set your sights higher, Phyllis."

"I pray to God and wish on stars, Mom. How high do I have to get?"

She almost laughed, but was too intent on dissuading me. "What about your music? What about things that really matter?"

"I'm reading the Book of Mormon, and I go to church three times a week and seminary every morning at six forty-five, even though the teacher has sawdust for brains."

"Watch your mouth, Phyllis," she said sharply as she ripped the string from a pod and funneled a handful of peas into a quart jar.

"Why does everything have to be the way you want it?"

"Young people are so blind." She washed her hands with a worn bar of Ivory, a long discolored brown crack in the soap. She wiped the water from her wedding rings with a stained dishtowel. "Deep in your heart you know what's important. You know your purpose on this earth."

"Oh, and what's that?"

"Letting your light shine, Phyllis. The light of Christ who is the light of the world. Jesus didn't need to be a Rhythmette to be loved. Neither do you. The real joy in this life is in God's plan—being a mother and multiplying and replenishing the earth. Not in some trumped-up organization like the Las Vegas Rhythmettes. It's phony."

On a hot April night, 127 girls and I filtered onto the shining gymnasium wood, tiptoeing around the edges of the sacred black and red Las Vegas Wildcat painted mid-floor. The wooden bleachers were pushed against the walls. Everything shone—our scrubbed faces, our hair, our eyes, the bright overhead lights. Some of the girls came in groups of two or three friends, some with their parents who lingered at the heavy green doors and watched wistfully while their daughters signed their lives over to Miss Stuckey.

One paper we were asked to sign asked for our consent for up to twelve hours a week and up to twenty-five when rehearsing for the show of shows—the Rhythmette Review. Another was a questionnaire on why we wanted to be a Rhythmette, what the word meant to us, how dedicated we thought we could be.

"Being a Rhythmette means I can be a representative of Las Vegas High School," I wrote. "I can learn discipline; I can learn how to work with a group of young people my own age in a constructive manner."

The paperwork completed, Miss Evelyn Stuckey told us to sit on the floor. Cross-legged or on one hip, everyone sat tall enough to be noticed in their coordinated outfits, bermuda shorts, striped blouses, ponytails, frizzed bangs, curled eyelashes, plucked eyebrows. Every girl, I supposed, saw at the back of her mind an image of herself full-faced on the Ed Sullivan Show, the center of the screen. Or had an idea of herself following the footsteps of the Rhythmette once chosen runner-up to Miss U.S.A.

I, too, scented the major leagues, a chance to jump the never-stopping train I was on where the rolling wheels repeated mile after mile: "Obey God's word, obey God's word." More important than any-thing—obey God's word. I and 127 other girls sat on the gymnasium floor, sniffing the scent of opportunity and wanting a piece of it. How could I not step on this golden rung, follow these urgings toward the big times—dressed in a formal evening gown and being introduced "MISS PHYLLIS NELSON" at the Rhythmette Review, the most glamorous show in all of Nevada outside the hotels and casinos? ("Wholesome glamour," Miss Stuckey claimed in an interview in the *Las Vegas Review-Journal*.)

I looked at the black painted lines marking the basketball court boundaries and sensed there were no boundaries for me if I could only be a Rhythmette. Then I noticed the gymnast's horse shoved against the wall of the gym. If only it would come alive and gallop to me in a show of favoritism. I'd jump on its back, race across the gym-nasium floor, and rein to a stop by Miss Stuckey. "Madam," I'd say. "Ultra rhythm, at your service."

"If you're chosen to be a Baby R," Miss Stuckey was saying, look-ing over the tops of her reading glasses at every face in the group while every heart skipped two beats, "we expect your best. If you can't give it, don't stay a minute longer." She had angelically curly hair and a charming southern drawl which barely covered the iron will we'd seen snatches of during PE. "Anybody want to leave?" Not a stir on the floor, not anybody shifting position or tying shoes, noth-ing. Over the easygoing collar of her wool plaid shirt, her eyes swept our faces with one more hawk-like gaze.

"All right. Then I understand each of you is willing to give your A-1, all-time best effort to the Rhythmette organization?"

We all nodded solemnly.

"The senior Rhythmettes will supervise this tryout," Miss Stuckey added, "though all my girls will teach you the routines. I wish every one of you could make it, but, sad to say, there are only six places in the line, plus one alternate. One hundred plus just doesn't fit into that number." Her laugh was something out of the slow South, a high chicken sort of claim on the barnyard. "If you don't make this cut, come to me and I'll tell you what might help you next year. Let's get rolling."

I wish I'd been more aware as I listened to Miss Stuckey that night. There was a Big Wheel rolling across the gymnasium floor of the Las Vegas High School gym with its immaculately shining floors, overhead lights glaring like hospital operation room lamps onto the wood's waxed surface, the smell of April and watered lawns and warm nights. A Big Wheel, a Plan, a Purpose. Round turnings, rollings, me a miniscule part of the tide, rolling along, singing a song, thinking I could bust out by becoming a Rhythmette. I wish I'd known how to listen to the quiet, offbeat side of me that didn't need to prove itself or make a major statement. But I could only hear the public side of myself, so indiscriminate, a sucker fish snapping at the bait, a marionette jumping at every chance to be on stage, the part of me insistent on forcing the bloom.

As I sat there, trying to concentrate, the moom shone through the high smoky windows in the gym and said, *Hey, Phyllis. What are you doing in that tight little box of a gym?*

Moon, I answered. *This is important.*

And why don't you wish on me instead of the stars?

Nobody wishes on the moon, I whispered.

Why not? the moon's lips crumpled. *I'm more like you than the stars are. They gradually burn to death, while I only change my faces and pull the tides.*

What do you mean?

You'll find out. Meanwhile, don't waste your time in that gym. You've got big rhythm, like me. We're sisters.

Joyce Ahern introduced herself. "I'll be your teacher tonight, but first I've got to tell you that Rhythmettes is one of the greatest things that could ever happen to you. It's really fabulous if you make it."

There were eight of us in her group. Joyce was nothing short of a porcelain beauty, white skin and upright eyelashes curled to perfection by the cage of an eyelash curler. Could my thin nose and what felt like chicken-bone arms ever translate into something like Joyce, her black hair turned gently under at her shoulders? How could I ever get my stick-straight hair to curve like that?

The music started. "Tequila," by the Champs, a routine the Rhyth-mettes had performed at the state basketball championship, their best ever. Afterward, everyone in the bleachers stomped their feet and jumped in the air yelling, "Tequila! Tequila!" in a wild, mad frenzy of school spirit.

"Roll your arms," Joyce said, "like in a mambo." We learned the part that went with the arms—rolling back on one heel while stepping on the other foot. Then we clapped our hands, put them on our hips, and jump kicked.

I had the grades to qualify, the dedication, and I learned quickly, so I made it through the first and second cuts. But on the following Thursday when it came time for the final judging, the braces on my teeth caught the entire spray of light from the overhead lamps, and I knew the four judges sitting in a tight clump on the bleachers would be blinded to the real Phyllis Nelson, the girl who believed in answers to prayers and wished on stars. My skin felt like a tight nylon stocking over my real dancing self, and my lips quivered.

When I heard the needle drop into place on the record and the sound of scratchy space before the Champs started strumming their guitars, my body started acting up, working against my will, and slipping out of control. I forgot part of the routine; I crossed my legs when I should have kicked them, and I didn't sink into the beat of the music.

I've always wondered what happened that night. Maybe my body was in league with my mother despite my intentions to the contrary. Or it may have wanted to stretch out under the moon on the desert sand when everything was velvet and still, when the tarantulas and horseflies were asleep, wherever they slept. It may have preferred the black night, a reprieve from the pressure of my mother standing in a window framed by sunlight, shaking her finger at me, always reminding me I had a purpose to fulfill, a rhythm I couldn't escape even amidst cold wars, communists, Sputniks, stories about Bugsy

Siegel and the Mafia drilling holes in his skull, pictures of the show
girls in the *Review-Journal*, relaxing on chaise lounges by swimming
pools, their derrieres rounded like rising suns, and more pictures of
such things as Miss America, Miss Nevada, Junior Miss Nevada,
Missy Nevada, or even the Rhythmettes.

I finally worked up the courage to go to Miss Stuckey's office in
the locker room and ask her why I hadn't made it. She reached for a
clipboard bulging with paper and leafed through the pages.

"Phyllis Nelson, hmmm." She kept leafing. "Here it is. They've
marked the box that says your sense of timing needs work. But you
did quite well otherwise." She looked up at me and eyed me as if I
were a new product at the grocery store. "You just might have a
chance next year if you can work on your rhythm somehow. See what
you can do."

I was so excited I wanted to leapfrog over the locker room
benches. Rhythm was the problem, not shyness, awkwardness, or my
undeveloped body. I could fix that in no time. I could already keep
four beats to the measure when I played the piano, I danced the
rumba with my father sometimes, and I could feel that rhythm beating inside me. I knew I had it. My rebel body was to blame the night
of tryouts, making me get out of step just slightly.

"Dear God," I beseeched again as I knelt by my bed to pray that
night. "If you'll help me with my rhythm, I promise I'll always and forever obey the Word of Wisdom. No tea, coffee, cigarettes, beer. I'll be
chaste, too, a pure vessel for thee, dear Lord." Then, as I snuggled
into the mattress, I vowed to discipline my knees and thighs and
arms so absolutely that there'd be no mistake next year.

.   .   .   .

April. Sophomore year. Now or never. I knew I had to steel my way
through this, not allow my body to rebel on me—my knees to shake,
my nose to shine. With my babysitting money, I bought a glue-like
deodorant to block all perspiration. I applied waterproof mascara
and eyeliner to make my eyes large and cat-like with techniques I'd

learned from my friend Ronnie Freed. I minimized my lips with a dark line drawn on by a new lipstick brush that clicked when the bristles came out and clicked when they went back inside. When the moon tried to talk to me and make me lose my concentration, I covered my ears with my hands.

And I kept my mother at bay. At the tryouts, I was like a Rototiller breaking up the soil, a disturbing machine determined to be noticed, determined to be a Las Vegas Rhythmette. Nothing else mattered.

In addition to the Saturday night dances, I'd stretched my legs into the splits all year to equip me with the highest kick, done 100 sit-ups a night for a flat stomach, repeated exercises to increase my bra size. I chanted "I must, I must" while I pressed the heels of my hands together and pumped. And I watched for any idiosyncratic disruptions of solid rhythm. My heart was calcified.

On the day the new Rhythmettes were to be announced, I stood tightly packed in the middle of the twenty finalists who waited behind the locker-room door, listening to the castanets of "Lady of Spain" while the senior Rhythmettes did their last routine for the student body of Las Vegas High School. When the applause ended, the seniors lined up in a row at the opposite end of the gym. A thin black microphone stand had been set in place.

The finalists were hidden behind the locker room's slightly open door. Some were clinging to Saint Christopher medals, some were checking their hair in the mirrors, some were mumbling silent prayers. But everyone was secretly anticipating the sound of her name sailing across the empty gym floor, floating over the heads of all the students crammed into the bleachers, her name spoken into the microphone loudly enough for everyone in Las Vegas High School to hear, a name to be reckoned with and remembered.

The announcements started from the short end of the Rhythmette line. The shortest senior walked toward the microphone. She was handed an envelope. She opened it. She read it. She spoke the name. Cheryl Henry screamed and almost tore off the door's hinges getting out to the gymnasium where the green-painted bleachers were filled to capacity. Through the crack in the door that had been pulled closed again, I watched Cheryl run across the gym floor, her arms wide open until she slammed into the arms of the senior Rhythmette who'd called her name. They hugged and jumped like mayflies.

The next senior stepped out of her place in the line and up to the microphone.

I can't remember what happened then because the sound of the next name was so alien to the sound of mine. "Nancy Atkinson!" My ears went numb, Arctic, and the whole room seemed a blizzard, with me huddling in animal skins, waiting for the cutter to break through the ice, throw a rope, and lift me. But I heard something through the storm's howling. Names being called. My name being called. Hands pushing me through the crowd.

"Phyllis, you made it."

I don't remember the trip across the gymnasium floor. I don't remember if people cheered or just clapped politely. After all, there were people out there who hadn't made the finals, people whose girlfriends hadn't made the finals, and here was I, Phyllis Nelson, a dark horse, walking, stumbling, running. I'd won. I'd controlled the elements, despite all the nattering from the moon.

I was slotted into place at the tall end of the line, and the music began. Squeezed between two other girls, shoulder to shoulder, I started across the floor. But a tiny moment of claustrophobia flashed through my head, so small I only remember it now. It had to do with eighteen dancing dolls and their choreography—always using the left foot to begin, turning their heads every eight counts, holding their shoulders back, tucking in their stomachs, smiling, always smiling as instructed by Miss Stuckey.

Crushed into my place in line and thinking in sets of four and measures of eight, I felt shut in for a brief second. What had I purchased? Another train ticket? For one small second I felt myself marching away from real rhythm where dancers threw themselves against the shadows of fire while the earth and the moon beat the drums. Real people howling at the moon, shaking their fists at the wind and the rain.

The new and the old Rhythmettes marched across the wooden floor. The line of girls was not the straight arrow line for which the Rhythmettes were famous, however. It rippled like water. We were Baby Rs, on our way to being grown-up and bounteous and leggy and ready for the grown-up world where our prancing legs would someday spread apart to make babies and birth babies or avoid babies or wonder why we couldn't have babies, all in accordance with the plan. We were being danced on our way by our hormones, by the mandate for procreation, by the rhythm of life, not knowing it was bigger than we were.

Dancing fools, me first among them, kicking headlong into our purpose on earth—to multiply and replenish. Miss Stuckey doing her part by preparing us with manners and stage presence, but really preparing us as gifts for the men who watched, men subject to their own hormones as we strutted and paraded across the stage, displaying our wares for them, the particular curve of our hips, the winning smiles.

The claustrophobia passed, however. I was one of the girls. A Las Vegas Rhythmette. I was somebody, and the football players and James Deans would have to reckon with me. I counted now.

The bright colors of the moment caught my attention, and I exalted in the fact that I, Phyllis Nelson, had arrived. God bless America. And the stars and the moon. Even my seminary teacher. It didn't matter when I overheard someone in the crowd filtering out of the gym saying, "How did Phyllis Nelson make it? She's so skinny. She walks like a primate."

And it didn't matter when my mother pretended to congratulate me. Her "Good for you, Phyllis," sounded hollow, echoing all the arguments we'd ever had about the importance of not getting sidetracked from God's work of being a lighted candle, virtuous, lovely, and of good report.

On that day in that time of my life, I could overlook all slights and forgive and bless everybody. I had arrived. I could dance up the stairway to the stars, clapping my hands and turning in synch with all the other women who were ever girls. I didn't know my mother didn't need to worry. I wasn't privy to what the moon already knew. There's no escaping rhythm.

I watched the New York Philharmonic as they gathered on the makeshift platform. Some of the musicians looked as if they could use a transfusion. They'd probably been out all night gambling and who knows what else. After all, they were in Las Vegas.

Even though I was disillusioned from my encounter with Lenny the night before, I was excited for his baton to start the music that was supposed to be purer than anything I'd ever heard. I sat with the Young Friends of the Symphony in the balcony tier of the convention center's round auditorium dressed in white gloves and a black velvet frock. We sat behind the orchestra, face to face with Leonard Bernstein, rubbernecking to get a good look at this God of the East and All Things Musical.

"Lenny's such a man," Mrs. Dickinson had told us the week before at the Young Friends of the Symphony meeting held in her living room. "He's such a lion," she added, almost growling as she spoke. She was the choral director at Las Vegas High School and the driving force behind the Young Friends.

"We've pulled off the greatest coup this side of the Mississippi!" She was backlit by an oriental lamp with a gathered fabric shade and was almost dancing in front of us thirty some high school students recruited from the marching band, orchestra, and choir at Las Vegas High School. We'd been promised an A for the term if we joined up. Not a bad deal, especially if we'd be cleansed of our cultural impurities as the choir director, Mrs. Dickinson, said we would.

The conductor, who had walked past me like a specter the night before, lifted his baton higher, but neither the noise nor the light in the convention hall was dying out. People were pointing, laughing, and turning every which way in their folding chairs. I imagined the audience had imprisoned the New York Philharmonic and herded them into the center of this Roman coliseum to play for their lives. For a minute, they seemed bigger lions than Lenny, waiting to devour him and the orchestra. They were dressed in everything from net shawls and red tuxedos to bell-bottoms with fringe sewn down the sides, bolo ties, leather vests, a few cowboy hats, peacock feathers poked in stiffly sprayed bouffants.

I had a good view of the tense muscles in his cheeks, the raptor eyes glowering as the raised baton failed to hush the unruly crowd. None of the woodwind players, string players, or percussionists were moving a muscle, totally attentive to their leader, but the audience wasn't following suit.

He lifted the baton even higher, trying to stand taller in his shiny patent-leather shoes, trying to subdue Las Vegas, if not with the tapered baton, then with the force of his imperial self.

The Young Friends of the Symphony had been trained when and when not to clap; we'd been taught to say "Bravo" if we especially liked the performance (though we all said "Brave-O" at the meeting to scare Mrs. Dickinson). We were all trying hard to sit at attention on the turquoise-colored cushions, our hands folded in our velvety laps, our attention riveted on the conductor. I was trying not to feel superior to those who didn't know symphony etiquette or to the technicians who'd left the overhead lights shining brilliantly on the conductor and his orchestra. This was the basketball crowd, after all.

Impatiently, Lenny's arms fell to his sides. He motioned to a man sitting on the front row dressed in a powder blue tuxedo who hustled to the stage pronto. The man's pleasant smile turned into panic as he listened to Bernstein's words. Then he hurried for the door. Lenny paced the stage like a caged animal until finally, the balcony lights dimmed. But those on the main floor did not.

As I watched like a spying angel from the balcony, a technician in a seaweed green jumpsuit moseyed up to the stage, mañana style. Lenny knelt at the platform's edge and pointed to the ceiling. The technician shook his head no, no way, you're out of luck, buddy. Then I watched The Lion turn on the technician, who seemed to grow smaller and smaller as the blast from the conductor melted his contours.

From her place on the front row, Mrs. Dickinson appeared between them, flapping her hands as if they were tiny wings. The technician backed away. The conductor dropped his fists to the sides of his cutaway jacket.

Meanwhile, the man in the powder blue tuxedo had climbed the stairs onto the platform, picked up the length of cord leading to the microphone, and was speaking into the public address system, "One, two. One, two. Testing," and an electronic scream pierced our ears.

After calming the storm, Mrs. Dickinson climbed the wobbly stairs carefully in her rhinestone-covered shoes, radiant in her strapless emerald green gown with a basket of black netting around the shoulders.

"Ladies and gentlemen," she said into the cavernously echoing microphone. "Ladies and gentlemen, please. Technical difficulties aside, we have some of the best musicians in the world here tonight who need to be treated with respect." She wagged her finger at the audience. "Let's show them Las Vegas knows its p's and q's." She patted the conductor sympathetically on the back and returned to her seat, and an uneasy quiet spread over the audience.

The first five minutes went well. The pastoral gamboling in Beethoven's Sixth settled the audience, and I closed my eyes to visions of woolly sheep grazing on uneven hills. But then, I became aware of small agitations beginning as if they were clothes in a washing machine window. Ring-covered fingers reaching, earrings sparkling, bow ties twitching, people leaning to whisper, a baby bouncing on its mother's knee, Brownie attachments flashing. A woman in the orchestra seats who hadn't removed her lynx coat or tinted glasses sent her maid through a pair of double doors. The maid wore a starched ruffle bobby-pinned to her hair and a short black dress which stopped short of her knobby knees. A few minutes later, she returned with a tray of popcorn and cellophane-covered Cokes in red cups. A small trickling of thirsty people followed suit, and the lights on the main floor showed everyone in high relief, every cough, every yawn, every pair of jaws chewing gum, every nodding head.

I pretended to be appalled by all this. I said "shhh" and sent death wishes loud enough for other Young Friends to hear. "They should be so ashamed," I whispered. But inside I was not totally sorry the conductor and the New York Philharmonic seemed to be drowning in the Vegas Valley Sea between the peaks of Sunrise and Mount Charleston.

. . . .

The following day, the day after the concert, I heard that Lenny said he'd never come back to Nevada: It was impossible to perform for such an audience; conditions were too difficult. But nowhere in any of the newspaper interviews did he mention that the Las Vegas Rhythmettes had welcomed him at the airport, or that the Young Friends of the Symphony had sat above him so appropriately, their young bodies molded from the desert sand and wind, sitting stiffly in black dresses, black suits, and white gloves to pay respect.

The breath of culture, given so briefly, was taken away suddenly. . . .

But Lenny, you didn't have to leave in a huff. Didn't you notice the Young Friends of the Symphony? We tried, Lenny. And I was prepared. I learned complicated rhythms and studied scales. I had three piano teachers.

You couldn't see, Lenny. I am music; the desert is music, too. You decided too soon. Your judgment was swift, and maybe, just maybe, it was wrong. Lenny, Lenny, why didn't you notice?

. . . .

If you've ever been to Las Vegas, you've been to Fremont Street. You may not have noticed the street itself because of the thousands of persistently flashing lights that confuse night and day and make you think you've arrived at the palace of the end of the world. But it's there beneath the speedway light bulbs racing off and on and inviting you inside for a game of roulette, craps, or keno.

Fremont Street. I can't think of it as a street, actually. There's always the shine of light on its surface as if it were patent leather. Maybe it isn't a street, but a way into a world where you can't close your mouth, or into a cave where you find the wizard who'll teach you all you need to know about escaping.

When I was there, Fremont Street seduced me with the mystery of the shifting bodies on its surface—winos, losers, Nellis Air Force Base flyboys who sometimes whistled at me, big-time spenders looking for the next game. It seduced me with the sound of money, with the blaring clothes people wore, with the possibility of dying my hair champagne pink and gluing rhinestones to my forehead.

The street was a temptress, leading to wide doors where guards said, "No, you can't come in here." But the doors weren't doors, they were giant sucking machines inside of which money fell into slot machine trays, stacks of chips grew tall and short on green felt tables, and men with I-know-the-world-and-everything-about-it-and-you-can't-faze-me expressions were dressed in green aprons, their faces pointed like foxes.

Protected by the seagull-wing fins of a '59 Chevy, my friends Karen, Cheryl, and I dragged Fremont street on warm nights, the windows rolled down, all of us craning our necks to see something to gasp about. Carloads full of teenagers, tourists, and flyboys cruised the street to the Union Pacific station, turned around, cruised back. Up and down Fremont.

Sometimes flyboys would yell at us: "Hey, baby, what's happening?" Karen gunned her engine to say we weren't interested. We wanted something else from Fremont Street—a genie to puff out of a light bulb, casino doors to vacuum us inside before we could protest, the golden nugget on the neon sign to fall and make a crater on the hood of Karen's Chevy.

But the street, as animated as it seemed when we drove or walked on its surface, was only a street after all. It couldn't give anything to anyone. It could only lie in the sand and let pass what would. We were only another moving molecule on Fremont Street—into its brightness, out of its brightness.

When we drove onto the side streets and away from Fremont, we saw the backside of the casinos sagging under the weight of millions of light bulbs screwed into their sockets, the buildings with nothing but alleys and shadows behind them. And behind those shadows were even darker streets where the shapes of our everyday houses waited for us. Only the moon, the dim streetlights, and Karen's head-lights illuminated the pathway to our own front doors.

The lower end of Fremont Street wasn't far from the high school, one block away. At lunchtime, when the air was throbbing with cheap sunlight, Cheryl, Karen, and I descended the stairs of the pink-stuccoed high school and tripped down the sidewalks in our C. H. Baker pointed shoes (pink, baby blue, orange, avocado, pur-ple, and chartreuse for $8.99 a pair—whatever matched our out-fits). We passed the girls and boys gathered into an elite knot on the front lawn, making our usual comments about the girls in their cashmere sweaters beaded with tubular glass, their wool tartan skirts with jewels embedded in brown squares. No one seemed to notice our departure. We crossed Bridger Street and walked past apartments with drawn shades where night people waited for blood to return to their heads.

Once a month, we saved our money for lunch at the El Cortez, a hotel on Fremont Street. It was a second cousin to the casinos nearer the depot, but we felt big time as we ordered open-faced turkey sandwiches from a waitress in a thigh-length wench cos-tume, two-thirds of her breasts rising like yeast below her lifeless face.

I crunched my kosher dill and laughed with Cheryl and Karen about how, when we got rich, we'd rent a helicopter and Elvis and land on the front lawn of the high school and see who was elite then. We'd buy angora sweaters and a Cadillac convertible and maybe a miniature poodle with a diamond collar for the back seat. We'd buy matching felt skirts with pink poodles prancing across the hemline.

Even as we talked, I could hear the handles of slot machines in the other room being pulled and pulled and pulled. I wondered where the money came from, even considered the possibility of the machines incubating their own coins and giving birth to the money, money, money while lights flashed and bells rang.

For some reason, though, I knew this money could never be mine, even if I had a truckload of coins to spend and pulled the same machine's handle all night long. It would be devoured again and again, the nickels and dimes and quarters food for the hungry slot machines rather than extra cash for Phyllis.

It seemed to me, as I cut into the turkey on my open-faced sandwich with my water-stained knife, that somewhere, in some great sky, someone had chosen the lucky and the unlucky, the winners and the losers. Luck wasn't granted because someone needed or deserved it, or I'd be the luckiest one alive. I deserved a boyfriend, a nomination for Homecoming Queen, even a few curves in my body, after all. But I hadn't been chosen. Someone must have made some decisions even before Fremont Street was laid in a straight line on the desert, before bricks were stacked or boards were nailed into casinos.

As much as I wanted a helicopter with Elvis on board, a gold Cadillac, and a chance to prove myself to the students who ruled the front lawn of the high school, I knew the money in the other room would never be mine. It belonged to Fremont Street and to the lucky. I'd have to get what I wanted in some other way, maybe from God if I kept saying my prayers every night before bedtime.

In May, the town celebrated Helldorado Days. There were a kangaroo court, a full-fledged carnival, and major parades on Fremont Street. Local businesses sponsored floats; the veterans marched in ranks; the schools sent their drum majors, majorettes, and marching bands with glockenspiels to compete for first place; and the horsey people blanketed their mounts in thousands of pounds of silver tack and waved to everyone, even as their horses plopped road apples on Fremont. When Budweiser Beer Clydesdales pranced in front of us, their heavy, white-feathered legs clopping on the street, we clapped and cheered from the sidelines, but mostly because someone or something would soon step into their huge mounds of fresh-steaming, green manure.

Because of Helldorado, I had a chance for Fremont Street to give something back to me—a chance to be noticed by the clique on the front lawn as well as the people of the town, a chance to ride high above the pavement in the light of full day, not overshadowed by the blinking lights and the sound of money. I'd already marched with the Las Vegas High School Rhythmettes in last year's Oldtimers' Parade and kicked my share of road apples to the side. But that wasn't enough. I'd never quite felt noticed.

Miss Stuckey received telephone calls almost daily with requests for a Rhythmette to appear on television, have a picture taken with the mayor, model for a local fashion show, serve as hostess for a Rotary wives' tea. Everyone in the community seemed anxious to show support for the youth of Nevada.

"I received a call this morning," she said as I exited the shower in the girls' locker room. I was dripping water on the minuscule tiles. "It was from the executive secretary of one of the casinos on Fremont Street. The owner wants to have one of the senior Rhythmettes be the queen of his hotel's float for the Beauty Parade. They're going to use real flowers, even for the queen's costume. Would you be interested?"

I almost dropped my towel when I realized how big the door was that was opening before me. A queen. No one had ever asked or nominated or elected me for such a thing. *Queen*, I said to myself as I continued to drip on the tiny tiles. *Queen Phyllis*.

I'd watched "Queen for a Day" on television; I'd seen young women crowned for Miss this and that; I'd read about chorus girls being past queens of cities and counties. I liked the idea of Queen Phyllis, even for one float for one day of the year.

"I'd like that," I told Miss Stuckey.

"All right," she said. "The secretary said to be at the casino for a fitting this afternoon. Go over there after school, and take the stairs next to the roulette wheel. If a security guard stops you, tell him you're on your way to the administrative offices. It's at the top of the stairs. And the parade is two weeks from Sunday."

Sunday, I suddenly realized, panic tightening my lungs. I pulled the towel more tightly around myself. *The parade was on Sunday. My parents! The day of rest. The Lord's day.* My stomach clenched. My forehead perspired. Here was good versus evil again, set on a table before me, waiting to be examined: a good Mormon girl's joy comes from obedience to commandments versus Phyllis Nelson's chance to be queen.

As I walked down the narrow passage between the hardwood bench lined with smelly sneakers and other girls dressing in front of their marine green lockers, I felt the old feeling of being bumped to the outside of life. So often I'd stood apart while I longed to wander from the tight circle of the righteous just once. This time it was only to ride on the top of a float in the bosom of flowers and crepe paper and tinsel. A queen on the float gliding above the crowd cheering for the late, but lovely, bloomer as she passed. The queen.

But never on Sunday.

I turned to see if I could catch Miss Stuckey's attention and tell her I'd forgotten something important I had to do on that Sunday, but she'd gone back to her tiny office covered with newspaper clippings of the Rhythmettes marching at the Pikes Peak Rodeo and the Pendleton Round-up, smiling their thousand-tooth smiles for the cameras, their page-boy hairstyles glistening with highlights. "My babies," she called the Rhythmettes. She herded us like fine sheep, watched whom we dated, checked our grades every term, told us to stand up straight, told us to be proud of ourselves as not everyone was able to make the marks required to be a Las Vegas High School Rhythmette. She'd turned her sweatshirted back to me and was busy examining a schedule on her clipboard. What could I say to her anyway? I'd already said yes.

Why did it always have to come to this? I wondered as I towelled

the last water from my calves and the arches of my feet. I only
wanted to ride on a float in the open air and sunshine and wave to
the people, to be dressed in flowers which were one of God's most
beautiful creations, to make my mark on Fremont Street. I wouldn't
be fornicating or lying. I wouldn't be taking the Lord's name in vain.
But I wouldn't be honoring my father and mother, either. They
wanted me to keep the Sabbath day holy and follow the commandments given to Moses, then to the Israelites, then to us. I needed to
obey if I wanted to find my way back to God.

Please, God, I prayed as I pulled my brassiere off the hook in my
locker. Please, God. Understand about this. I hooked my bra together, then
climbed into my underpants labeled Wednesday. You're the King. I only
want to be queen for a few minutes. Have a heart. You wouldn't mind just this
once, would you?

I could hear water dripping in the shower stall and the echo of the
solitary drops, one by one, hitting the tile, splashing the floor, the
sharp sound of water working its way through the tile, wearing it
down in the course of time. Time was so long. If I was only one drop
of water to God in one split second of time, what would it matter if I
rode on a float down Fremont Street? One small ride didn't have
anything to do with God.

The casino was one of the biggest. I recognized the owner's picture,
bigger than life, in the lobby, a shiny black and white of him with his
arm around his son, Ted, who went to the high school and was already an alcoholic, though a desirable one—lots of black, curly hair,
a king of hearts smile. I hoped I wouldn't run into Ted because he
might tell his father he'd chosen the wrong girl to ride on his float, a
girl outside the knot that owned the front lawn of the high school.
He'd say his father should have done more checking rather than
trust Miss Stuckey. Luckily, he was nowhere in sight. Neither was his
father. The secretary smiled, her eyes peeking out of cat-eye rhinestone rims.

"You must be Phyllis Nelson," she said, pursing her lips and tipping her head slightly as if to say, "How cute you little high school girls are, and isn't this casino wonderful to care about our city's homegrown?" She tugged at the string connecting her glasses to her neck.

"Come this way, and I'll take you to Mrs. Rubinstein. She'll fit you for the costume." When she rolled her chair back and stood up next to me, she looked surprised. "My, you're one of the tall ones, aren't you?"

"I'm on the tall end of the line, yes."

"And you're rather thin, too," she glanced back at me nervously as she opened the office door. "Well, follow me. Mrs. Rubinstein knows how to fix anything."

She walked down a long hall with marbled carpet—browns, golds, oranges, rusts, swirling in the hallway. She swayed when she walked, her buttocks sharply accenting each step, her high heels sinking into the cushioned carpet and leaning to the insides. She stopped to rub her finger on one of the hall light fixtures. "Dusty," she said. We walked and walked, up stairs and down stairs, each step feeling heavier to me. What was I doing here? Why was I following this woman down long halls? Where was she leading me? And each step became burdened with the argument again.

"You only want temporal pleasures," one side of me said.

"You want to keep me from having any fun," the other said back.

"It's such a puny thing," side one said, "to be a queen on a float. That that should be more important to you than keeping God's commandments says more about you than I'd like to hear."

"Why shouldn't I be a queen? Who am I hurting? Absolutely nobody."

"Except yourself," said side one.

"Give me a break!"

"This way," the secretary said as she opened a door marked wardrobe. "Mrs. Rubinstein will take care of you." She patted my arm as I passed through the door, then held onto the inside and outside doorknobs, leaned back, and scrutinized me one last time. "Mrs. Rubinstein, this is Phyllis Nelson for the Beauty Parade float. You'll know just what to do, I'm sure. She's one of the Rhythmettes, you know—the ones you see in the newspapers all the time. Have fun in the flowers, honey." She closed the door.

I turned to look at Mrs. Rubinstein, who was a marked contrast from the rest of the hotel. She was small, her hair pulled severely to the nape of her neck and secured in a bun. She wore pince-nez and looked at me over the tops of them. Her lips were colored a slight coral, but she wore nothing more on her face. She looked both very young and very old in her transparent long-sleeved blouse of white nylon. Underneath the fabric, two obvious straps dug into her shoulders, pulled tight by heavy breasts and a slightly round stomach. As Mrs. Rubinstein hunched over gathered fabric and leaned close into her work, she reminded me of a leaf turning colors under the autumn sun, slightly brown at the edges, yet still a vibrant gold in the center. Something about the gold made me say what I said, the words out of my mouth before I even thought them.

"I love God," I said before she had a chance to say anything.

Without looking up, she gathered her eyebrows together, then opened her basket of thread, needles, thimbles, and tapes. "Good for you, dear." She narrowed her eyes even further, raised her head, and looked intensely through rather than at me, no words. Then, re-membering our business, she picked up a small green notepad.

"What is your waist size?" she asked. "Hips? Bust? Hat size?" She wrote on the green pad and measured the questions I couldn't an-swer. And while she slid the tape around my hips and breasts, I promised myself I'd pray the whole time I'd be riding on the float. I'd think about God and his sunshine and his people all the time I rolled down Fremont Street. I'd light my candle for him, and my smile would be filled with his grace. When people looked up at me, they'd see God's essence, not Phyllis Nelson dressed as a float queen. If I wasn't actually on the float, it would be okay if I was there.

"We'll beef up your chest," she said. "God didn't give you much in the way of breasts, did he?" She reached into a drawer and pulled out two sizes of foam pads. She put one size over one of my breasts, then the other, and as she did, I noticed the pale blue numbers slipping out from under the lace at her wrist.

"We'll use the thickest one," she said, and made notes to herself on the pad. "And I want you to come in at twelve o'clock on the day of the parade. Our makeup artist can give you some glamour, bring out the beauty in your face, fix your hair to show off your features. You shouldn't let it hang in your eyes, dear. We'll make you into a first-class beauty. False eyelashes, pluck the eyebrows, plump up the chest. You'll be a beautiful queen in a raiment of flowers. Do you like the idea of being dressed in flowers? Novel, isn't it?"

I wanted to talk to Mrs. Rubinstein. I wanted to forget about the flowers and ask about the numbers. I wanted her to tell me about those people—how they put the numbers there and if they hurt her, or if they pushed her if she stepped out of line, or if they ever stopped to notice she was God's child.

"Were you my age?" I pointed to the numbers on her wrist.

She looked directly into my eyes, and I saw large slivers of time— fierce, sad, dank—and I knew she'd never worried about riding on a float down Fremont Street or whether she was a queen or not, except when the nights were long and she shivered under a thin blanket and called out to God, who didn't hear her. Maybe she wondered if there was any love at all, not the least bit concerned with the kind of love that would ask to be honored as a queen.

"So you love God, do you?" she said.

"Yes, I do," but then I suddenly saw the power of God staring out of her eyes, a bigger God than I'd ever seen before: a God so magnificent he was all the flowers in the world at the same time, a God so frightening he was all the withered flowers in the world. And then she sat down and lifted her needle, its thread, the amorphous blue metallic fabric onto her lap. She leaned back over her work as if I'd already left the room. I started to say something, but there were no words left between us.

As I walked over the swirling carpet, I knew I didn't have to ride down Fremont in a car, on a float, or even in a taxi. I'd telephone

Karen. I'd ask her to take my place. She'd be overjoyed to be the queen, just as I had been.

Fremont Street. I walked along its sidewalks in the late afternoon on my way to the bus stop. Shadows from the casinos across the street touched the curb next to my feet. They were long shadows of buildings housing treasures that were part of my wishes by day and my dreams at night.

But I'd been behind these buildings; I knew they were made of regular things like bricks, glass, stone, and clay, even though they were camouflaged by the lights and their storehouses of games, diversions, machines that seemed to manufacture money, tables where the lucky became rich, rich, rich when their hands curled around a stack of chips.

But as I walked along the concrete sidewalk lining Fremont Street, I imagined tables surrounded by men with slicked-back hair, standing at the tables forever until they were covered with cobwebs and their pointed fox faces stiffened with frost. Yet they still rolled the dice to decide who would be lucky or unlucky, who would win or who would lose, even though they suspected the decision was made before dice were invented.

If you've ever been to Las Vegas, you've been to Fremont Street. You've seen the flashing lights that hide the simple lines of the asphalt street, the fact that the street begins and then ends, the fact that no one ever stays there. You know it's only a street to walk on until you reach the doors that open in, then open out again. You know it's a black ribbon of asphalt rolled out on the desert floor until it passes through a bouquet of brilliant flowering lights which attract the honeybees and you and me. You sniff its scent, want to hold it in your nostrils like cigarette smoke.

But you know you're walking into a daylily in reverse, still open at night, inviting you to sniff its perfume. And you know when a flower never closes, it isn't a flower. It's only Fremont Street.

Alan Richman

·······························

Lost Vegas

Seen the show?" Ash Resnick asked. I was just off a flight from Fort Carson, still in uniform, and didn't know what show he was talking about. Resnick, who is in charge of gambling operations at Caesars Palace in Las Vegas, grabbed my arm and propelled me from the lobby to the show room, where he told the maître d' to seat me next to the stage.

The guy blanched. This was Thanksgiving of 1968, the week of Frank Sinatra's comeback to Vegas after the famous punch-out at the Sands. Dean Martin couldn't have gotten a table near the stage.

☞ From Gentlemen's Quarterly, November 1992.

Why me? Because I knew somebody who knew Ash, and that's the way Vegas worked back then. When I told my mother I was going to Vegas before my tour in Vietnam, she insisted I write Ash, a child-hood friend of hers. His reply was terse. He told me to page him at Caesars when I arrived. Ash never talked a lot, and he wrote even less.

For the next three days, Resnick treated me like a member of the family (albeit one he wasn't talking to). His wife, Marilyn, lent me her pink Grand Prix. Everything I did was with his family, and when it wasn't, it was on the house. Ash "had the pencil," the power to comp anything to anybody.

My last night in Vegas, he told me to go to the Stardust and ask for Al, a pit boss at the craps tables. He would take me into the *Lido de Paris* review. I valet-parked the pink Pontiac, asked for Al. Out strode a monster, the kind of guy who amuses himself by crushing dice with his teeth.

"Waddaya want?" he snarled.

I kind of wanted to still be in uniform. And carrying an M-79.

"Uh, Ash sent me."

Al beamed, not a picturesque sight.

"How many in your party?" he said, suddenly, sounding like Alistair Cooke.

"Just me."

"You mean Ash didn't get you a girl?"

I mumbled something about Ash, my mother and family values.

Al beamed again, this time with malicious intent. "Wait till I talk to Ash about this," he said.

He took me into the show. Front row of course. Afterward, I returned to Caesars, where I heard myself paged.

It was Ash. Al had called.

He handed me a key, said I should go on up to the room, she'd be along soon. It was the night I learned what I'd be fighting for.

❧   ❧   ❧

Almost a quarter-century later, I'm back at Caesars, still the classiest hotel in the city. My room's great. I've got a Jacuzzi with marble steps and gilded handles. I've got a mirror over my bed. A woman, I haven't got.

I don't know what's more depressing, bathing by yourself in a Jacuzzi or sleeping by yourself in a bed with a mirror over it. Jean Harlow's husband killed himself in a bed like this. I guess that's the answer.

I've spoken to one woman, a cocktail waitress. She liked me, hinted that I could see her after work. She was 51 years old, been here since '64, her feet were killing her, she had to work in a miniskirt, and the slot players were giving her 25-cent tips. She wanted to show me snapshots of her grandkids.

I stood in line behind some very attractive young women. They were unescorted. Also, they were about 12. They were in line for pizza slices at Caesars' fast-food court.

After that, I turned in.

It was kind of early to be in bed, not even 10 P.M., but I didn't know what else to do. I'd been thinking of taking in a show, but everyplace I looked there was a magic act. I remember a few years ago, you came to Vegas, the only thing you wanted to see disappear was the broad you woke up next to in the morning. Now, there's the "Prince of Magic" Kirby Vanburch, the "World Champion Magician" Lance Burton and, of course, Siegfried and Roy and their white tigers. I saw the white tigers. They're behind glass at the Mirage, doing what tigers do behind glass. Nothing.

The lounges, the ones that had Shecky Greene and Louis Prima and Don Rickles, are gone, swallowed up by video poker and slot arcades. I stopped at the Galleria Bar at Caesars, the one they used to call the Gonorrhea Bar because so many hookers hung out there. I didn't see any women, but they do serve complimentary hand-carved roast-beef sandwiches at happy hour that look pretty good.

The Strip has changed. It's got an amusement park for kids called Wet 'n Wild and a new cinder-block hotel, the Excalibur, 4,000 rooms and booked solid every day, maybe eleven kids to a room. I looked in, my eyes hurt from the purples: The decorator had to have been a prepubescent on a sugar rush.

No reason to get up early. Used to be nice, Vegas asleep, take a walk in the desert. Now, there are more than 800,000 residents, a yellow haze of smog dims everything, and radio stations have morning men chortling over traffic reports: "Tim, it's getting busier and busier. Backed up almost from the Strip to I-15. There's no escaping it this morning!"

Rush hour in the Mojave?

Don't misunderstand me. Vegas is a great place. Why, a man could live here and buff his gas grill and raise a family and never have any reason to regret that it's not what it used to be. I'm just wistful, is all.

"We had this thing called the Bed Toss at Circus Circus. That was back when the hotel first opened, and it was a kind of adult Disneyland. It was wild—you'd be shooting craps, some crazy bastard, an acrobat, would dive out of the ceiling at you. He was Jumpin' Joe Gerlach. We had an old-fashioned peep show. For a quarter, you'd see real naked girls. With the Bed Toss, we had two red satin beds, a round target over each bed. In the beds were two great, big, zaftig blondes in G-strings, laying there, covered. They were killers. You'd throw a softball, if you hit the target, they were thrown out of bed. They'd dance naked for you and go back to bed. These two broads were unreal.

"One of them had something going on with Jack Entratter, the president of the Sands, one of the real early pioneers, a very beloved guy with freaky sexual tendencies. Ted Kennedy was in town, speaking at the Sands at this $100-a-plate dinner, campaigning for Nevada Senator Howard Cannon. Peter Lawford, the whole Rat Pack, all hung out at the Sands, that was the connection to the Kennedys, how Jack Entratter became their friend. Jack called me, said, 'Doing any business at the Bed Toss?' It was a slow night. He said, 'Create any problem if you shut it down?' This was eleven or twelve o'clock. I said, 'No problem.' It wasn't a bad idea to do a favor for Jack Entratter, to have him in your debt. I shut *down, let the girls go, told them Jack would be calling. They said, 'What does he want with us?' I said, 'How would I know, I'm not your fuckin' social secretary.'*

"The next day, they came back, they said they had to tell me this. They said, 'You know what we did? We fucked Teddy Kennedy all night long.' I said, 'You're full of shit, nobody could fuck you two all night long, you'd kill two men and a boy.' They described him perfectly, and they didn't know politics from a polo shirt. They said he had to sit down every once in a while, put cold towels on his back— it was right after Teddy's plane went down. They said outside of his pain he could go all night. These two blondes were dumb as posts, they couldn't have made it up."

—a former Circus Circus executive on Ted Kennedy's
1964 visit to Las Vegas

Vegas never had a chance, not in America, the land of moral cleansing. Once a prodigious sanctuary of greed, indulgence, materialism and victimless crime, Vegas was doomed from the day Bugsy Siegel, who built the Fabulous Flamingo, started bragging about what a good time everybody was going to have. A town like Vegas ends up becoming a family-destination resort or it dies.

There's an argument, a reasonable one, that Vegas has never been better. Tourism has almost doubled in the past decade, to more than 20 million visitors a year. Gambling revenues are approaching $5 billion a year. If the city has also become a place where you can buy a house, raise a family and attend an Elks Club social without wondering whether the guy next to you is packing, what's so terrible about that?

Newcomers swear it's the greatest place to live the world has ever seen. Old-timers—anybody here before the Seventies—agree. And then they tell you how much better it used to be. "I want the town the way it was, but the worst thing that can happen to people is an inability to adjust," says Wayne Newton, the city's most revered entertainer, a showman who lives in the city and works twenty weeks a year at the Las Vegas Hilton.

Vegas is now the fastest-growing city in the nation and shows no signs of slowing, not with Howard Hughes's Summa Corporation turning 23,000 acres of desert—*that's thirty-nine square miles*—into a "planned, mixed-use community." Vegas has more than three dozen tanning salons—*yes, tanning salons in the desert!* It has artificial lakes that provide excellent recreational opportunities—*yes, paddleboats in the desert!* MGM is building a theme park, George Lucas is designing the special effects for a new hotel, and a people-moving magnetic-levitation train is in the works. It's the Disneyland Virus. There's no known cure.

More than anything else, what changed Vegas was righteous indignation. I've heard all the other theories: Howard Hughes and the Justice Department chased out the mobsters. Baccarat, an oddly addictive card game, broke the high rollers. AIDS ended the era of the hooker. The new, oversized hotels can only be filled by van-sized families. It all makes sense, but none of it is correct. America resented Las Vegas, couldn't tolerate it. Newton remembers that back in 1975, Dick Clark suggested to him that they buy a Las Vegas TV station together, then backed out after his advisers warned him that Vegas wasn't going to last. They were right, of course. It didn't, not the Vegas of memory.

The Las Vegas of the Fifties and Sixties was a small town. It would be years before residents, consumed by water lust, would baptize their planned communities with nonsensical names like Crystal Cove, Desert Shore and Rip Tide. The weather was dry, as yet untainted by artificial lakes and the ornate fountains that now spout everywhere. It was one of those mythical places where front doors were left unlocked, and there were more churches per capita than anywhere else in America. Wayne Newton had not yet declared bankruptcy, and who could have imagined he ever would?

There was more than that, of course. There was a sense of family, and if some of that was courtesy of the guys whose nicknames spoke of the unique ways in which they hurt people, well, Vegas was never a town to begrudge a man his past. Anyway, you didn't see much of fellows like Charlie "Trigger Happy" Fischetti, Jake "Greasy Thumb" Guzik and Tony "Joe Batters" Accardo, the bosses of the Capone gang in the Fifties, or of Icepick Willie Alderman, a part owner of the Flamingo. Guys like that sent more-polished cronies to look after hotel and casino interests, and while these envoys occasionally demonstrated their breeding by pistol-whipping a colleague, at least that sort of behavior was kept among themselves. Perhaps they were more than a little paranoid—Newton says he's walked through secret escape tunnels built under some of the older hotels—but you couldn't expect them to adjust to newfound gentility all at once. The city grew surprisingly fond of its gentrified hoodlums, and today this era of alleged Mob benevolence is recalled with tremendous affection.

"The people I suspect might have been involved in organized crime, from Moe Dalitz down the line, I was never treated in any but a nice way by them," Newton says. "If anything, I miss them."

Nobody deplores the passing of the old days more than Chicago Ray Lenobel, who got into the fur business in the Thirties and still runs a fur salon in the Dunes with his wife, Anna Nateece. His showroom is timelessly modern, with beige carpeting and chrome-and-glass tables. If Las Vegas furs by Anna Nateece are no longer compatible, it is not because Ray and Anna have slipped. It is because the city has let them down.

Let me tell you how bad the fur business has become: When I stop in to see Ray, he tries to sell *me* a coat. It's a good deal, too—$9,000 for a lynx.

Once, he was furrier to Liberace. He put Mr. Showmanship in Anna's most-dazzling creations: a Russian-lynx coat with hand-sewn rhinestones that would cost a million today, a sequined mink made from 400 skins. "He'd open the coats, blind people," Ray says. He sold his furs to Adnan Khashoggi, who once bought a $300,000 bedspread, and to Mike Tyson, who spent about $2 million at the shop. It's easy to tell, though, that his fondest memories are of the Mob guys, maybe because his sweetheart a long time ago was the daughter of a cousin of Al Capone's.

He was 16 when he started in furs, and it wasn't long before he ingratiated himself with the Chicago Mob by attending "every Italian wedding, every Italian funeral—when one of their own died, the bosses would come in, not the Mustache Petes but the Lucky Lucianos." At a time when every mobster had a wife at home who demanded nothing and a dame on the side who demanded everything, Lenobel quickly established himself as a necessary resource. "They liked me,"he says. "I kept no books. They'd call me up, say 'Virginia's coming in, go up to twenty-five.' That meant Virginia Hill got a $25,000 coat. A week later, somebody would come in, hand me the money. Their word was their bond. Unless they got killed, I got paid."

In 1953, he opened a shop in the Sands, the great Vegas hotel of that decade. There isn't a man of that era he doesn't speak well of, except for Howard Hughes, whom he calls "a skinflint." As the years passed, business only got better. "One girl at Caesars Palace, a cocktail waitress working the baccarat tables, she got seventeen coats in one season. She had femme-fatale looks," he says.

Lenobel sits down heavily, a big, shambling man in his early seventies who remembers the past with uncritical fondness. Today . . . well, he doesn't really like to talk much about today. It's understandable.

"Today, we got old ladies in gym shoes playing nickel slot machines. They come in, ask me if our furs are real."

Slot players.

"When we opened," he says, "the slot player was considered a worm."

The slot player is everything now. Video-poker machines are encroaching on casinos like some creeping alien body-snatching menace. Megabucks and Quartermania jackpots generate the kind of frenzy formerly indigenous to high stakes craps games. Slot players, once categorized as bloodless men or insignificant women, now account for well over half of all casino profits. Nobody has ever seen a slot player in an Anna Nateece fur.

Ray sighs. "I don't know how much longer I can hold out."

"When I first started dealing, in the late Seventies, early Eighties, the Mexican play was a monster. We're talking sixty Mexicans at one time, with $50,000 to

$100,000 *apiece, all of them at the Dunes, all of them playing baccarat. For Mexicans, it became the national game. They loved to banter with you, and they were good tippers. With the Mexicans you'd say 'Uno puesta para muchachos'—'Put a bet up for the boys.' If you had blond hair, blue eyes and spoke Spanish, they thought you were all right.*

"They'd all play, and they'd all stay until they lost it all. There seemed to be a basic pattern: Thursday night, they'd beat the casino for a half-million. Friday night, they'd beat the casino for a couple hundred thousand. Saturday night, the casino would get back $2 million. On Sunday, they all drank Cordon Bleu and lost the rest. If any of them were still there on Monday or Tuesday, it meant they had won on the weekend, still had money, and they were going to stay until they lost it all."

—Larry Gentry, baccarat dealer at the Riviera

High rollers are not like you and me. In fact, they want nothing to do with you and me. More and more, Vegas is becoming a segregated city, keeping the "haves" from the "have children."

The top floors of hotels, the ones with the gaudy high-roller suites, are usually accessible only with special keys. After major events, such as the Evander Holyfield–Larry Holmes heavyweight-championship fight at Caesars, areas with high-limit tables are monitored, and people who stop to gawk are asked (politely) to move along. Baccarat games are almost always isolated from the rest of the casino floor by velvet ropes.

The days when you could see a $500-minimum craps game in progress are gone. High rollers have almost vanished from sight, although Gentry insists that they're out there. He tells me about some baccarat dealers at the Tropicana who divided up a pool of about $800,000 in tips—$32,000 apiece. Two of the biggest gamblers in the world were playing at the same time, one of them Japanese, the other Australian, each putting up $500 for the dealers on every hand.

Assured of the existence of high rollers (now more commonly called "whales"), I go looking for them. I don't bother with the places where ordinary visitors gamble, the casino common. High rollers do not enjoy mingling with $2 blackjack players and slot players holding plastic cups filled with quarters. I set out to find the semiprivate gaming areas that some casinos utilize. These areas would be totally private except that state laws forbid it.

I start my search at the Mirage, which goes to extraordinary efforts to provide privacy for its high rollers, offering them their own gardens, swimming pools and putting greens. While striding across the casino floor, I spot an unmarked door with a sentry standing outside.

"Can I help you?" he asks.

"I'd like to go in," I say.

"It's for high rollers," he replies.

"What's that?"

"High limit."

"Well," I say, "can I go in?"

He nods, since to do otherwise would have been against the law. Behind the thick door and the heavy curtains is a mini-Versailles, posh and almost noiseless. One of the two rooms has a roulette wheel, a blackjack table, three baccarat tables and a small sitting area with flowers and silken chairs. The second, smaller room is set up for a dinner party. The long, polished wood table has gilded chairs of red brocade. The chafing dishes are silver. A wine, already uncorked, is ready to pour. Vegas hotels have traditionally served wines of impressive name and bad vintage to their high rollers, correctly assuming the gamblers might recognize the first but would have no idea of the second. Tonight's selection is Chateau Margaux 1984, a first-growth Bordeaux from a mediocre year.

As I walk through the rooms, my every step is tracked by a nervous floor supervisor. I don't know what harm he thinks I'd do, since the room is empty of gamblers. He's noticeably relieved when I leave.

At Caesars Palace, my next stop, the equivalent room is located on a discreet, semiprivate floor, near the Palace Court, the French restaurant. The room is not in use.

I try the Riviera, where Sinatra is performing. I have heard tales of the singer's legendary appeal to high rollers. In years past, he attracted so much action that money boxes, ordinarily emptied at the end of each shift, overflowed and had to be changed during shifts. In those days, Sinatra liked to hang around the casino after his second show, sometimes stepping behind a blackjack table, dealing cards and paying off every hand (with the casino's money, of course). Later in the evening, when the kid came by the lounge with the morning papers, Sinatra would sell the papers and let the kid sing.

When I look in at the Riviera baccarat tables after a Sinatra show, the action is modest, the chips mostly black ($100), the singer nowhere to be seen.

I hear mixed reports on the health of the high roller. Casino executives tell me they are more plentiful than ever and the perks offered them better than ever: lavish rooms, extravagant meals, limousines, Learjets.

From others, though, I hear that the devaluation of the peso has ruined the Mexican business, the decline of oil prices has devastated the Texas business, a federal law requiring anyone gambling more than $10,000 a day to show identification has ended the money-laundering business, and setbacks in the Japanese stock market have hurt the Asian business—notwithstanding reports that Ken Mizuno, a Japanese businessman and golf-course mogul, lost $60 million playing baccarat from 1989 to 1991.

One thing has not changed. I never hear of any female high rollers, and I presume they do not exist. I don't even know if they would be welcome. In Vegas, women have never been thought of as gamblers. They have always been something else.

"One night, between shows at the Aladdin, Eddie Torres said he wanted to talk with me. He had originally come out to Las Vegas with the guys who ran the Sands. Now he was my partner. We owned the Aladdin for a while. He was in the lounge. When I came in, he was glaring.

" 'I fixed them,' he said.

" 'Fixed who?' I asked.

" 'The hookers, the ones at the bar.'

" 'How did you fix them?'

" 'The barstools,' he said. 'I had a screw put in the barstools so they wouldn't swivel. Now they can't turn around and look.'

"I just looked at him. He didn't like hookers' staring at men in the lounge. It always amazed me, the things that occupied their minds. He was so proud of what he had done, as though he had built the second Boulder Dam."

—Wayne Newton

The swimming pools are the giveaways. They're filled with kids.

Swimming pools aren't supposed to be for kids, not Vegas pools. In Vegas, the pools were where you met women or, more accurately, where the women who wanted to be met found you. A grown man in Vegas didn't go to a hotel pool to swim.

You don't meet women at pools or bars or on the street anymore. George Knapp, a former TV reporter, recalls that "the hookers were so brazen eight or nine years ago, they'd accost men walking with their wives and girlfriends." Now, they're gone, chased away by a Clark County sheriff who does not condone prostitution. Who voted for this guy?

The dream of every unaccompanied male visitor is to meet a show girl. In the earliest days of Vegas, introductions were arranged solely by hotel management; it was a condition of employment that show girls mingle with favored customers. "You could not approach a table of show girls who hooked on the side," says Don Williams, a Vegas management and political consultant. "If you did, security would break your arms and legs and throw you out. The biggest whores in town were unapproachable." These days, show girls have a different lifestyle (as well as job description). Meeting them is still possible. The best place is at the day-care centers where they drop off their kids.

"Some of the girls are married and have families," says Jahna Steele, 30, star of the *Crazy Girls* review at the Riviera. "Some are in school. For some like myself, it's a career. I was married. I was divorced. Of course, I'd like to meet the prince who would sweep me off my feet, but in this day and age, the reality of that happening is slim. Times change. Old Las Vegas is gone. It's too corporate; they don't treat show girls the way they used to. In old Las Vegas, the show girls were chauffeured here and there. Now it's a job. You come in, do your time, go home, as simple as that."

You can find much more accommodating girls through the Yellow Pages, as you can in your hometown. In Vegas, you look under "Entertainers-Adult." These entertainers-adult call themselves Private Dancers, Harem Dancers, Untamed Ladies and so on. Singing and dancing is not their specialty. Another resource is magazines with names like *Calendar Girls* and *Nightlife*. They are dispensed from news racks on street corners.

Some of the best-looking women in the city dance topless at Crazy Horse Too, a nightclub on Industrial Boulevard. The featured attraction there is table-dancing, which demonstrates just how incredibly well behaved the Las Vegas destination visitor has become. For $20, a girl stands on your table and basically molds her body to your face without exactly touching it. Your obligation is to keep your hands pressed to your sides as though they were spot-welded there.

Another kind of club offers equally frustrating encounters, except these are with worse-looking women and cost a great deal more. These sex-tease clubs have names like Nasty's, Tabu, Black Garter, Chaser's, Alley's, Night Gallery and Expose. Basically, a man has to be brain-dead to go into one of them. Almost all are operated by Terry Gordon (whose brother, Jack, is the manager and husband of La Toya Jackson). Although Gordon has a dreadful reputation, he is in reality an engaging fellow who operates a smarmy business, precisely the profile of the Vegas figure everybody claims to miss so much.

At the Crazy Horse Too, a beer is a beer. At one of Gordon's places, a drink is a life's savings. Cokes are okay. A Coke costs $3, and it is a good Coke. The next—the only—step up is a bottle of nonalcoholic wine. The reason Gordon serves only nonalcoholic drinks is he then avoids contact with regulatory agencies that might find fault with his operation.

I visited the Black Garter, where Gordon sells his nonalcoholic Ariel White Zinfandel for $910 a bottle. The nonalcoholic Sante sparkling wine (which tastes as if it's made from burned grapes) is $2,410 a bottle. If you wish to be a sport—and anybody who visits one of Gordon's clubs is surely that—you might as well drop another $590 and spring for the Ariel Napa Valley Blanc de Noirs, at $3,000 per bottle.

The Black Garter is small, overheated and dark. The cheesy red-and-black decor must have cost Gordon at least the price of a bottle of Zinfandel. The background music is soft and slow. The overall effect is of a spooky junior-high-school Halloween party, the kind where young boys go to get kissed.

Customers who purchase a bottle of $3,000 almost-wine and head for one of the private back rooms with one of Gordon's somewhat-better-than-average-looking women have similar, but more ambitious, expectations. Why anybody would spend this kind of money for this kind of woman, even if sexual intercourse were the result (and it is not), is absolutely baffling. It has to be the moment. I suppose that when a woman is all over a man, something inside him is saying "Sign the damn credit-card slip."

The disappointment felt by customers when their expectations are not realized in a back room can be acute. Bomb threats are not uncommon. Two patrons of Pluto's, now closed but once called "the mother of sex-tease clubs" by George Knapp, obtained a refund at gunpoint. (Sympathetic police refused to press charges.)

I catch up with Gordon in the Jerry Willick Hair Design salon at the Las Vegas Hilton, where he is getting a manicure from a woman who tells me she is really a singer and a songwriter. A portly, black-bearded man of 50 who likes to roll two balls Queeg-like in his hands, Gordon insists that his businesses are no worse than any others in Las Vegas. He says guys go to the craps tables, they can shoot dice for $50 or they can shoot dice for $5,000. Guys go to his nightclubs, they can spend $50 or they can spend $5,000.

I ask him if the people who go to his clubs go home happy.

"People come, they spend a lot of money. Some are sad. Some are happy. Nobody's ever written me a thank-you note."

He says he has learned something from all his years in this business.

"Women are all different. Men are all the same."

.   .   .   .

"You're an ex-felon and you come to Las Vegas, you have to register within forty-eight hours with the sheriff. Johnny Roselli—they called him 'the Ambassador,' he's the bag man for the Desert Inn—is so high up in the Chicago Mob, he didn't bother. Roselli later was an emissary between the Mob and the CIA in the plot to kill Castro. He also ended up stuffed in a fifty-five-gallon drum.

"Now Ralph Lamb, the sheriff, even though he's a real cowboy, every day he's roping and shit like that, is a power, maybe the third- or fourth-most-powerful person in the state. And he has a sense of the theatrical. Every once in a while, he wants to let people know who's running this town.

"Roselli is sitting at a table at the Sands with Moe Dalitz and Peanuts Danolfo. Ralph tells this rookie cop to walk up to the table, tell Johnny Roselli he's a no-good-rotten ex-felon who better get his ass down to register. Ralph tells the kid, 'He'll tell you to get the fuck out, do what he says.' That's what happens. Ralph is sitting in his unmarked car outside with his undersheriff, a big Indian named Lloyd Bell. Ralph hands Lloyd a roll of quarters, says to him, 'I'm going in the front door and take Johnny Roselli out.' He tells Lloyd that the only guy likely to get up and give him shit is Peanuts, so he should come in the side door, up behind Peanuts, and if he didn't hospitalize Peanuts he'd be looking for a new job in the morning.

"Ralph comes in the front door, says, 'You greasy gangster SOB, you told one of my deputies to get out of here.' Johnny Roselli is a nice dresser. Ralph reaches across the table, grabs him, drags him across the table, flings him on the floor. Peanuts starts to get up, the way Ralph said he would. Dalitz sees Lloyd Bell coming to sucker-punch Peanuts with the bag of quarters. He grabs Peanuts's tie, jerks him down. Moe is the boss, so he sits. Now, Ralph is slapping the shit out of Roselli. He takes him outside, where the kid is waiting in the car with the lights and siren on, throws him into the backseat of the car, tells the rookie to take this SOB downtown and treat him like a bank robber, which meant delousing him.

Now, *everybody in the state is calling Ralph, telling him to let Roselli out. Ralph says, 'I run this town. You come to this town, I'm your first stop.' The next day, Roselli is out on bail. Shortly afterward, he buys a house in Las Vegas, becomes a permanent resident. He never again wanted to fuck with Ralph Lamb."*

—Don Williams

Gangsters never ran Vegas. Cowboys did. People forget that. They see too many movies, they think Bugsy Siegel was the mayor. There were a few people who made the old Vegas possible, and one of them was Ralph Lamb, the sheriff during the good years. Ralph was tough. He once rode to the edge of town and told the Hell's Angels to turn back. They did.

Cowboys and gangsters built Las Vegas (with considerable help from the Teamsters Central States Pension Fund). You might think they'd have turned the city into Beirut, but it never happened. They divided up the town, the cowboys assuming the political power and the gangsters the economic power. Or maybe it was just that the hoods sent to Vegas to look after Mob interests were in their forties and fifties when they arrived, a time of life when killing people isn't the thrill it used to be.

The rules under Ralph Lamb were simple and ensured that Vegas would remain a decent, if not exactly law-abiding, place: You did whatever you wanted, but you did nothing to hurt the town. Notoriously press-shy, Lamb once said "In those days, we just did what we thought the public wanted done." If he was a little easier on criminals than a peace officer should have been, you could blame the state government for setting a lax example. Until the Sixties, the prison at Carson City operated a gambling casino for inmates, allowing them to obtain additional funds from friends and relatives whenever they, financially speaking, busted out.

Back then, if Ralph took you in, Oscar Goodman got you out. Goodman represented Mob figures and just about any other local who got in trouble with the government. He's as good now as he was then. Sitting under a full-size chandelier that hangs precariously low over his desk, he ruefully admits that he has always been characterized as "Goodman the Mob lawyer." He asks politely if one small thing might be pointed out.

"The truth," he says, "is that these bad fellows I represent are found not guilty."

One of his clients was Jay Sarno, the impresario who built Caesars, the first great theme hotel. Sarno was as much a hotel pioneer of the Sixties as Siegel was of the Forties, but he was far from a beloved man.

"He was one of the great salesmen in the history of the world," says Goodman. "He also was charged with giving an IRS agent a $62,500 bribe. His codefendant was Stanley Mallin. Jay was fearful he would die in prison but perhaps more fearful that he would be convicted and Stanley acquitted.

"A lawyer named Harry Claiborne represented Stanley. Claiborne insisted on making a defense of character witnesses. I just as much insisted to Jay that I would not. Claiborne called the chancellor of UNLV to testify about the character of Stanley: 'Excellent.' Then a leading Las Vegas internist 'Excellent.' This went on and on, and Sarno's toupee started to turn, he was so mad. He kept insisting 'I want character witnesses!' The last character witness for Stanley was Robert L. Smith, a building contractor: Again, Stanley's character was 'excellent.' Jay finally forced me to question this witness on his behalf. I said, 'Mr. Smith, you have known my client, Mr. Sarno, for fifteen years. Tell the ladies and gentlemen of the jury of his reputation for honesty and integrity.'

"He looks at the jury: 'Fair.' "

Sarno was acquitted, of course.

Weren't they all?

"I was walking with Ash when this guy comes up to me looking for a handout. He asks for a hundred dollars. He can tell I'm Lebanese. He said the Jews threw him out of his country. I can see he's a phony. He goes up to Ash, tells the opposite story, says he's a Jew and got thrown out. Ash gives him the hundred, says to him, 'There's another hundred if you tell me what you really are.' "

—Fred Doumani, former owner of the Tropicana Hotel

Something else happened that Thanksgiving weekend, something I recall vividly whenever I walk into a casino. After the Sinatra show, I played some blackjack and lost $50. It doesn't sound like much, but in those days, $50 bought two nights at Caesars, and it was most of the cash I had with me. When Ash Resnick came looking for me, I told him I needed to cash a check.

"What do you need money for?" he asked.

Feeling irrationally contrite, I confessed.

He took a roll of bills from his pocket, peeled off a fifty, handed it to me, took my arm, led me into the casino, sat me down at a blackjack table, took the $50 bill out of my hand, put it on the table. The dealer exchanged the bill for chips, and Ash put them on the betting line.

He nodded. The hand was dealt. The dealer's upcard was a queen. I had fourteen, almost certainly a fatal hand. Before I could make a decision, hit or stay, the dealer started taking cards for himself. He busted.

Ash picked up the $100 in chips, put them in my hand, practically lifted me from the table.

"Let that be a lesson to you," he said. "Don't gamble."

I never saw Irving "Ash" Resnick after that weekend. I wrote to him once, suggesting he write a book. I heard he got the letter, but he never replied. It didn't surprise me.

I'm told there once were a lot of men in Vegas who lived the way he did, but I don't believe any were his equal. Bob Stoldal, the former news director of Vegas station KLAS-TV, says of Ash, "You looked at him almost as though he were the father figure of Las Vegas."

According to those who knew him, Ash was a gambler (without question), a provider of women (well, he was nice to family friends), a shylock (allegedly collecting interest on markers) and an unqualified soft touch. He didn't build hotels, but he was associated with at least seven of them, including the Thunderbird, the Tropicana and Caesars. There were at least two attempts on his life. He wasn't scratched. He has been credited with inventing high roller junkets, introducing baccarat and conceiving the idea of hotel-sponsored championship boxing, which would make him, if all three are true, one of the most influential entrepreneurs in Las Vegas history. He took care of Joe Louis when Louis got old, and he counted Sonny Liston as a friend, even though *Sports Illustrated* printed rumors, almost certainly false, that he had Liston killed.

When he died of cancer, in 1989, everyone mourned. And some, of course, wondered. Was he part of organized crime?

"If anything, it was disorganized crime. He wasn't part of organized anything," says his daughter Dana, now 31.

Ash grew up in New York and played basketball with the Original Celtics. His gambling career may have coincided with his basketball career, a conflict of interest frowned upon even then, but he had left the game by the time he started booking bets. One of his close friends was Lem Banker, whose father ran an illegal bookmaking operation out of a candy store in Union City, New Jersey.

Banker, now a professional gambler living in Vegas, recalls the career move that prompted Ash to go west. He took a $100 bet on a horse that went off at 72–1; when the horse won, he didn't have the $7,200 he owed. This was particularly unwise, because the man who made the bet was Albert Anastasia, the head of Murder, Inc.

After that, Ash decided his future lay elsewhere, and he left for Vegas. There he met and married Marilyn; a singer and show girl who had made her first visit to the town in 1953, when she was 16. Marilyn remembers Betty Grable swimming in their pool, Cassius Clay eating in their house, Elvis sitting next to her in the coffee shop at Caesars. She remembers that when she was a show girl in the Fifties, "we were treated like movie stars."

She and Ash had two children, Dana and Lara, 25, who lived the most wonderful of lives, a fairy tale *noir*. Dana says that long after she was grown, she'd run into Sinatra, Dean Martin and Sammy Davis, and they'd always remind her of the times her father brought her into the steam room at the Sands. "I don't remember it; I was 3," she says. She went up onstage with Eddie Fisher and Paul Anka, who sang to her, and she remembers Joe Louis taking salt and pepper

shakers from the dinner table and putting them down her lace an-
klets. She and Joe and her father would ride around golf courses in a
cart, going as fast as it would go, her father driving and Joe holding
her outside in his big hands as they sped up and down the hills. She
once turned in a class paper on the two Louis-Schmeling fights and
received a low mark because she'd left the *c* out of Schmeling's
name. "I told the teacher, 'But Joe Louis told me how to spell it.' She
didn't believe me."

Although almost unknown outside of Las Vegas, Ash was all-
knowing within. He wasn't a Mob guy, but he worked with them all.
He wasn't on the side of the law, either. No question about that. He
ran into trouble with the government in the Seventies, something
about skimming $300,000 from Caesars, but it was a minor difficulty
and he beat it, as he beat most things. He was a hard man to cate-
gorize, but Mel "Red" Greb, a fight promoter who first brought big-
time boxing to Vegas, does a good job of it.

"Ash was a hustler, second to none," Greb says. "He was a bull-
shitter, a salesman, but he could produce, I'll say that. He was a likable guy. He'd fuck over his mother, but he was a nice fellow in spite
of it all."

*"Some of the worst characters who ever lived, they lived in this town. You
couldn't help liking them. As long as you didn't cause trouble, you were fine, and
if you did cause trouble, it didn't matter who you were. You pushed these guys too
hard, they pushed back. But nobody ever killed anybody in Las Vegas. If you're
like Gus Greenbaum and his wife, dumb enough to go to Phoenix, they killed you
there."*

—Don Williams

On October 1, 1990, Joey Cusumano, a man whose name is often
preceded by the adjective "reputed," was pulling his black Mercedes
500SL convertible into his Las Vegas home when he noticed something funny about the car: The radio, the headrest, the dashboard
and the windshield were exploding around him, leather and gen-

uine-wood trim being blown apart by bullets from a silenced 22-caliber handgun fired by a man in a ski mask. Some disguise. You see a man in a ski mask in the Mojave Desert, you pretty much know it isn't Jean-Claude Killy.

The guy had jumped out of the bushes, followed Cusumano's car into the garage as the remote-controlled doors closed behind it. Actually, "garage" isn't quite accurate. Joey doesn't have a garage. He parks his car in his living room, on a marble floor, and he has been known to smile and admit that when you park your car in your living room, you've got to watch for oil leaks. So this guy was practically in Joey's living room, firing away, shot after shot, hitting everything but Joey. He was popping away from five feet at a guy in a convertible with the top down, and he was *missing*! Some shooter.

Joey's house is a fortress, which could have something to do with his close association with the late Anthony "Tony the Ant" Spilotro, the despised street enforcer of the Seventies and early Eighties. Spilotro was sent by the Chicago Mob to look after its Las Vegas concerns, and he ruled with an extremely heavy hand—his idea of a heavy hand, according to legend, was putting a man's head in a vise and squeezing until his eyeballs popped out.

Finally, a shot hit Joey's right shoulder, grazing the bone. Then he was struck twice more in the back, both shots going in below the left shoulder as he dived down on the seat. While he was lying there, he slammed the car into reverse and sat up, waiting for the automatic transmission to engage. That's when he saw the guy for the first time. He also saw the gun inches from his head and the trigger finger tightening.

The gun misfired.

Joey thought the gun misfired once, but later, three unspent bullets were found in his car. Three times the executioner tried to put a bullet in Joey's brain. If you're going to be in that line of work, you've got to remember that a gun with a silencer jams if you shoot it too many times.

The guy was still pulling the trigger when Joey floored the car and battered apart the garage doors, which open outward, like a hinged gate. He drove himself to a hospital, where he was fixed up. His car received equally good reconditioning. He drives it today.

Joey now has a little pain in his right shoulder where the bullet grazed the bone. He has a couple of slugs still in his chest, one of them so close to the surface he lets friends touch the bump. Thirteen bullets left that pistol, and Joey drove away, his smile, good manners and courtliness intact. Nobody was ever arrested, and Joey has denied knowing who did it, why they did it or why they didn't try again.

Joey, who is no killer, once did two years in a federal work camp for conspiracy and interstate racketeering, something to do with an ill-advised telephone call across state lines. He is in the Nevada Gaming Control Board's "black book," forbidden to enter any casino. While he was closely associated with Spilotro, nobody has ever accused him of sinking to Tony the Ant's level. (Actually, Spilotro sank to an extremely low level; he was found beaten to death and buried seminude in an Indiana cornfield, in 1986.)

Among the current cast of Vegas characters identified as "alleged," Cusumano is in a class of his own. He is old Las Vegas, articulate, well-liked and civil. If he is in line, as some speculate, to be the boss of Vegas, successor to Johnny Roselli, Marshall Caifano and Spilotro, he could restore a certain style to the city.

It won't happen, of course. Joey doesn't want the job, and even if he did, Las Vegas doesn't need someone like him.

Las Vegas is no place for a mobster, alleged or otherwise.

It has become a great city, a family town, as pristine as a Mormon picnic.

It couldn't have turned out better.

That's right, isn't it?

Richard Meltzer

Who'll Stop the Wayne?

THINGS YOU CAN ONLY LEARN BY TRAVELING—In case you thought L.A. has the monopoly on Raleigh Hills execu-drunk tanks, they also got one in Vegas (so who knows where else) and they even got Gale Storm. Yes I was in L.V. (on business), saw MUCH GOOD TELEVISED SHIT (the business of watching teevee), really fine up-chuck I will share with you in the hope that you'll watch it too (next time you're in Puke City yourself).

CHANNEL 3: Ample Duds commercial featuring STILL PHOTOS of fatties in the latest up to date blimp attire. "Big, beautiful women,

☞ From L.A. Is the Capital of Kansas (*Harmony Books*, 1988).

when you're in Vegas come to Ample Duds." (Sizes 36-60.) "You get more of the things you *love* . . . at Pizza Inn." (I LOVE A DONUT, but did not have time to check what flavors they got.)

CHANNEL 5: Every ten minutes they plug EVERY SHOW THAT'S ON SAT. & SUN. ShaNaNaCharliesAngelsLaverne&ShirleyBurns&AllenCrummyCartoonsMoviesYouveSeenSixTimes—2 seconds of everything. Governor Lisk of Nev. as Smokey the Bear: "Our forests are tinder- dry," he warns.

CHANNEL 8: Jack Concannon (3rd rate QB with the Eagles and Bears, '64-71) does the sports at 11, interviewing the only black faces you'll see in town (besides Redd Foxx and Bill Cosby), those amazing athletes of UNLV.

CHANNEL 10: Crash course in the high cost of entertainment, the making of a "must-see" Vegas show. "You've gotta be a T.V. STAR, lotta television exposure, *maybe* some hit records. Wayne Newton on the other hand is *more than* an enigma, he's a Vegas institution. He worked his way up thru the boondocks, his feel for an audience is *phenomenal*. But he may be a VANISHING BREED."

CHANNEL 13: "Family Shoes is *going out of business forever*," spoken with a certain *affirmative joy*, the kind of a.j. you're bound to have with a great catchy name like Family Shoes. Ben Stepman Dodge (in Henderson): "We're the *other* Dodge dealer." Whoever the *other* other might be it's no big sweat t' guess why (duller than a CARPET COMMERCIAL). 11:30 sign-off editorial: "What percent of auto accidents in Clark County involve at least one driver who has been drinking?" Ans.: 65. Tho no actual *opinion* is given they welcome your response.

Capsule summary of the sheer greatness of LVTV: Three steps "down" from L.A. (if that's possible), probably on a par with Fargo or Sarasota. The town that TV (i.e., Johnny Carson) put on the map has certainly got its TV "act" together, consistently delivering the Buddhist/Hindu/LSD massage that LIFE IS LOSS—of small-biz staying power, mind-set tenacity, aesthetic acuity, and the integrity of actual needs (as well, of course, as wages)—and who're WE to grumble when it could be "worse"? We could be living in Mormon Penis, Utah (for inst) or Mumps, Tennessee.

Everything in Vegas feels like (and ultimately *is*) TV and I'm not talking *Let's Make a Deal* or *Joker's Wild*. The casinos now have slot machines with *electronic images* of oranges & cherries in lieu of the customary stamped or painted whatsems. You go to jai alai at the MGM Grand and the chain-link grid between you and the players, coupled with the colors and lighting, makes the whole thing look like TV dots blown up *too many times*—jolting your eyes and making you "doubt" what you're seeing. There isn't *one* cocktail waitress who couldn't be a regular on *Three's Company* or *Flamingo Road*. The whores all resemble Phyllis George. The best food in town is (believe it) Denny's. IHOP is second.

So after two days of gambling/losing, eating/drinking and digging the tube-writ-small, I figured it was time for a mega-dose of the REAL THING, a hefty tune-in on TV per se at its most ersatz, grandiose and fucked—the sort of BOGO-SIMULATION-OF-LIFE you can only get LIVE at any of the town's fabulous "rooms." Quick perusal of the entire Strip offered 16,000,000 TONS of hot worthless pathetic ugh—Liberace, Mac Davis, Charo w/ David Brenner, Ann Margret, the Royal Lippizan Stallions (in their worldwide debut anywhere other 'n turf), Neil Sedaka w/ Fred Travalino, etcet. But none of these jerks, be they equine or human, had the goods on y'already know who I'm talkin' about: the one the only mr. entertainment himself WAYNE NEWTON. At the Aladdin which he owns. If TV sez he's the man he's the man.

At 30 bucks a pop (plus 15 3/4 % "entertainment tax") for 2 drinks and a show, it's got to mean I take my work seriously. Seen the guy on Johnny and a telethon, and already know he's gotta be the biggest no-talent dork ever to simultaneously be the biggest thing in contempo-squaresville make-believe, but still I ain't seen the TOTAL DIMENSION(S) of the thing and fuck if I'm gonna pass up the chance. Besides, Liberace (second choice) is only $17.50 so that must mean the poor bastard's over the hill, and what I'm lookin' for in worthlessness is MR. NOW. The Dadaist in me sez go with Wayne and lemme tell ya DADA NEVER HAD IT SO GOOD.

For starters consider this: *The* first Elvis medley (anywhere ever) comprised SOLELY OF BALLAD SWILL—"Are You Lonesome Tonight?," "Love Me Tender," "Can't Help Falling in Love with You." It's dedicated, naturally, to the man Himself, "a giant of the entertainment industry I had the good fortune to call a close personal friend during his final days on earth"—which is prob'ly even true, and prob'ly says more about CULTURAL ENTROPY than umpteen *This Is Elvises*. Speaking of which, even after he'd turned to shit himself, Elvis still had the pipes to at least sonically distract you from an obvious retrograde lyric; this was therefore the first time I actually managed to catch the *words* to "Lonesome" and Wayne's TOTAL NON-MASTERY OF SINGERLY NUANCE has gotta be why. Even some demi-quasi-*semi*-pro like let's say Diane Keaton could proably've dredged *something* out of the tune, while this boy comes up empty 'cept for I-miss-you-do-you-miss-me you could cut with a butter knife. Which has gotta be the dandiest OUT-OF-CONTEXT FORCED-ATTENTION TRIP in yrs., the sheer inadvertency of which (not to mention its in-the-cards *inevitability*) hasta put him one up on Marcel Duchamp getting the bumpkins of his day to ogle a urinal.

But don't let ballads fool you, Wayne's a rocker from *way* back, as his hobbling, bobbling renditions of the Elks Lodge R&R Songbook adequately proved to all outpatient "geris" in from Cripple Creek. Average age hadda be somewhere around 67 or 68, and these folks were ALL SMILES as the puffboy in the Slim Whitman 'stache yanked 'em, by the numbers, from "Good Hearted Woman" to "Polk Salad Annie" to that guaranteed showstopper "Johnny B. Goode." And by showstop I ain't kidding, twice the band lurched into "J.B.G." overtime when Wayne insisted on ROCKIN' SOME MORE and each time the show just dead fucking STOPPED. And by smiles I'm saying that's all there was, *the ecstasy was minimal*; was more like these slaphappy sexagenarians were pleased as punch seein' the NICE YOUNG MAN—who could eas'ly be their bouncy beloved GRANDSON—be oh so tasteful & harmless WITH THE MUSIC OF NIGGRAS & REDNECK BEASTS. If he'd done "Midnight Hour" (some sets maybe he does) it wouldn'ta raised a hackle.

Which is not t' say the customers did not at times get *carried away*. They got carried away exactly TWICE. One, a standing ovation for Wayne's stirring (lame & literal) reading of "MacArthur Park"— Tommy Velour could not of read it better— accompanied by fright- eningly authentic fake lightning, fake thunder and FAKE RAIN. Two, "God Bless America" (slide show of clouds and a *heap* of uninten- tional wrong wds.—if they'd been on purpose *somebody* woulda chose 'em a mote less dumb) had 'em on the edge of their seat in silent googoo-eyed communion with their LORD (prob'ly ashamed they couldn't kneel), an appropriate response to what had to be the apex—the acme!—of the show; if L.A. is the cultural capital of the republic (for which it stands) then Vegas is the RELIGIOUS CAPITAL, the capital of capital.ism, a truism if there ever was one (and truism is the hick version of irony).

But hicks in Vegas also need DIRT, a passel of smut to give 'em a guilty "thrill" that would only embarrass them and make th'm fear for the social order back in _____ (tired of making up silly hometown names). With his "phenomenal rapport" w/ an audience on the line, Wayne *had the smut*; told this utterly *bizarre* sexist joke that filled their quota and more. "Has anyone out there ever had a COYOTE DATE?" Members of the band say me-me-me. "No, *you* guys don't count. Oh excuse me, you don' know what a coyote date is? Well first lemme assure you this *does not apply* to any ladies in attendance tonight. Let's say you're at a bar . . ." He then goes thru this whole routine of after you've had a few the uggle at the end of the counter is finally not too bad. "So you take her to a motel, I won't even say what the two of you *do* but you wake up in the morning with a head-splitting hangover and this *weight* on your arm. You're afraid to open your eyes and *look*, finally you muster the courage and she's WORSE THAN YOUR WILDEST NIGHTMARE. You've got to get *out of there* before she wakes up, but if you remove your arm that's exactly what she'll do. So you do what coyotes do when caught in a trap . . . YOU CHEW YOUR ARM OFF!" Haw haw hoo as the aforementioned bandboys wave empty sleeves of their tux.

Yes, the rapport is phenom'nal, for a guy with *no discernible charisma* he sure knows how to occasionally get a rise. (Could be he's learned the skill by doing "time" with encounter groups brought in just for him.) At other times tho he falls flat on his nose with self-deprecating INDIAN JOKES (claims now he's part Native-Am., wears feathers on his silver buckle: niftiest way IMAGINABLE to get you t' stop thinking *Mafia*) which expose an itchy inability to even be overtly *in* sincere. (He is not your garden-variety "Vegas phony.") Obviously he knows (to some extent) he ain't got nothin' but success (like nobody's *that* stupid), question remains to what extent he maybe fancies himself as a *charlatan* behind it all—how much actually boils down to (what could pass for conscious) "manipulation." In any event, the setup seems to be for everyone (8 million L.V. tourists a year) to see Wayne ONCE—and once is sure as heck sufficient.

But I haven't even mentioned (& I'm sure you'd like to KNOW) the final segment of th' show, the part where he PROVES BEYOND A SHADOW OF A DUCK he is one helluva competent practiced Musician. Earlier, on "Johnny B. Goode," he toyed with a guitar, *possibly* the playing was his, a mere TEASER for his hogwild romp thru the wonderful world of strings-other-than-bass. With malice aforethought he flaunts his virtuosity on BANJO (bandleader holds up the sagging mike), documents it on amplified VIOLIN. For the rousing grand finale ("Saints Go Marchin'") he even grabs a TRUMPET, hits four-five notes before laying it down, geez this cat can play 'em! . . . nice t' know what it was *about* was MUSIC.

Bravo, bravo, halfassed applause (no encore tonight) and then we're herded out to this stack o' discs. On the Wayneco label—natch— for the bargain price of six bucks (hold the tax) a throw; still plenty time to throw away even more on blackjack, roulette. At this point I can't see ANY WAY I will wager a wooden quoit, not after the total-loss farm of 90 minutes of Wayne. Formula for all this must take into account how much the idiots're likely to bet & lose B.W.— before Wayne—'cause after Wayne it's bound to noticeably diminish . . .

Okay, I did my bit for world TV knowledge, live version of TV has gotta be 50 times more noxious than the basic small-screen gig; please don't 'spect me to do it again—soon or otherwise. Only personal "benefit" from my Vegas stay is after Vegas EVEN MELROSE LOOKS FUNKY. (If you're planning to somehow *vacate* L.A., y'oughta take a quick one to Vegas and L.A.'ll look like San Francisco.)

Jim Sloan

"Melvin and Howard": A Nevada Fairy Tale

The following is based largely on interviews and court records. In cases where participants weren't available for interviews, their recollections are based on their own public statements, transcripts or other published accounts.

ARNOLD DUMMAR: We weren't the richest folks in Nevada. When Melvin was a boy we lived in a trailer some of the time, moving around to where I could find work. I did some mining and I worked

☞ *Excerpted from* Nevada: True Tales from the Neon Wilderness (*University of Utah Press*, 1993).

a lot of road construction. Back then they were putting in some of the major highways and Melvin would come out and see this clean, smooth stretch of pavement that his daddy built and then he'd see one of those big, roaring cars, like a Tucker or a Bel Air, come sailing through the desert on that road and he'd imagine the prospects of life just over the ridge. Even though we didn't have much, I think Melvin always saw the promise of things. He had dreams; he always had dreams. His momma was working in a motel for a time and I swear even years later when we'd drive by the place, the tears would well up in his eyes and he'd think of his momma cleaning up for strangers, making almost nothing and never seeing a tip from the rich men who could afford to stay in the rooms. Maybe he saw that Bel Air parked out front, I don't know. It's funny though. When we all heard about the will and how Howard Hughes had left Melvin—what was it, about a hundred and fifty million?—none of us was surprised. I mean, if it was going to happen to anyone, that kind of fairy tale, it was going to happen to Melvin. He wanted it so much.

MELVIN: I'd stopped in Tonopah to get something to eat and play a few hands of blackjack and then I was back on 95, heading south. It was dark, and I was on my way to L.A. to see my daughter. Linda and I had split up, but that's another story. I'd steamed open her love letters. I stopped somewhere outside of Beatty, not far from that whorehouse—the Cottontail Ranch, I guess it's called—to relieve myself. I drove down a dirt trail a ways out into the sagebrush and started to unload when I noticed this old guy sprawled out in the desert face down. He was trying to lift himself up, and was on his hands and knees when I got to him. He was real skinny—it was like lifting up bones with real soft flesh—and I asked him if he was all right and he said something like, "I'm all right," but the truth was that he was shivering and couldn't stand up straight. I thought I had a wino on my hands. He said he didn't want anything to do with hospitals or cops, that he just wanted a ride into Las Vegas and would I take him. I said sure, it was right on the way.

ARNOLD: This boy's a hustler, a real go-getter. Never drives by a hitchhiker. Can't stand turning people down! But I'll tell you, picking up this hitchhiker was the best job he ever done.

MELVIN: He gave me the creeps. Kept staring at me. He had blood on his shirt and a scar or something below his left eye, and since he didn't say much I just did all the talking. I told him I was working up in Gabbs for Basic Industries bagging magnesium and that I'd been a milkman in L.A. and a plasterer for my father. I told him jobs were hard to get and keep, like the one I wanted so bad down at Hughes Aircraft down in L.A. That's when he spoke. He said he knew all about Hughes Aircraft because he owned it. He was Howard Hughes. I look over at him to see if he's serious but you can't tell, so I'm laughing and thinking to myself, "Hold onto yer nuts 'cause the squirrel's out tonight." I started singing some of my songs to him. I had written some pretty good ones, and my favorite was "When A Dream Becomes a Reality." It's about how with hard work, faith, and courage you can conquer anything. So I sang it to him. He must have thought I was crazy because he just sat there. Later they'd say I got him to sing "Santa's Souped-Up Sleigh," but I hadn't even written that song yet and I don't remember him singing at all. He just sat there actually, enjoying my singing I guess (I'm a good singer; I've always been able to hold a tune). When we got to Las Vegas he asked me for some change and I gave him a quarter and that was that. Until 1976 when I got a call about the will.

NOAH DIETRICH: I was skeptical at first. Although Howard and I had worked together for thirty years—I helped build his empire for God's sake—we'd gone our separate ways in 1957, and not entirely as friends. Why would he make me the executor of his will? I had sued him for $1 million! And the will didn't really sound like him. He called his cargo plane the Spruce Goose in the will, yet in real life he hated the name. Still, there was no telling what the prospects of death had meant to the man. I imagine his thoughts, as he wrote the will, had turned to power and wealth, and in his mind those pleasures were inexorably linked to my early years with him. He was still a teenager when he hired me, with the simple instructions: "Make me the richest man in the world." Then, of course, he was free to practice his golf, fly his planes, produce his ridiculous films, all those things that drained off the profits I worked so hard to secure for him. His reputation as an inventor was dramatically overstated—my God! He spent several days designing an uplift bra for Jane Russell!—and in many ways he was the oddest man I ever met. He had a completely unfounded and paranoid fear of germs and sudden heart failure, and he constantly feared eavesdroppers, even from passing cars on the highway. He also had an almost childlike dependence on me and others who worked for him, and when I read of his last days—how he'd lived in almost total seclusion in a Las Vegas penthouse and later in the Bahamas—I was not surprised. He was a man who could never be happy. He could isolate himself, but he would only dream about the times he still walked freely on the earth. The time I was with him. His last words to me had been, "Noah, I can't exist without you."

HAROLD RHODEN: Noah called and said he thought the will was genuine. I was his personal attorney at the time and I thought Noah, who was terminally ill, had lost his legendary cogency. News of the will was already all over the papers, and it was madness to think it was genuine. Howard Hughes writing out a handwritten will? Dispensing his massive fortune in a three-page note, written in chickenscratch, filled with misspellings? It had to have been a forgery. The man had only been dead a few weeks and already there were a dozen wills dismissed by the courts because they were forgeries. And this one was worse than the others because of this one clause that left a sixteenth of the estate—at the very least a hundred and fifty million—to a man called "Melvin Du Mar." Out of the blue. Gee, do you think Melvin might have helped old Howard write his will? Curiously, the will had been found on a desk in the Mormon Church in Salt Lake City. Melvin was living in Ogden at the time and reportedly studying to be a church official. Gee, do you think there was any connection? Also, I understood that he'd once been accused of forging a check. I told Noah that I thought we could both lose a lot of money if we tried to get the will probated.

DIETRICH: There was a lot of money to be made.

RHODEN: A longshot, at best.

DIETRICH: Howard had died a lonely, sick man. He ate poorly, injected pain killers in his groin. He weighed ninety pounds when he died, and his teeth were rotten and his bedsores ate away his skin down to the bone of his shoulder blades. He was at the mercy of his aides, whom he communicated with through memos. Always writing memos, hatching wild schemes, indulging in his wild delusions. His sorrowful handwriting reflected his mind, which after a time was poisoned by the kidney disease brought on by the painkillers he abused. He came to hate those he depended on most, and he often taunted them by telling them he'd written a will out by hand, and that they would never find it. Two weeks before he died he told one of his aides, "Don't bother to look for my will, you're never going to find it. It's safe. I've given it to someone I can trust." But he never said who. He once mentioned the will in a memo, using almost the exact same words that appeared in the Mormon will. He told his aides not to worry about the will, that when the time came, it'll be there.

ARNOLD: I love my boy. He grew up different from the other kids—more sensitive, I guess—and we didn't question that, just accepted it. Our family was always big on affection, hugging and kissing, what have you, and even when he got older Melvin would cry if he saw a sad program on the television. He hurt when others hurt, but he sang when others sang, too. After the will was found we started to think that maybe it was some kind of test from God, some kind of message from God or something, and that Melvin was being singled out for some reason. All that money. Would it change our lives? Would it change Melvin? Would we do the right thing with the money? Would we learn, or would we forget?

RHODEN: I remained doubtful until after I'd had a few handwriting experts examine copies of the will. It was my first exposure to the hideously fickle winds of the handwriting analysis world and I was still naive. So when my experts all said it was unquestionably the hand of Howard Hughes, I became convinced, ingenuously awed by this graceful science. Note the way the author went over and over that certain letter. A forger would never do that. And a forger would never attempt three pages when one would do. And note the odd pen lifts, where the author would pause where a man with an unpoisoned reason would never have stopped. This is Howard Hughes. Even the Mormon Church hired a handwriting expert, someone who had already examined many of Hughes's memos and letters, and she, too, was convinced it was his hand. I was ecstatic but for one lingering doubt in my mind—Dummar. How could Hughes have done this to us? Dummar was by far the weakest link in the case, and the bequest was just large enough—and just suspicious and unlikely enough—to make it worthwhile for Hughes's relatives to contest the will. And for me to drop the case.

MELVIN: Well, we didn't know whether we'd get any money or not. I was afraid to let myself think it. My attitude has always been that if good fortune comes, it comes. You can work at it, but after a point it's in the hands of fate.

RHODEN: Shortly after the will was found I had occasion to catch Melvin's act on television. The reporters had flocked to his gas station in little Willard, Utah, to ask him how he knew Hughes and I sat and watched Melvin tell the preposterous story. I watched his little eyes drip tears down his chubby cheeks as he told of tossing Hughes a quarter—Melvin's investment in his first hundred and fifty million—and I told a colleague that if the Mormon will were a forgery, Melvin Dummar would have had to have been in on it and that that would have been simply impossible. Why? I was asked. Because Melvin Dummar, I said, is just too dumb. Too dumb to have forged the will, and too dumb for any self-respecting forger to use as a frontman. It was, as I think back now, at that moment that the most frequent and convincing defense of the Mormon will was launched. It was so unbelievable, it had to be true.

MELVIN: It was a crazy time, that's for sure. I wasn't ready for all the television. It just kept coming, the questions kept coming and all manner of crazy people started stopping at the station. One man pulled a knife on Bonnie, my wife, and said he wasn't going to pay for the gas because he knew we was filthy rich and that was that. Lots of people thought we were rich and tried to get something out of us. But we weren't rich. We were really poorer, because we had to hire an attorney. Finally it all got to be too much for me and I just shut the door and wouldn't come out of the house. My brother-in-law was talking about writing a book about me but we only got about a hundred pages because I really hadn't done that much. And then there was talk of selling T-shirts and what not and I just wasn't ready for it. I remember thinking at one point that maybe Bonnie'd written the will. She liked to sometimes spell our name Du Mar—like it was in the will—because somebody'd told her it had more class than Dummar. And I started to think back on how after I told her the story of meeting Howard Hughes she would ask me if I thought Uncle Howie would leave us anything when he died. She was just joking, you know, but I was crazy.

BONNIE: It was a tough time for Melvin. There was just all this constant attention. It was all anybody would ever talk about! I met Mel when we were both living in L.A. and one of my sons set his trash can on fire. We didn't talk much until one night there was an open house at school and he asked if I would take his daughter. He stayed home and cooked us a dinner of burnt pork chops and cold peas, which made him seem all the more sweeter in my heart. There was a kindness, a gentleness about him that I loved. He works harder than any man I know. One time he had a snowmobile accident out in the middle of nowhere in the Utah mountains and he broke his leg, a compound fracture. But he set that leg himself and crawled through the snow to a road and got a ride to the hospital. The doctors didn't know how he did it. So, when all this business about the will came along I thought two things: One, he deserved the money, and two, he didn't deserve having a lot of people call him a liar and a forger. I could see what it was doing to Melvin. I could see the way he started to clench his jaw that way.

RHODEN: Dummar kept me awake at night, the thought of him.

Was he too dumb to write that will, or just dumb enough to try something that outrageous? He tormented me.

MELVIN: I didn't like this Rhoden guy at all. He really pissed me off. Eight months after they found the will I had to give him a deposition and the whole time he was coming at me and puffing up like rooster looking to get laid and I just got sick of it. I was thoroughly pissed off, to the point where I wanted to kill someone. He kept saying he knew I forged the will and that if I didn't confess I'd go to jail.

RHODEN: I told him he'd rot in prison until he couldn't get it up anymore. Look, I wanted to know if the guy was a liar! Before I chucked my career and my savings defending a will, I wanted to make sure this guy hadn't forged it. I was very cagey, too. I suggested minor details or omissions to his story that would have made it more solid, such as that he might have given Hughes some mouth-to-mouth or done something else to save his life. Something besides giving him a quarter, something that would have given Hughes more incentive to leave him all that money. A business tip. His last sandwich. Anything. But Melvin stood fast. That's all that happened, he said. Then I told him I knew he was lying, that I had proof and that I'd turn it over to a prosecutor if he didn't just confess and save me a lot of time and agony. "I don't know nothing about who wrote that will if Howard Hughes didn't," he said. But how did it get to the church? "I don't know." Who delivered it, Melvin? "I don't know." Finally I relented. "I lied when I told you we have evidence that the will is a forgery," I told him. "We have a great deal of evidence that it's not. We believe you, Melvin." And you know, he tried to smile, but he couldn't. He was crying too hard.

MELVIN: It was a relief to hear that somebody believed me. Most of the time I never heard that. Nobody believed me.

ARNOLD: Some people would say Melvin was a liar, but we always knew it as just his way with exaggeration. It wasn't lying, it was just Melvin's world, which was bigger and more spread out than other people's. He never lied to hurt anyone, but sometimes his recollection of things was bigger and more dramatic than what might have been the true facts of the matter. But that's what Melvin believed, it's what he saw. You understood that when you got to know him better.

RHODEN: Two days after that deposition—and just before we were to have a probate hearing in Las Vegas—I got word that the FBI had found a fingerprint on an inner envelope containing the will. It wasn't Howard Hughes's, and it didn't belong to one of his aides. It wasn't a church official's either. It was Melvin Dummar's. Needless to say I was absolutely furious. I watched Melvin go on television and claim the thumbprint wasn't his, that it had been planted there, that it was some kind of setup to discredit the will. As I sat there I knew I was watching a miserable, sniveling liar. Melvin even had the utter gall to publicly demand that the man who delivered the will to the church come forward! He said someone was trying to keep the Hughes fortune together. "I believe in the golden rule," Melvin said. "Them's that got the gold make the rules." I remember thinking just how totally trite that was, how so typical it was of the persecuted plebeian.

MELVIN: I had my reasons. Who was going to believe me? I was gonna go back to the church or call, but by the time I got home it was all over the news and some people were saying a mysterious woman had dropped it off. I thought, "If that's what they want to believe, let 'em believe it." I just thought the whole world wouldn't believe the truth, what really happened. I was trapped. I told everybody a lie that I hadn't seen it or had anything to do with it and I didn't know how to stop it.

RHODEN: I scheduled another deposition for the following month and told Melvin that all the attorneys in the case were going to be testifying to a grand jury and that he was bound to be arrested for forgery, perjury, and a whole slew of other offenses befitting a liar. He sat there saying nothing. Finally he admitted he'd taken the will up to the church himself, and that he'd read it over and over before delivering it. But I didn't write it, he said. I swear. His eyes teared up and his voice broke. I just found it on the counter in the station after this one guy had stopped to buy cigarettes. He'd left it there, and I took it over to the church. Who would have believed it if it just turned up in my gas station? He broke down then, fully weeping, and I sighed. With that kind of anguish—how could he be lying?

JUDGE KEITH HAYES: The occasion was supposed to be a probate hearing of some sort, but the real purpose of the proceeding was to try to get Melvin Dummar to tell the truth. It was the strangest day in court I believe I've ever experienced. People lined up early for seats, and at one point a fight broke out between two men who wanted the same seat in the front row. Television and newspaper reporters, that slovenly lot, made themselves at home in my jury box, sketching or taking notes on anyone who came or left. One reporter—I believe someone told me later that he was from Houston and had never been to Las Vegas before—spent the entire time reading a book on how to win at blackjack. When Dummar came into the courtroom he was stalked by television cameras and people shouting questions at him, and at one point one of the cameramen leaped on my clerk's desk to film the other cameramen filming Melvin. They told me Melvin had a penchant for game shows, that he loved them dearly and had some special ability to get selected as a participant on them, and I found myself thinking that this very hearing—this hearing that I had somehow allowed in my own court—had descended to that depth. It was a game show, with all the hype and manufactured tension of "Hollywood Squares" or "Let's Make a Deal."

RHODEN: It lasted three and a half days, glacially paced and tedious. The attorneys for the family, which was contesting the Mormon will, picked at Melvin the way I had, the way I had learned was useless, and after a time I began sketching a portrait of Dummar. We saw so much in him, imagined he carried with him so many intriguing secrets, but the truth was that he was a vacuous man, and if he'd had a deep secret it would have bubbled to the surface almost immediately. He was not deft. So I drew him. I am not a bad artist, and I tried to capture that hollowness, those otiose eyes, and I succeeded to where I believed there was a message in my art. That, of course, was that Dummar was simply too stupid to have carried off the kind of fraud we all were imagining. I gave a copy of the picture to the judge, thinking it might help my case, and by the third day all the members of the press had copies. They crowded around Dummar in the lobby, requesting his autograph. I remember vividly the boyish pleasure he took in this. This, if nothing else, will fulfill at least some of his dreams, I thought.

PAUL FREESE: I was representing some of the family members in this matter, and we felt we had plenty of evidence the will was a forgery. Dummar's aunt, Erma Dummar, was putting together an article for *Millionaire* magazine about the time another writer was doing a piece on Hughes. We had reason to believe Erma had gained access to copies of Hughes's memos and writing and was able to dig up information from those documents to give authenticity to the will she or someone else forged. When we'd asked her about whether she'd forged the will, she took the Fifth Amendment! And Bonnie was no fine, upstanding citizen either. We believed she was in on it. We asked her under oath to spell certain words that in the will had been hideously misspelled: revolk, devided, companys, one furth and exutor. She spelled them all pretty much the same way. She also liked to spell her last name Du Mar because a children's-book author once told her it sounded more sophisticated. Melvin's last name was spelled Du Mar in the will. Is this all beginning to sound a little funny to you, too? It gets better. We found out that Melvin had gone to the library and examined copies of *Life magazine that had examples of* Hughes's writing in it, and that he'd cut out pages of another book about Hughes where some of Hughes's memos had been reproduced. It all added up to a forgery. A forgery by Melvin and his family.

MELVIN: They kept coming at me about this stranger who had delivered the will to my gas station. Who was he? Why had he done it? I didn't know. All I know is that just a short time before I found the will next to my school books—I was taking some college classes at the time and was thinking about being a priest in the church or going to law school—a man wearing a fine suit and driving a blue Mercedes had stopped at the station for a while. Hughes had been dead three weeks and this guy had asked me what I thought of Howard Hughes dying and then he'd said wouldn't it be nice if a guy like you were in Howard Hughes's will? Then I found it. I steamed it open and read it over and over again. I couldn't believe it. Then I took some other envelopes and took some glue off them and put them on the original and drove into Salt Lake. I was going to explain to the church president what had happened and then I was going to pray with him. But I couldn't find him . . .

JUDGE HAYES: Enough! I told him to turn his chair around and face me. Brother Dummar, I said, where did that will come from?

MELVIN: I told him I thought it was the man in the blue Mercedes and that . . .

JUDGE HAYES: I was furious. Do you know who wrote it? I asked. He averted his eyes, lowered them, but I could hear him say no. Did you participate? I did not, he said. I told him I thought he was lying, that if I asked everyone in that courtroom to raise their hands if they agreed the palms would shoot to the sky, a lush foliage of affirmation. There are a few things that are truly valuable, Melvin, I told him. Freedom. Good health. The love and respect of your family. Your own self-respect. Doth it profit a man if he gain the whole world and lose his soul? Well, Melvin, I said, I'm not worried about your soul anymore. It's your hide that worries me. I will make it a duty to have a piece of your hide. If you are convicted of perjury or any other crime, you will go to prison. It is no country club.

RHODEN: Again, there was nothing in his eyes. No fear, really.

FREESE: My wife said that when she'd seen Melvin all misty-eyed on television after the will had been found, it had reminded her of one of those contestants on the game shows. Exuberant in a contrived, naive way. When we started to investigate him, we found out that he'd been on just about every game show on television. He'd been on some of them several times, under assumed names because it was against the rules to appear more than once. His first wife told us how Melvin had coached her on how to get picked to deal with

Monte Hall. You screamed and jumped up and down, even when they told you not to. It gave you the edge on the other contestants. He and Linda, his ex-wife, had been on "Let's Make a Deal" four times (once wearing rainbow afros and another time wearing duck hats with signs saying "Quacking up for a deal") and he'd been on "The Dating Game" (he'd lost) and "Truth or Consequences" and "Hollywood Squares." I thought I understood what motivated him. When I was a kid in New York during the Depression, I remember thinking how much I wanted a package of gum to fall off one of the delivery trucks. I fantasized about it constantly. The next step, of course, would have been to steal the gum, or arrange to have it bounced off the truck. And this, in a sense, is what Melvin had done. He'd dreamed so hard about being rich, about being rewarded by Howard Hughes, that he'd arranged to have the gum bounce off the truck. So I told him, Melvin, let's you and me make a deal. Tell us the truth. Tell us you forged that will, and I will testify on your behalf and try to get you probation for the perjury and conspiracy charges you will face. That is my pledge, that is my deal.

HAYES: Freese's technique was superb, but Melvin just sat there. Then he asked, "Am I supposed to say something?" I told him he could reply.

MELVIN: Well, I just told them the truth. I didn't know whether the will was forged or not. I told them if it was, then I hadn't forged it. That's all I had to say.

RHODEN: I was relieved in a way, for now I could drop the case with little doubt in my mind. There was no way even I could take this case to a trial. I had, as they say, sprung a few dogs from the kennel before, but this case now had the putrescent aroma of a loser. A short while later the FBI came out with another report concluding that the will was a forgery. It was based on handwriting experts, and even though I could match them penlift for penlift on that front, it would cost me a fortune and where would it leave me? And all this business of the mysterious bagman dropping the will at the gas station—that simply could not be corroborated. We were dead in the water. Aunt Erma later testified that she had nothing to do with the will and that she'd taken the Fifth because her attorney, fearing she would be charged with something, told her to. But the damage had been done. Then Melvin told me he'd torn out those pages after he'd gotten the will, just to verify in his own mind that that was Hughes's writing. But Melvin, I asked, did it occur to you that if you'd checked the book out there would have been a date on it and you could prove that it was after the will came out? Of course it didn't occur to him. Finally I told him that unless the man in the blue Mercedes reappears, there is no hope for this case.

ROGER DUTSON: I was Melvin's personal attorney at the time when I got the phone call from LeVane Forsythe. I don't know how he got my name. It was a short phone call. His voice was gravelly, like he'd lived a long, wearisome life of late nights and early mornings, and the crackle in the line told me it was a long distance call. He refused at first to give me his name, but he told me in an even, matter-of-fact voice that we should believe Melvin's story because the will had, in fact, been delivered to the gas station three weeks after Hughes had died. I'm the guy who delivered it, he said.

LEVANE FORSYTHE: I don't know. I could have just kept my mouth shut. Hughes had already paid me. But I read about that poor asshole Dummar and how he was going to get screwed out of his dough and I just made the call. I told them, "I don't want any money, and I don't want any fuckin' subpoenas. Just believe the man; he's tellin' you the truth."

DUTSON: We convinced him to meet with us, so Rhoden and I flew up to Anchorage, where he was living, and found out he was a contractor there. He told us he'd made as many as fifty deliveries for Hughes, mostly to politicians and other people Hughes was trying to influence. He delivered what he presumed was cash in manila envelopes, always getting paid cash in his own manila envelope. But he wouldn't give us any names of people he'd paid off. That was between him and Hughes, he said. He said he and Hughes had met in 1946 when Forsythe was a construction foreman for the crews building sets on Hughes's RKO studios. He said Hughes liked him because he'd told on some workers who were goofing off and stealing lumber, and that over the years he always received his instructions in secret from Hughes himself. He'd been holding on to the manila packet for Dummar for four years.

RHODEN: Forsythe was the perfect character to join this adventure. His story had just enough truth to make it convincing, and just enough holes to make you doubt it. It's called verisimilitude. It had the hint of truth. He had a deposit slip for the $2,800 he said Hughes paid him, and we talked to the teller who took the deposit. She remembered it because the bills were old but looked brand new and she had thought at first they were counterfeit. Forsythe also had the plane ticket for his trip to Salt Lake the day he delivered the will. He said he always traveled under an assumed name, and this day it was Finn Trudell—Finn for final and Trudell for true delivery. Only the ticket agent got it wrong and wrote Glenn Trudell. What was also very nice was Forsythe's reluctance to enter into the case at all. He wasn't after money and he wasn't after publicity. He just hated to think his last job for Hughes had been botched. Hughes had once written in a memo that he had "a trusted envoy . . . a man with whom I would trust with my life." It was my opinion, when all the facts were weighed, that Forsythe was that trusted envoy.

FORSYTHE: Well, I hadn't botched nothin.' They didn't believe I knew who Dummar was so they flew him up to Anchorage and put him in a crowded bar and told me to pick him out. I spotted him right away. "Kid, you sure did fuck this one up," I told him.

JAMES DILWORTH: The trouble was that LeVane Forsythe was a pathological liar. We found out he'd been accused once of forgery.

RHODEN: Accused . . . and acquitted.

DILWORTH: And that one judge had called him a "fanciful fabricator" when he claimed to have seen Hughes being carried out of the Desert Inn in 1970. That was when there was a big power struggle over the Hughes empire, and this Forsythe fellow just couldn't stay out of it. He had a thing about Hughes. The mystery of Hughes's world allowed him to indulge in his own fantasy—of being Hughes's "trusted envoy." If the Mormon will was found to be genuine, you can bet LeVane Forsythe would line up for the money that would have been doled out under one of the clauses to all of Hughes's "aides." My word! These two men—Dummar and Forsythe were cut from the same cloth. I was representing one of the family members, and I wasn't about to let millions of her money go to a pair of liars such as these two.

DUTSON: It was easy to say Forsythe was a liar. That is until LeVane took a lie detector test for us. We asked him if he had received an envelope from Hughes in 1972, if he had received a phone message in January 1976 (just after Hughes's death) to deliver it, and had he then, three months later, delivered the envelope to Melvin Dummar? He answered yes. A minus score would have meant he was lying. A positive score meant he had no knowledge he was lying. Anything over a plus six meant he was telling the truth. LeVane Forsythe scored a plus 14. That's a pretty real fantasy world.

RHODEN: Our case grew stronger in other ways. The rollercoaster headed skyward. Not long after Forsythe emerged from under his rock, we learned the will had been written with a certain type of Papermate ink that was in use in 1968, the year the will would have been written. The ink hadn't been put into pens since 1972, and it was the same ink found in many of Hughes's memos. It turns out Hughes's aides bought him Papermate pens by the boxload; it's all he ever used. In a market that had 3,000 pen inks in use, the odds of a forger picking precisely the right ink for 1968 seemed staggering. It would have been impossible for a researcher to learn what ink to use, since Papermate keeps that secret. Anyone who forged this will would have had to be blessed with remarkable foresight, research skills, and luck. Melvin Dummar, who stomped up to the twenty-fifth floor of the Mormon Church in broad daylight to drop off this precious document on a stranger's desk, just didn't seem to be that kind of guy. With this information, I had to go to trial.

JUDGE HAYES: The proceedings were accompanied by their characteristic hoopla, but the glamorous sheen wore quickly from this trial. Each side felt obliged to run out their handwriting experts, and for a time I suspected the opposing attorneys felt victory would come in sheer numbers, or that they could simply numb the jury into submission. For months it was all talk of tremors, overlinings, pen lifts, broken connections and inconsistently written "ofs." One expert talked on consistent inconsistencies. Hundreds of thousands of dollars were spent on these so-called experts, and in the final examination, the same inconsistencies that convinced one expert the will was forged was evidence to another it was genuine. It was maddening to listen to these calligraphic mercenaries; at least two had "revised" their opinions of the will after being hired by the contestants to examine it, and two others flipflopped completely. One gentleman was particularly decisive in a most confoundingly ambiguous way:

"I am more positive that the will in question was not written by Mr. Hughes than that it was."

"You mean that you are positive that Hughes wrote the will? And you are positive that he did not? But you are more positive that he did not than that he did?"

"I cannot explain my findings any clearer."

It was stupefying!

MELVIN: When they put me back on the stand, it was the same thing all over again. Melvin, why did you lie? Melvin, did you write this will? Some days I sat there and clenched my jaw so hard a couple of my teeth broke. I just told them my story and admitted my lies. I admitted that I thought Bonnie done it at first, and I admitted lying about taking the will over to the church. But the rest of it, I swore, was true. I never asked anything of Howard Hughes and I didn't expect anything from him. If I found him out in the desert, I'd do it all over again. It gets to you after a while; you do things for people, you treat them with respect, and then you turn around and somebody's calling you a liar. I got so tired of being called a goddamn liar. I made some mistakes, but I wasn't out to cheat or hurt nobody. That whole thing would have made a cheat or a liar out of anybody, at least in the public's eye. Because the public don't think anybody deserves $150 million.

JAMES DILWORTH: It boiled down, really, to whether you believed Dummar's story about finding Hughes in the desert like that. Here was a man, nearly invalid at times, under twenty-four-hour supervision, who sneaks out of his hotel penthouse and is picked up at two in the morning a hundred and fifty miles away. He was in the middle of some very intense business deals at that time in his life; he'd just made $450 million selling his shares in TWA, and he was looking for another investment to avoid paying any taxes. He was buying casinos all up and down the Las Vegas Strip! Is it logical that a person could be out in the desert, near death, at two or three in the morning and then return to his penthouse suite and work on the complex kinds of things Howard Hughes was involved in during those days? A thing you had to consider as you weave through this mishmash was Hughes's fear of kidnapping. He had a phobia about people seeing him and a terrible phobia about being kidnapped. He wouldn't even sit next to a window! Melvin Dummar sure as heck didn't pick up Howard Hughes because we know where Hughes was and the man who Dummar said he picked up looked as much like Howard Hughes as a zebra looks like a gnat.

RHODEN: The truth was, Hughes did leave his suite—often. He plotted ways to sneak out without anyone knowing. He especially liked going on his secret missions when one aide in particular—Howard Eckersley—was on duty, and that man was on duty the night Melvin found Howard Hughes in the desert. "I feel better doing something highly secret like this when Howard is on and it is at night," Hughes wrote once in a memo to another aide. Hughes wasn't just selling airlines and buying casinos during that time, he was also buying up mining claims, thousands of them, and he loved roaming the desert and inspecting them himself. We had an engineer testify that he'd been at a hotel in Tonopah about the time Melvin found Hughes in the desert and that all of Hughes's people were racing around frantically, saying they couldn't find the old man, that he'd been missing two or three days. We had the father-in-law of one of Hughes's executives recalling how Hughes would some- times take off into the desert without anyone's knowledge and that once he'd been brought back in someone's car. Of course, we had no proof, but the other side had no proof either. It was just as easy to believe Hughes would emerge and roam among his new mining claims as it was to believe he remained a captive in his own pent- house, the windows and blinds shut, the movie projector spinning out "Ice Station Zebra" for the hundredth time. Besides, you had to believe Melvin's story. It was too bizarre to be a lie, even if your liar is as talented as Melvin Dummar.

DILWORTH: Mr. Rhoden argued that because the desert pick-up story is unbelievable, no liar would have made it up and that's why you ought to believe it. That isn't a reason to believe it! That it's un- believable is a reason not to believe it. Isn't it?

RHODEN: It took me four days to go through my closing arguments, an elaborate effort to lend credence to what was on its face a pre- posterous tale. I called on the jurors to summon up their imagina- tions and to picture justice and fairness in a fictional world. For that is where Melvin Dummar and Howard Hughes lived; that is the life they shared. Melvin lived in a fantasy, a world where anything was possible. Deals were made, fortunes could be won. It was a place where the golden rule had become twisted, but for a few hours alone in his car with a scared, broken man, the world spun according to his rules, so he told the old man of his troubles and of his hopes and he sang for him one of his songs, "When a Dream Becomes a Reality." And when this old man, living alone in his own tormented mind, heard this, he, too, saw the possibilities of life. He saw his power personified. He once wrote in a memo: "Nobody gives a damn about me, all they want is my money." But Dummar asked for nothing. He even gave up a few coins for the old man. So Howard Hughes joined Melvin Dummar's world, played by his sense of justice.

DILWORTH: Wouldn't it be wonderful if life were like fairy tales. But life is not. Life is raw and lonely and deceitful. The truth: Melvin Dummar is deceitful.

RHODEN: And to think that Dummar would have dreamed up such an incredible story to support a will he had forged . . . well, it just didn't make sense. Why would Dummar, even if he'd heard the news reports that no Hughes will was found right after his death, think Hughes might write one by hand—had, in fact, told several aides he'd written one by hand. How could he know what ink he should use? How could he have known about some of those handwriting quirks? And how could anyone as careful about those details be so careless as to walk up to the Mormon Church in Salt Lake City in broad daylight, rubbing his greasy fingers all over his carefully forged document, and deliver his artwork in person? And think of the lonely man, Howard Hughes. He lived a sad, vacant life, and he had few dreams. There was no romance. When one of the hundreds of movies he watched came to a love scene, he called in an aide and asked him to fast-forward it, to push it past the "mushy parts." To think that such a man could suddenly, in his death, take control of his legacy, to find in himself a pocket of sentiment, lends a credence to life and human nature itself, doesn't it? Don't you want to believe that Howard Hughes—a frightening, enigmatic symbol of corporate greed and the weakness of the human spirit—could salvage his soul with a simple act of kindness like this? Believe it! Somehow it makes his whole life easier to understand, easier to accept. And it says something about our world; by believing this will we're not just saying that Howard Hughes was capable of this kindness. We're saying we're all capable of it, that this kind of thing can really happen. Melvin's story is that in December, at midnight, off the main highway, he found an old man alone in the desert, at twenty degrees above zero, in his shirtsleeves. And Melvin gives us no explanation of what Howard Hughes could have been doing there. Would anyone wanting to be believed make up a story like that? I don't know why Howard Hughes named Dummar in his will. None of us will ever know. But he did.

❧   ❧   ❧

RAY DUMMAR: Melvin had trouble finding work after the trial so I let him run the cafe here in Gabbs for a while but it didn't work out. You can't have live lobster on the menu here 'cause people take one look at it and think it's a giant bug or something. That's my brother for you, always dreaming. He's back in Utah now doing something, working for a liquidation firm I guess. The number of times he's been broke, I guess that makes him an expert. I gave a sermon over to the church the other day and talked about how Melvin lied and how it was a mistake to lie. He didn't do what he was supposed to do; deliver the will. Instead he's got to steam it open and read it and then try to pretend he'd never done anything like that. He acted just a little too sneaky. Then he goes to the library and does some research to see if all that's written in the will could be true, and instead of checking the book out he's got to tear out the pages. Wrong again. Just the other day I saw where they sold one of Hughes's companies and I started figuring it up and I said, "Hey, Melvin. You would have made a hell of a lot more than a hundred and fifty million." He just said, "You're a big help."

MELVIN: I was playing with a band called The Night Riders at a church dance when the verdict came out. There were a lot of reporters, so Bonnie and I went outside and sat on the hood of a car while they took pictures and tossed questions at us. Was I disappointed? No. What will I do with my life? Just keep on living, I guess. Are all your dreams broken?

BONNIE: I think it was a relief just to have it over.

MELVIN: I was driving a beer truck then, making three dollars an hour, but my name was so well known that some of the guys in the band talked about playing full time. I didn't want to be a gimmick, I wanted to make it on, you know, our talents, but three years later it was like we had to do something to play off the Howard Hughes thing. So I wrote a song called "Thank You, Howard," and I opened the show with it, strolling out on stage wearing white gloves. The joke was that I didn't want to leave fingerprints. "All you ever left me was frustration/I'll never see the millions you left me/I wish you'd come back one day and save me from all these critics/All you left me was frustration and I'll never be the same/But I thank you just the same." Then the guitars would pause and I'd whisper into the mike, "Thank you, Howard." People seemed to like the song and we actually played in a couple Reno casinos before the jobs ran out and the band broke up.

BO GOLDMAN: They came to me about writing a screenplay about the whole thing and I just wasn't interested. I was bored with Howard Hughes. But I flew out to meet Melvin and something just clicked. There was something almost mythical about the whole thing; help an old lady across the road and she rewards you with a fabulous inheritance. The trouble was that Melvin didn't inherit any money; the jury threw the will out. The executives all said the movie wouldn't make any money because Melvin had lost, but in my mind, that was the proper ending. The myth gives way to an even higher truth—the reality of money and lawyers and the danger of believing in those things you wish for so desperately. But it turns out the executives were right; the movie lost money.

BONNIE: Melvin wanted so badly to play himself. They went around and around on that one. They finally gave him one line. He's behind a ticket counter and he lends somebody a knife and tells them not to cut themselves. If you blink you miss me. I'm in the background somewhere.

MELVIN: I still want to be an actor. That's why I went on the game shows so much. I wanted to be a game show host, too. I still aspire to be an actor. It's just that it takes so much time. You have to take classes and then support yourself while you're doing handyman commercials or something. It's just that all my life I've had to work. Everything I have I've had to work for—I've never had a lick of pure luck in my life. You need luck to be an actor, I guess. Sometimes I feel like I'm just trapped.

Merrill Markoe

Viva Las Wine Goddesses!

So the other weekend I went to Las Vegas on a date. At first I had my doubts about our choice of venue, and consulted friends, who fell into two camps: those who found the excesses and depravities of the place to be the very definition of hilarity and those for whom the identical elements were at the heart of a searing existential depression, which, they felt, could only lead to a loss of the will to live.

I can confirm that there is real truth to both perceptions, and it seems to me that the best way to avoid passing from the first camp

☞ *From* New York Woman, March 1990, *and* What the Dogs Have Taught Me *(Penguin Books, 1992).*

to the second is to be very careful about the length of your stay. *This must not*, for any sensitive and reasonably intelligent adult, *exceed thirty-six hours*. For those of us blessed (or cursed) with a hyperactive sense of the ironic, Las Vegas, taken in small doses, is a specialty act without peer. And so I present you now with a kind of handy guidebook for your own short visit. Think of it as something you might get from that *big* travel writer—I forget his name—the one who writes all the "Rome on five dollars a day" things, if he weren't too big a weenie to write it.

Merrill's Guide to Thirty-Six Hours of Vegas Fun

Las Vegas is but a hop, skip and a jump from Los Angeles. But since fewer and fewer people rely on any of the above for their transportational needs, you have your choice of flying or driving. We drove— through mile after mile of pale orange landscape, dotted with tiny specks of black and pale green that are either sagebrush or tumbleweed or rock—until we reached Las Vegas.

Of course everyone knows what the Las Vegas strip looks like from a million movies and videotape montages. But they ill prepare you for how really, really bizarre it is in three dimensions. Almost everywhere you look, a building is screaming a visual or verbal insanity at you. The overall effect is of something you made up in a feverish dream one night when you drank too much tequila and ate too many pepperoncini.

TIP NUMBER 1: *Stay at the Gaudiest Hotel You Can Afford.*

Why? Because the whole point of going to Las Vegas is to have the Las Vegasiest time you can have. I heartily recommend Caesars Palace, which I found to be the wackiest luxury hotel that I have ever been in, around or near. It's not just because the employees wear costumes or because of all the oversize antiquities, friezes and historical references. How about those moving sidewalks that carry you into the complex—passing through a miniature temple type of structure, with gold columns and horns to announce your arrival— and then abandon you to the regular old stationary sidewalks for your exit?

Many movies, such as *Rain Man*, have shown us in loving detail the lavish suites full of grand pianos and chandeliers that are provided for the high rollers. We, however, had an economy priced room right next to food services, just a short distance down the hall from accounting. This simple room did not have even a regular-size piano, but it did feature a giant raised marble bathtub. Okay, fine, I can definitely follow the concept of a giant raised marble bathtub/shower combo, but the concept kind of goes south in the small economy rooms where the tub has to serve instead of a stall shower. And since these tubs are located nearly in the center of the floor—only feet from the bed and the TV and the window—suddenly you are faced with a far-from-glamorous situation, namely, one where bathing must be done in the presence of all people in the room. This is less than ideal, *especially* if you happen to be sharing a hotel room with someone you barely know.

Now you might be muttering to yourself, "What kind of moron would share a hotel room with someone she barely knows?" but that is not something I want to discuss. This is, after all, my essay. The point I am making here is that maybe you never need to know someone so well that you lose altogether the option of showering privately. And in this particular room, your roommate, who may be pretending to sleep or watch TV, is, unquestionably, just watching you shower.

Which brings us to the in-house viewing selections. There was a tape showcasing the various wining and dining opportunities in our very own hotel complex, such as "Cleopatra's Barge" for dancing and "The Bacchanal Room," where you dine in splendor, served by the lovely "wine goddesses." There was also a learn-to-gamble-with-Larry-Manetti tape that my date must have watched about 300 times. In this, a blond woman in a fur and the older guy from *Magnum* P.I. who is not Tom Selleck take some pointers from Larry

Manetti (I forget just who he is). But in a hilarious twist of fate they end up beating him at his own game . . . and then the fun begins!!!! Once your sides have stopped aching from laughter (and once you have gotten over the shock of showering in front of someone who doesn't mind watching Larry Manetti for hours on end), it's high time to get the hell out of the room and experience some of that world-famous Las Vegas nightlife!

TIP NUMBER 2: *Go to a Show.*

Somewhere in your room is a book that lists every show in town. I selected *Nudes on Ice* for our viewing enjoyment because . . . well, it was the stupidest-sounding show available. Now, I realize that not everyone selects their entertainment according to this criterion (and, by the way, aren't you glad you don't have to travel with me?), but everything on the list sounded pretty stupid to me, so I felt that attending the stupidest one of them all would be the most Las Vegasy thing to do. (I actually came very close to selecting *Boylesque*, but in the end I felt that Las Vegas men pretending to be women would be less interesting than the men pretending to be men and the women pretending to be women.) And I was not disappointed. I don't know whether or not partially nude women so bored with their jobs that they could barely keep their cigarette butts lit constitutes a "sexsational revue" (as the program advertised), but it was interesting to note that the more breast that was exposed, the less skating was required. I guess this equation is relevant in every walk of life.

Especially memorable for me was Act 5, which was called "A Russian Fantasy" and which seemed to my nonexpert eyes to be a recreation of that period of Russian history when, because of a crop shortage or something, the czar apparently decreed that only a percentage of women in the royal court could be fully dressed.

Honorable mention goes to the comedian who came out and devoted a third of his act to dirty balloon animals (always a rollicking good time). This is entertainment that you cannot see anywhere else in the world, and for a very good reason. Why in the world would you want to?

TIP NUMBER 3: *Win a Bunch of Money.*

Let me begin this section by saying that I have never been remotely interested in gambling. I have always felt that nothing ventured is nothing lost. I have never been able to see the fun in losing $5 and then winning back $3.50. Which gives you an idea of the kind of stakes I usually play. But, influenced by my date, I picked the right number at roulette and immediately won $400. And before the evening was over, we had won $1,200. I cannot recommend this too highly. If it hasn't occurred to you, win $1,200 and see for yourself. It's very energizing and really adds to your Vegas fun.

TIP NUMBER 4: *Dine Among the Wine Goddesses.*

By now you will have seen the ad on your color TV (while you were trying not to watch someone else shower). What sort of Las Vegas visitor would you be if you didn't give the wine goddesses their due? At least this was my rap right up until we were seated at our table and I saw the wine goddesses in diaphanous harem outfits circling my date, offering to give him some kind of theoretical eye massage. Maybe I wouldn't have gotten quite so ticked off if there had been wine gods available for the gals. Maybe then we all could have had a great big laugh about it. Ha, ha, ha. As it was, I, for the first time in my life, felt it necessary to threaten restaurant help with my Swiss Army knife.

There were other highlights to the meal besides the much-loathed wine goddesses. For instance, it's not every restaurant that offers you what look like 3-D fiberglass replicas of the available entrees to examine before you order. For those of us who have never actually seen what a real veal chop looks like, this is extraordinarily helpful. But the biggest dinner highlight was definitely the arrival of Julius Caesar and Cleopatra, heralded by the crash of a giant gong.

Dressed in full historical regalia, this important couple had come all the way through time with nothing more on their minds than to find out how we were enjoying our meal. And I confess I tried to use what little clout I had with the great Roman emperor to see about getting the wine goddesses pulled off the face of the earth.

TIP NUMBER 5: *On Your Way Out of Town,* *Be Sure to Visit the Liberace Museum.*

Now, I don't want to say too much here. I know the man came to a tragic end. But let me just suggest that you slow down while passing through the portion of the museum devoted to Lee's brother George, and observe that in a glass case both his driver's license and his frequent flier card have been mounted and preserved. On sale in the gift shop are a variety of swell items. Because I was ahead my half of the $1,200, I was able to purchase the Liberace paper clips, the coffee mug, the photo-embossed Christmas ornament, the key chain, the extra-large postcard of Liberace posing by his closet and the box of scented soaps, each shaped like a grand piano and emblazoned with his name.

TIP NUMBER 6: *Now Get Out of There and Don't Look Back.*

And so we say good-bye to the city of Las Vegas, remembering that we'd better not overstay our thirty-six hours. Taking with us a whole lot of free money and a bunch of silly stuff . . . and leaving behind the goddamn wine goddesses. And they'd better stay the hell out of Los Angeles if they know what's good for them.

Faith Fancher and William J. Drummond

······································

Jim Crow
for Black Performers

The movie "Bugsy" tells the story of how the mobster Bugsy Siegel
changed Las Vegas from a collection of desert shacks into a multimillion-dollar entertainment and gambling oasis. Benjamin
"Bugsy" Siegel has another claim to fame in the history of Las Vegas. He was the man who ushered in Jim Crow, segregation, keeping blacks out of the hotels and casinos unless they were performing on stage. Ironically, just as a gangster instituted segregation,
the Mob was instrumental 13 years later in removing the color bar

☞ From All Things Considered, a production of KNPR-FM, Las Vegas. Air date July 4,
1991.

in Las Vegas. This part of the story, which is ignored in the movie, is described here by Faith Fancher who prepared this report.

FANCHER: Las Vegas is so strongly identified with Sammy Davis, Jr., entertainment and gambling that it's hard to conceive of a time before the Strip and the Glitter Gulch existed. Show business veterans Peter Lynn Hayes and his wife, Mary Healy, who make their home in Las Vegas, remember those days. Healy says what they found when they got to southern Nevada in the early '40s was far from glittering.

MARY HEALY: When we came to Vegas the first time, there was nothing on the Strip. I mean, it was desert, like it looks somewhat between here and L.A. It was all desert. El Rancho was the first. Then the Frontier came next. Now, in between all these places, nothing but desert.

FANCHER: Las Vegas was just a dusty railroad town during most of the early part of this century. Then came the Boulder Dam project in 1928. Gambling was legalized in 1931. El Rancho Vegas, the first really classy entertainment palace, opened in 1941. As a youngster, Peter Lynn Hayes watched the growth of Las Vegas from the vantage point of a bar stool at his mother's saloon, called the Red Rooster.

PETER LYNN HAYES: And strangely enough, back in those days, starting in '47, '48, '49, '50, all of the great black entertainers—Lena Horne, Pearl Bailey, Nat King Cole, Louis Armstrong, Joe Williams, Count Basie—they could all play the fabulous places on the Strip, but they were not allowed to dine there or to live there. Now, my mother had no color line at the Red Rooster. As long as your money was green, she was open for business.

HAROLD NICHOLAS (Dancer): At one time, they had blacks all over the Strip, in all of the clubs, you know—headliners, too.

FANCHER: Harold Nicholas of the famous Nicholas Brothers dance team was one of the headliners in the early days of Las Vegas.

NICHOLAS: It was really like—like the Strip had—had turned black, shall we say. Oh, everybody was there. They had them all there—Billie Daniels and all of them

FANCHER: To build the desert town into an international entertainment mecca, Bugsy Siegel and the other casino and hotel own-ers relied on big-name black entertainers. But it was Siegel who de-cided that segregation of the races would be the policy in the hotels. Siegel was afraid that if blacks were allowed to patronize the hotels, whites would not come in to spend their money. So Siegel installed Jim Crow when he opened the Flamingo on Christmas Day in 1946. Blacks could entertain on stage, but they could not live at the hotel or gamble in the casino.

Segregating the hotels and casinos was in keeping with the pre-vailing racial climate of Las Vegas at the time. When civil rights leader Woodrow Wilson arrived in Las Vegas in the early '40s from Chicago, he found that city ordinances had just been passed confin-ing blacks to housing on the west side of town.

WOODROW WILSON (Civil Rights Leader): When I came here, it was only a few blacks living in west Las Vegas because there wasn't any-place to live. It was a horrible situation because—no water, no sewer and people had to eventually put down small lines—pipelines for water-spigots throughout the area and had outside privies.

FANCHER: Lena Horne appeared at the Flamingo Hotel in the sec-ond week of January 1947. She refused to accept accommodations on the black side of town. Bugsy Siegel relented and gave her a ca-bana outside the main hotel building. Woodrow Wilson was the head of the Las Vegas NAACP and recalls that Lena Horne won a mixed victory.

WILSON: The housekeeper would have the maids every day burn the—the—bedding—the linen from the bed that she was sleeping in, but still, Lena stayed in. She stuck in there and would not accept it. But they—each day, her linen was burned.

FANCHER: Segregation laws were imposed on the city in the early 1940s during the influx of Southern whites, first to work on Boulder Dam and later in the defense industries. The popularity of Jim Crow laws earned Las Vegas the nickname "Mississippi of the West." An-thropology professor Roosevelt Fitzgerald of the University of Nevada says the city was out of step with the rest of the country.

ROOSEVELT FITZGERALD (University of Nevada): One thing that I find very interesting with this is that at the same time that Las Vegas was sort of moving backwards, beginning with the late 1940s, the remainder of the country was beginning to move forward. I always find it ironic that a year before Jackie Robinson breaks into major league baseball, Las Vegas slunk into segregation, while integration is—was the order of the day in other places. I've never been able to figure that out, and I don't know if I ever will.

FANCHER: Even during World War II, Jim Crow laws were firmly observed. Sara Knight Preddy, a longtime Las Vegas resident, recalls that Japanese-Americans headed for internment camps received better accommodations than local blacks.

SARA KNIGHT PREDDY (Las Vegas resident): They had a convoy came through here, and they were a convoy of the Japanese people, I believe, or it was foreigners, and when they came through here, they housed them in one of the hotels downtown, and the drivers of the trucks was black, and they couldn't live down there and neither could they go in. They had to come on the west side and stay. They wouldn't let them sleep down there or eat either.

FANCHER: The same kind of embarrassments were suffered by many entertainers at the hotels. During those years, dancer Harold Nicholas found that the only door open to blacks was a stage door.

NICHOLAS: They give you that old "I'm sorry" business, you know. "It's not—not our fault," you know. "I—it's not us." It's—sure, we've been through it. I've had it—they've refused me. I've had it done to me in one of the Vegas hotels. They have asked me out of the casino, you know. They—surely they did.

Of course you resented it, you know. That was a bad feeling that it would put inside you, you know, but you had to go through, and you had to go on. You couldn't just give up, you know. And I guess we weren't about to get in the street and start yelling and fighting and carrying on, you know, but—so we just—we did it by trying to entertain the people and educate them in our way.

FANCHER: Nobody forced the Negro stars to perform at the Jim Crow hotels. Why did they do it?

PREDDY: Money. Money.

You know, most blacks that came to Las Vegas had never made that kind of money. This place paid more money for entertainment than anywhere in the world, and I think this is the reason that most blacks always tried to get in—to play in Las Vegas—not only blacks, white, too.

FANCHER: The hotel management kept a watchful eye on the entertainers. Once a reporter from E*bony* called the Sahara, wanting to interview one of the Negro stars. The reporter was met at the airport, watched the show from the wings, did the interview and left on the next plane. Some of the black entertainers resisted being humiliated, sometimes physically.

NICHOLAS: Billy Eckstine never, never went for any of that kind of stuff—of them bossing him around, pushing him out of things and all that—because Billy Eckstine would knock you down in a minute, you know. He didn't care, you know, because he went in the club, and some little guy came along and start giving him a whole lot of mouth. "Well, you can't be in here. What are you doing here?" And all this. And he looked in the glass and saw this guy coming behind him that was going to try to hit him and knock him down or something. So Billy got out of the way and took a thing and knocked the guy through the glass. Yes, right in Vegas.

FANCHER: Billy Eckstine was the exception. For 13 years while segregation was observed, the black performers complained privately, but the show, nevertheless, went on.

HAYES: I think they were humiliated, and I think it was such a gross oversight and such a dreadful thing to do to any other human being that I think they'd—they'd just rather bury it.

FANCHER: Peter Lynn Hayes, the veteran actor and comedian, was intimately involved with the early days of Las Vegas entertainment. He recalls that Jim Crow rules in the hotels had no effect on the personal relationships between black and white performers. Once, at an appearance featuring his pal Sammy Davis, Jr., Hayes used the occasion to poke fun at the race issue.

HAYES: So I introduced Sammy by saying that, "All of my life in vaudeville, everybody always said that the greatest entertainer that ever lived was Al Jolson." And I said, "I take exception to that. I think Sammy Davis is the greatest entertainer that ever lived. After all, he's a fabulous dancer. He's a terrific mimic. He has tremendous hit records on sale year after year. Of course, there's one thing that Al Jolson could do that Sammy couldn't do. Occasionally, Al Jolson worked in white face." And Sammy—Sammy went right out of his chair.

FANCHER: They joked about it, but the color bar remained firmly in place. Casinos were established on the west side to cater to blacks. Some of these places also attracted many whites because it was such a lively scene.

JOE WILLIAMS (Blues and Jazz vocalist): I remember that Bob Bailey had a club over there called Sugar Hill. And he threw a party for me over there one night, and I looked up—here was Johnny Carson and Ed McMahon, the Mills Brothers—all kinds of people, black and white, from the Strip—you know, the ladies of the ensemble, the dancers and the showgirls—everybody showed up. It was a gas. We had a ball, and about 8:30 in the morning, I remember—Carson leaned over and whispered in my ear and said, "Bed check." And I split.

FANCHER: As time passed, hotel owners on the Strip began to soften the Jim Crow policy according to how much clout a black entertainer might have. Singer Harry Belafonte was at the height of his popularity when the calypso singer played the Versailles Room at the Riviera Hotel on the Strip. The Riviera's manager, Ed Torres, decided to give Belafonte a room.

WILLIAMS: And Torres called a meeting of the Hotel Association . . . And told them, "I'm bringing in this man. My room is sold out for eight weeks." And he said, "I'm going to give him the same suite—penthouse suite that Alan King is in right now." That was the end of that. And Harry told me he came in, he told his son, "Put on your swimming trunks." He said, "What, Daddy?" "Put on your trunks." He said he took him downstairs and threw him in the pool.

FANCHER: In 1955, Sammy Davis, Jr. opened in the Venus Room at the new Frontier. In the audience, seated in front, was his grandmother, stepmother and his sister. This was the first time blacks were allowed in the audience on the Strip. The national civil rights movement, which was just getting off the ground with the Montgomery bus boycott and the freedom riders, was beginning to have an effect in Las Vegas.

WILSON: Accepting the status quo had come to an end.

FANCHER: Woodrow Wilson, who was to become the first black elected to the Nevada State Legislature, had helped reinvigorate the local NAACP in the late 1940s. Then, in 1960, he and other civil rights leaders organized the opposition to segregation in the hotels and casinos.

WILSON: Black people were going to stand up for their rights as citizens of this country and this community. They were going to be a part of it. And I think that the message came through loud and clear that we were moving in another direction and that things had to change or else.

FANCHER: Younger professional blacks, imbued with the fervor of the civil rights movement, were moving into Las Vegas, and according to UNLV history professor Eugene Mooring, this group was instrumental in sparking the changes.

EUGENE MOORING (UNLV): The key was when Dr. James McMillan and Dr. James West moved—one was a doctor, one's a dentist—they brought real leadership to the black community, and it was those two who decided they were going to march on the Strip on March 26, 1960, if Mayor Orrin Greggson and the county commissioners did not require the downtown hotels and the Strip hotels to open their public accommodations to blacks.

FANCHER: Who deserves the credit for achieving the peaceful end of segregation in the hotels and casinos in Las Vegas is a tough question to resolve. When the situation came to a head in March 1960, the mayor and other civic leaders wanted to avoid demonstrations because they would mar the city's image and scare away business. According to Dr. James McMillan, there was another, silent partner in those negotiations.

DR. JAMES MCMILLAN: And at that time, the Mob, I guess as you have heard, they were owners of all these hotels, and they came in to find out what was going on. They wanted to protect their investment, and we had talked to some of those people, and they finally decided that we were interested in really eliminating segregation because that would enhance their—their business.

FANCHER: It was a mobster, Bugsy Siegel, who segregated the city's casinos, and 13 years later, it was the Mob that was called upon to decide whether to eliminate Jim Crow in those same places. Dr. McMillan sensed that mobsters tended to be conservative when they had money invested. They didn't want to rock the boat. The black dentist says his mediation effort was undertaken with some fear for his personal safety.

McMILLAN: I was really worried because I thought that these people could do what they wanted to do with individuals, and it was a known fact that, you know, if a dealer didn't do right, they'd break his hand or set him out, and I thought maybe I was going to get hurt. But after they had found out what we were talking about, then they said, "OK, fine, we have no problem," and they OK'd it.

FANCHER: At 6 P.M. on March 26th, 1960, segregation began to collapse in Las Vegas because the owners voluntarily removed the color bar. Gradually, all the casinos and hotels opened their doors regardless of race. Segregation disappeared so fast that Peter Lynn Hayes says jokes about civil rights actually became popular.

HAYES: Dean Martin did one of the funniest things I've ever seen on a nightclub stage. He came out one night with Sammy Davis in his arms—holding him in his arms—and he said, "Ladies and gentlemen, I want to thank the NAACP for this award."

FANCHER: More than 30 years have passed since segregation ended. A whole new generation of black entertainers is making big dollars on the Strip. Many of them don't know what black performers in the '40s and '50s went through.

JOE WILLIAMS (Singer): Well, maybe it's a good thing, and I hope that they never know. If that's happening, it might be a good thing if they don't know that there are barriers or that there were barriers, you know. Sometimes that knowledge can affect people negatively.

FANCHER: Today the patrons of the Las Vegas gambling halls, hotels and casinos are among the most racially integrated crowds to be found anywhere in American society. Truly, in Las Vegas, the only color that counts is green. As for the underworld figure whose vision started it all, he never really was able to see his dream completed. Just six months after he opened the Flamingo, Bugsy Siegel was shot to death in Los Angeles on June 20th, 1947.

Edward Allen

·······················

Penny Ante

I can't understand it. I've done everything right all day: left my ill-starred blue shirt home, brought along the sunglasses that have been so good to me, avoided abbreviating any of the items on my grocery list. And, of course, I have labored carefully over the exact placement of that certain hidden object, which I have pinned with much seriousness beneath my clothes.

What's more, I have been a careful driver, covering the fifty miles between my house and town without causing a single Toyota to honk at me angrily. I have taken care to be equally well-mannered with my

☞ *From* Gentlemen's Quarterly, *May 1992.*

shopping cart, there in the corridors of the bag-it-yourself discount warehouse, where love songs, nothing but love songs, filter down all afternoon, soft as asbestos, from the barnlike ceiling. Those tender lyrics, mostly about individuals learning to live with or without someone else's precious love, still echo through my head as I wheel my week's groceries through the parking lot, wandering in search of my car through the vague, frostless chill of a winter night in Las Vegas.

Now, with shopping over, half my supper eaten and the other half doggie-bagged, an inconclusive fortune-cookie chit folded in my shirt pocket and a clump of third-rate Mongolian beef sitting heavy on my stomach, I am an unhappy man. I am unhappy in that crushed and chastised way of a student who has been yelled at unfairly in front of the class. I can feel my face flush with the shame of it—the shame of someone who has no reason to deserve the kind of humiliation I see laid out on the table in front of me, hand after hand, here in a room where all the other blackjack players and crapshooters and roulette-wheel watchers seem, from their buzz and clamor, to be getting as rich as sweepstakes millionaire David Brumbalow.

I want to tell you that these are the thoughts of a man who prides himself on his common sense, who likes the efficiency of combining this weekly Las Vegas shopping trip with a quick and strictly budgeted run at the casino tables, a man who answers no chain letters nor dreams of buying real estate for no money down, someone to whom Nostradamus is nothing, someone who will never call in to Time-Life Books to order its *Illustrated Encyclopedia of Spooky Noises*. In short, I am a reasonable American, registered to vote, sitting at a blackjack table, losing, with a $2 bill safety-pinned to the front of my underpants.

What I like most about gambling is that it does not make sense. I find it comforting that in pursuit of its admittedly fraudulent promises, I don't have to pretend to make sense myself. The hobby of gambling, even at my wimpish betting level, allows me to believe things that I know are not true. It lets me be a devotional weirdo, without requiring me to dress funny. It gives me a chance to apply the most-Byzantine rules and structures to my most ordinary actions, all in search of that compelling fiction known as luck.

In short, gambling invites me to take an hour's recess from adulthood, to play in a well-demarked sandbox of irrationality and to look at the world as a magical place, which, of course, it is when the light hits it at the right angle. Those people who stubbornly remain adults and who look upon gambling's happy meaninglessness from within the logic of the real world will see something quite different. They will see a phalanx of games controlled by the indomitable law of averages, games that from an adult's wintry perspective you cannot hope to master. Those adults will see me, and the people sitting next to me, giving our money away week after week to people who do not love us.

One reason it's so hard to keep from getting angry tonight is that this casino has been very good to me on occasion. I do not believe in telling you the name of this establishment or how well I have done before, but I will say that in the past, on a summer night, I have stepped out onto the Las Vegas Strip with a smile on my face that you couldn't have wiped off with a shovel. I have walked past where the Caesars Palace loudspeakers blend flutes and drums to produce what I guess is supposed to sound like Cecil B. De Mille slave sacrifice music, have walked with the kind of stride that can only indicate the presence of multiple hundreds in the wallet. If I were a mugger, I would pay close attention to the way people walk.

But tonight, everything is terrible: The air is thick with carpet shampoo and cigarettes; the happy voices around me seem as empty and shrill as untrained parrots. Nothing falls together right. I chose this dealer for her kind face, yet there seems a ferocious hopelessness to the cards she tosses me. As she deals me a jack to bust another hand, I can hear, at the far end of the casino from beyond a bank of slot machines, the strains of "I've Got to Be Me" in the amplified voice of a lounge singer who I'm sure would rather be almost anybody else. Everything around this little $5 blackjack table seems wounded, like a country that has just devalued its currency.

One of the reasons I find gambling so much fun is that the adventure is not limited to the times when you are doing it. In fact, the moments when you are actually doing it will frequently stink, as they do tonight. For me, the subsidiary thrill is just as important, as well as much less expensive.

The surrounding excitement can stretch out in either direction. For hours before, on a Las Vegas shopping day, as the time draws near for me to leave my house in the desert and drive into town, I find an almost-religious excitement in the preparation for a session, complete with my own private rules, rituals, prohibitions. And coming home, blessed or wounded, I am allowed to wrestle again with the mystery of what I did wrong and what I did right; I must also try once more to find some way to recognize the difference in advance.

One of the things I know, though it doesn't matter on these local trips, is that I must never again permit myself to drive through another state and out again without stepping on the ground of that state. This is a superstition that I developed on my own, and I am rather proud of it. Somehow it seems right, a mandate for some kind of geographical integrity. I would be even prouder of it if it worked.

Particularly important in the moments of preparation is to avoid putting on any article of clothing in which I have had a bad night in the past. Unfortunately, a too-strict observance of this rule always leads to a problem with shoes because I have only a limited number, and I've had terrible nights in every pair I own. The best I can do, as a sort of nervous compromise, is always keep a second pair in the car so that if I get hurt in one casino, at least I can change shoes before trying the next.

Do I really believe any of this stuff? I do, in the sense that within the skewed world of gambling it is no crazier to believe it than not to. And at the purest level, the irrationality is its own payoff. I don't know if anybody in the world shares this feeling, but for me, to walk around in a place as public as a casino with a $2 bill fastened to the front of my shorts is an unqualified pleasure, whether it works or not. (It doesn't work. I will be honest now and admit that this account is narrated retrospectively and that I have since retired the $2 bill, which is the only reason I'm willing to mention it. That bill let me down one too many times—meaning somehow that it must have lost the power I knew it never possessed. I am trying to be scientific about these things. As I said, I pride myself on my rationality.)

So here I am, delivering more of my money to the absentee investors in a casino I won't name, on a night I could be reading a good book or maybe writing one. Why do I bother? This question always comes up when I talk to non-gamblers, and I never have a decent answer. Why is an activity with so little to offer so appealing to so many people, enough to make it one of the few growth industries in a retreating economy? Why should so many people fly so many thousands of miles to stay in rooms where the drapes never quite come together in the middle, and drop so many thousands of dollars at games that really aren't very interesting, all in pursuit of a chance that anybody with more brains than a state lottery player knows is mathematically remote?

In my experience, what makes it worthwhile is the idea that something as tyrannical as the law of averages can be turned upside down, if only for an hour or a weekend, and that what does not make sense can be forced to make sense. That logical turnabout is in itself a pleasure worthy of any number of spongy hotel mattresses. Deep down we all know, unless we are of the intellectual caste who smoke cigarettes but find airplanes too dangerous, that we are suckers. But that's okay; we're in good company, and we're here to have fun. All day and night, the law of averages grinds away at our frail chances, immutable in its pronouncement that if you keep playing long enough at a game that has a negative expectation built into it, you will have to lose.

In other words, you can't even break even. But we also know that people have been known to have astonishingly good nights, even when they are playing like idiots. And the best players can, and will, get slapped in the face. It's not fair. That's another thing I like about gambling. It's value-free. You'll have a great night sometime, and the greatest thing about that night will be that you did nothing to deserve it.

I suppose that when I described some of my own private superstitions, I might have sounded like someone who has forgotten to take his medication. But I think I can demonstrate that such craziness makes at least some kind of sense.

Superstitious gambling behavior makes sense because even the smallest and most meaningless actions can be shown to affect, in some way, the random interconnectedness of all physical processes. By this logic, everything you do can be said to transform the world. If I cough once at the card table, or lean back in my chair, or audibly riffle my chips, I may distract the dealer during that magically important process of shuffling the cards. The outcome of the game will thus be changed completely—every hand, every possibility, turned upside down.

The example I use in my forthcoming novel has to do with what will happen if you bend down to pick up a penny as you are walking into a crowded casino.

The first thing that will happen is that you will get to the crap table a few seconds later than you would have without having bothered with the penny. A man who walked in the door before you, who would have been behind you if you had left that penny alone, will now get where he's going a few seconds earlier. The shooter about to roll the dice at your table will see you out of the corner of his eye and will shake the dice in his fist one less time, and the throw will come out showing a different number.

Because of that last throw, or because of all the throws following it, which have been changed as well, somebody will eventually leave your table. And it is a physical law that whenever someone leaves one place, he or she has to move to another place. When that happens, the progress of the game at whatever table that person ends up at will be changed utterly. Because of that change, a few who would otherwise have left their tables will stay, and others who might have stayed will leave. Where will they go? It doesn't matter. Wherever they go to will never be the same.

In time, every game in the whole casino will be changed utterly, because of that penny. The change will be so pervasive that eventually a man who would otherwise have been lavishly in the money will get discouraged and grab a taxi downtown (and, of course, the interference of that cab in traffic will delay by a few seconds another cabload of gamblers bound for Caesars, whose night, now, will never be the same, and they will never know it).

Thus, when our discouraged man gets downtown, Binion's Horseshoe Casino will be transformed by his effect on the games he buys into there, which effect again will multiply from table to table in a chain reaction, a process something like that film they played for us in elementary school to illustrate atomic fission, showing a floor covered with thousands of mousetraps armed with Ping-Pong balls, onto which one triggering ball (the neutron?) is dropped. Those people chased out of Binion's by the change this man has caused will wander around Fremont Street, extending the process you have begun, carrying it from street to street, mousetrap to mousetrap, from Pioneer to Golden Nugget to Four Queens.

When you look around town a few hours after picking up that earthshaking penny, everything will seem normal. But I believe that if you were able to go back, like George Bailey in *It's a Wonderful Life*, and see both worlds, with penny and without penny, the Strip would be a different place. People would still walk in and out of the same doors, but they would not all be the same people; cars gliding up and down the Strip would catch the traffic lights in a different sequence. Those two possibilities of the Strip would look much alike, but they would in reality be as different from each other as Jimmy Stewart's old Bedford Falls was from the soulless alternate reality of

Pottersville. (Actually, I have to admit that I've always liked Pottersville better; every time I see that movie I wish I could drop into the Indian Club for a Christmas Eve martini.)

And more: I suspect that in one of these casinos there is a man who because of that penny will have the luck of his life. This guy will end up with so much money that he will choose to spend some of it on a young woman who is not his wife. If the girl does not turn out to be a police decoy, this man's casino session will culminate in her arms, with the result that later, on the too-soft Beautyrest, he will disappoint his wife by turning over and going to sleep—which means that the baby who would otherwise have been conceived that night will never be born to fulfill his appointed destiny, whether that be to develop sugar-free cotton candy or to blow up the world. That child's existence is now canceled, as thoroughly as all the other Pottersvillean ghosts have been canceled by all the other people who have bent down to pick up pennies in front of all the other casinos.

Like many other trains of thought, this one takes us to only a limited number of terminals. As crazy and metaphysical as the idea of interconnected events is, there's not much you can do with it, mostly because we can't ever see the alternative possibilities that our actions have preempted. All we can do is pay attention, go on with our strategies, not worry too much about what could have been and try to play as intelligently as we can. We will find, among other things, that intelligence does not help us.

Although the mathematics are pretty clear, any psychological observations I can make about the gambling will be almost as shaky as the hands of a poker novice holding the first full house of his life. The reason I know so little about anybody else's gambling experiences is that, even though it doesn't look that way, gambling is a profoundly solitary activity. In the crush around the casino tables, surrounded by the high spirits and camaraderie of players, one is really walking among thousands of strictly personal experiences. When I mention the irrational (or maybe I can be fancy and say *pararational*) behavior that I have no idea if it applies to anybody else. It's not the sort of thing we talk about.

I feel the same ignorance whenever I get into a discussion about the phenomenon of the compulsive gambler. From within my minimum-risk style, the cruelty of that disease seems incomprehensible. And although I don't think I'm likely to end up like that, the picture frightens me. Among those who consider ourselves noncompulsive, the specter of the toxic gambler, the driven and tortured person we have seen on television, with his face hidden from the interview camera, and who deep down we all fear we could turn into, waits at the edge of every table, his flamboyant sickness looming over our careful play the way the shadow of alcoholism hovers over the early social drinking of every young man with a family history.

Whenever the subject of compulsive gambling comes up, it is usual for someone to cite the many sources who believe that what the compulsive gambler really wants to do is to lose, that he is trying to reconnect with a distant parent, who will comfort him in his hour of loss and take him in. I don't know. I wonder if in some cases, the problem has more to do with rationality.

My admittedly unstudied theory is this: If "healthy" gambling is in part a vacation from rationality, then perhaps sick gambling is for some a failure to escape that rationality. Perhaps, the sick gambler suffers from bringing too much rational baggage along, into a part of the world where it does not work. I am thinking in particular of the principle of fair play, the idea that there exists some sort of moral balance sheet between getting and deserving.

A normal gambler knows the dice and the cards and the wheels and the video chips will play anything but fair; cards will fall (as they have been falling for me on this rotten night) in a sequence that only a malevolent deity (or the always-suspected, but highly unlikely, crooked casino) could have engineered.

The healthy gambler winces, gets disgusted and finally writes it off, knowing the universe is unfair. I think some compulsive gamblers fail to understand this. The compulsive, frantic on a losing night, seems to believe both in fair play and in the inherently balanced nature of the universe—and so goes on losing disastrously, laboring under the conviction that the universe will relent, will show just a touch of human decency and will force the cards to pay the wronged player back for all those previous acts of cruelty.

I suspect also that some compulsives are simply drawn into their illness by the pure sensuality of the betting moment. When we see the misery that the compulsive gambler brings down upon himself, it is natural to imagine him the worst of masochists. But just because he almost always ends up ruined doesn't mean that the ruin itself is what he sought. To use an example from another illness: If we were examining the case of an alcoholic who every night gets so drunk that he throws up, we probably would not be taken seriously if we concluded that this person's real problem is that he's addicted to vomiting.

Instead of being a masochist, perhaps the compulsive gambler loses control because he is enjoying himself so much. Even if he seems miserable most of the time, there is something very powerful about the instant the dice are thrown, the second the deciding card is turned over, the moment the little ball takes its last spastic bounce into the numbered slot.

In my own timid experience, I've felt something of that thrill a few times. On those rare occasions, when a series of successful blackjack hands has allowed me to increase my bet to the grand total of, say, $30, the moment when the card comes down, while everything hangs in the balance—that's where the thrill is. It is a neurological jolt made up of greed, lust and excitement mixed together with a strong dose of fear. Whenever my game gets raised to such a level, then I can feel myself coming alive in a way that seems to redeem all those previous hemorrhogenic hours I have spent on those stools, busting sixteens.

There is another thing that attracts me to casinos, and it may help explain why it felt so appropriate for me to pin that $2 bill to my shorts. For many people, and on many levels, gambling is strongly associated with sex.

On one level, it's easy to understand why that should be so: Money gained through the accident of luck comes with few restrictions on how it is to be spent. And even though Las Vegas is trying to put on a clean face for the benefit of its most profitable tourists (meaning the retirees and the young parents, devoted slot-players all), there remain plenty of young women ready to provide more-traditional forms of entertainment—after they have checked your ID and asked you all sorts of questions to make sure that you are not a cop.

But even for those players who would never call the Room-Service Showgirls escort agency nor board the free limousine that ferries patrons to the out-of-town, legal brothels, something of the old sexiness still hangs in the air above the real games, the ones still played on green felt instead of video terminals. I'm sure it is no accident that the prettiest employees in a casino are always the women who bring gamblers their free cocktails, encouraging them, without saying a word, to drink more, bet more, lose more.

Although the narrow-tied swagger of the Rat Pack is long forgotten down the endless corridors of Circus Circus RV Park, although the city seems determined to insulate the "slots-and-tots" crowd from any disturbing memories of how sexy this place used to be, although the public-relations industry seems bent on changing the symbol of Las Vegas from the painted showgirl to the painted clown—still, something filters through here and there, in the agitated light of the Strip when it catches your eye from an unexpected direction, in the climactic squeal of a Chicago secretary blessed with beginner's luck as she rolls another winning number.

And then there is the ubiquitous $100 bill, the controlling scrip against which all clattering chips and wrinkled twenties are measured. It is the only piece of American currency that cannot be called ugly. The reverse side is especially attractive, with its leafy green and that sort of Frederick's of Hollywood laciness in the scrollwork around the edges.

Even the most uxorious conventioneer knows that if an escort-agency transaction ever should occur, it would involve bills of this denomination. To handle one bill is perhaps to be remotely involved in all the adventures that that bill has helped to capitalize. That moment at the casino cage, as the cashier counts your chips and crisply deals out the stacked hundreds, remains, I think, an erotically charged moment—no matter that you have already earmarked that money to resurface your driveway.

Marc Cooper

Searching for Sin City and Finding Disney in the Desert

No, this is not a good town for psychedelic drugs. Reality itself is too twisted.

—Hunter S. Thompson,
Fear and Loathing in Las Vegas, 1971

LAS VEGAS—Heeding the good Doctor Gonzo's advice, I did not repeat his mistake of 22 years past and cart across the Clark County line two bags of grass, 75 pellets of mescaline, five sheets of blotter

☞ *Originally appeared as "Fear and Lava: Looking for Blackjack and Finding Fanny Packers. A Tale of the New Las Vegas" in* The Village Voice, *November 30, 1993.*

acid, a salt shaker of coke, or a galaxy of uppers, downers, scream-
ers, and laughers. But just as Thompson had brought his Fat
Samoan Attorney in tow to the Vegas Strip, I thought it prudent to
invite along my corpulent Neapolitan literary agent, the Big Vig, for
my visit. The Big Vig was invited strictly for moral support. As a semi-
compulsive gambler, I needed someone to sit next to me at the 21
table. Who better to approve each more reckless maneuver with a
knowing nod than another irretrievable card-and-dice junkie?

And so far my strategy had worked. No sooner had we dumped
our bags in our Tropicana Hotel "garden suites" (both with a commanding view of the neatly furrowed rows of cars in the hotel parking lot) than we sat down at the blackjack table and within no time
at all were experiencing financial free fall. "Better double up or even
triple your bets now if you wanna win back what you're down," the
Big Vig wisely advised as he rummaged in his Bugle Boys for yet another crumpled C-note.

Not that we were at this table on a fully voluntary basis. Actually
we were more like indentured servants. Checking into the Tropicana
nowadays, or just about any other Strip hotel, is like signing up for
a sting in debtors' prison. The balding gnomes who run these outfits—infinitely more sinister than their mob predecessors—have
come up with a fantastically evil device to keep you glued to your
casino seats. No, not the fabled free drinks. Nor the blasts of arctic
air and rushes of pure oxygen pumped through the gaming rooms in
quantities sufficient to raise an army of Haitian zombies and burnish
them with baby-pink glow. Not the absence of clocks so that you forget to check in with your baby-sitter, nor the dearth of pay phones
just in case you do remember.

No. Instead it was a devilishly simply ATM-like card, handed to
us at check-in, already embossed with our names in gold letters.
We were now members of the Island Winners Club. And, we were
told, our $85-a-night room charge would be waived—for two
nights—if we simply played the quarter slots or $5 blackjack tables
for only four hours over the next two days. Hey, just like the Big
Rollers, we were going to get "comped." We just had to hand the

card over to the dealer when we sat down or stick it into the bar code reader now attached to every one-arm bandit. Computers would clock our gaming.

"How in the hell can 14 minutes pass so slowly?" the Big Vig asked, a hint of alarm spreading over his broad visage, his Manhattan pallor turning a Southwestern rust color under the effects of casino air. He had just run his Winners Club card through one of the—very few—electronic meters in the casino that would read out our time logged at the table. Here we were, three hours and 46 minutes of gambling away from free rooms, if not freedom itself, and so far we were down $300. Sitting back at the 21 table, and being dealt, during my 15th and 16th minute, a series of stiff hands—13s and 14s—with the dealer showing Jacks, Queens, and 10s, it seemed ever more that calling us members of the Island Winners Club was a little like dubbing the guys in Cell Block B participants in the Indoor Chess and Weight Lifting Society.

Things took a disorienting turn for the worse when the Ohio schoolteacher next to me split a pair of 10s against the dealer's seven and then *won* both hands even though the dealer drew to 19. That move made about as much sense as people voting for Republicans because they want "a change." But she won. I, playing by the book, lost, choked out with an 18. "Harv, we better go now," the schoolteacher said to her husband, scooping up her green and orange chips and checking her watch. "The Volcano goes off in eight minutes."

In fact, the Volcano in front of the Mirage Hotel just down Las Vegas Boulevard goes off every 15 minutes until midnight, and, being that it was eight minutes to 11, its impending belching session was a perfect excuse for the Big Vig and me to take a gaming hiatus.

We zoomed up the Strip, the oven-dry night lit with an atomic glow from the 100 megatons of neon around us, and soon found the Volcano. Difficult to miss. For, on the sidewalk in front of it, packed behind a protective railing, were hundreds, perhaps as many as a thousand people obediently waiting for the scheduled volcanic blowout.

Here was ground zero of the New Las Vegas. The traditional sleaze and cheese that had always made this place a great weekend refuge from the monotony of an ordered and decorous life are being swept away by a lava flow of respectability and Family Values. Anxiously gathered at the foot of the Mirage Volcano was this herd of beefy middle Americans, almost all dressed in short pants, T-shirts, and baseball caps, and enough of them wearing those pastel-colored fanny packs around their waists that the city looked as though it was immersed in a continuing convention of colostomy patients. If Bugsy Siegel had walked by at that moment, half of these lookie-loos would have called the feds. If so much as one old-time Vegas showgirl had shimmered by in boas and pasties, this assembled decency league would have stoned her to death.

As the Volcano began to rumble—that is to say as the sound effects cassette began to play through the weatherproof loudspeakers hidden among the faux rocks of the volcanic lagoon—the awestruck crowd, henceforth to be known at the Fanny Packers, first hushed and then in its own way erupted as whole batteries of handheld camcorders recorded the scene for later viewing in dens and family rooms from Omaha to Oshkosh.

We only knew this structure in front of us was a volcano because that's what the management at the Mirage calls it. What it looks like is a rather squat, mostly symmetrical, triple-tiered, 54-foot-high, concrete pump-driven fountain-cum-waterfall that empties into an oversize pool with a lot of pumice stone glued to its sides.

Its scheduled eruption consists of the aforementioned soundtrack, accompanied by dozens of red floodlights flashing on and off. As the drama builds, a piped vent just clearing the top surface of the volcano begins to blow out puffs of steam. Then a gas jet next to the steam pipe ignites, and a large flame politely reaches toward the sky, soon setting off five or six rows of similar gas burners running down the slope of the slab and into the pool, making the whole thing look like a slightly damaged kitchen stove on steroids. The flames burn a gassy bluish-yellow for about a minute, and then—suddenly—the show is over. But the onlookers all agreed that this was marvelous, worth the wait, worth seeing again, worth filling an 8mm tape with, worth having lost title to their home and boat to come to Vegas to witness.

This is where, customarily in an article like this, the reporter is supposed to come up with some pithy, penetrating observation. Something about how this scene in front of the phony volcano revealed some new insight into the national zeitgeist, how it symbolized something about a culture where people prefer simulation over the real thing, or how in a country where everything is screwed up and nothing works anymore (or as Vegas philosopher George Carlin has noted, "Where we can't even build a VCR worth a fuck") Americans now find their only solace in the worship of technology, even technology at this infantile level, solely because it works.

Or, perhaps, the writer should be compelled to expound on how a TV-dominated culture has erased the line between adulthood and childhood, how kids and grown-ups spend all their time watching the same TV shows and therefore it should come as no surprise that young and old both now eat food with their hands, that they all dress like Beavis and Butt-head, and that therefore this mechanical volcano brings equal glee to the gathered 10-year-olds *and* their parents. Anything like that could be said here. But it was the Big Vig who, gazing out at the gas flames and burping steam, put it best. "It makes me nostalgic for my childhood," he said, remembering lazy summers spent collecting industrial artifacts in the shadow of chemical refineries and cracking plants. "It looks just like Elizabeth, New Jersey."

Vegas may seem like old times to the Big Vig, but to the rest of America it has become the last chance at a future. It laughs at the thought of recession, this last boomtown in America. Make that boom city. For Las Vegas is the fastest growing metropolitan area in America. As New Jersey, New Hampshire, Texas, California, and about 45 or so other states went down the toilet in the '80s, Las Vegas saw its population double from 465,000 in 1980 to 925,000 today.

Las Vegas is also quickly becoming America's favorite tourist stop, logging some 22 million person-visits per year, the Strip casinos piling up about $3.5 billion in annual revenues.

But there's a glitch in this rosy scenario. Las Vegas has never before had so much competition. As everyday economic life in America has become a breathtaking risk, when it's an all-out crapshoot whether you'll still have a job next month, an even bet whether your insurance will really pay off your medical claim, and a roulette spin as to whether you can make the next mortgage payment, who needs to travel to Vegas for gambling thrills? The recession-ravaged infrastructure of America is being retooled nationwide for gambling. There is not only Atlantic City, but new riverboat gambling in the heartland and waterfront betting in the south. Mining town gambling in the Rockies. Cruise boat gambling in the Pacific and the Caribbean. Indian reservation gambling in the southwest and New England, and of course multimillion-dollar lottos and lower-stake lottery tickets in just about every supermarket and corner convenience store in the country.

Fifty percent of Americans have now been inside a casino, up a dramatic four points just since 1991. But less than a third of that group has been to Las Vegas. Now Las Vegas wants to lure the 85 percent of Americans who have yet to set foot in this desert paradise. To do that a couple of Vegas casino kings are remaking the face of the city, pouring in $2 billion of capital.

But I couldn't care less about *their* capital. After the volcanic parenthesis and a midnight nosh, it was 1:40 A.M. and the Big Vig and I were trying to win back our capital, engaged in hand-to-hand combat on the slippery slopes of the so-called Island of Las Vegas—the Tropicana casino. Some Fanny Packer moron next to me at the blackjack table insisted on hitting 13s and 14s while yelling out, "Come on, eight! . . . Come on, seven!" The dealer kept busting her out, wickedly snapping down one face card after another. As my pile of chips atrophied, I asked the Big Vig just how much he figured we could lose during our mandatory four hours. But I'd lost him. Down about $400, the Vig just stared at his cards, absolutely intent on climbing back out of the hole.

I knew the answer, anyway. Betting $5 or $10 a hand, you can easily blow a hundred in five minutes—maybe $500 an hour, $2000 or more in the required four hours. I had about an hour and a half logged on my debit card, and I was $375 in the hole.

But then the cards turned. Sarge, who's been dealing 22 years, started busting. I hit three hands in a row. Then I got a blackjack on a $20 bet. I let the $30 in winnings ride. I got two deuces, the dealer showing a six. I split the deuces into two separated hands and now had a hundred on the table on two $50 bets. My first card was a Queen, so I stayed on that hand, a limp 12. My next draw was nine. I put down another 50 to double down on one card. A red King! A cool 21. The dealer flipped over his hold card. A nine, giving him 15 and forcing an obligatory hit. Another nine and he was out. My $20 bet of two minutes ago had morphed into $300.

I was on the upswing. The Vig was also winning now and told me he was about even on the day. I was reborn. The lump was gone from my throat, the tightness in my chest had eased, time was passing much more quickly, I was drinking Wild Turkey with a bit more abandon and, though I was freely tipping Sarge, by about 2:30 A.M. I was actually ahead $75. The Vig, who was up a hundred, packed off to bed and advised I do the same. I told him I'd be up in five minutes. Which turned into 10, then 15, and I was losing again. Disgusted with myself, I took a bathroom break and pulled $400 cash out of my pocket and stuffed it into my shoe, leaving me $300 or so to play with.

Resuming play, I might as well have stepped into a draining whirlpool. Down within minutes to one 10 stack of $5 chips, I knew sure as shit that I was going to lose everything. Sarge bravely countenanced my world-weary chatter, my increasingly feigned nonchalance, and keenly eyed my evaporating stash, knowing full well that he'd seen the last tip from me for the evening. And then, about 4:00 A.M., it was all over. The last chip was consumed, and only my bone-deep fatigue kept me from dipping into my shoe-covered reserve.

But there was a certain existential epiphany, a veritable frisson, that I always feel as the last, lost chip is swept away. All the previous hours of chitchat, of know-it-all exchanges between the ice-cool dealer and the jaded writer from the big city, the kibitzing with the T-shirted rubes and the ponytailed sharpies around me, the false promises of the casino, the little stories you tell yourself while you're sitting at the table—all of this comes to an abrupt, crashing halt because when your last chip is gone so are you. No seats for the on-lookers. And the other players at the table, the dealer, and the pit boss, who a moment before were your buddies, can no longer give a fuck whether you live or die. And that's when I feel that perverse thrill. Because it's one of the only fully honest interludes you have in modern America. All the pretense and sentimentality, all the euphemisms and fairy tales are out the window. You are out of money? OK—get lost.

I had, however, fulfilled my four-hour obligation. My $85 room would be free for two nights. And it had only cost me $310.

Alan Feldman, the vice-president in charge of public relations for Mirage Resorts, Inc., looked at my business card and then across his desk at me and asked, "Hey, you're not going to write one of those cynical stories about Vegas are you?"

Cynical? I thought, before answering. Moi? Cynical about a place that suckers you into its casinos with $4 prime rib dinners, $3 lunch buffets, and 93-cent shrimp cocktails? Cynical about a town that puts slot machines in the 7-Elevens, the gas stations, gas station bathrooms? Cynical about this being the only place in the world where pawn shops are open 24 hours a day, including the Dante-esque automobile pawn shops? Cynical about casinos that bus in old people from 300 miles away, give them a book full of two-for-one scrip, force them to amble from gambling hall to gambling hall for eight hours after a five-hour bus ride, and then turn around and bus them back home through the middle of the desert night?

"Cynical?" I answered. "No way. I'm here to write about the New Las Vegas."

Of course, what Feldman had in mind when he said cynical was something very specific. His company was just about to open a place next door called Treasure Island—"an adventure resort"—which would feature not an erupting volcano, but a once-an-hour nine-minute battle royal between a 90-foot pirate ship and a full-scale British frigate, replete with cannon blasts, sword fights, and more than 30 real, live actors. T.I., as this new $300 million property is called, is one of three new wave resort hotels in Vegas.

Also just open for business is the $400 million Luxor, owned by the Circus Circus company; in December, it'll be joined by Kirk Kerkorian's $1 billion MGM Grand. The Luxor boasts a 30-story, 2526-room, glass pyramid hotel, a 10-story sphynx, a piercing mega laser beam that can be seen by planes 250 miles away over Los Angeles, a winding Nile river, barges that float you to your elevator, a seven-story movie screen, an 18,000-square-foot video arcade, including virtual-reality games, a replica of King Tut's tomb, and an atrium lobby that claims to be big enough to hold nine 747s stacked on top of each other (perhaps a final resting place for those unfortunate jetliners downed by the hotel's blinding laser beam).

Across the street is the MGM Grand, a mammoth collection of aqua and black glass block, like a repository of every leftover office building in Dallas. The Grand will debut as the "biggest hotel in the world," with 5005 rooms, 33 acres of adjoining theme park, the "biggest casino in the galaxy," measuring in at 171,000 square feet, an 88-foot-high MGM lion whose mouth you suggestively walk through to enter the complex, and lobby and room decor based on MGM's *Wizard of* Oz, including emerald green carpets, a yellow brick road through the casino and into the amusement park, and paintings of Dorothy, Toto, the Tin Man, the Lion, the Scarecrow, and the Good Witch of the East on the walls, thereby confirming to dazed but awakening gamblers that they are, indeed, no longer in Kansas.

Taken together, these three hotels mark the conversion of Las Vegas into what is now called a "multi-dimensional resort destination where entertainment resorts are the rule, rather than the exception," to quote the marketeers who kicked off this new phase when they opened the Mirage in late 1989. In other words, a sprawling Disneyland.

So when Feldman worried about me being "cynical" he worried that with so many Egyptian mummies, swashbuckling pirates, and dancing munchkins taking up residence on the Vegas Strip I might get the same wrong impression that other reporters have recently gotten, that this new adolescent-minded Vegas is up to something really dirty, like hooking a new generation of gamblers by getting them into the hotels while still in diapers—you know, the Joe Camel strategy.

"The fallacy about what's really going on here is the concept of the family. Family is the 'F' word here. A casino is no place for kids," Feldman swore. "Las Vegas is not going after kids. But we have to find a new public for Las Vegas, and the biggest untapped pool are those people who won't travel without their kids. So we're giving a little something for the kids to do too. What we are really after is what Disney said. He's not after the kids, but rather, the kids inside all of us. We are building adult theme parks. We are playing in the tour and travel market now, not just the gambling market."

Feldman really didn't need to explain to me that Vegas was simply catering to an increasingly adolescent national culture. Coming to Las Vegas since toddler age, I have seen the town's rapid transformation from mobster and starlet hideaway to haven of sin and vice to low-roller heaven. The latter phase began in 1974, when Circus Circus started offering rooms for less than 20 bucks, 24-hour circus acts, and a mezzanine full of carnival games for the kiddies. The family revolution took a quantitative leap four years ago when the 3049-room, $630 million Mirage opened and quickly became the most successful hotel in Vegas history.

Mirage boss Steve Wynn beat the odds by raking in more than $1 million a day, a figure the naysayers had predicted he'd never reach. ("The Volcano has been key to that success," noted Feldman. "It brings by thousands of people every day.")

Today the 51-year-old Wynn, the highest-paid executive in the nation ($34 million a year, according to *Fortune*) also stands as the most powerful force in the Vegas desert. Now he's posed to enter state politics. He personally led a drive to register his employees, 97 percent of whom are now on the voting rolls—and boasts that his workforce accounts for a full 10 percent of the people most likely to vote in Clark County.

But most of all Wynn, more than any other corporate power in Las Vegas, has understood the gestalt of entertainment and diversion in modern America. Give 'em spectacle, spectacle, and then a little more spectacle. Age, class, educational differences wither under the wow 'em neon and the knockout theatrics. The ultimate populist, he seems to be able to geometrically reduce the lowest common denominator on a daily basis. His concept of Las Vegas is to Bugsy Siegel's what MTV is to *Playhouse* 90.

I mean, sure, Vegas, *is* trying to hook the kiddies. But as Feldman argued, that's not the real point. Nor is the signal truth here that American grown-ups have kids lurking inside them. Simply, it's that America's adults have become kids. As I walked out of Feldman's office and drifted through the Mirage, the actual number of kids I saw was minimal. But the public spaces of the hotel were thronged with adults, undoubtedly drawn by the Volcano.

Veritable mobs of Fanny Packers pointing to, photographing, and posing in front of the 20,000-gallon saltwater aquarium that takes up the whole wall behind reception (God help the clerks when the next 7.8 shaker hits!). More Fanny Packers flocking around the Mirage's 10-foot-long glass-enclosed mock-up of Treasure Island, all jostling for room from which to take the best video shots. Hundreds more Fanny Packers oohing at a pair of exotic (and very real) Royal White Tigers forever imprisoned in what the Mirage calls "spacious accommodations." Ecologically correct Fanny Packers capturing on video the captured bottle-neck mammals of the dolphin habitat. Even more Fanny Packers videocamming the plastic and rubber flowers in the 90-foot-high atrium and Tropical Rainforest by the front exit.

As I left the air-conditioned paradise of the Mirage and walked out onto the parched concrete of Las Vegas Boulevard, I thought of Alan Feldman's parting line: "What we do for entertainment tells us who we are." Walking out toward the Strip I shut my eyes tight, not only as protection against the snickering sun, but also to blot out that godawful Volcano starting to vibrate again in front of me.

By the time I got back to the garden wing of the Tropicana, the Big Vig had been reduced to watching Monster Truck races on ESPN. Boris Yeltsin, he had heard, was doing something dramatic to save Russian democracy, like firing tank shells at Parliament, but the Vig could get no confirmation. Like most Vegas hotels, the Tropicana refuses to carry CNN, lest continuing coverage of some trivial event out in the World distract you from your unfinished business downstairs in the casino.

The Big Vig, however, had completed his four-hour sentence at the Trop while I had been plodding through the Mirage rain forest and, unlike me, had come out with his free room *and* 80 *bucks*. Which meant . . . we were free! Free from the Tropicana, white, and over 21, we could choose among dozens of round-the-clock casinos.

After a ceremonial burning of our Island Winners Club Cards, which created enough of a toxic cloud to set off the smoke alarm but, fortunately, not enough to trigger the in-room sprinklers, we debated where best to satisfy our swelling urge to play. Maybe the last outpost of elegance, the Desert Inn. Maybe the hangout of the open-shirted high-rollers, Caesars Palace. How about the Stardust? The

Hacienda? The Sands? Nah. If visiting any of those places was like searching for a date with Lady Luck, then what we were about to do was equivalent to a back-alley encounter with anything but a lady. The decision was in. We were going as low as humanly possible, on a beeline up the strip to Vegas World.

Vegas World is the creation of self-styled "Polish Maverick" Bob Stupak, whose public rep in Vegas registers two ticks lower than Charles Keating's among Sun City pensioners. But Stupak could give a fuck what the locals think. For Vegas World is perhaps the world's only direct-mail casino. Every month Stupak mails out tens of thousands of invitations to lunch-pail Joes and Jills: For only $400 a couple Stupak offers two nights' lodging, $200 back in cash, and an armful of worthless freebies (mostly two-for-one gimmicks that require additional spending), which essentially means that any Bozo who takes him up on it is forking out 100 bucks a night for a room that can be had anywhere else in the city for $24.95.

But then again, Stupak goes one step beyond the mechanical reproductions of the Mirage and T.I. He even beats the King Tut simulation at the Luxor. Stupak actually takes celebrities you swore (or at least hoped) were dead and brings them breathing, kicking, and crooning onstage. "See stars like Allen & Rossi, Zsa Zsa Gabor, Frank Gorshin, Jerry Lee Lewis, Helen Reddy, Mickey Rooney and Donald O'Connor," his brochure teases. (What's wrong, Bob, you couldn't find Tony Orlando?)

And don't think Stupak isn't in step with Steve Wynn and the New Vegas. At a cost of $50 million, the Polish Maverick is going 20 feet higher than the Eiffel Tower and completing his 1012-foot Stratosphere Tower . . . that's right, "the tallest tower in America," which will feature $6 elevator rides and four revolving wedding chapels at its summit.

Stupak reeled me and the Big Vig in with a different come-on: a blackjack variant called Double Exposure 21. Played just like normal 21, with one twist: *both* of the dealer's cards are dealt face up. How's that for leveling the playing table? But old Bob had it all figured out. What he gives with one hand he takes away with the other. In this case, the dealer handed me a Double Exposure rules card that was only a bit denser than the Government Printing Office's new two-volume set of NAFTA regulations. All I know is that somehow or other I was dealt three 21s in a row and never won one chip. The Vig got pissed as well when the dealer kept winning on ties (a no-no in pure 21), wandered off, and developed a passion for $1 video poker.

I stuck it out at Double Exposure, striking up a table friendship with a palsy-ridden San Franciscan named Lennie who, on this final night of his two-night package deal, was about $750 and a quart of Jack Daniel's down. "Hey, you take care of me, I take care of you," Lennie slurred, nodding toward the dealer, pushing him over a fiver chip. But down Lennie went. Another hundred, then another. "This is all I got left man, not even anything for a taxi when I get home," he said, showing me six or seven $5 chips. "What should I do?" Before I could shout: GETTHEFUCKTOBEDLENNIE! he went on. "My plane outta here isn't till noon tomorrow, man. I gotta play, but maybe I'll take a food break." Lennie motioned to the nearest pit boss. Dino or Vinny or whatever his name was kept slowly chewing his gum as Lennie explained he had been playing 15 hours straight, and wanted the casino to "comp" him a breakfast so he could charge his batteries. Any other place in town that would be no problem. What's a $3 meal against keeping the johns playing? But this was Bob Stupak's Vegas World and Dino/Vinny hung tough and shook his head. "If I comp you, big guy, gotta comp everyone else," Dino/Vinny managed to articulate. "No can do."

I thought Lennie was going to pass out. But taking a deep breath, and quivering on the verge of tears, he put his last $30 on the betting line and somehow got a hand that the Double Exposure rules let him win. Now, with a $60 stake, Lennie forgot about food, cut his bets down to the $3 minimum, and had enough capital for another half hour or so. Revived, he tossed the dealer a silver dollar and said: "Take care of me and I'll take care of you."

That bout took care of it for me, however. I did some quick figuring in my head and estimated after my ups and downs I was still $250 in the hole. The Vig was still ahead a hundred bucks and suggested we head downtown, where Binion's Horseshoe casino draws in the locals with its 25 cent craps and dollar blackjack tables. Downtown, separated from the Strip by a two-mile stretch of motels that all seem inspired by the Jetsons, and flanked by round-the-clock wedding chapels, is Fremont Street, the original Glitter Gulch.

Downtown, kitty-corner from the Horseshoe and Steve Wynn's yuppified Golden Nugget, is the real bottom feeder of all Vegas casinos—Sassy Sally's. But where Vegas World is real sleaze, Sally's can be accused only of a totally innocent kitsch. The brocaded floor carpets are worn to the padding, held together by strips of gaffer's tape. There are not tables here, only slot machines, and they have been presided over by neon lamps shaped as prairie dogs, cacti, and covered wagons since long before anyone heard of Southwestern decor.

On the rear wall is a huge digital clock counting down the minutes before "Double Jackpot Time." Every 15 minutes at Sally's, a bell rings and for the next 60 seconds any slot jackpot pays double, provided you've been playing the machine for at least four minutes. It was five minutes to the next double-up period and the Big Vig and I were ripping through two rolls of quarters.

Suddenly the bell rang, a siren wailed, a red-and-blue bubblegum lamp began to twirl, and a scratchy tape that sounded eerily like the Chipmunks started: "It's dubba, dubba, dubba, dubba, dubba, dubba, Double Jackpot Time! . . . Dubba, dubba, dubba, dubba, dubba, Double Jackpot Time!" And the Vig and I were singing along at full volume, still pumping in the quarters.

We won *bubkes* of course. But it was the best minute I had in Vegas.

Walking outside for air we ran into Mr. Ed. That's what he calls himself. And appropriately, because Ed's job in the New World Order is to stand in front of Sally's from early afternoon till midnight and pass out two-for-one scrip while wearing a yellow foam-rubber ten-gallon hat and a matching apparatus around his waist that makes it look as though he's a riding a yellow foam-rubber horse. "Best god-damn town on earth!" Mr. Ed assured us. To break the monotony he told us his life story: "Came here a year and a half ago after a big bust up with the old lady. We were livin' in New Mexico and I owed the IRS, so I just sold my truck. A real beauty. A '57 Apache, 3100 Series with the big block. I got two grand for it and came out here, and I love it. Love it. I work seven days a week and nine hours a day, but I got my apartment and my bills paid, and who doesn't love this 24-hour-a-day lifestyle. It's a happening place, brother. No place like it in the world."

"You can say that again," said the Big Vig.

So Mr. Ed did. "No place like it in the world."

Every month, 2300 more people become Las Vegas residents after landing, for the most part, jobs like Mr. Ed's. Unemployment in Las Vegas is at 6.2 percent—a figure that 20 years ago would have been considered catastrophic, but today sounds like full employment.

Consequently, 41 percent of all new Clark County drivers' licenses this past year were given to transplants from recession-scorched California. Twenty-five percent of new homeowners are also from the Golden State. And with 18,000 new jobs coming with the opening of the Luxor, T.I., and MGM Grand, you'd expect incoming traffic to be backed up to the BQE. So far an estimated 100,000 people have applied for those jobs.

Las Vegas is, after all, a great place to live, even a better place to raise your children, according to the dozen or so recently arrived hotel and casino employees with whom I spoke. That means two things: Housing is still cheap. And Las Vegas is still one of the most segregated cities in America. In this sense also, Vegas is a model for America's future: a whole desertful of low-paying service jobs for a displaced white working class. In return for their allegiance to the new downsized order, these white workers are offered a city without the ills of urban America. Taxes are low, schools are functional, and people with different skin colors are on the other side of the local Maginot line. In this case, literally, on the west side of the railroad tracks that border the Las Vegas Strip.

Dear departed Bugsy Siegel helped set the racial tone here back in 1948, when he hired Lena Horne to sing at the Flamingo but banned her from walking into the casino and then ordered her room linen burned after she used it.

The casinos were ordered desegregated in 1960, but blacks still lag far behind in city employment. The current economic boom has leapfrogged right over the city's blighted Westside, where there isn't a single supermarket, fast food outlet, or even a casino.

When Los Angeles erupted in April 1992, Las Vegas had its own $6 million disturbance, which took one life. The 1350-member Las Vegas Metropolitan Police Department—8 percent black—immediately hit the streets and stopped enraged blacks from arching into the casino district. In the aftermath, Mayor Jan Laverty Jones appealed to the casinos to dampen tensions; the city's major hotel and gambling concerns all agreed to hire three blacks each as dealers, bartenders, and cocktail waitresses.

Taking a suggestion from Mr. Ed, the Big Vig and I evacuated the Tropicana and moved across the street and through time to the medieval-themed Excalibur—a whipped-cream white monstrosity topped by massive gingerbread towers. "Best place in town," Mr. Ed had assured us.

"All they need is straw on the floor to make this place a total barn," the Vig affectionately noted as we stood in line to check in. Another line snaked behind the counter where the Fanny Packers bought tickets to the "twice Knightly" dinner-jousting show. Yet another triple file lugubriously filtered into one of the eateries offering Lance-A-Lotta Pizza. There were more lines in front of the casino cashier windows, purposely kept scarce to deter you from cashing in

your chips. There was even a human traffic jam in front of the elevators, as hotel security demanded a valid room key before allowing
passage. The Excalibur, it was turning out, was what Camelot would
be like if the East German Interior Ministry had seized it.

Comrade Walter Ulbricht's men had certainly designed the Ex-
cal's guest rooms, definitely Dungeon Lite. Dizzying brocades on the
rugs and drapes, hot pink wallpaper imprinted to look like . . . well
. . . the brick walls of a dungeon. Ceilings so low that, at five foot
three, I could actually spring up and touch them.

"Let's get out of here, let's hit the casino," I said to the Vig as soon
as we put our bags down.

But the Big Vig had gotten religion. The oversize oaf was up $160
since we arrived and was so self-satisfied, so self-righteous, so goddamn cheap, that he was about to become a Fanny Packer before my
very eyes. "You know," he said to me, "Las Vegas has other things to
do besides gamble."

A pregnant pause as we *both* wondered what he'd say next.

"You know they have wonderful museums here," he said and
pulled me out the door.

I have to say I was a lot less impressed than the Vig was by the
combination Elvis/Antique Doll/Boxing museum that Chicago
George runs, paying only $21,000 a month in rent. ("I'm 100 feet from
the MGM Grand," he explained.) As french-fry fumes and the odor of
charred beef floated in from the burger joint next door, and as the
Big Vig snapped up a MIKE TYSON IS INNOCENT T-shirt and an Elvis clock,
my thoughts drifted to the 21 tables that by now were holding $500
of mine. In fact, I could think of nothing else until Chicago George
spoke up.

"When you boys are done here, go over and see my wife Bunny,"
he said. "She works over at the Liberace Museum."

Blackjack could wait another hour or two. A 10-minute jaunt
down Tropicana Road we found the one-story Spanish Colonial–
style building, humanity's monument to a great pianist, holding
down the corner of yet another shopping mall. The Liberace Museum is the Third Most Popular Tourist Attraction in Nevada (mean-

ing there must be a *big* drop off after number two), pulling 150,000 visitors per year. For just $6.50 you get to tour the three buildings of the museum, all oddly separated by other mall shops, including a religious bookstore and an Armenian deli, and ponder the accumulated memorabilia of a Great Artistic Life as the maestro's recording of "Bewitched, Bothered and Bewildered" tinkles demurely in the background.

Far be it from me to rob the reader of the joy of discovering the contents of this temple on his or her own, but let me advise that when you make the pilgrimage, don't forget your sunglasses. The glare is vicious: here's the rhinestone-covered Baldwin grand piano, the coordinated rhinestone-covered Rolls-Royce (if you have trouble finding it just look for the Rolls painted like an American flag next to it), the rhinestone-covered Excalibur motor car (no relation to the hotel), the rhinestone-*and*-coral pink convertible VW with a Rolls grille, the collection of rhinestone-studded velvet capes, yet one more rhinestone-covered grand piano, and the rhinestone-covered frame around the picture of Liberace with Tony Orlando (quick, call Bob Stupak!)

In the third and final room of the museum, just beyond the Liberace Library, which has no books but lots of Czech Moser crystal, and right past the Liberace death chamber—the re-creation of his private bedroom complete with a chinchilla bedspread—that is to say, inside the Liberace Gift Shop (where we found the Liberace snowstorms to be the best buy), we discovered Chicago George's wife, Bunny, furiously puffing away on a brownish More while she gift wrapped a piano-shaped ashtray.

"Say," the Big Vig said to her. "I didn't see any explanation of how Liberace died. Do you know how?"

"He was old, he just died," Bunny said through a nicotine cloud.

"Oh," the Big Vig said. "Funny, I thought it was AIDS."

"His heart went," Bunny said diplomatically. "What killed him was the heart attack, honey."

We would have liked to discuss these necro-nuances with Bunny further but were pushed aside by streams of bubbly Fanny Packers just arriving on two buses, part of an organized tour from Arkansas. Americans, even these elderly women with blue rinses and aging men with paunches hanging over the conch buckles of their wide leather belts, are quite forgiving of celebrity and wealth. Liberace is still an untarnished hero in many of the same parishes that today are embarked on campaigns to outlaw gay rights.

Soon we were back at the Mirage, where we had to pick up a couple of comp tickets Alan Feldman had gotten for us for the Siegfried and Roy show, the longest-running spectacle in Vegas. After so much high culture, I was ready to relax at the 21 table when I remembered that the Vig had gone cold turkey.

"Can you hang on just 10 minutes?" I asked him, as I sat down at the third base seat at a $10 table. Before I could answer, the Vig took up his position at first and announced to me in a voice so dispassionate that it chilled my soul: "I'm going to play, too." I don't know what had come over him, what had suddenly led him astray from his newfound path of thrifty rectitude, but, whatever it was, you can be sure he deeply regrets it today. As do I.

Never had I seen such a stretch of pure rotten stinking bad luck. With every hand we played things got worse. Double down on 11 and draw an ace. Split aces and draw two sixes. Stand on 20 and watch the dealer take a stiff 14, draw a deuce, then a five. Worse, the Vig and I were mesmerized. Our table was one of the few equipped with Steve Wynn's continuous action, automatic eight-deck shuffling machines (patent pending), which meant the game progressed like a brushfire through Malibu. And the deeper in we got, the harder it became to stand up and leave. Too much was invested. Somewhere, midway through the massacre, I had to go to the casino's bank of ATM machines and pull cash for both of us from my bank account and my American Express credit line. When that wad was shot, we had no choice but to retreat. Between the two of us we dropped $1100. In maybe 45 minutes. Probably less.

I staggered out the door and, sick to my stomach, handed the car keys to the Vig. I got in the rented Mercury, put the seat back, and closed my eyes. I had not really slept in three days. I awoke when the Vig slammed on the brakes and I saw us face-to-face with a barbed wire and concrete antitank barrier.

"Just what the doctor ordered," the Big Vig said, regaining some of his composure. Drawing on the experience of previous debacles in Vegas, the Vig had brought me to the most therapeutic place in town—the Survival Store.

"We are here to rent some Uzis," the Big Vig proclaimed to the guy behind the counter, who made up for his nerdishness by wearing a .357 Magnum on his hip with two auxiliary fast loaders of ammo.

"Will that be semiautomatic, or automatic, sir?" asked the Nerd.

"Fully automatic, please," the Vig answered, knowing that Nevada was one of 38 states where machine guns are legal. For $20 (40 seconds worth of casino play) plus the cost of ammo, the Survival Store rents a fully automatic Uzi and lets you shoot it off at its indoor firing range. I let the Vig take the one available Uzi, while I opted for the more politically correct .50-caliber semiautomatic Desert Eagle handgun, the ultimate gangsta piece. "Nevada's a great place," the Vig said as I hefted the Eagle over the counter.

"A lot better than there," the Nerd said, motioning his head toward a bumper sticker reading THE PEOPLE'S REPUBLIC OF CALIFORNIA. At that, I decided to let the Vig put the charges against his New York ID instead of mine from the Sacramento DMV.

As we blasted and fired away, I looked at the holes being ripped in the paper targets and tried to imagine the heads of Steve Wynn, Bob Stupak, and every bleached-blond and Grecian-formulaed dealer I'd sat against over the last three days.

But when the smoke had cleared and we were turning the guns back in, I told the Vig that this really hadn't made me feel much better. Overhearing me, the Nerd had a brainstorm. "If that didn't do it for you, sir, I've got a World War II .50-cal machine gun off a B-17. Wanna try it?"

I told him thanks, but I was out of money.

No more than five minutes into the Siegfried and Roy show, I was hoping for floods, earthquakes, and firestorms. I was hoping those Royal White Tigers I'd seen penned up in the lobby and that were now onstage would shake off what appeared to be their PCP-induced stupor and put us all out of our misery by simply chowing down on the two Austrian Nazis at the center of this pageant. The Big Vig just sat and moaned.

This was a Sound and Light Version of *Marat/Sade* meets *The Wizard of Oz* meets the Vault with a soundtrack by the jet-motor engineers at Boeing. The first hour was about five minutes of mediocre magic and 55 minutes of explosions, dry ice smoke, computerized dragons spitting out more gas fires, a cast of dozens strapped into brass suits and trundled off in a death march to the sound of thunderous timpani, Siegfried—or maybe it was Roy—flying out over the audience like Peter Pan on a cable, oodles of chains, bushels of whips, a few torture boxes, and even a good old-fashioned rack. Come back, Liberace, all is forgiven! Come back, Buddy Hackett, for that matter.

At halftime, the Götterdämmerung receded as the two boys—both in shiny knee-high black boots—came out to chat with the adoring audience. Arte Johnson had nothing on their accents as Siggy waxed serious and said how much he and Roy, really how all of us, needed to "preserve nature in all its *vohn-der*."

To thunderous applause, the room blacked out, and a giant screen dropped down over the stage. A pumped up home video of Siegfried and Roy romping around their "jungle palace in the desert" with a pack of domesticated white tiger cubs elicited squealing approval from this crowd, whose members had probably just voted down the last school bond measure but somehow were not offended at the thought of having plunked down close to $150 per couple to watch TV in a big room.

I really was not having fun anymore, yet I had to keep watching to see what outrage would come next: Siggy rolling with a couple of creamy cubs; Roy, dressed only in a bikini bottom, riding on the back of a full-grown tiger across the mansion backyard. But when the film cut to the "natural vohnder" of Siegfried and Roy frolicking in their frigging swimming pool with a pair of 600-pound tigers, and when the audience around us began to ahhh as if it were looking at one of those paintings of big-eyed waifs, the Big Vig and I headed for the exit.

Used to tallying multiple digits in our heads, we came up with these numbers: Siggy and Roy perform six nights a week, two shows a night, about 480 performances a year. Every show is a near sellout, drawing an average of maybe 1500 people. That's about 720,000 viewers per year, at about 75 bucks a pop, adding up to a gross of around $54 million a year. "I must be a real putz," the Big Vig said, turning deadly serious, a sure tip-off of a profound existential crisis. "Here I've been struggling 11 years as a literary agent, busting my ass so that a *good* book might bring in 50,000 readers and gross a million. Where did I go wrong?"

Having fallen asleep at dawn, I slept till noon. The Big Vig had left me a note, saying that the tiger show had left him suicidal and he thought it best that he take the 10 A.M. flight home. At least I think that's what the note said. My left eye was swollen almost shut and hurt like hell.

An ophthalmologist on Paradise Road who outfitted me with a grotesque eye patch said I had probably broken a blood vessel from stress or fatigue. I knew it was both. Even in the doctor's office, the nurse saw me off, not with a "Good-Bye," but with a "Good Luck!"

Was it that obvious? Even to strangers? That the only thing I had on my mind, even while the doctor was patching me, was to get back to the tables? True, I was in a panic. The Last Day Panic. I had faced the music and totaled it up. Eight-hundred-fifty dollars was the damage so far. I had to be home that night and that meant only a handful of hours were available to win it all back. Like Truman beat Dewey, I'd pull it out at the last moment.

I chose Bugsy's old place, the Flamingo, to make my last stand. But the Last Day Panic means you do everything wrong. You hit 15s. You split 9s. On the way from one table to another you put $5 down on your wife's birthday on the roulette wheel. You lose and then you try your birthday, your weight, your IQ, which is now down to double zero. You buy $10 worth of Keno cards every 10 minutes and play your social security number, your address, your body measurements.

Or you take the big plunge and try a whole new game. I found Caribbean Stud Poker. An absolutely brilliant game—for the casino. This one was designed by computer. Every card game in the world punishes the player when the dealer has a good hand. But Caribbean Stud Poker also punishes you when the dealer has a *bad* hand. That's to say, your good hand doesn't really count if the dealer doesn't have a minimum, or so-called "qualifying hand." Which means you lose on both ends of the spectrum. Truly fantastic.

So why do people, why did I, sit down to play? Because the game is nifty. It's played on a table that looks like 21, but here there is no tension among the players because everyone plays only against the dealer. Unlike blackjack, you can't screw up someone else's hand by making a bad move. There's also a perfect balance of technology and humanity. An automatic shuffling machine and little slots that suck your ante down off the table and right into some casino accounting room.

The dealer has plenty of space to ham it up. My dealer, Kevin, was terrific. He didn't even make a joke about my eye patch (perhaps mistaking me for a pirate on leave from T.I.). Like a carnival barker he entertained us as we got fleeced. Showing a King? "A cowboy!" said Kevin. "You know those cowboys don't ride alone!" A trey? "Treacherous Threes!" warned Kevin. A Queen became "Twin Sisters," or "Little Girls." A Jack, we were told, hinted at a full-scale "Jack Attack!" Not just plain sevens, but "Easy Sevens."

This game, I would say, objectively, is near impossible to win. But it's addictive, the most fetching I've ever seen. Its genius is that it is s-l-o-w. You lose, all right, but it takes a long time. And that's finally what it cost me near $1000 to learn. I could have read it for free in a study on gambling by Harrah's Casino that I picked up after I left town. The study said the number one reason people gamble, more than a chance at winning, is the ability to "socialize"—with "the dealers and the other patrons of the casino."

I hadn't yet read this report when I played Caribbean Stud, but I could see it right there at the table. Gambling, much more than the Volcano, or King Tut, or Treasure Island's Buccaneer Bay, is the ultimate fantasy in America. Because in a society in which the only currency is currency, and where most of us are absolutely irrelevant and powerless economic entities, to sit down at any Vegas table creates at least the illusion of empowerment. As long as our money holds out, we are real players—if not outside the casino doors, at least at this table, for this moment. And while we are there we can talk the talk and sit in close proximity to the only person we know whose blood pressure registers no variation as he handles hundreds of thousands of dollars each day: the dealer. And while we are there, no one will ask how much money we really have or don't have, what we do for a living, what we feel or want or yearn for. While at the table, it's enough to know we are one of those powerful enough to throw money down the sewer. In our hearts we know we will lose. But, God, let it be slow. Let it be as long as possible before I'm returned to civilian status, to being one more sorry-assed Fanny Packer relegated back to my sofa, watching Oprah and Ivana and Robin Leach flaunt it in front of me.

My last hundred lasted a magnificent three hours at Caribbean Stud. When I busted out I felt the same depraved tingle I had two nights before when I bombed at the Tropicana. Kevin, the dealer, asked me politely to buy more chips or get up as there was a line of people waiting for a place.

I started up the Mercury and headed west toward LA on I-15. My head was light from no sleep, my one good eye started to cloud. I hadn't eaten a real meal in two days and a pit burned in my stomach. And not just from hunger. But then I remembered I was only 40 miles away from Stateline, Nevada—home to two super casinos joined by a monorail running over the highway, the final legal gambling oasis before reentering California.

In this America, in this land of endless opportunity, I was being offered one last shot at redemption.

NOTES ON THE CONTRIBUTORS

EDWARD ALLEN has taught creative writing and literature at Rhodes College and Ohio University. Formerly a resident of Pahrump, Nevada, Allen is a writer-in-residence at the University of Central Oklahoma. His stories have appeared in *The New Yorker*, the *Mendocino Review*, GQ, and other publications. He is also the author of two novels, *Straight Through the Night* and *Mustang Sally*. An avid fan of gambling casinos and TV game shows, he once appeared for three straight days on *Jeopardy*.

A. ALVAREZ, poet, critic, and author, was born in London in 1924. His books include *The Savage God: A Study of Suicide*; *Life After Marriage: Scenes from Divorce*; *The Biggest Game in Town*; and three novels—*Hers*; *Hunt*; and *Day of Atonement*. He writes regularly for *The New Yorker* and has been published in many other magazines and periodicals on both sides of the Atlantic. He is married with three children and lives in Hampstead, London.

ROBERT ALAN AURTHUR, writer and producer, was one of the leading dramatists of the golden age of television. Throughout his career he wrote for stage, screen, and television as well as writing magazine articles, short stories, and books. His column, "Hanging Out," appeared in *Esquire* from 1971 to 1975. His film credits include *Edge of the City*, *Warlock*, and *All That Jazz*, which he also produced.

PHYLLIS BARBER, a freelance writer and professional pianist, is currently on the faculty of Vermont College's M.F.A. in Writing Program. Her books include *And the Desert Shall Blossom*; *The School of Love*; *How I Got Cultured: A Nevada Memoir*; and two books for children. She won first prize in the novel and short story categories in the 1988 Utah Fine Arts Literary Competition. She lives in Dillon, Colorado.

SUSAN BERMAN was a long-time journalist for *The San Francisco Examiner* and also a freelance writer for *New York* and *Esquire*, among many other publications. She is the author of *Driver, Give a Soldier a Lift* and *Easy Street*, for which film rights were bought by Universal. She is presently writing a novel.

KATHARINE BEST and KATHARINE HILLYER first met in London in 1943 when they were working for the Office of War Information. In Ms. Hillyer's words: "The British asked us so many questions about America that we finally woke up to our vast ignorance about what went on beyond the Alleghenies." This led to a country-wide tour by car that eventually covered 250,000 miles. Their articles appeared in numerous publications, including *Reader's Digest*, *Holiday*, *Saturday Evening Post*, and *Esquire*.

MARK COOPER'S articles, essays, and interviews have appeared in dozens of publications, including *Rolling Stone*, *Mother Jones*, *The Nation*, and the *Washington Post*. He is a staff writer for the *Village Voice*, and since 1981 has taught journalism and Latin American studies at California State University. His most recent book is *Roll Over Che Guevara: Travels of a Radical Reporter*, published in 1994.

NOËL COWARD (1899–1973) was a playwright, composer, actor, and author best known for his witty, sophisticated comedies about the British leisure class. Among his many successful plays and musical revues are *Hay Fever*; *Blithe Spirit*; and *Song at Twilight*. He also wrote a two-volume autobiography, *Present Indicative* and *Future Indefinite*; a novel, *Pomp and Circumstance*; poetry; and nearly three hundred songs.

JOAN DIDION was born in Sacramento, California. She has written four novels and five books of nonfiction as well as several screenplays (co-written with husband John Gregory Dunne). She lectures at various colleges and universities and is a contributor to *The New York Review of Books* and *The New Yorker*. She and her husband live in New York with their daughter, Quintana Roo Dunne.

JOHN GREGORY DUNNE is the author of the best-selling novels *True Confessions*; *Dutch She, Jr.*; *The Red White and Blue*; and *Playland*. He's also written four books of nonfiction and two collections of essays. He has written screenplays and is a frequent contributor to many publications, including *Esquire* and *The New York Review of Books*. He is married to Joan Didion.

FAITH FANCHER and WILLIAM J. DRUMMOND have been National Public Radio correspondents. Faith Fancher now works at KTVU/Fox in Oakland, California. In 1993 she received the Bay Area Black Media Coalition's Beverly Johnson Award for Journalist of the Year. William J. Drummond is presently a professor on the faculty of the University of California, Berkeley.

ALBERT GOLDMAN is best known for his writing on music and popular culture, particularly the biographies *Ladies and Gentlemen, Lenny Bruce!*; *Elvis*; and *The Lives of John Lennon*. He died in 1994 at the age of sixty-six. At the time of his death, he was working on a biography of Jim Morrison.

MICHAEL HERR was born in Syracuse, New York, and attended Syracuse University. In addition to *The Big Room*, he is the author of the books *Dispatches* and *Walter Winchell*, and co-author of the screenplays for *Apocalypse Now* and *Full Metal Jacket*. He lives in New York State.

DANIEL LANG was a prominent American author and staff member of *The New Yorker* for forty years. His books include *Early Tales of the Atomic Age*; *The Man in the Thick Lead Suit*; *From Hiroshima to the Moon*; *A Backward Look*; and *Casualties of War*.

A. J. LIEBLING was a long-time staff member of *The New Yorker*. He was also a reporter, columnist, war correspondent, and satirist who wrote *The Wayward Pressman*; *The Road Back to Paris*; *The Telephone Booth Indian*; *Chicago: Second City*; *The Sweet Science*; *The Earl of Louisiana*; and many other books. He died in 1963.

MERRILL MARKOE, the author of *What the Dogs Have Taught Me* and *How to Be Hap-Hap-Happy Like Me*, was the original headwriter for *Late Night with David Letterman*, for which she won four Emmy Awards. She has also been a correspondent for NBC-TV's *TV Nation*; written, directed, and starred in a number of HBO specials; and received the Writer's Guild and Ace awards for her work on *Not Necessarily the News*. Markoe writes for several national publications and has a regular column in *Buzz* magazine. She lives in Malibu, California, with her dogs Lewis, Tex, Bo, and Winky.

RICHARD MELTZER is the grandfather (uncle?) of rock criticism, a genre he disowns with a passion, as well as the author of close to eleven books, including *Gulcher* and *L.A. Is the Capital of Kansas*. He has spent the last six years on a seminal novel, *The Night (Alone)*, for which he either will or won't receive the National Book Award.

JANE O'REILLY is the author of *The Girls I Left Behind* and *No Turning Back: Two Nuns Battle with the Vatican over Women's Rights to Choose*. Her articles on family, money, the media, and politics, and her groundbreaking essay on the Women's Movement, have appeared in numerous publications, including *New York*, *McCall's*, *Atlantic Monthly*, *Vogue*, and *Ms.*, for which she is a founding editor. She lives in Vermont.

J. RANDALL PRIOR has written for *Spy* magazine and other publications.

ALAN RICHMAN is GQ's special correspondent, and since 1992 the magazine's food and wine columnist, for which he won the James Beard Journalism Award for Restaurant Criticism in 1993 and 1994. He has also written for *People*, and worked at a variety of newspapers, including *The New York Times*, *Montreal Star*, and *The Boston Globe*. He lives in Manhattan.

JIM SLOAN lives in Truckee, California, with his wife, Karen, and their daughter, Emma. He is a journalist by trade, and his fiction has appeared in *The Boston Review*, *Permafrost*, and *The Chattahoochee Review*.

HUNTER S. THOMPSON lives in a walled compound on the outskirts of Woody Creek, Colorado. His reporting and essays appear in numerous publications, including *Rolling Stone*, where he has long been the National Affairs Desk. He is the author of nine books, including *Fear and Loathing on the Campaign Trail '72*; *Hells Angels*; and *Fear and Loathing in Las Vegas*.

NICK TOSCHES is the author of two landmark biographies—*Dino* and *Hellfire*—as well as *Cut Numbers*; *Trinities*; and many other books.

MICHAEL VENTURA'S works include a book of essays, *Letters at 3A.M.: Reports on Endarkenment*, and a novel, *The Zoo Where You're Fed to God*. At present he is writing a novel about Las Vegas titled *The Death of Frank Sinatra*.

TOM WOLFE is the author of such best-sellers as *The Right Stuff; From Bauhaus to Our House;* and *The Bonfire of the Vanities*. His other books include *The Kandy-Kolored Tangerine-Flake Streamline Baby; The Electric Kool-Aid Acid Test;* and *The Painted Word*, to name only a few. He has also worked as a reporter, and his writing has appeared in *New York, Esquire,* and *Harper's*. He lives in New York City.

ACKNOWLEDGMENTS

"Who'll Stop the Wayne?" from L.A. Is the Capital of Kansas by Richard Meltzer. Copyright © 1988 by Richard Meltzer. Reprinted by permission of Harmony Books, a division of The Crown Publishing Group.

"'Melvin and Howard': A Nevada Fairy Tale" is an excerpt from Nevada: True Tales from the Neon Wilderness by Jim Sloan (Salt Lake City: University of Utah Press, 1993). Permission courtesy of the author and the University of Utah Press.

"Viva Las Wine Goddesses!" from What the Dogs Have Taught Me by Merrill Markoe. Copyright © 1992 by Merrill Markoe. Used by permission of Viking Penguin, a division of Penguin Books USA Inc.

"Las Vegas: Mississippi of the West or Promised Land?" A production of KNPR-FM, Las Vegas. Air date July 4, 1991. Written and produced by William J. Drummond and Faith B. Fancher.

"Penny Ante" by Edward Allen. Reprinted by permission of Irene Skolnick Agency. Copyright © 1992 by Edward Allen.

"Searching for Sin City and Finding Disney in the Desert" by Marc Cooper, originally appeared as "Fear and Lava: Looking for Blackjack and Finding Fanny Packers. A Tale of the New Las Vegas" in The Village Voice, November 30, 1993.

Grateful acknowledgment is made to the following for permission to reprint illustrations on the listed pages: Michael Abramson: 40, 313; Susan Berman: 103; Jefferson Graham: 59; The Las Vegas News Bureau: xi, 25, 95, 127, 211, 218, 247, 304; The Las Vegas News Bureau, UNLV Library: 195; Richard Menzies: 276; Mary Ellen Mark/Library: 175; Nepwork Photos: 119, 158; Phil Stern Photo: 139; Sylvia Plachy: xv, 45; R.T.S.I.: 325; Fred Sigman and Charles Morgan: 269; Chip Simons: 148; Stanley Tretick, The Library of Congress Collection: 1, 298; The Riviera Hotel: 170.